COMPA ATES:
BRITAIN IN I ONTEXT

FAMILY LIFE AND SOCIAL POLICY COURSE TEAM

Melanie Bayley, Editor

Ann Boomer, Secretary

David Boswell, Senior Lecturer in Sociology

Hilary Canneaux, Course Manager

John Clarke, Senior Lecturer in Social Policy

Allan Cochrane, Senior Lecturer in Urban Studies (Course Team Chair)

Juliette Cowan, Secretary

Rudi Dallos, Staff Tutor, Social Sciences

Harry Dodd, Print Production Controller

Peggotty Graham, Staff Tutor, Social Sciences

Pauline Harris, Staff Tutor, Social Sciences; Open University Tutor

Tom Hunter, Editor

Bernie Lake, Secretary

Mary Langan, Lecturer in Social Policy

Jack Leathem, Producer, BBC/OUPC

Vic Lockwood, Senior Producer, BBC/OUPC

Eugene McLaughlin, Lecturer in Criminology and Social Policy

Ione Mako, Production Assistant, BBC/OUPC

Dorothy Miell, Lecturer in Psychology

John Muncie, Senior Lecturer in Criminology and Social Policy

Roger Sapsford, Senior Lecturer in Research Methods

Esther Saraga, Staff Tutor, Social Sciences

Jane Sheppard, Designer

Richard Skellington, Project Officer, Social Sciences

Paul Smith, Social Sciences Liaison Librarian

Margaret Wetherell, Senior Lecturer in Psychology

Fiona Williams, Senior Lecturer in the School of Health, Welfare and Community Education

Michael Wilson, Senior Lecturer in Research Methods

David Wilson, Editor

Consultant authors

John Baldock, Senior Lecturer in Social Policy, University of Kent

Elizabeth Barrett, Training Officer, Ford Motor Company Ltd., Basildon, Essex

Rosaleen Croghan, Research Assistant; Open University Tutor

Sally Foreman, Research Psychologist; Open University Tutor

Norman Ginsburg, Principal Lecturer in Social Policy, South Bank University, London

Hilary Land, Professor of Social Policy, Royal Holloway and Bedford New College, University of London

Lynne Segal, Principal Lecturer, School of Psychology, Middlesex University

George Taylor, Senior Lecturer in Social Work, De Montfort University, Leicester

External assessors

Hilary Graham, Professor of Applied Social Studies, University of Warwick (Course Assessor)

Kum Kum Bhavnani, Lecturer in Applied Social Studies, University of Bradford

Caroline McKinlay, Publications Officer, Women's Aid Federation, England

Raymond Taylor, Prinicpal Training Officer in Social Work, Central Regional Council, Stirling

Tutor panel

Rosemary Collins, Open University Tutor

Helen Cowie, Senior Lecturer in Social Studies, Bretton Hall, University of Leeds; Open University Tutor.

COMPARING WELFARE STATES: BRITAIN IN INTERNATIONAL CONTEXT

EDITED BY
ALLAN COCHRANE AND JOHN CLARKE

SAGE Publications
LONDON • NEWBURY PARK • NEW DELHI

PUBLISHED IN ASSOCIATION WITH

The Open
University

The Open University, Walton Hall, Milton Keynes, MK7 6AA.

First published 1993

SAGE Publications Ltd
6 Bonhill Street
London EC2A 4PU

SAGE Publications Inc
2455 Teller Road
Newbury Park, California 91320

SAGE Publications India Pvt Ltd
32, M-Block Market
Greater Kailash–1
New Delhi 110 048

British Library Cataloguing in Publication Data

Comparing Welfare States: Britain in international context

I. Cochrane, Allan II. Clarke, J.

ISBN 0–8039–8845–1

ISBN 0–8039–8846–X Pbk

361.30941

Library of Congress catalog card number 92-051048

Edited, Designed and Typeset by the Open University.

Printed in the United Kingdom by Butler and Tanner Ltd, Frome and London.

This text forms part of an Open University Third Level Course, *D311 Family Life and Social Policy*. If you would like a copy of *Studying with the Open University*, please write to the Central Enquiry Service, The Open University, PO Box 200, Milton Keynes, MK7 6YZ, United Kingdom.

CONTENTS

PREFACE   xi

ACKNOWLEDGEMENTS   xiii

CHAPTER 1
COMPARATIVE APPROACHES AND SOCIAL POLICY

ALLAN COCHRANE

1	WHY COMPARISON?	1
2	DEFINING WELFARE STATES	3
3	MOVING TOWARDS COMPARISON: STATISTICS AND WELFARE REGIMES	5
4	INCLUDING THE EXCLUDED	10
5	MODELS AND STRUCTURE	12
6	CONVERGENCE OR DIFFERENCE?	16
	REFERENCES	17

CHAPTER 2
THE BRITISH WELFARE STATE: FOUNDATION AND MODERNIZATION

JOHN CLARKE AND MARY LANGAN

	INTRODUCTION	19
1	FOUNDATION	20
1.1	THE BRITISH WELFARE REGIME: STATE, MARKET AND FAMILY	23
1.2	NATIONALIZING INFRASTRUCTURE: HEALTH AND EDUCATION	24
1.3	WELFARE IN THE POST-WAR ECONOMY	25
1.4	MEANS-TESTING: RESIDUAL NEEDS AND RESIDUAL BENEFITS	26
1.5	CITIZENSHIP: THE COSTS AND BENEFITS OF WELFARE	27
1.6	1945 AND ALL THAT	29

2   EXPANSION AND MODERNIZATION   29
2.1 THE EXPANSION OF STATE WELFARE   30
2.2 NEEDS AND PRIORITIES: THE CHANGING SHAPE OF WELFARE   35
2.3 MODERNIZATION AND REORGANIZATION: THE CORPORATE
     MANAGEMENT STATE?   41
2.4 THE FAMILY AND THE STATE   44
2.5 THE BEGINNING OF THE END?   46

     REFERENCES   47

CHAPTER 3
RESTRUCTURING WELFARE: THE BRITISH WELFARE REGIME IN THE 1980s

JOHN CLARKE AND MARY LANGAN

INTRODUCTION   49

1   SOWING THE SEEDS OF DISILLUSION: THE THREE Ds   50

2   ROLLING BACK THE STATE?   53

3   TIGHTENING THE NET: WELFARE BENEFITS IN THE
    1980s   57

4   VARIETIES OF PRIVATIZATION   62

5   MANAGERS AND CITIZENS: DELIVERING WELFARE   67

6   A NEW REGIME? WELFARE IN THE 1990s   69

    REFERENCES   74

CHAPTER 4
GENDER, 'RACE' AND CLASS IN BRITISH WELFARE POLICY

FIONA WILLIAMS

INTRODUCTION   77

1   CHANGING ISSUES AND CHANGING EXPLANATIONS   77
1.1 CLASS AND CAPITAL: AGENCY AND STRUCTURE   78
1.2 THE DIVERSITY AND INTERRELATIONSHIP OF SOCIAL DIVISIONS   79
     GENDER   79
     DISABILITY   80
     'RACE'   81
     A FRAMEWORK   82

2   FAMILY, NATION AND WORK: THE EARLY YEARS   83

3   POST-WAR BRITAIN: THE CIVILIZING MISSION
BROUGHT HOME   84
3.1 THE IDEAL, THE REALITY AND THE PATHOLOGY   85
3.2 CONTRADICTIONS IN WELFARE   88

4   FAMILY, NATION AND WORK: THE NEW RIGHT AND
BEYOND   90
4.1 THE INTENSIFICATION OF INEQUALITIES   91
4.2 THE REWORKING OF FAMILY, NATION AND WORK   94
4.3 CONCLUSION: CONTRADICTION, CHALLENGE AND
CHANGE IN THE 1990s   96

REFERENCES   102

CHAPTER 5
HONG KONG: A RESIDUAL WELFARE REGIME

EUGENE MCLAUGHLIN

1   LIBERAL APPROACHES TO WELFARE   105

2   THE CONTEXT   106

3   SOCIETY AND SOCIAL POLICY: 1945 TO THE 1960s   109
3.1 THE GOLDEN AGE OF VOLUNTARISM 1945–1965   110
3.2 SOCIAL CRISIS AND DEMANDS FOR SOCIAL WELFARE   113

4   THE CONFIGURATION OF CONTEMPORARY SOCIAL
POLICY   116
4.1 PUBLIC HOUSING   118
4.2 EDUCATION AND HEALTH   119
4.3 SOCIAL SECURITY   122

5   THE DELIVERY OF SOCIAL WELFARE   124
5.1 THE FAMILY AND SOCIAL WELFARE   124
5.2 THE VOLUNTARY SECTOR AND CONTEMPORARY SOCIAL
WELFARE   130

6   MAKING SENSE OF SOCIAL WELFARE IN HONG
KONG   131

7   CONCLUSION   136

REFERENCES   137

CHAPTER 6
THE GERMAN WELFARE STATE: A CONSERVATIVE REGIME IN CRISIS

MICHAEL WILSON

1	GERMANY AS A CONSERVATIVE WELFARE REGIME	141
2	THE DUAL SYSTEM I: THE SOCIAL SECURITY STATE	143
3	THE DUAL SYSTEM II: SOCIAL ASSISTANCE	148
4	SOCIAL ASSISTANCE AND THE PRINCIPLE OF COMPENSATION	152
5	FAMILY, WELFARE AND THE LABOUR MARKET	153
6	THE STRAINS OF UNIFICATION	159
7	THE IMPACT OF UNIFICATION ON WOMEN IN THE EAST	163
8	CONCLUSION: THE FUTURE OF THE GERMAN WELFARE REGIME	166
	NOTES	169
	REFERENCES	169

CHAPTER 7
SWEDEN: THE SOCIAL-DEMOCRATIC CASE

NORMAN GINSBURG

1	WHY SOCIAL-DEMOCRATIC?	173
2	INCOME MAINTENANCE POLICIES AND OUTCOMES	176
2.1	INCOME INEQUALITY AND POVERTY	176
2.2	OLD-AGE PENSIONS	179
2.3	SOCIAL ASSISTANCE	180
2.4	UNEMPLOYMENT AND LABOUR-MARKET POLICIES	181
2.5	WOMEN, THE LABOUR MARKET AND INCOME MAINTENANCE	184
3	MINORITY ETHNIC GROUPS AND THE WELFARE STATE	187
3.1	MIGRATION	187
3.2	THE STATUS OF MINORITY ETHNIC GROUPS	188

4	WOMEN AND FAMILY POLICIES	190
4.1	IDEOLOGY AND FAMILY POLICY REFORM	190
4.2	LONE MOTHERS	193
4.3	DAYCARE AND PARENTAL LEAVE	194
4.4	THE NEW PATRIARCHY?	196

5	CONCLUSION: THE END OF AN ERA?	198

	REFERENCES	200

CHAPTER 8
IRELAND: CATHOLIC CORPORATISM

EUGENE MCLAUGHLIN

1	CATHOLIC CORPORATISM	205

2	HISTORICAL LEGACIES	207
2.1	CHURCH AND STATE	207
2.2	MOTHER IRELAND	210

3	THE POST-WAR TRANSFORMATION OF THE IRISH STATE	212

4	TOWARDS A WELFARE STATE	214

5	THE IMPACT OF THE SHIFTS IN SOCIAL EXPENDITURE	216
5.1	EMPLOYMENT	216
5.2	TAXATION	218
5.3	WELFARE EXPENDITURE OUTCOMES	220

6	WELFARE IN CRISIS AND THE QUEST FOR CONSENSUS	222

7	WOMEN, FAMILY LIFE AND THE IRISH STATE	225
7.1	DISCRIMINATION	225
7.2	REFORM AND REACTION	227

8	CONCLUSION	232

	REFERENCES	233

CHAPTER 9
LOOKING FOR A EUROPEAN WELFARE STATE

ALLAN COCHRANE

	INTRODUCTION	239
I	THE GLOBAL CONTEXT	240
2	EUROPEAN WELFARE STATES	250
3	A EUROPEAN WELFARE STATE?	253
4	A WIDER EUROPE	261
5	CONCLUSION	264
	REFERENCES	265
	INDEX	269

PREFACE

Our aim in *Comparing Welfare States* is to show the value of adopting a comparative approach to the analysis of social and family policy, by setting the British experience in a broader (largely European) context. Such an approach is not only important because it introduces us to a wider range of welfare regimes, but also because it helps to clarify the nature of the British system itself. After outlining some of the principles of comparative study, we use them in practice by looking at the contrasting experiences of welfare states in Britain, Hong Kong, Germany, Sweden and Ireland. As well as highlighting the diversity of national experiences we explore their shared features, and conclude by considering whether a transnational European welfare system is emerging. Each chapter moves between national and comparative questions, emphasizing the need to bring the two together if we are to grasp the full complexity of existing and developing welfare regimes.

This book is one of a series published by Sage which is concerned with the relationships between families and the development and practice of social policy. The other two books in the series are *A Crisis in Care? Challenges to social work* (edited by John Clarke) and *Social Problems and the Family* (edited by Rudi Dallos and Eugene McLaughlin). Each of the books in the series looks at the ways in which professional and state-sponsored interventions help to shape the experience of family life in different contexts. And each also considers the ways in which particular notions of the family influence the development of social policy. We believe that only by bringing these debates together is it possible to understand key aspects of the welfare regimes being constructed in the 1990s.

This series of books was initially written as part of an Open University course, D311 *Family Life and Social Policy*, which is, as its title implies, principally concerned with the complex interrelationships between the family and the state. The family is frequently understood as a private arena within which individuals are essentially free to determine how they live their own lives. The state, on the other hand, is often presented as the complete antithesis, at worst seeking to interfere in matters which should be left to private decision-making, at best helping to provide a wider – public – context within which individuals and families may interact.

The course questions these dichotomies and explores the greater complexities of family life in the United Kingdom at the end of the twentieth century. It uses insights from psychology, social policy and sociology to develop its arguments, starting with a focus on the internal life of families, moving through a consideration of forms of social and professional intervention towards a comparative analysis of social policy in Europe and a consideration of possible futures. At the core of the course are concerns about the relationships between the public and private spheres, about the need to acknowledge and explore diversity in the lived experience of families and about the ways in which power and inequality work themselves out within and between families. These concerns are also central to all the books in this series.

The chapters of this book have been substantially informed by debates within the Course Team, drawing on ideas, evidence and methods from a range of disciplines. In other words they are the products of a genuinely interdisciplinary process in which we have all learned from each other. Without these debates and regular discussion it would have been imposs- ible to produce this book. In such a collaborative process it should be clear that important contributions have been made to all of the chapters by people who are not explicitly named as authors.

An Open University Course Team stretches far beyond the core of aca- demics who write for it, to include consultants, tutor-testers and assessors who give invaluable advice, a course manager who somehow brings the pieces together, editors and designers who make it all look good, and secretaries who manage – against all the odds – to produce high-quality manuscripts to deadlines which everybody else does their best to forget. The work of all of these people is reflected in this book as well as in other parts of the course. We thank them for it.

ACKNOWLEDGEMENTS

Grateful acknowledgement is made to the following sources for permission to reproduce material in this book:

FIGURES

Figure 2.2: Central Statistical Office (1982) *Social Trends,* No. 12, reproduced with the permission of the Controller of Her Majesty's Stationery Office; Figure 2.3: Halsey, A.H. (ed.) (1988) *British Social Trends Since 1900: a guide to the changing social structure of Britain,* Macmillan Press Ltd; Figure 2.4: Gough, I. (1979) *The Political Economy of the Welfare State,* Macmillan Press Ltd; Figures 3.1, 3.2, 3.3, 3.4, 3.5: Hills, J. (1990) *The State of Welfare: the welfare state in Britain since 1974,* Clarendon Press, an imprint of Oxford University Press; Figure 6.1: Voges, W. and Rohwer, G. (1992) 'Receiving Social Assistance in Germany' in *Journal of European Social Policy,* Vol. 2, No. 3, 1992, Longman Group UK Ltd; Figure 8.1: *The Irish Times,* 4 September 1992; Figure 8.2: *The Economist,* 16 January 1988.

TABLES

Table 2.2: Sleeman , J.F. (1979) *Resources for the Welfare State: an economic introduction,* Longman Group UK Ltd; Table 2.4: Central Statistical Office (1982) *Social Trends,* No. 12, reproduced with the permission of the Controller of Her Majesty's Stationery Office; Tables 2.5 & 2.6: Halsey, A.H. (ed.) (1988) *British Social Trends Since 1990: a guide to the changing social structure of Britain,* Macmillan Press Ltd; Table 3.1: Hills, J. (1990) *The State of Welfare: the welfare state in Britain since 1974,* Clarendon Press, an imprint of Oxford University Press; Table 4.1: Johnson, N. (1991) 'Politics of Thatcherism: social policy in retreat?' (Conference paper delivered to 25th annual conference of the Social Policy Association, University of Nottingham 9-11 July 1991); Table 5.1: Chow, N.W.S. (1986) 'A review of social policies in Hong Kong' in Kwan, A.Y.H. and Chan, D.K.K. (eds) *Hong Kong Society: a reader,* Writers' and Publishers' Cooperative, Hong Kong; Table 5.2: Roberts, D. (1991) *Hong Kong, 1991,* Hong Kong Government; Table 7.1: O'Higgins, M., Schmaus, G. and Stephenson, G.(1990) 'Income distribution and redistribution: a microdata analysis for seven countries' in Smeeding, T., O'Higgins, M. and Rainwater, L. (eds) *Poverty, Inequality and Income Distribution in Comparative Perspective,* Harvester Wheatsheaf; Table 7.2: Sawyer, M. (1976) *Income Distribution in OECD Countries,* Organisation for Economic Cooperation and Development; Table 7.3: O'Higgins, M., Schmaus, G. and Stephenson, G. (1990) 'Income distribution and redistribution: a microdata analysis for seven countries' in Smeeding, T., O'Higgins, M. and Rainwater, L. (eds) *Poverty, Inequality and Income Distribution in Comparative Perspective,* Harvester Wheatsheaf; Table 7.4: Smeeding, T., Rainwater, L., Rein, M., Hauser, R. and Schaber, G. (1990) 'Income poverty in seven countries: initial estimates from the LIS database' in Smeeding, T., O'Higgins, M. and Rainwater, L. (eds) *Poverty, Inequality and Income Distribution in Comparative Perspective*, Harvester Wheatsheaf; Ginsburg, N. (1992) *Divisions of Welfare: a critical introduction to comparative social policy*, Sage Publications Ltd; Table 8.1: *Social Indicators for the European Community*, Eurostat, 1984; Table 8.2: *Ireland – A Directory 1992*, Institute of Public Administration, 1992; Tables 9.1 & 9.2: *The Future of Social Protection*, OECD Social and Policy Studies, No. 6 , 1988, Organisation for Economic Cooperation and Development; Table 9.3: Office for Official Publications of the European Communities (1991) *Eurostat: Basic Statistics of the Community*, 28th edition 1991, European Community; Table 9.4: Pfaller, A. *et al.* (eds) (1991) *Can the Welfare State Compete? A Comparative Study of Five Capitalist Countries*, Macmillan Academic & Professional Ltd.

CHAPTER 1
COMPARATIVE APPROACHES AND SOCIAL POLICY

ALLAN COCHRANE

1 WHY COMPARISON?

This book has two main aims. The first is to show the value of cross-national comparison in the analysis of social policy. Whilst recognizing the difficulties we aim to show not only that comparative analysis is possible, but also that it can deliver useful insights by highlighting alternatives to existing arrangements which are frequently taken for granted. This leads directly into the second aim, which is to develop a fuller understanding of welfare systems in a range of countries, both to see whether broad international trends can be identified and to use the experiences of others to inform domestic (British) debates.

If the growing number of books (and journals) promising comparative analysis is anything to go by, it is perhaps no longer necessary to make the case for a comparative approach to the study of social policy; on the contrary, it may now be single-country studies which need to be justified. It is increasingly assumed that reaching a full understanding of developments in any particular country is only possible if its experience is set in the context of those of other countries. It is also increasingly acknowledged that developments in any single country cannot be explained without setting them in the context of wider – global – changes. Yet there is a danger that the new orthodoxy may make it rather too easy to espouse a comparative approach without ever being quite clear why, or what questions can be most helpfully illuminated through comparison. We need to be clearer about the reasons for adopting this approach. Comparative study is only of significant value if it helps us to understand supra-national trends as well as highlighting what is specific to individual countries.

The value of comparison can be illustrated negatively by considering the way in which the development of the British welfare state has generally been interpreted. Traditionally, its growth until the late 1970s has been explained as a more or less inexorable progression from Poor Law to Department of Health and Social Security, with the welfare state receiving its endorsement in the implementation of the ideas of Beveridge and Keynes by successive governments after 1945. This has been described as an evolutionary process (Fraser, 1973) and, however modified by the consideration of historical detail, it has always read like a story of the triumph of rational social administration over the forces of darkness – or, in its least determinist form, of reluctant collectivism over anti-collectivism (George and Wilding, 1976/1986). It was easy to believe in the uniqueness and perfection of the British welfare state, at least until the (equally British or, at least, English) Margaret Thatcher began to 'reform' it in the 1980s.

But this approach missed the extent to which similar moves were taking place at the same time in many of the countries of the developed capitalist world especially in Western Europe and North America. It also ignored the extent to which other models of welfare might have been more effective than that of Britain, whether judged in terms of income maintenance, social support or the reduction of social and economic inequalities. In practice, a narrow focus on Britain made it easier to perpetuate the myths which helped to sustain Britain's peculiar form of political consensus after 1945, despite the tensions within it (see, for example, Johnson, 1977, Chs 1 and 2; Leys, 1989, Chs 4 and 6).

Equally importantly, analysis of this kind tended to ignore the global context within which the development of the British welfare state took place. Once this is taken into account, it is difficult to ignore the extent to which events in the UK were part of a wider international settlement, dominated by the economic and political power of the USA, but also influenced by a widely perceived military and ideological threat from the Soviet Union. Some analysts have gone beyond this to argue that the post-1945 boom years represented the high period of what has been called global Fordism (see, for example, Lipietz, 1987). Global Fordism has been characterized as having three main components:

- a monetary settlement at international level (institutionalized in the Bretton Woods agreement) which underpinned the continued expansion of world trade

- a combination of mass production linked to mass consumption at national level within the richer countries

which in turn was supported by the states in these countries through

- a mix of Keynesian economic policies and universalist forms of welfare which found their institutional expression in the so-called Keynesian welfare state.

Although the notion of global Fordism has been widely criticized, not least because it implies the existence (and apparent 'necessity') of a more or less unified system, the advantage of such a global focus is that it encourages an interest in the framework, structural constraints and dynamics within which welfare states were constructed in the developed capitalist countries after 1945.

Paradoxically, perhaps, it also makes it easier to explore some of the special features of individual cases which are equally important. Staying with the example of Britain for the moment, the experience of the Second World War confirmed its secondary status, setting up a continuing debate (rarely explicitly formulated by leading politicians) about whether it should continue to seek an international (global) role as deputy to the USA or accept an apparently more modest role as part of Europe (see, for example, Brett, 1985, Ch. 6). '1945' also heralded a gradual retreat from the formal trappings of Empire, often under pressure from national movements in the old colonies. The new welfare state implied a recognition that the UK's citizens (particularly the working class) could no longer rely on a successful Empire to provide economic and social benefits. The move towards a welfare state was not accompanied by similar reforms in its remaining colonies, but rather by increasingly restrictive controls on entry to the UK, thus effectively excluding their residents from welfare citizenship.

There are, therefore, essentially two sides to the comparative approach as it is developed in this book. The first is the strictly comparative one – which identifies and explores the similarities and differences between countries and their experiences – while the second has the rather different (although related) aim of setting those experiences within a wider global context.

2 DEFINING WELFARE STATES

The chapters which follow all look at countries which have been described as welfare states, but the implications of such a description may not always be clear, since the differences between them sometimes appear to be as important as any similarities. It is important not to impose any excessively tight definitions at the start, because, if we do so, the conclusions are likely to follow inescapably from the definition. Some countries will meet the standard and others will not. But a loose working definition is required to make comparison possible in the first place. So, what do we mean by 'welfare state'?

Mishra (1990) argues strongly that a commitment to full employment needs to be seen as a central component of mid twentieth-century welfare states, and it is an argument with which we have sympathy. After all, one of the most effective ways of reducing poverty (if that is one of the aims of welfare) is to ensure that access to paid employment is easily available. And, of course, where insurance is a major part of the welfare system, it is difficult to see how benefits can be maintained at reasonable levels without close to full employment (thereby ensuring that contributors outnumber beneficiaries).

In the end, however, we have excluded a commitment to full employment as a defining characteristic of a welfare state, not least because the general move away from full employment policies is so well recorded in all but a very small (and reducing) number of countries. In that sense it is already clear what the direction of change has been, and we would immediately be having to find a new term for the states in which we are interested. There is also a more fundamental problem with a focus on full employment, because it has an inherent gender bias. Most definitions of 'full employment' generally leave women in low-paid and part-time work on the continued assumption that most of them will be married and that the welfare needs of married women will be met through 'their breadwinner husbands' (Chamberlayne, 1991/2, p. 7).

This difficulty with 'full employment' is a particular expression of a more general problem in the analysis of welfare, when attempts are made clearly to differentiate between the public and the private domains – so that, for example, care which is undertaken by those employed by the state (in the public domain) is likely to be understood as part of the welfare state, whilst care undertaken in the domestic sphere (and probably not, or only marginally, funded by the state) is likely to be considered as outside the welfare state. As a result Dominelli chooses to work with a much broader definition, suggesting that 'the welfare state comprises ... those public and domestic relationships which take as their primary objectives the well-being of people' (1991, p. 9). Again we have a great deal of sympathy with this definition, but in this case find it difficult to know quite how to use it in practice. On one interpretation this could include almost every sphere of human activity: even the most profit-maximizing of entrepreneurs might justify their activity in terms of providing services to people. On another it could exclude most of human activity: even the most apparently selfless of individuals might explain her (or even his!) actions in terms of dedication to God, or to the benefits she got from her relationship to the person being helped. At least some of those working in the welfare state do so for the money, rather than out of any concern for the well-being of others. The conception of the state embodied in the definition is also difficult to utilize since it allows little scope for the state itself to have any power.

As a result, we have chosen to take a rather more limited definition as our starting-point. We shall principally (although not solely) be concerned with those policy areas generally associated with a relatively narrow use of the term 'welfare state', namely the involvement of the state in social security and social services. So, while acknowledging the potential importance of labour-market policies, we plan to start by looking, more modestly, at areas which are more widely understood as being to do with social welfare, that is those in which states take on responsibility for providing a range of welfare services and/or benefits to their citizens rather than those connected with the development of macro-economic policy and the maintenance of full employment. Because we acknowledge the dangers of sharply distinguishing between public and private, we shall focus particularly on the ways in which different welfare states have developed (implicit or explicit) family policies. Doing so should make it easier to explore the complex relations between social policy and ordinary life, acknowledging that states themselves help to define the domestic sphere.

This definition and its associated focus should not be taken to imply that direct state provision is a necessary or defining characteristic of welfare states – on the contrary, we start from the assumption that there is likely to be a 'mixed economy' of welfare, whose precise mix will itself be different in different countries, involving the state, the market, non-statutory organizations and networks of 'informal' carers. In other words it will be possible to identify different regimes in different countries. Equally, how-ever, we also accept Mishra's argument that the move to a more or less 'mixed economy' may not simply be a neutral one, in which one set of providers is seamlessly replaced by another. On the contrary, he suggests, it may mean a shift in emphasis: in some cases, for example, a 'disentitle-ment' to services may be buried within a process labelled 'privatization' (Mishra, 1990, p. 111). One of the reasons for developing a comparative approach is to explore the implications of these different mixes for welfare distribution in different countries.

Our concern with 'family' policies has both a pragmatic and a more basic justification. Pragmatically, it makes it possible to be a little more consist-ent about the examples developed and explored in the different countries considered in the book. But the choice of family policies in particular also reflects our understanding that a central feature of social policy in devel-oped capitalist countries is to be found in the way it defines and con-structs families as sources of informal welfare supply and – when families 'fail' – as causes of social problems. This focus makes it easier for us to consider the extent to which changes in 'mixed economies' of welfare may be encouraging 'disentitlement' for some families, and shifts towards placing of new (or additional) responsibilities on some members (usually women) of some families. Looking more closely at these policies helps to confirm the significance of gender-based differences in the operation of the welfare system, and to call into question the gender-neutral language of benefits, entitlement and citizenship.

3 MOVING TOWARDS COMPARISON: STATISTICS AND WELFARE REGIMES

If there is widespread agreement about the need to develop comparative analysis, there is much less on quite how this should be done or on the implications of doing so. One widely acknowledged pitfall of comparative work is that it is difficult to avoid interpreting the experience of other countries in terms of one's own. There is a risk that the home country of the researcher becomes some sort of a norm, against which everything else is judged. This is compounded by the difficulty of understanding the social and political 'rules' which are simply taken for granted in appar-ently similar, as well as widely different, systems. Similar terms may have quite different social meanings in different places. Although most countries have local governments, for example, the understanding of their role within different national political structures may be subtly different. Ashford draws a contrast between the historically subordinate status of local government in the United Kingdom and its higher status (if not greater power) in France. In official discussions within the UK it is frequently suggested that its mechanisms of democratic decision-making at local level may interfere with the local government's efficiency in delivering nationally agreed services. Ashford (1980) argues that such a distinction could not be made in France where mayors think of themselves as 'part of the democratic fabric of Republican France' with their own specific legitimacy (p. 96). In Germany the Constitutional Basic Law guarantees local government autonomy within the framework of law; in the UK it is assumed that the responsibilities of local government are delegated from the centre.

It will be clear to anyone who has travelled outside their own country that we understand the unspoken 'rules' of our own countries, but feel less secure about apparently similar situations in other countries. We are often unsure how to behave, even where – as in the case of the United States for English speakers – language is not a problem. Language differences merely highlight these difficulties. At its most basic, all translators of foreign languages know that words which 'mean' the same may conjure up quite different images in different societies. Even apparently the most straightforward words such as 'flat' or 'apartment' may imply significantly different living arrangements (or social relations) in different countries, although we generally use them as if they mean the same. And, of course some words – such as *Schadenfreude* and *Weltanschauung* – are often described as untranslatable. If these problems arise with ordinary language, how much more complicated things are likely to be in the highly contested fields of welfare and social policy.

The danger of pursuing this acknowledgement of differences too far, of course, is that it makes comparison impossible: everything becomes unique and little can be shared across cultures. So, in general, social scientific teeth are gritted, problems acknowledged and comparisons undertaken. But the legacy of these fears often survives and is reflected in collections of case studies of individual countries in which little attempt is made to explain how they link together, or even why they have been put together, except in the most general terms. Simply cataloguing different experiences is assumed to be worthwhile, encouraging readers to move from narrow parochialism, to open their eyes to the importance of difference. This is a justifiable but inherently limited position, since collections of case studies rarely allow enough space to explore differences effectively. Often attempts are made to draw out superficial similarities, while key differences are missed. Unless it is clear that chapters really are focusing on equivalent activities, comparison becomes impossible. A great deal of supposedly comparative work looks rather too much like an unconnected series of chapters (usually written by national experts) each summarizing the experience of one country and expecting the reader to draw his or her own conclusions.

One way out of this impasse has been to move away from the detailed study of individual countries, which are later brought together in a linked series of case studies, towards the study of more aggregated data, increasingly available from international agencies such as the United Nations and the Organisation for Economic Cooperation and Development (OECD). Using such data makes it possible to develop comparisons across a range of indicators, such as public expenditure on particular activities (for example, levels of social and defence spending) and patterns of income distribution. With the help of statistical analysis it is possible to draw conclusions about some of the factors which might have influenced differences, exploring a range of hypotheses including 'the impact of economic growth, the openness of the economy, demographic structure, the role of political parties, forms of interest mediation and so on' (Castles, 1989, p. 5). One conclusion of this research has been that party political control has had an impact on levels of social expenditure, with parties of the right resisting its growth and social democratic parties encouraging its increase (see, for example, Castles, 1982; Esping-Andersen, 1985; Heidenheimer *et al.*, 1990).

The advantage of approaches which utilize existing, internationally available aggregate data is that it is possible to identify broad trends and draw equally broad conclusions, but the gaps they leave remain frustratingly large. Whilst accepting the existence of a correlation between party political control of governments and levels of welfare spending, for example, one still wants to know what factors caused different parties to succeed in different places, and whether overall levels of spending conceal significant differences in the form of spending. This may be compounded by problems with the data used for comparisons. It is not always clear whether the data are strictly comparable, since different countries may use slightly different definitions and, for example, the exclusion of publicly regulated insurance schemes in one country and their inclusion in another may make it difficult to assess the allocation of resources to welfare. Allowances can be made for some of these (for example, by translating spending levels into standardized international units) but there remains a continuing concern because the data are supplied by the governments whose spending is being compared. It may be the case (as Castles suggests) that there is a high degree of standardization, but it does not take a very cynical observer – particularly one who has seen the ways in which definitions of unemployment were changed in the UK through the 1980s – to imagine how figures could be manipulated to suit the interests of the various governments.

Even without manipulation, serious problems may arise if aggregate figures are simply taken for granted. As we have already indicated, support for full employment can be seen as a central element of some welfare states, yet one consequence of high levels of unemployment may be increased expenditure on unemployment benefit. In the aggregate figures, therefore, a move away from a commitment to full employment (one measurement of the existence of a welfare state) may be reflected in terms which suggest an increased commitment to welfare spending (another measure of the existence of a welfare state). Again taking the UK as an example, although the governments of the 1980s were committed to and implemented a range of policies intended fundamentally to reshape the welfare state, the rise of welfare spending to meet the income support and benefit costs of rising unemployment may have obscured the actual extent of this shift.

Concerns such as these can perhaps be dealt with through careful – and sceptical – analysis of the easily available data. More importantly, however, as Castles acknowledges, the data only cover some areas, not all those of interest in the comparison of welfare states. As Castles explains:

> The initial thrust of comparative policy analysis had a very strong tendency to be concerned with topics for which comparable, and most specifically, quantitative data were readily available – public expenditures and macroeconomic outcomes in particular. Far less was it concerned with qualitative issues or intrusion into areas in which governments had not seen fit to provide standardized data. In other words, the appropriate domain of comparative analysis was conceptualized in terms of officially defined functions of the modern state, not so much because of the values that social scientists brought to their analysis, but rather because governments were themselves deeply implicated in those aspects of the domestic political economy and considered it useful to gather information on such matters. Until quite recently, it is fair to say that comparative policy analysis followed the primrose path of doing what it was easiest to do on the basis of information gathered by others.
>
> (Castles, 1989, p. 5)

Despite these concerns, at its best this method has been highly productive, making it possible to develop helpful typologies as a framework for exploring particular cases. Esping-Andersen (1990, pp. 26–30) uses it to identify what he calls three regimes of welfare capitalism – conservative, liberal and social-democratic – around which he suggests most welfare states can be clustered.

Conservative welfare regimes are those in which corporatist arrangements are most pronounced. Esping-Andersen defines these in terms which stress the ways in which state welfare is used to maintain (and even reinforce) existing class and status differentials, thus encouraging social and political stability and continued loyalty to the state. The state (rather than the market) is likely to be important in the delivery of welfare, but not in ways which encourage redistribution or equalization. These welfare regimes tend to dominate in those countries in which Catholic parties are strong, parties of the left weak and there has been a history of absolutism and authoritarianism. Because such regimes tend to be highly influenced by the Church, they are also usually committed to the maintenance of traditional family forms, and the state intervenes only when it is felt that the family cannot resolve the problems of its members. The entry of married women into the labour market is discouraged and benefits tend to encourage motherhood, while collective forms of childcare provision are underdeveloped. Esping-Andersen suggests that Austria, France, Germany and Italy can all be seen as regimes of this type.

Liberal welfare regimes are principally characterized by an emphasis on market-based social insurance and the use of means-testing in the distribution of benefits. Levels of universal transfer payments and forms of social insurance are 'modest' and welfare is largely oriented towards a class of the poor dependent on the state. Benefits are limited and stigmatized, because the model assumes that higher levels of benefit will reduce incentives to work. Private schemes are encouraged for those who wish to go beyond the minimum, and in some cases may be actively subsidized. Such regimes are, therefore, highly differentiated and stratified, with 'a blend of a relative equality of poverty among state-welfare recipients, market differentiated welfare among the majorities, and a class-political dualism between the two' (Esping-Andersen, 1990, p. 27). Examples of this model are said to include the USA, Canada and Australia.

In contrast to the other two, the social-democratic regime is characterized by principles of universalism and equality. This regime tends to encourage equality across classes, based on high standards, rather than the minima endorsed elsewhere. In order to achieve this, services and benefits had to be provided at levels acceptable (and attractive) to middle-class groups, and members of the working class were to have access to the same rights as those of the middle class. According to Esping-Andersen, 'This model crowds out the market, and consequently constructs an essentially universal solidarity in favour of the welfare state. All benefit; all are dependent; and all will presumably feel obliged to pay' (1990, p. 28). The attitude to the family within this model contrasts with those of the other two, because the state takes on and socializes many aspects of traditional family responsibilities (such as in providing support for children and the old) effectively encouraging individual independence, particularly for women who choose to work. Full employment is a central element in this regime, both because it provides income support and because it makes it possible to pay the costs of welfare. The Scandinavian countries provide the best examples of such regimes.

The power of such comparison is clear. It enables analysts of social policy to develop a picture both of patterns of difference and of broad directions of change. It allows them to raise their heads above the details of legislative programmes and their implementation in individual countries and to consider the importance of more general tendencies which cut across national developments. It provides a starting-point from which the significance of differences can be explored more fully. As Esping-Andersen makes clear, none of the regimes he identifies can be found in a perfect or pure form. Instead, each particular welfare state will have elements of all three in its make-up, and some may have quite distinctive features which are not reflected in the types he has identified. The UK provides a good example of a system which fits uneasily into any of the three regime types, although Esping-Andersen (1990, p.26) suggests that it is closest to the liberal one.

4   INCLUDING THE EXCLUDED

Despite its overall strength, some of the weaknesses associated with research based on international statistics are also apparent in Esping-Andersen's writing. The main policy areas which he explores are social security expenditure and pension expenditure (in Chapters 4 and 5) and labour-market policies (in Part II) (Esping-Andersen, 1990). These are the areas in which his conclusions about the importance of class alliances or coalitions might be expected to find their greatest support. And they are also the areas for which internationally comparative data are most likely to be available in a reasonably standardized form. If one were looking for policy areas in which non-class interests might be mobilized, or, indeed, those in which other forms of class politics were important (for example in the workplace), then other sources of evidence would be required. This is perhaps most obvious in areas such as childcare provision or reproductive rights, in which one might expect the role of women's organizations to have been significant but which are not well represented in international statistics.

The most striking absences from these statistical approaches – and indeed (except in asides) from Esping-Andersen's regimes – are those relating to gender. And yet it is clear that the welfare arrangements in different countries are all based on key assumptions about the different positions of men and women in the labour market. One of the problems with Esping-Andersen's approach is that it tends to underplay this. Although, as we noted above, he points to some important differences between the ways in which the regimes he identifies deal with families, and women within them, he does not follow up these issues in his more detailed analysis of statistics. Langan and Ostner note that 'Women appear almost by accident and then vanish again', because they are not central to the theoretical framework utilized by Esping-Andersen and they only appear when the statistics make that necessary (for example in the discussion of labour markets) (Langan and Ostner, 1991, p. 130). More often the discussion deals with apparently non-gendered categories, focusing on the extent to which different regimes allow a greater or lesser 'decommodification' of labour, that is, 'the degree to which individuals, or families, can uphold a socially acceptable standard of living independent of market participation' (i.e. without paid employment) (Esping-Andersen, 1990, p. 37).

Of course, this fails to acknowledge the extent to which women already operate in a 'decommodified' domestic sphere and the extent to which their involvement in that sphere is a necessary basis for the 'commodification' of labour. Langan and Ostner argue that 'men and women are "gendered commodities" with different experiences of the labour market resulting from their different relationship to family life' and stress the importance of appreciating the domestic division of labour 'in understanding the gendered nature of the welfare state and its associated social stratification' (1991, p. 131). Taylor-Gooby develops this point, arguing that: 'the gender division of care coincides with patterns of access to and status in paid employment that, despite national variations, deny women equal opportunities in this sphere' (1991, p. 101).

These points are reinforced when consideration is given to 'welfare services provided free by women in the domestic economy' (Dominelli, 1991, p. 8). These, of course, find no expression in aggregate statistics, yet may be of crucial importance in making judgements about who gains and who loses within particular welfare regimes – or particular 'mixed economies of welfare'. One attempt – by the Family Policy Studies Centre – to estimate what it would cost to pay wages to those currently involved in providing unpaid care in the UK puts it at between £15 and £24 billion per year (Evandrou *et al.*, 1990, p. 258). If anything, this is likely to be an underestimate. As Dominelli goes on to argue, this makes it necessary to move away from approaches which sharply distinguish between the public and private spheres, since 'treating these worlds as unconnected to each other enables non-feminist theories to ignore the contribution the domestic economy makes to sustaining and reproducing public welfare relationships' (1991, p. 9).

If gender is one factor which is absent in much comparative work, 'race' is another. Yet a crucial element in most modern welfare states is that they have developed to a large extent in response to changing understandings and interpretations of 'race' and that they have in turn helped to shape and reshape the ways in which racial divisions are understood in the societies of which they are part. The Western European welfare states were created in part as a means of defining the continued status of their residents and citizens, in sharp contrast to the outsiders for whom access was to be limited. Throughout the years since 1945 one of the recurrent themes of popular newspapers in most Western European countries has been the extent to which outsiders of one sort or another (usually black and frequently defined as 'immigrants') have been seeking to 'take advantage' of their welfare benefits and other provisions. Welfare citizenship has been a means of including some people, while excluding others. As with the case of gender, the racial division of labour within the welfare system has also served to reinforce and reproduce fundamental divisions. Since a high proportion of the support and service jobs within Western European welfare states are held by black people, and these jobs are usually low paid, this helps to confirm their position at the bottom of the social system, within what Fiona Williams has called 'a racially and patriarchally structured capitalism' (1990, Ch. 6). Dominelli has listed a number of factors which need to be considered in the analysis of welfare in this context. They include: 'the exclusion of black people from access to positive welfare resources ... the over-representation of black people in its punitive elements ... [the] use of black people's labour to finance welfare provisions on the cheap ... and the detrimental impact of policies on black families' (Dominelli, 1991, p. 2). Few of these can be identified in the easily available international statistics.

5 MODELS AND STRUCTURE

Comparative work based on aggregate statistics produces a useful starting-point, as much for the questions it raises as for the conclusions it offers. But the gaps – what is not explained – are as important as what is explained. In order to move on, it becomes necessary to return to more detailed studies of individual countries or groups of countries, both in order to go below the level of official statistics and explore the content of welfare policies, and to fill in some of the gaps, to understand why particular welfare states do not quite fit the various types. In moving in this direction we are following the route advocated by Castles in his discussion of comparative public policy. He argues that although comparative analysis cannot deliver a model of welfare able to identify convincing and continuing regularities from a bank of official statistics, it is able to identify 'puzzles' which need to be explained and looked at in the context of a more limited number of cases (Castles, 1989, p. 10). In other words, if one starts from a belief that there are substantial differences between two countries and the available statistics suggest their welfare outcomes are similar in some particular respects, then it might be worth asking why. Conversely, where similarities are expected and differences are apparent, questions may need to be raised. This is a more modest form of comparison, but not a retreat back to a belief in the need for an endless catalogue of unique cases. On the contrary, it is only recognition of the interdependence of welfare states within a wider set of international arrangements that provides the basis for a return to particular cases.

Despite the weaknesses which have been considered above, the three welfare regimes identified by Esping-Andersen are helpful in providing a starting-point for comparative analysis, particularly if they are not restricted to the areas on which he concentrates. It is possible, for example, to point to ways in which the different regimes might also imply different positions for women within them (Taylor-Gooby, 1991, pp. 102–3). They may also provide the starting-point for a more systematic analysis of particular welfare states. This is the method which we have adopted here, setting out to follow the approach described by Ginsburg (1992) as one of 'structured diversity'. This acknowledges the wide range of differences between welfare states but also understands that they exist within wider economic, social and political frameworks which help to structure that diversity.

It is in order to emphasize the importance of this that we start with an extended investigation of the development of the British welfare state since 1945. This may seem rather paradoxical: a return – despite all our high ambitions – to the usual quick run through from Beveridge to Thatcherism. But our argument does not take Britain for granted as a focus of study, as a paradigm of the 'welfare state' against which those of other (less fortunate) countries have to be judged. On the contrary, we set out to use the Britain as a case study of a welfare state both in order to help us to understand what is distinctive about it and what it shares with other welfare states. We seek to explore and identify what was historically specific about Britain within a wider set of international arrangements (welfare state construction and restructuring). Our starting-point is the wider international settlement (or settlements) which were arrived at in the wake of the Second World War. The bases of these are, of course, to be found in earlier periods, but '1945' effectively settled the ground rules for the next three decades, endorsing already apparent directions. These will be explored more fully in Chapter 2, but it should be clear that European welfare states developed in the context of the economic and political dominance of the USA and the perceived threat of conflict with the Soviet Union. An important justification for our approach is to explore the consequences of the break-up of these arrangements and the coterminous (if not necessarily causally related) crises faced by many of the modern welfare states.

The first part of the book concentrates on the British experience, not because it is in some way more important (or more 'normal') than that of other countries, but because it is the one with which we as authors based in Britain can connect most easily. Chapters 2 and 3 look at Britain as if it were a case like any other, seeking to identify its special features and those which link it to other welfare states. They highlight the ways in which the British welfare system has been shaped and reshaped since 1945, questioning the notion that there was a welfare consensus which was unchallenged until 1979. At the end of the first part the British model should be clear: it is, as Esping-Andersen notes, a rather uneasy mix of universalism and the market, although Esping-Andersen's own assessment of this mix seems substantially to underestimate the significance of universalism in the British case. Chapter 4 explores many of the implicit assumptions made about family structure and 'race', which helped to define the meanings of welfare 'citizenship' in the UK. Its welfare state was a post-imperial one, constructed around a particular vision of the white (English) 'respectable' working-class family, headed by a male breadwinner.

In the second part of the book we move on to consider other cases, which have been chosen partly to exemplify the regime types developed by Esping-Andersen, but with the clear understanding that these types only provide a starting-point and that the actual experience of welfare in each may bear little relationship to what might be expected from the model. The chapters do not focus on Esping-Andersen's own relatively narrow concerns with pension rights and labour markets, but instead seek to consider a wider range of power relations and welfare provisions, in the job of providing more rounded discussions of the particular cases, without losing sight of our broader comparative ambitions. Two examples of conservative/corporatist states are considered, in order to help clarify the range of differences which may exist within one model (see Table 1.1). Each case has also been chosen because of its relationship to the UK or because its approach to welfare is likely to inform our understanding of the British welfare state. In addition, the cases chosen are intended to help clarify the extent to which there is a degree of convergence between welfare states within Europe and ultimately, as Chapter 9 asks, whether it is possible to identify the first signs of the development of a European welfare state. We have not attempted to produce a comprehensive survey of all possible forms of welfare regime, but have retained a more limited focus, with Britain at its centre. This means that we explicitly chose not to include any substantive discussion of the USA, of the post-Stalinist regimes of central and Eastern Europe (although there will be some reflection on these changes as they have affected Germany), or of welfare arrangements in the Third World (except in the discussion of Hong Kong).

Table 1.1   States and welfare regimes

State	Regime type
Hong Kong	Liberal/market
Germany	Conservative
Sweden	Social-democratic
Republic of Ireland	Conservative

Chapter 5 provides a bridge from Britain to a wider international context by looking at the development of social policy in Hong Kong since 1945. Although its experience is linked directly to its status as a British colony, Hong Kong's welfare regime is fundamentally different to that of Britain. At the same time as the Beveridge Report was introducing elements of universalism to the British welfare state, in Hong Kong the same government was creating a more residual, liberal or market-based system that was also being justified in terms of Chinese traditions, particularly in terms of what was claimed to be the Chinese approach to family life. All the different cases are important as examples of the working out of the different models in practice, but this case highlights some of the uncertainties and confusions to be found in the British model itself. Elements of the liberal approach are, of course, to be found in Britain as well as in Hong Kong. But the Hong Kong case is also significant because it confirms the extent to which the welfare states of the developed capitalist countries (particularly in Europe) were not seen as appropriate for export to their colonies or other countries of the Third World. The welfare states of the prosperous countries at the core depended on the continued existence of marginal systems in the poorer countries of the periphery.

The next chapter focuses on Germany as an example of more corporatist arrangements. The strength and resilience of the German system and the ways in which it provides welfare support may come as rather a surprise to British readers who are more used to comparisons with the USA as *the* model of market capitalist welfare. Here is another country fundamentally (and apparently successfully) committed to market capitalism yet with quite a different set of arrangements in the welfare field. If the USA offers a mixed economy dominated by the private sector, the mixed economy of welfare in Germany is a rather different one, deeply rooted in a wider range of voluntary and church-based organizations, and organized around a clear notion of 'partnership' between the different sectors. The German system is explicitly based on the notion of 'subsidiarity', according to which welfare provision should always be the responsibility of the most basic unit possible, on a range from individual through family and voluntary sector to the different levels of the state. The state will only intervene when the family is unable to support its own members. But there is also an equally clear understanding that the state retains an important role in maintaining social norms and encouraging particular social relationships – most notably in terms of gender relations, but also in defining those who may be accepted as 'German'. The absorption of East by West Germany (the German Democratic Republic by the Federal Republic of Germany) in the early years of the 1990s makes it easier to explore some of the tensions within the system, since although the East-ern model (of enforced universalism) was largely rejected, it continues to raise questions about attitudes to childcare, abortion rights and support for women in paid employment. It also highlights some of the difficulties of giving rights to insurance-based benefits to those who have never been part of insurance schemes.

Chapter 7 turns to Sweden, which has generally been used as the classic example of the social-democratic – universalist or socialist – model. Many of the aspects of the model are indeed to be found in the Swedish welfare state, particularly in the extent to which the middle class as well as the working class benefits from the welfare state, and the extent to which women have greater access to the labour market and there is more sup-port for childcare than in other countries. But the difficulties of sustain-ing the model in a time of economic difficulties is increasingly apparent, as are some of the underlying assumptions of universalism and the prom-ise of economic independence for women. The extent to which women may be effectively disadvantaged by some aspects of the welfare system is considered, as well as the ways in which in Sweden, too, it is used to define citizenship, particularly with respect to minority populations.

The fourth case – focused on the Republic of Ireland – is an example of more conservative, corporatist arrangements, maintaining status differ-entials with extensive involvement from the Church, and clearly con-servative attitudes to the position of women. As in Germany, the assumption is that women tend to leave the labour market on marriage, but the welfare system does not provide the same levels of financial support as in Germany – nor are levels of 'breadwinner' income compara-ble. In Ireland the mix of different elements cutting across regime types, in particular involving a heavy dose of liberal approaches, is noticeable, too. But the mix is significantly different from that in Britain. If Britain is an example of an uneasy mix between liberalism and universalism (or social democracy), the Irish system is an equally uneasy mixture of cor-poratism and liberalism. Most explicitly of all the cases under consider-ation, Ireland's welfare system has begun to be influenced by its relationship to a wider European context through membership of the European Community. This begins to raise questions about convergence at a European level that are discussed more fully in the book's final chapter.

6 CONVERGENCE OR DIFFERENCE?

Running through all the cases and through the book as a whole is a concern to understand the nature of the crises through which all the welfare states under discussion have been passing, with a view to assessing how far these crises have been resolved, in what ways, to whose benefit and at whose expense. An underlying issue in a great deal of comparative study is the extent to which welfare policies are becoming more or less similar. One argument which has been put strongly (for example, by Esping-Andersen, 1990, Ch. 9) is that the US-influenced liberal model is becoming, or is likely to become, dominant across welfare states, and in the face of this perceived shift others have argued for a form of social corporatism as a viable alternative which should be adopted more widely (see, for example, Mishra, 1990)*. The conclusions of our own surveys are certainly rather more equivocal. There still seems to be a high degree of confusion and uncertainty in the field of welfare, with solutions or clear future directions difficult to identify.

It is, however, perhaps possible to draw rather more definite conclusions about some other continuing features of welfare states which are more widely shared. In their different ways all of them make assumptions about the roles to be played by women and informal carers (also often women), and in the 1990s it looks as if that role is going to be of increasing importance, with increased pressures on those performing it. It is also increasingly clear that welfare – however universally it is defined – is only available to those recognized as citizens. Different groups have different rights and different access. Paradoxically, it is frequently those employed at the lowest levels of the welfare system who are most explicitly excluded from its benefits.

Western Europe is becoming more integrated economically, and this is having fundamental impacts on systems of welfare, some of which are discussed more fully in the final chapter of the book. One aspect of this has been described as the development of 'Fortress Europe', that is, a Europe whose main justification is to sustain high levels of welfare and employment within it, while excluding those from outside who also wish to benefit (see, for example, Gordon, 1989). In the 1990s this means not only that groups like Germany's *Gastarbeiter* (guestworkers) will only be allowed entry on strict conditions and that it will be possible to exclude the feared stream of migrants from the countries previously part of the Soviet bloc, all looking for the promise of wealth in the West, but it will also undermine the position of existing populations which are seen as 'non-European', including the Algerians in France and Britain's black and Asian people. Baldwin-Edwards (1991) argues strongly that most of the countries of the EC are effectively moving towards a model (pioneered by the Benelux countries, France and Germany) characterized by strict

---

*Mishra's notion of social corporatism is close to Esping-Andersen's 'social democracy' and the cases he examines are those of Sweden and Austria (Mishra, 1990, Ch. 3).

immigration control, 'permitting only economically necessary guestwork-ers and humanitarian considerations of family reunification and refugees' (p. 219). Refugee status is becoming increasingly tightly defined through-out Europe as a means of restricting the numbers able to seek asylum in these countries.

The promises (or threats) of harmonization of social as well as economic policy within the European Community reinforce the urgency of clarify-ing the different models in contention. The current expectation seems to be that the welfare regimes of the northern parts of the EC will appear too costly in comparison with the cheaper welfare regimes of the poorer south and that this is one of the pressures leading towards what is predicted to be the ultimate victory of liberal approaches within Europe. Even if these are the dominant pressures, however, it is not clear that liberal market approaches will necessarily be the most effective (or cheapest) in deliver-ing welfare. It is possible to envisage a residual version of all the welfare regimes, even if it is not always easy to see how each would be able to sustain legitimacy in such a context. It may be more appropriate to acknowledge that the complexity of the mix between regime types is likely to increase. There may also be pressures working in other direc-tions, resisting moves to residualization. It may be too early to dismiss the positive benefits to employers as well as welfare citizens from welfare states closer in form to social-democratic and conservative regimes and Esping-Andersen holds out the hope of democratic class struggle as a means of constructing popular (and expensive) welfare systems. Alterna-tives might also be available if alliances are built across class lines, recognizing the particular position and needs of women and of groups such as 'guestworkers' and Britain's black population within existing welfare states. We hope that this book will make its own contribution to informing debates about future welfare strategies in Britain and more widely within Europe.

REFERENCES

Ashford, D. (1980) 'A Victorian drama: the fiscal subordination of British local government' in Ashford, D. (ed.) *Financing Urban Government in the Welfare State*, London, Croom Helm, pp. 71–96.

Baldwin-Edwards, M. (1991) 'The socio-political rights of migrants in the European Community' in Room, G. (ed.) op. cit., pp. 189–234.

Brett, E. A. (1985) *The World Economy since the War: the politics of uneven development*, London, Macmillan.

Castles, F. (ed.) (1982) *The Impact of Parties: politics and policies in democratic capitalist states*, London, Sage.

Castles, F. (1989) 'Introduction: puzzles of political economy' in Castles, F. (ed.) *The Comparative History of Public Policy*, Cambridge, Polity Press, pp. 1–15.

Chamberlayne, P. (1991/2) 'New directions in welfare? France, West Germany, Italy and Britain in the 1980s', *Critical Social Policy*, no. 33, pp. 5–21.

Dominelli, L. (1991) *Women across Continents: feminist comparative social policy*, Hemel Hempstead, Harvester Wheatsheaf.

Esping-Andersen, G. (1985) *Politics Against Markets: the social democratic road to power*, Princeton, NJ, Princeton University Press.

Esping-Andersen, G. (1990) *The Three Worlds of Welfare Capitalism*, Cambridge, Polity Press.

Evandrou, M., Falkingham, J. and Glennerster, H. (1990) 'The personal social services' in Hills, J. (ed.) *The State of Welfare*, Oxford, Clarendon Press.

Fraser, D. (1973) *The Evolution of the British Welfare State*, London, Macmillan.

George, V. and Wilding, P. (1976 and 1986) *Ideology and Social Welfare*, London, Routledge and Kegan Paul.

Ginsburg, N. (1992) *Divisions of Welfare: a critical introduction to comparative social policy*, London, Sage.

Gordon, P. (1989) *Fortress Europe? The meaning of 1992*, London, Runnymede Trust.

Heidenheimer, A. J., Heclo, H. and Adams, C. T. (1990) *Comparative Public Policy: the politics of social choice in America, Europe and Japan*, New York, St Martin's Press (3rd edn).

Johnson, N. (1977) *In Search of the Constitution: reflections on state and society*, Oxford, Pergamon.

Langan, M. and Ostner, I. (1991) 'Gender and welfare' in Room, G. (ed.) op. cit., pp. 127–50.

Leys, D. (1989) *Politics in Britain: from Labourism to Thatcherism*, London, Verso (2nd edn).

Lipietz, A. (1987) *Mirages and Miracles: the crises of global Fordism*, London, Verso.

Mishra, R. (1990) *The Welfare State in Capitalist Society: policies of retrenchment and maintenance in Europe, North America and Australia*, Hemel Hempstead, Harvester Wheatsheaf.

Room, G. (ed.) (1991) *Towards a European Welfare State?*, Bristol, School for Advanced Urban Studies.

Taylor-Gooby, P. (1991) 'Welfare state regimes and welfare citizenship', *Journal of European Social Policy*, vol. 1, no. 2, pp. 93–105.

Williams, F. (1990) *Introduction to Social Policy*, Cambridge, Polity Press.

CHAPTER 2
THE BRITISH WELFARE STATE:
FOUNDATION AND MODERNIZATION

JOHN CLARKE AND MARY LANGAN

INTRODUCTION

This chapter and the next deal with the organization of social welfare in Britain in the period since the Second World War. They examine how different sectors – the family, the market and the state – have been coordinated in a 'mixed economy of welfare' and how the balance of that mixed economy has changed during the period. Although we are concerned with the relationship between the three sectors in this mixed economy, in both chapters we give disproportionate attention to the state. This is not because the state necessarily plays the primary role in *providing* welfare but because it is the state which is the *organizing* force that establishes the 'mix' between the sectors: the balance of familial, market and public provision which makes up social welfare at any particular time.

Our concern, then, is to highlight the political choices, the settlements between different interests, which have shaped and re-shaped the composition of the mixed economy of welfare. In these two chapters we have referred to the different patterns of mixed economies of welfare as 'welfare regimes'. This is both a less cumbersome phrase than 'mixed economies of welfare' and highlights our concern to focus on political choices and the state's role in coordinating the different components of welfare provision. Because of this focus, these two chapters are specifically about Britain rather than the UK. Although Northern Ireland is subject to the same welfare legislation, the nature of the state and the forms of political organization there have meant that welfare has a relatively distinct social and economic character (see, for example, Ditch and Morrissey, 1992).

This chapter begins with a discussion of the constellation of international and domestic political factors which provided the context within which the welfare regime emerged. We then divide the period into two phases, the first from the mid 1940s up to the mid 1960s, during which the broad framework of the welfare state was established, and the second from the mid 1960s to the mid 1970s, when considerable expansion and modernization took place on the foundations established in the immediate post-war decades. In each period we consider the particular relationship between the state, the market and the family in the provision of welfare.

The distinctive feature of the early post-war years was the expanded role of the state in providing benefits and services and in economic management, by comparison with the pre-war period. The comprehensive package of reforms affecting education, health, housing and social security introduced between 1944 and 1949 established a welfare regime in which the state promoted the principles of universal provision. However, both the market and the family continued to fulfil important welfare functions while the state sector itself retained important elements of an earlier individualist/selectivist model of welfare alongside a wider commitment to collectivist/universal principles. Although the post-war welfare regime came under growing pressure as a consequence of rising unemployment and other social and economic changes from the mid 1970s onwards, it remained substantially intact until the Conservative governments of the 1980s.

In our survey of the post-war welfare state we are particularly concerned to draw out the – often unstated – assumptions of welfare policy about the role of the family, the position of women and the nature of social citizenship. It is clear that from the outset the welfare state assumed as the norm the respectable, white, working-class family, headed by a securely employed father, with wife-and-mother in an appropriately dependent and subordinate role. Indeed the British welfare state, based on this model family, was presented to the world as a great national monument, attained in the face of imperial decline. However, as unemployment, immigration, divorce and family breakdown, not to mention poverty and homelessness, increased during the post-war decades, the problematic character of the citizenship rights offered through the welfare state became increasingly apparent.

I   FOUNDATION

Like the other western nations, Britain faced major tasks of social and economic reconstruction at the end of the Second World War. The form of welfare state that emerged was the outcome of the particular balance of international and domestic social forces in the immediate post-war period. A complex combination of conditions framed the new world order that took shape in the late 1940s. Although the Allies emerged victorious from the war, popular confidence in the capacity of unrestrained market forces to guarantee either economic or political stability had been severely undermined by the events of the pre-war decades. Free market economies had been seriously discredited by the worldwide slump of the 1930s and by the slide of much of Europe first into fascist dictatorship and then into war. By contrast, the Soviet Union had emerged with unprecedented prestige from the war, its system of state planning apparently vindicated. A wave of popular radicalization throughout the west insisted on 'no return to the thirties' as the price to be paid for the sacrifices of the war years. Social, as well as economic, reconstruction were central issues for post-war governments.

The issue for capitalist societies in the west was how to combine the 'economic engine' of the free market with arrangements for ensuring social peace domestically. Reconciling these needs focused attention on economic management (rather than state ownership as in the Soviet model) to minimize the fluctuations of the free market and on social policies directed at the promotion of social harmony. As Esping-Andersen (1990) has shown, different countries developed different solutions to these problems, creating a variety of 'welfare capitalisms'. The creation of the British welfare regime was framed by these same conditions, overlaid by the nature of its position in the world order which emerged at the end of the Second World War.

A central feature of this position was Britain's subordinate place in the 'Western Alliance' under US leadership, an alliance whose defining characteristics were increasingly sharply etched in opposition to the 'eastern' or 'Soviet' bloc in the Cold War. US leadership of this alliance combined military, economic and political power, most clearly expressed in its domination of the post-war reconstruction of Europe: rebuilt using US funds, shaped by US concerns about the Soviet threat and enthusiastically courted as a market for US economic expansion. Britain was locked tightly in that alliance – the 'special relationship' celebrating close military, economic and cultural ties which linked Britain and the USA and creating an 'Atlanticist' rather than 'European' orientation in British politics (Calvocoressi, 1987).

This new world order provided the framework within which the British welfare state took shape. The traditional British establishment was deeply tarnished by bitter memories of the long depression years, by the shame of appeasement and by its early incompetence in the conduct of war, symbolized by Dunkirk and savagely caricatured in the figure of 'Colonel Blimp'. Even Churchill's wartime role could not save the Conservative party from the landslide defeat of 1945. The leadership of the Labour party, experienced in earlier minority governments and in the war cabinets, now stepped forward to implement a national revival programme largely drafted by two Liberals – John Maynard Keynes and William Beveridge. The legislative reforms that inaugurated the welfare state met the social needs of economic reconstruction. They also addressed the demands of a labour movement which articulated the egalitarian and democratic ethos engendered by the experience of wartime mass mobilization.

The creation of the welfare state was to play an important role in enhancing national prestige abroad, compensating to some extent for the loss of status to the USA and for imperial decline. In the post-war period Britain placed great emphasis on its capacity to give the world a moral lead, through the vitality of its democratic institutions (which had stood firm against fascism) and the values of citizenship and social solidarity (upheld by its comprehensive and progressive welfare system). The eugenic themes of the Beveridge Report, with its imperialist emphasis on the role of mothers in 'ensuring the adequate continuation of the British race and British ideals in the world', reflected this outlook (Cohen, 1985). Richard Titmuss, the pre-eminent figure in post-war social administration, endorsed the prevailing concern about the 'future of the white peoples' and drew attention to the way in which western civilization had 'slowly evolved a higher way of life', insisting that it was 'our duty to help and guide the teeming millions of India and Africa to a more abundant life' (quoted in Jacobs, 1985, p. 10).

At the same time the terms of Britain's subordination to the USA constrained the development of the welfare state. In the late 1940s US economic pressure reinforced domestic political opposition to social reform and spending on social services (Brett, Gilliatt and Pople, 1982). As early as 1947 the burden of financing US loans precipitated a balance-of-payments crisis, leading to the curtailment of the council housing and school building programmes (Morgan, 1984). By 1950–51 the high defence budget required to sustain British support for US involvement in Korea resulted in further welfare cuts and the imposition of charges for false teeth and prescriptions. From the outset, the British post-war welfare state was circumscribed by its subordinate position in the Atlantic Alliance.

These economic and political conditions framed the internal reconstruction of the British economy and state. They form the boundaries of the post-war political consensus which oversaw the creation and development of the British welfare state. While the consensus allowed scope for considerable domestic political disagreement, keeping the major dimensions of party alignment alive and active, the external conditions were accepted by all three major parties (Conservative, Labour and Liberal) as establishing the limits within which governments were able to act. More than this, the consensus extended to agreement over the major directions which governments would pursue within those limits. At the core was an acceptance that a level of government intervention in economic management was necessary to overcome the inherent instabilities of a free market economy and to promote full employment.

Macro-economic policies aimed to achieve a number of objectives: to promote Britain's competitiveness in a more complex world market; to minimize the economic and social disruptions brought about by the cycles of slump and boom to which unregulated free markets seemed prone (and to which the crises of the 1930s presented stark testimony); and to encourage the politically significant goal of full employment. While parties differed on the level and form that such macro-economic management might take (for instance, over whether nationalization of key sectors was desirable), the principle of intervention was widely shared. This commitment to intervention owed much to the experience of the wartime 'command economy' and its perceived effectiveness in promoting national efficiency.

The state was accepted as having a national 'coordinating role' in both economic and social management. Nonetheless, the stress both in wartime and the subsequent decades was firmly on the principle of coordination – improving the functioning of what was to remain a fundamentally capitalist or free enterprise economy in which nationalized or public-sector production was to play, at most, a supporting or infrastructural, rather than leading, role. Equally, the Keynesian policies of economic management adopted in the post-war period were geared to smoothing the workings of a free market through affecting the conditions of demand which formed the economic environment of individual enterprises, rather than the direct management of production implied in a fully fledged 'command' economy.

1.1   THE BRITISH WELFARE REGIME: STATE, MARKET AND FAMILY

The post-war reconstruction of welfare in Britain involved the elaboration of a new set of relationships between the state, the market and the family. In assessing that set of relationships it is useful to think of welfare provision not as a unitary structure ('the welfare state') but as a complex and changing pattern of relationships between the state, the market and the family. It is probably best captured by an analogy with the term used to describe the British economy in the same period – the 'mixed economy'. What was constructed between 1944 and 1948 was a new mixed economy of welfare.

Although most attention has been given to the expansion of state provision in this period, this expansion was framed by the presumption that most welfare needs would be satisfied by the family and the market. Only in some instances, notably education and health, was it the state's role to be the primary agency of provision and even here private provision continued alongside the work of the state. As we have seen, Britain's relationship with the United States established an external constraint on welfare spending which influenced both the structure and standards of the welfare state from the outset. Equally importantly, the social relations of the market-place permeated the new system, creating a 'social division of welfare' that reflected deep-rooted class inequalities in British society (Titmuss, 1958). To the extent that welfare remained a matter of 'private' concern, the structural inequalities of individual income and family wealth were able to exercise a significant influence on access to 'welfare goods'.

In addition to its direct role in the provision of health care and education, the state was required to support the institutions of the market and the family, filling gaps where the market and the family failed, but with no intent to replace them as the main source of support to individuals. In their different ways the programmes of public housing, income maintenance, services to neglected children and so on, assumed that needs would be met primarily through (male) waged work and the services which the wage can buy, and through the services provided within the family by wives/mothers. Even in the income maintenance programmes, the predominant mode of providing for benefits was to be social insurance, which presumed a pattern of sustained employment in order to accrue a contribution record.

In these ways the foundation of the post-war welfare state assumed a particular type of 'mixed economy' of support for the individual's well-being based on an economic and social architecture in which the 'family wage' was the lynchpin, linking the labour market to the distribution of social roles and dependency by age and gender within the family. Embedded in this structure is a clear view of a gendered division of labour. The idea of the 'family wage' justified differentials between male and female wage rates, men's higher rates reflecting their role as 'breadwinner' for dependants. Within the family, women traded housework, childbirth and child-rearing and physical and emotional caring as 'labours of love' in return for economic support (Finch and Groves (eds), 1983). In practice, much 'welfare work' was expected to be undertaken within the family either by spending some of the 'family wage' (on insurance policies or at the chemists) or by women 'looking after' young children, ill family members or dependent relatives. The provision of state welfare was intended to supplement and support this hidden welfare work and the family economy.

1.2 NATIONALIZING INFRASTRUCTURE: HEALTH AND EDUCATION

In the areas where the state intervened most extensively through the post-war welfare reforms – health and education – 'market' or private provision was marginalized but not abolished. Both the Education Act 1944 and the National Health Service Act 1946 extended and integrated previously existing state provision in their respective fields, creating national systems which were – significantly – free at the point of use. Universal access to secondary education and health provision marked major advances over pre-war patterns of provision and access, in particular the structures of class advantage associated with being able to pay privately for education and health services.

Nonetheless, these developments rearranged rather than removed the private sector in education and health services. The development of both proposals ran into strongly entrenched interests intent on defending private-sector provision. In health, this resistance was marshalled by the British Medical Association which preserved the right of both hospital consultants and general practitioners to continue with private practice alongside their National Health Service work, as well as to remain in private practice outside the state sector. In education the Fleming Committee reported on the future of the private sector, recommending the continuation of 'independent schools' together with their closer integration with the state sector. Although permissive powers were established, allowing for the use of up to a quarter of private places for pupils from the state sector in return for subsidies to private schools, these powers were little used. As later research was to reveal, the architecture of both class and gender inequalities was reconstructed rather than dismantled within the new secondary education system. The independent sector retained its privileged position and was supplemented by the creation of the grammar school stream. For most working-class children the expansion of access to secondary education led straight to the gates of the secondary modern.

Both the health and the education changes bore the marks of the wartime experience. The home front had revealed the limitations of the pre-existing systems of health care and education, while the coordination of wartime services (such as the Emergency Medical Service and the evacuation of schoolchildren) indicated the possibility of the state playing a more enhanced role in the organization and provision of welfare. Although such possibilities were doubtless moved forward by particular political interests and lobbies, the experience of state coordination during the wartime economy provided the springboard for post-war reforms.

The reconstruction of education and health around principles of universal state provision resembled the processes of 'economic' nationalization. Both were prefigured by state direction of the economy during wartime but, post-war, this was concentrated on the nationalization of infrastructural industries or what were identified as core public utilities. Health and education can be seen as major infrastructural provisions in the social rather than economic field – being taken into 'public ownership' and thereby 'socializing' the costs of providing the minimum national health and educational standards seen as essential to the post-war reconstruction of British society.

1.3 WELFARE IN THE POST-WAR ECONOMY

The key economic foundation of the post-war welfare regime was the presumption that a managed economy would deliver full employment as a political objective. Such conditions were the starting-point for William Beveridge in *Social Insurance and Allied Services* ('The Beveridge Report', 1942) which established the principles of an integrated system of welfare benefits. This report placed the insurance principle at the heart of welfare, drawing on the earlier systems of old age, sickness and unemployment insurance introduced during the Liberal governments of 1906–14. The Beveridge reforms integrated these into a more systematic approach to social insurance, on the principle that contributions paid by employers and employees would fund basic insurance for the three main categories of need: old age, ill health and unemployment.

Embedded in this system were three core assumptions. First, it rested on the view that waged work was the primary source of income and that the state's role was to provide a limited substitution for loss of income suffered by individuals through no fault of their own (right from the start those making themselves 'voluntarily unemployed' were penalized). The principle of limited substitution was important in the way it assumed that the level of state provision should not act as a disincentive to either looking for employment or making individual provision for misfortune or the future (for example, by individual investment in private pensions).

Secondly, it embodied the assumption that the political task of maintaining full employment would be achieved, thereby minimizing the costs of one element of the insurance scheme – that part paid out as Unemployment Benefit. Without the maintenance of full employment, the insurance principle would be very severely tested, both by demands made upon it by those out of work and by the lack of incoming contributions from those who would have been in employment. Further, the failure to achieve full employment would mean an inability on the part of individuals to build up the record of contributions necessary to fund the benefits which they might claim in the future (affecting pension rights in particular).

Thirdly, it assumed that full employment meant full *male* employment. Despite the expansion of women's waged work during the war, both the Beveridge Report and the benefit system flowing from it viewed women's waged work as a secondary or peripheral activity. Although women might work for a period before marriage, this would be merely a transitional phase on the way to their 'normal' condition of housewives and mothers. On this basis, women were structurally positioned in the benefit system as dependants, in that their access to income was assumed to be via men. In 'normal' conditions men would be the wage-earners, bringing in the 'family wage' from which the wife and other dependants would be maintained. In 'abnormal' conditions (such as sickness or unemployment) the interruption of earnings would be substituted for by state benefits payable to the wage-earner and *his* dependants. One index of this gendered hierarchy was that married women were not expected to be separately insured for sickness benefit since their sickness was assumed to involve no loss of income. As a result, it was anticipated that most women would pay reduced National Insurance contributions since they were not expected to be claiming benefits in their own right.

1.4 MEANS-TESTING: RESIDUAL NEEDS AND RESIDUAL BENEFITS

From the outset, the benefit system rested on the assumption that income was to be derived from labour-market activity or its linked substitute, insured benefits. For Beveridge there was to be an increasingly residual role played by a further layer of non-insured benefits, National Assistance. National Assistance was intended to fill the gaps left by employment income and insured benefits and was to be strictly means-tested. Like the insured benefits, National Assistance embodied a set of assumptions about gender relations and the family. It continued what had been known as the 'liable relative' rule in Public Assistance, whereby men were assumed to be financially responsible for the women with whom they lived. This barred 'cohabiting' women from independent access to the National Assistance system, deeming that they would be economically supported by their male cohabitees.

A variety of changes between Beveridge's conception and the implementation of the National Insurance and Assistance programmes ensured that Beveridge's original view that means-tested benefits would play a residual and declining role was never fulfilled. From the start, the benefit rates for National Insurance were set below the carefully calculated subsistence levels worked out by the Beveridge Committee, affecting unemployment and sickness benefits and state pensions. This led to recipients having to apply to the means-tested National Assistance for 'topping up' to bring their benefits up to the subsistence level determined by National Assistance criteria. Unemployment benefits were then time-limited to 52 weeks, requiring the long-term unemployed to resort to means-tested benefits after that point. A range of benefits directed to what Beveridge termed 'the marriage needs of women' (relating to widowhood, divorce, separation and sickness) were withheld, tightening the economic dependency of married women on their husbands.

Finally, the introduction of family allowances, for which feminist groups had long campaigned, established them below the realistic cost of child maintenance, requiring both National Insurance and Assistance to build in allowances for dependent children to their benefit rates. This was to have particular significance for National Assistance (and its later incarnation as Supplementary Benefit) as the numbers of lone-parent households grew (a category of need to which Beveridge had attached low priority). The combined effect of these changes was to ensure that means-tested benefits were to play a central rather than peripheral role in the British state's provision of income support during the post-war decades.

1.5   CITIZENSHIP: THE COSTS AND BENEFITS OF WELFARE

The post-war construction of welfare enormously extended the range of the state's support for individual welfare. It created wider access to the basic health and education services, increased access to public-sector rented housing, extended the numbers covered by insurance benefits, and extended access to uninsured benefits (National Assistance). In 1938, 1.3 million people were in receipt of some form of state income support while by 1950 this had risen to 2.3 million (Parker and Mirlees, 1988, pp. 494–5).

The expansion of services meant a continued enlargement of the share of Gross National Product devoted to public spending. Central government spending was the area of substantial post-war expansion, followed by growth in the local government share. The funding of state activities followed wartime trends, based on increasing rates of both personal and corporate taxation and lowering the thresholds at which personal taxation became payable. This expanded tax base combined with the revenue from National Insurance contributions to establish the financial settlement for the development of state welfare.

The combination of NI contributions and taxation in funding welfare expenditures is reflected in tensions about the nature of welfare 'rights' in the British welfare state which are particularly visible in relation to income support. On the one hand, the insurance or contributory system is associated with the idea of benefits being 'earned' – claims on such systems are legitimated through a contribution record. On the other hand, non-contributory benefits are funded from general taxation and represent cash transfers from tax-payers to the non-working population. This distinction underpins the more grudging nature of the 'rights' of individuals to non-contributory benefits. From the outset, non-contributory benefits involved an apparatus of means-testing and investigation designed to prevent fraudulent claiming, which continued pre-war attitudes to the 'undeserving' poor (those who had not 'earned' their benefits). Many surveys undertaken during the intervening years have confirmed that the social stigma associated with means-testing, combined with a relative lack of knowledge about entitlements, resulted in substantial under-claiming of non-contributory benefits.

Such processes raise significant questions about the nature of the status of 'citizenship' which is commonly identified as being expressed in the creation of the post-war welfare state. The idea of 'citizenship' reaches back to the 'New Liberalism' movement of the early twentieth century, in whose hands it became a key term for defining the expanded responsibilities of the state in establishing the conditions for all members of the society to take a full and productive role in the nation's life (Langan and Schwarz (eds), 1985). Beveridge himself was much influenced by New Liberalism and by the development of the idea of citizenship within Fabian thinking in the inter-war years. His use of it in the Beveridge Report fed into wider concerns with post-war social reconstruction towards a more egalitarian society (Calder, 1969).

The classic view of citizenship, formulated by Marshall (1977), describes the development of three fields of rights established between the state and its subjects which promote a formalized system of equality. The first is the field of *legal* rights (equality before the law), the second the field of *political* rights (universal suffrage) and the third the field of *social* rights (universal access to welfare benefits and services). The post-war welfare state, although often conceived of as establishing the last of these conditions, falls some way short of establishing universal access. We have seen that, in some respects, benefits were conditional rather than unconditional. We have also seen that, in the case of married women, access was as dependants rather than as individual citizens in their own right. (This parallels the uneven gender development of both legal and political rights in British history.)

Citizenship also imposed limitations based on birth and residence through the nationality tests which have been used to distinguish citizens from aliens in defining eligibility for benefits and services (see, *inter alia*, Gordon and Newnham, 1985). The 'universalism' of citizenship is, in these ways, deeply circumscribed – a highly conditional universalism which presumes a family-based social and economic structure. It addresses an indigenous population at whose heart are wage-earning males supporting families surrounded by a set of dependent populations positioned by age (both young and old), by gender (the 'anomaly of the married woman'), by infirmity and by 'race' (the 'alien' non-citizen).

1.6   1945 AND ALL THAT

In the preceding sections we have been attempting to establish some of the structural limitations of the immediate post-war welfare reforms. One reason for this focus is that the 'moment of 1945' is profoundly wrapped up in what might be called myths of recent British history which make it difficult to discern the precise character of the welfare regime which was created. On one side, '1945' is a triumphal moment – the point at which British society was transformed and a peculiarly British variety of 'socialism' was installed. Here, the welfare state, nationalization and the managed economy are seen as a decisive break with the bad old days of pre-war Britain. Opposed to this mythology is a demonology of '1945' which treats it as the point of origin of a British version of the 'totalitarian' state: an excessive and excessively interfering structure which undermined British freedoms, and the free market in particular (Hayek, 1944). Although the triumphal tone of '1945' as the start of a new Golden Age dominated public and political discourse in the 1950s and '60s, the demonology of 1945 came to occupy an increasingly significant role in the 1970s and '80s as the welfare consensus constructed around the post-war settlement came apart.

Our attention to the structural conditions and limitations of the creation of the British welfare regime is intended to offer a more cautious view of the achievements of '1945'. What was created was considerably more cautious, partial and conditional than either of the mythologies about the creation of the welfare state allows. It is also important to trace the structural conditions under which the state involved itself in welfare because many of the subsequent changes in welfare in Britain represent attempts to come to terms with different aspects of the legacy of '1945'. Subsequent events only make sense in the context of this settlement. The limited nature of British 'universalism'; a recognition that the 'welfare state' was only part of a larger mixed economy of welfare; the problems implied by lower than projected National Insurance benefit rates; and the dependence of this mixed economy of welfare on conditions of economic growth – these mark out the founding conditions of the post-war welfare regime. The following sections explore what happened when the unravelling of these founding conditions met changing social and economic circumstances.

2   EXPANSION AND MODERNIZATION

Although Britain's welfare regime underwent little qualitative change until the late 1970s, the international post-war economic boom allowed a dramatic expansion in the scope of welfare services within the framework established in the 1940s, a pattern common throughout the west. Common demographic trends in advanced capitalist society – a combination of a baby boom and a growing number of older people – increased the demand for welfare. At the same time growing prosperity and, in the sphere of health in particular, scientific and technological advances encouraged higher expectations – and spiralling costs. However, the welfare state in Britain came to occupy a distinctive political position in the 1960s because of the fact that, although the British economy had grown consistently in the post-war decades at a faster rate than at any time in the twentieth century (at an average of 3 per cent a year), it was still falling behind its major industrial competitors (whose average rates of growth were around 5 per cent a year). In response to the widespread perception of relative decline, the Labour party put welfare services at the heart of a programme of modernization and national revival.

In Harold Wilson's vision of the 'white heat' of technological revolution, an expanded and improved education system (including the harnessing of 'wasted talent' by the Open University) had a vital role to play. Grand housing and development schemes would remove the slum housing and inner-city blight that had resulted from 'thirteen years of Tory misrule'. Even social security policy – with the introduction of earnings-related sickness and unemployment benefits – was linked to the modernization project: 'in a period of rapid industrial change it is only elementary justice to compensate employees who, through no fault of their own, find that their job has disappeared' declared Labour's 1964 manifesto (MacGregor, 1981, p. 112).

2.1   THE EXPANSION OF STATE WELFARE

If '1945' marked the foundation of the welfare state in Britain, the follow-ing thirty years saw its development into a systematic structure. That pattern of development changed little by way of the basic principles around which the mixed economy of welfare was originally structured. In those domains where the state had taken on the role of primary provider (particularly education and health), the state continued to expand – par-ticularly in secondary, further and higher education. In some respects, the expansion of the state's role in education and health (to the extent that there was a closer match of need and resources) expressed Labourist commitments to greater egalitarianism and increasing access to edu-cational and health services.

But even where the state was the primary provider, private-sector alternatives continued and, in some areas, flourished. Table 2.1 records the growth of occupational pension schemes and private health insurance in the post-war period, together with the survival of private education. We have not discussed housing within this chapter, but it is worth noting that although the number of properties in the public rented sector increased from 2.5 million in 1951 to 7 million in 1980, the number of owner-occupied properties rose from 4.5 million to 12 million over the same period (*Social Trends*, 1982, p. 149). That growth was heavily subsidized by a little regarded 'welfare benefit' – mortgage tax relief – which represented a major transfer from the public to the private sector in terms of tax revenue forgone.

Mortgage tax relief is one reminder of the continued presumption that it was through the market that most needs would be satisfied. Changes in

Table 2.1 Private welfare in the United Kingdom, 1951–80

	Pensions (percentage of labour force in occupational pension schemes)		Health care (millions of members of private health insurance schemes)		Housing (millions of houses in tenure categories)			Education (percentage of pupils in independent schools)
	Men	Women	Subscribers	Pensions insured	Owned	Council rented	Private rented	
1951	30	12	0.06	0.1	4.5	2.5	7.5	5.0
1956	39	19	0.32	0.7	–	–	–	6.2
1961	50	25	0.50	1.1	6.5	4.5	5.5	7.7
1966	62	26	0.75	1.6	–	–	–	7.2
1971	55	34	1.0	2.1	9.0	6.0	4.0	6.1
1976	65	50	1.1	2.2	–	–	–	5.6
1980	68	55	1.6	3.4	12.0	7.0	2.5	5.8

Source: Taylor-Gooby, 1984, Table 5; data from Social Trends, 1981 (pensions); Seldon, 1981, p. 56 (health care); Social Trends, 1982, p. 149 (housing); Social Trends, 1982, p. 47 (education)

the systems of income support were made within the continuing underlying assumption that waged work was the primary source of economic support. What did change, though, were the numbers of people who were excluded from the labour market – by virtue of age, responsibilities for dependants, disability or (in the shape of things to come) unemployment. This growth of the dependent population (rather than great increases in the level of benefits) underpinned the substantial rise in spending on social security between 1945 and 1975.

In other respects changes in the nature of insurance benefits underscored the importance of the market. The shift to earnings-related contributions and benefits tied one's prospects for income support more closely to one's fortunes in the labour market and less to one's 'universal' position as citizen. Given the structuring of the labour market by patterns of class, gender and ethnic inequality, the effect of introducing earnings-related benefits was to ensure the reproduction of labour-market inequalities inside the system of state income support.

Table 2.2   The relative growth of different categories of public expenditure, United Kingdom

| | As percentage of Gross National Product | | | | | | |
	Social services	Economic services	Environ-mental services	Defence	Debt service	Other services	Total
1910	4.2	1.8	0.7	3.5	0.9	1.7	12.7
1938	11.3	2.9	1.0	8.9	4.0	1.9	30.0
1955	16.3	3.2	1.1	9.6	4.2	2.1	36.6
1970	23.2	6.1	4.0	5.6	4.6	3.7	47.1
1975	28.0	8.2	4.2	5.6	4.5	4.3	54.7

| | As a percentage of total public expenditure | | | | | |
	Social services	Economic services	Environ-mental services	Defence	Debt service	Other services
1910	33.1	14.2	5.5	27.6	7.1	13.4
1938	37.7	9.7	3.3	29.7	13.3	6.3
1955	44.5	8.7	3.0	26.2	11.5	5.7
1970	49.1	12.9	8.4	11.9	9.8	7.8
1975	51.2	15.0	7.7	10.2	8.2	7.8

Note: Totals may not be exact due to rounding.
Source: Extracted from Sleeman, 1979, Table 3.1

Between 1950 and 1975 the share of GNP taken by public expenditure (that is, by central and local government spending) rose fairly steadily. Given that GNP itself was growing on average by 3 per cent per annum through much of this period, this meant a simultaneously larger slice of a

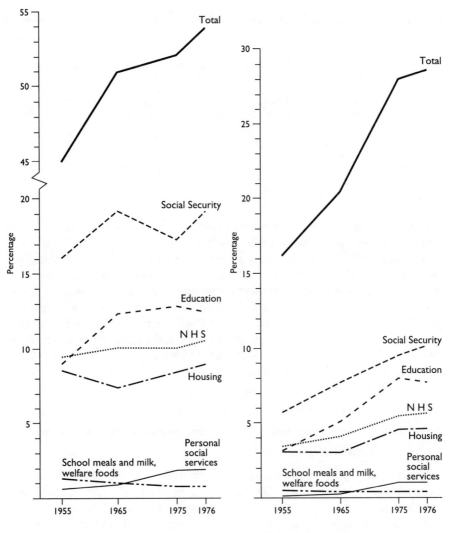

(a) **Welfare expenditure as percentage of total public expenditure**

(b) **Welfare expenditure as percentage of Gross National Product**

Figure 2.1   The growth of expenditure on the main branches of the social services, United Kingdom, 1955–76

Source: Data from Sleeman, 1979, Table 3.2

larger cake for state spending. Within this framework, it was spending on welfare services which accounted for the largest part of the growth of public spending. Figure 2.1 shows the changing shares of GNP taken by different elements of public spending up to the mid 1970s. Spending on welfare services rose from a share of 11.3 per cent in 1938 to 16.3 per cent by 1955 and to 28 per cent by 1975 (see Tables 2.2 and 2.3).

Table 2.3   Total social welfare expenditure as a percentage of total public expenditure and GNP, United Kingdom, 1955–76

| | Expenditure as percentage of: | | | | | | | |
| | Total public expenditure | | | | Gross National Product | | | |
	1955	1965	1975	1976	1955	1965	1975	1976
Total social welfare	44.9	50.9	51.2	53.9	16.3	20.6	28.0	28.6
Total public expenditure	–	–	–	–	36.4	40.8	54.7	53.1

Source: Extracted from Sleeman, 1979, Table 3.2

Figure 2.1 shows how different elements of the welfare system experienced divergent patterns of growth within the overall expansion of welfare, and in subsequent sections we shall consider some of the changing patterns of needs and priorities which account for these divergences. But it is important not to take the bare economic facts of the growth of state spending and its share of GNP at face value, since there are specific political and economic decisions which shape that growth, in particular the means by which the state appropriates a proportion of the GNP to its own use. Public expenditure in general, and welfare spending in particular, is funded by a combination of four sources of finance:

1   National Insurance contributions;
2   general taxation (both direct and indirect);
3   local taxation (rates/community charge/council tax);
4   borrowing by the government.

Although employers' and employees' contributions nominally covered the expenditure on insured benefits, the bulk of welfare spending was funded from general taxation. In the mid 1960s, local taxes and NI contributions accounted for only 16 and 15 per cent respectively of the state's income (Sleeman, 1979, p. 67). In part, the general economic growth experienced during the period provided a steadily increasing flow of money to the state without any change in taxation policies. But, in order to divert an increasing share of GNP to state spending, taxation patterns had to change.

Figure 2.2 indicates one significant area of change in taxation policies: the steady lowering of tax thresholds relative to average male earnings. The effect of such changes was to widen the tax base (the number of people paying income tax) by drawing in greater numbers of those on below-average earnings. Lower thresholds were accompanied by a tendential increase in the *rates* of taxation through the period, although these were subject to regular variations from government to government, particularly between Labour and Conservative terms of office. The expanding range of personal taxation made it clear that, if the newly discovered citizenship brought social rights, it also brought economic obligations.

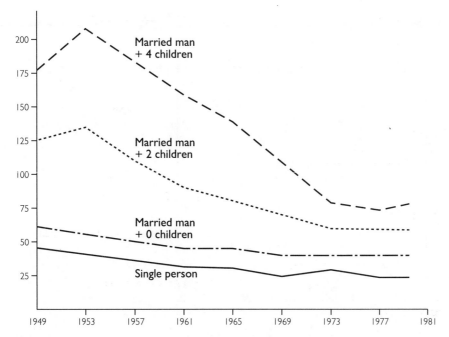

Figure 2.2   Tax thresholds as percentage of average male earnings

Note: The diagram takes family support through family allowance, Child Benefit and child tax allowance into account so that it is comparable over the whole period.

Source: Taylor-Gooby, 1984, Figure 2

2.2   NEEDS AND PRIORITIES:
THE CHANGING SHAPE OF WELFARE

The expansion of welfare through to the mid 1970s can be seen as the product of the conjunction of three elements: changing patterns of need, changing state priorities and changing costs of welfare. Demographic patterns affect the level of demand for welfare. As Figure 2.3 reveals, one of the key demographic shifts which has borne increasingly upon the welfare state has been the growth in the proportion of the population beyond retirement age. This shift has two key features. One is the overall growth in the numbers of people over 65, the other is the effect of increasing longevity such that some analysts find it appropriate to distinguish two age groups beyond retirement age: pensionable age to 74; 75 and beyond.

Such changes have multiple implications for the provision of welfare. First, there are increasing numbers of people eligible for pensions. Secondly, there is an increasing demand from an older population on health services. On average, those beyond retirement age incur roughly double the health service costs of the general population, and those aged 75+ about four times: see Table 2.4. Thirdly, an ageing population creates more demands for social as well as health care, ranging from accommodation to personal support, which may be forthcoming from a variety of sources – kin, voluntary groups, personal social services or purchased

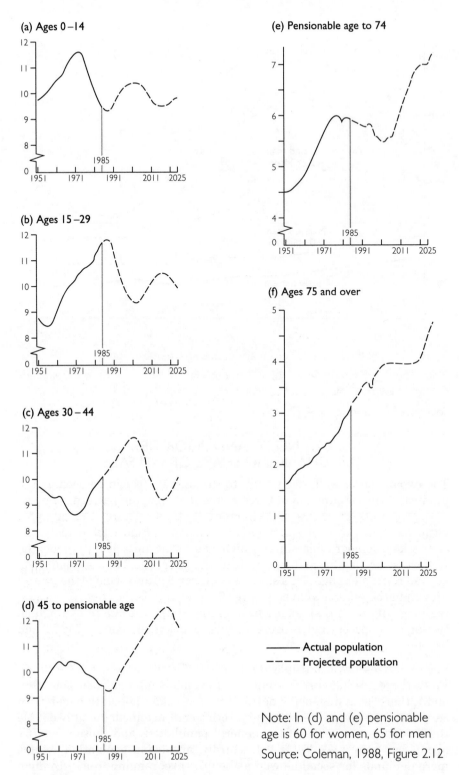

Figure 2.3   Actual and projected home population by age-group, England and Wales 1951–2025, in millions

from the private sector. Finally, as the proportion of the population beyond retirement age (and not merely the absolute numbers) increases, so the social costs of a growing non-working sector has to be met from the revenue generated by a relatively smaller economically active sector.

Table 2.4 Average National Health Service costs of older sections of the population compared with average costs in 1979 (£ per year)

	Men	Women
All ages	126	146
65–74	268	244
75+	507	623

Source: Taylor-Gooby, 1984, Table 2

Poverty and inequality first re-emerged as political issues in the United States, partly in response to the black civil rights movement and partly as a result of a growing recognition of the persistence of poverty in an age of affluence. The complacency of the post-war world order, with its theories of 'convergence', 'post-industrial harmony' and the 'end of ideology', was undermined by the emergence of new forms of social conflict and widespread evidence of a decline of social cohesion. In the USA a series of social investigations, notably Galbraith's indictment of 'private affluence, public squalor' in *The Affluent Society* in 1958 and Michael Harrington's *The Other America: poverty in the United States*, published in 1962, led to the 1964 'war on poverty' launched by the Johnson administration; parallel studies of poverty and anti-poverty initiatives were taken in Australia, Canada, Sweden and France (see Atkinson, 1975).

In Britain 'the rediscovery of poverty' resulted from the pioneering work of Dorothy Wedderburn, Brian Abel-Smith and Peter Townsend. The publication of *The Poor and the Poorest* by Abel-Smith and Townsend in 1965 had a major public impact and put social security policy back on the political agenda for the first time since the Beveridge Report. It also led directly to the launch of the Child Poverty Action Group which, as well as spearheading a forceful 'poverty lobby', influenced the growth of a wider 'welfare rights' movement over the next two decades (see Alcock, 1987). This movement included professional associations (representing groups working within the welfare state), charitable bodies (representing particular patterns of need, such as neglected children or forms of disability), activist groups emerging around new needs (such as homelessness and lone-parent families) and groups contesting patterns of discrimination (around 'race', gender and sexuality), newly defined welfare constituencies (people in mental hospitals, older people, claimants) and groups emphasizing links between First World industrialized affluence and Third World poverty and dependency. This expansion of the 'voluntary sector' added the political tasks of raising public consciousness and political lobbying to the work of direct provision of assistance which had historically been the focus of voluntary agencies.

Table 2.5 Number of persons receiving insurance grants, 1950–80, Great Britain (thousands)

	Insurance benefits					Maternity benefits		Children attracting family allowances[4]	War pensions
	Retirement pensions[1]	Widows, orphans, guardians etc.	Average number[2] incapacitated by sickness and injury	Industrial/ disablement pension	Unemployment Benefit[3]	Maternity grants awarded during year	Maternity allowances awarded during year		
1950	4,152	474	917	59	226	757	124	4,756	1,047
1960	5,563	549	957	173	192	867	198	5,764	724
1970	7,363	551	978	207	305	829	233	6,955	519
1980	8,918	457[5]	1,096	196	709	664	351	13,304	354

Notes: [1] Men over 65, women over 60. [2] Not including death benefit. [3] Average number of claims during the year. [4] Before April 1977 family allowance was payable to a family with two or more children; Child Benefit, introduced in April 1977, applies to all children. [5] 1979 figures.

Source: Parker and Mirlees, 1988, Table 2.25; data from CSO, *Statistical Abstract for the United Kingdom*, relevant years; Ministry of Labour, *Abstracts of Labour Statistics*; *Ministry of Labour Gazette*; Treasury, *Return of Expenditure on Public Social Services*; DHSS, *Social Security Statistics*, 1976 and 1985

Table 2.6 Number of persons receiving National Assistance/Supplementary Benefits, 1950–80, Great Britain (thousands)

	Total no. persons benefitting from assistance	Total no. of weekly allowances	Dependants		Old[1]		Sick		Unemployed		Others		Non-contributory pensions in payment without supplement
			Adults	Children	With*	Without*	With*	Without*	With*	Without*	With*	Without*	
1950	2,289	1,350	272	351	677	106	114	102	38	39	96	178	316
1960	2,724	1,857	385	436	1,075	111	139	128	43	85	65	211	46
1970	4,238	2,739	674	825	1,745	156	164	159	71	157	274		—[2]
1980	4,972	3,115	692[3]	1,165[3]	1,590	101	57	148	176	678	365		—

Notes: *With/without contributory benefit. [1] Men over 65, women over 60. [2] No longer separately counted. [3] Includes Northern Ireland figures.

Source: Parker and Mirlees, 1988, Table 12.24; data from Ministry of Health, *Annual Reports*; National Assistance Board, *Annual Reports*; CSO, *Statistical Abstract for the United Kingdom*, for relevant years; DHSS, *Social Security Statistics*, 1976 and 1985

The impact of these pressure groups and the 'social administration' lobby on Labour policy may be discerned in the introduction of earnings-related benefits, the replacement of the limited family allowance scheme with the more comprehensive Child Benefit and the strengthening of entitlements to means-tested benefits (see Hills (ed.), 1990). However, it must also be noted that real benefit *levels* were little improved and Child Benefit in particular fell far below the costs of childcare, while the rising numbers of the long-term unemployed and lone-parent families produced growing reliance on means-tested benefits with their concomitant problems of stigma and lack of take-up (section 1.5 above).

Other demands on the welfare system also increased substantially between 1950 and 1970. Tables 2.5 and 2.6 show the changing pattern of income maintenance benefits paid out by the state in the post-war years. With few exceptions, most categories of benefit reveal steady increases between 1950 and 1970, with the largest rises being for pensions in both the insurance and means-tested benefit payments. The growth of needs for income support of all kinds enlarged the share of public expenditure taken by income maintenance (sometimes referred to as 'transfers'). But other services encountered rising demand as well in a complex mixture of new or growing needs (health), changing population patterns (numbers of children entering the education system) and changing political priorities. Substantial rises in education spending, for example, followed two major initiatives – the major expansion of higher education begun in the 1960s and the raising of the school-leaving age (ROSLA) for secondary schooling combined with moves towards comprehensivization.

At the same time, it is clear that not all the rise in welfare expenditure could be attributed to the processes of meeting new or expanding needs. The welfare state suffered from differential price inflation – the costs of providing its services rose faster than the national rate of inflation through the 1960s and '70s. This phenomenon was visible for welfare services in all the western industrialized countries during this period and is based on the way in which costs are incurred in the provision of such services. Figure 2.4 provides a breakdown of the factors involved in the rising public expenditure on three areas of welfare between 1965 and 1975 in Great Britain. It separates out four elements:

1   the 'real increase' per person;

2   the 'population effect' (changing demographic patterns);

3   the relative price effect; and

4   general inflation.

It can be seen that a significant proportion of the increased costs of each service are generated by the 'relative price effect' of the provision of public services. Gough (1979) argues that this effect primarily results from the comparatively *labour-intensive* nature of such services. Where other forms of economic activity were increasingly substituting machinery for labour, many of the services provided by the state offered few oppor-

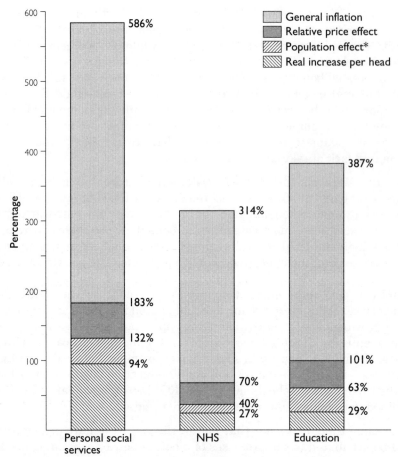

Figure 2.4   Percentage increases in government expenditure on services, 1965–75

Note: *This assumes the following increases in 'need' stemming from population changes alone: education + 27%, derived from a calculation of the increase in the 5–14 year-old age-group; NHS + 10%; and personal social services +20%, using the figures in *The Government's Expenditure Plans* (1977), vol. II (HMSO), p. 80, for the second half of the 1970s.

Source: Gough, 1979, Figure 5.2

tunities for such substitution in that they involved what might loosely be termed 'people work' and did not fit the general industrial and commercial trend towards 'labour-saving devices' (for example, teachers were not displaced by teaching machines, nor nurses by robots). Such conditions meant that welfare services were disproportionately affected by rising labour costs throughout the post-war decades, although this only became visible as a political issue in the period of more militant public-sector trade unionism in the middle and late 1970s (Gough, 1979, pp. 85–6).

Nevertheless, the potential impact of labour costs on the provision of welfare services was mitigated by its characteristic employment patterns. The expansion of the public-sector services in the three decades following the war involved the staffing of such services drawing disproportionately on women and black people; their position in the labour market meant that average wage rates remained significantly lower in the public compared to the private sectors of the economy. Without such wage differentials, deriving from the effects of gender and ethnicity in the labour market, the costs of welfare would have been considerably higher.

2.3   MODERNIZATION AND REORGANIZATION: THE CORPORATE MANAGEMENT STATE?

The response of the state to this complex network of needs, priorities and costs was to focus on the need to modernize the organizational structures through which welfare was provided. Between the early 1960s and the mid 1970s, the British state underwent a fevered range of restructuring and reorganization affecting central government, local government and the NHS. All of these reforms aimed at creating administrative and managerial systems in place of what were identified as archaic and ramshackle systems which had evolved over the previous 150 years and whose lack of integration presented a major stumbling-block to the efficient coordination and management of public services.

The modernizing impulse of the Labour governments under Harold Wilson in the 1960s produced a major reorganization of government ministries into a new departmental structure of 'super ministries' (see Figure 2.5), starting with the creation of the Department of Education and Science in 1964 and, most significantly, the creation of the Department of Health and Social Security in 1968 which brought together the main structures of welfare services and benefits. This followed on the reform of the National Insurance and National Assistance systems of income maintenance. Both government reports and other research had demonstrated structural flaws in the system of income support: the inadequate level of insurance benefits which meant recourse to National Assistance; the inadequacy of family allowances; and the problems of low take-up and stigma associated with means-tested National Assistance.

The Labour reforms brought some significant changes, most notably the extension of graduated benefits and contributions in the National Insurance scheme affecting sickness and unemployment benefits and, in 1970, pensions through the introduction of the State Earnings Related Pensions Scheme (SERPS). The National Assistance Board mutated into the Supplementary Benefits Commission, though much of its personnel, methods and rules remained the same. The resulting schemes of income support were not as redistributive in their effects as the original plans, nor did they accomplish sufficient increases in benefit levels (or family allowances) to remove the reliance on 'top-ups' from means-tested

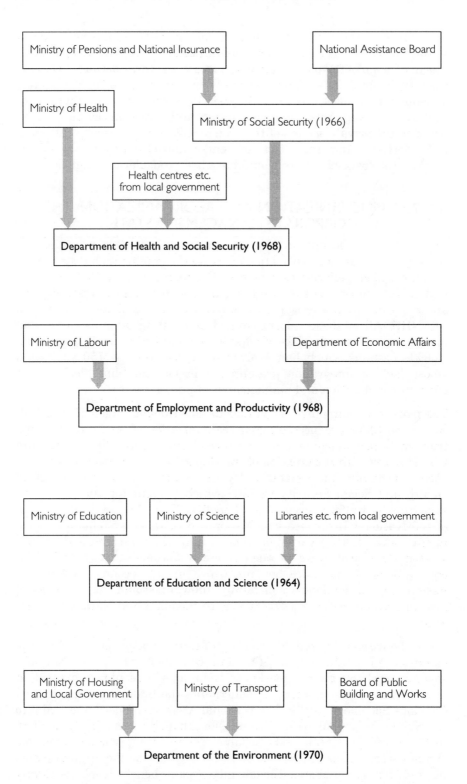

Figure 2.5   The administrative reorganization of British government during the 1960s
Source: Taylor-Gooby, 1984, Figure 1

benefits. In fact, the decade of the 1960s saw an *increasing* reliance on means-tested benefits: among pensioners from 1.3 million in 1961 to 1.9 million in 1971; among unemployed people from 140,000 to 400,000; among sick and disabled people from 280,000 to 320,000; and among women with dependent children and no insurance entitlement from 80,000 to 220,000.

Local government was also a major object for reform, not least because a wide range of welfare services – education, housing and personal social services – were delivered through the local state. The Kilbrandon Committee (Scotland) and the Seebohm Committee (England and Wales) produced plans for the integration of what had been widely scattered aspects of 'personal social services', creating integrated social services departments delivering a range of provision to a variety of client groups. The expansion of state welfare involved local authorities spending a greater share of the GNP, rising from 9.8 per cent in 1951 to 18.6 per cent by 1975 (Gough, 1979, p. 97). At the same time as local authorities' share of public expenditure was rising, the proportion of government revenue raised by local taxation (rates) declined, the gap being filled by increasing transfers from central to local government. A variety of reports addressed the changing role and position of local government, eventually resulting in a major restructuring in 1974 which created new and larger authorities responsible for the bulk of service provision: the aim was better management structures combining with larger client populations to produce more efficient service delivery.

The National Health Service was also to undergo major reforms through the same period, also culminating in a major restructuring in 1974. In 1962 a substantial hospital building programme was inaugurated, and the hospital sector was to lay claim to a rising share of NHS expenditure through the 1960s. As in local government, concerns with the efficient allocation and use of resources dominated policy discussions through the period – originally around the concentration of services through district hospitals and eventually emerging in the form of regional and district tiers of management in the 1974 reorganization.

The concern with the organizational structure of the NHS was paralleled by concern over the way resources were distributed in relation to health needs. The pattern of resources and needs at the inception of the NHS and for much of the ensuing period gave rise to what was known as the 'inverse care law' which described the concentration of services in the areas of lowest need and the relative lack of services in areas of highest need. The reorganization of 1974 followed previous initiatives aimed at redistributing resources to a closer fit with need, and was accompanied by the establishment of the Resource Allocation Working Party (RAWP) whose purpose was to establish new principles for matching needs and resources.

All of these reforms shared significant common features. They involved greater *centralization,* a commitment to a view of *managerial efficiency* and were part of a movement towards greater *public expen-*

diture and resource planning by central government. The response to the growth of state spending, and the coterminous growth of the state as the largest employer in the country, was to look for mechanisms which would improve coordination. Increases in scale (whether in the form of the 'super' departments, larger local authorities or the regionalization of the NHS) represented public-sector adaptations of the economic wisdoms of the private sector – that large corporations represented the best integrated and most cost-effective form of organizing production.

Similar lessons were learned from the private sector in the view that such large, integrated organizational structures were best steered through systems of 'corporate management' – a cadre of senior managers capable of developing and carrying out long-term planning and of managing the efficient allocation of resources to accomplish the plans. This view of integrative planning also applied at the highest level of national government with an increased commitment to both long-term economic planning and greater economic management in which the Treasury played a leading role. The result was a system in which centralized planning and budgetary systems took on a core role in the organization of public services.

2.4   THE FAMILY AND THE STATE

By 1975 the family occupied a rather more complex position in relation to state welfare than might have been predicted from the comfortable assumptions of 1945. The core presumption of the conventional nuclear family as the cornerstone of social care still prevailed and the demeaning conceptions of heterosexual cohabitation still dominated social security provisions. But there were also growing signs that reality was failing to live up to this ideal, which led some commentators to criticize reality. Among the causes for concern were: the increase in married women's employment (= children not being looked after properly); the rising divorce rate (= the possible collapse of the family); the growing number of lone-parent families (= the possible collapse of the family); the growing numbers of illegitimate births (= growing immorality); and the increasing numbers of older people dependent upon public rather than familial care (= the loss of 'family feeling' and obligation on the part of younger generations). The bracketed 'equals' signs here represent the most pessimistic interpretations of these changes.

This growing gulf between the ideal and the reality of family life placed contradictory demands on social policy. On the one hand, the state provision of care had developed around the assumption that the family would normally provide support for its members and therefore state support would be the exception. As the exceptions (and the concomitant demands on the state) increased, there was concern that the very existence of state support itself was producing the deviations from the ideal. This argument, sometimes referred to as the 'perverse incentives' of insurance

(Parker, 1983), was expressed with especial vigour in relation to lone-parent families. Critics claimed this was a deviation encouraged by the knowledge that Supplementary Benefit was available to compensate for the loss of male income (the vast majority of lone-parent families being headed by women).

At the other extreme were the efforts made to ensure that some sections of the population did not have families or, more accurately, did not have dependants who might seek to benefit from state provision. Although, as we have noted, public services benefited disproportionately from the employment of migrant workers, the 1960s and '70s saw a constant tightening of restrictions on immigration to Britain from the Commonwealth Immigration Act of 1962 through to the Immigration Act of 1971. The growing restrictiveness of the legislation was disproportionately directed at black and Asian migration. This oppressive trend culminated in the 1971 Act's distinction between 'patrials' and 'non-patrials': only those who had a parent or grandparent with UK citizenship were eligible for the right to live in the UK. Others wishing to enter became simply migrant workers with no rights of settlement or citizenship. 'Dependants' became a major focus of attention, with increasingly rigorous and discriminatory tests being applied to prevent entry of those who might become 'a charge on the public purse'. In these conditions, proving 'citizenship' became an increasingly significant test of eligibility for services or benefits – a test to be taken by those from ethnic minorities whose skin colour was taken to suggest that they were 'alien' rather than British (Gordon and Newnham, 1985).

The family also played an ambiguous role in one of the other significant policy development of the 1960s and '70s – the expansion of personal social services. The creation of local authority social services departments focused explicitly on the provision of a 'family service', which positioned the family in a number of different ways. Like other policy domains, it assumed both the normality and desirability of the nuclear family, and aimed to address concerns about 'family failure' by providing social work services to improve family functioning (**Clarke (ed.), 1993**).[*] In an uneasy alliance with the NHS, social services were also responsible for those who, for one reason or another, were not being cared for by or within families and thus required (or were seen to need) public institutions or residential care.

The dual function of personal social services, linking family intervention and institutional care for dependent populations of older, young and disabled people, put social workers at the forefront of the movement towards 'community care'. This policy combined critiques of the ineffectiveness (and costs) of institutional regimes with a view of the desirability of individuals living 'independently' in the community. At its heart was an assumption that networks of care would or could be available within the

---

[*] An author's name in bold indicates another book or another chapter in a book in the Family Life and Social Policy series.

community to provide support. This rested on the belief that networks of 'primary carers' rather than professional carers would play the dominant role in providing such support. In that context, primary care was identified with the family and – through the usual gendered logic – with women as wives, mothers, daughters and sisters of those who needed care.

2.5 THE BEGINNING OF THE END?

The British welfare regime continued to expand up to the mid 1970s, along the intersecting axes of state, market and family laid down in the 1940s. In part this expansion continued in the 1960s and '70s in response to the perception of national decline, out of the conviction that more high-tech health care and a well-housed and better-educated population would be better equipped to revive Britain's national fortunes. In part too, welfare services – and welfare spending – continued to increase in response to the growing pressure from those excluded from the labour market, lone-parent families and the increasing proportion of older people. As the pace of economic expansion began to falter in the late '60s, and was replaced by recession in the early '70s, the difficulties of sustaining the pattern of state welfare in its post-war form emerged as a persistent focus of public and political debate.

In 1974 the Labour party was returned to office on the basis of a counter-crisis programme and the promise of a 'social contract' – a deal between the government and the unions to preserve welfare services in return for restraining demands for wage increases (Panitch, 1976). In the first two years of the Labour government real wages fell as inflation raged and the unions acquiesced to incomes policy. As the nation's economic plight deteriorated, the government was obliged to seek assistance in the form of a loan from the International Monetary Fund. The forms of the loan obliged it to cut public expenditure on welfare, drastically curtailing capital projects in health and education from 1976 onwards. The Labour government's shift towards austerity welfare policies at a time of rapidly rising unemployment produced a combination of widespread protest against 'the cuts' in various public services and more general disillusionment with Labour's programme.

The Callaghan government's persistence in trying to hold down the wages of some of the lowest paid public-sector employees finally provoked an upsurge of union militancy in what became known as 'the winter of discontent' in 1978/9. The Labour government's attempt to create a social-democratic or 'corporatist' response to the problems exposed by the first major post-war recession was generally judged a failure. The breakdown in the consensus of support for the welfare state in the 1970s reflected the erosion of the underlying assumptions of the post-war welfare regime. Where the Beveridge system had assumed and required full employment for its successful operation the decline of the British economy created growing numbers of unemployed. Where the system assumed a patriarchal family supported by the family wage, neither the wage nor the family lived up to expectations. Where Beveridge assumed a declining role for means-tested benefits, the combination of growing numbers of unwaged people and the low rates of insured benefits ensured the steady expansion of means-testing. Most significantly, where economic growth had allowed potentially conflicting interests to be reconciled in the post-war consensus, the arrival of recession meant the collapse of the post-war settlement. By the end of the 1970s 'welfare' in Britain became the explicit focal point for a number of conflicts – between tax-payer and welfare scrounger, between rate-payer and 'profligate' local authority, between rich and poor, between the 'general interest' and 'special interests' and between citizens and 'aliens' – all framed by the question of 'what the nation could afford'.

REFERENCES

Abel-Smith, B. and Townsend, P. (1965) *The Poor and the Poorest*, London, Bell and Hyman.

Alcock, P. (1987) *Poverty and State Support*, London, Longman.

Atkinson, A. B. (1975) *The Economics of Inequality*, London, Oxford University Press.

Beveridge, W. (1942) *Social Insurance and Allied Services*, (The Beveridge Report) Cmnd 6404, London, HMSO.

Brett, T., Gilliatt, S. and Pople, A. (1982) 'Planned trade, Labour Party policy and US intervention: the successes and failures of post-war reconstruction', *History Workshop Journal*, no. 13.

Calder, A. (1969) *The People's War*, London, Calder.

Calvocoressi, P. (1987) *World Politics since 1945*, (5th edn) London, Longman.

Clarke, J. (ed.) (1993) *A Crisis in Care? Challenges to social work*, Family Life and Social Policy series, London, Sage/The Open University.

Cohen, S. (1985) 'Anti-semitism, immigration controls and the welfare state', *Critical Social Policy*, no. 13, Summer.

Coleman, D.A. (1988) 'Population' in Halsey, A. H. (ed.) op. cit., pp. 36–134.

Ditch, J. S. and Morrissey, M. J. (1992) 'Northern Ireland: review and prospects for social policy', *Social Policy and Administration*, vol. 26, no.1, March, pp. 19–39.

Esping-Andersen, G. (1990) *The Three Worlds of Welfare Capitalism*, Cambridge, Polity Press.

Finch, J. and Groves, D. (eds) (1983) *A Labour of Love*, London, Routledge and Kegan Paul.

Fleming Committee (1944) *Report of the Committee on Public Schools and the General Educational System*, The Hon. Lord Fleming, MC (Chair), London, HMSO.

Galbraith, J. K. (1958) *The Affluent Society*, Harmondsworth, Penguin (4th rev. edn, 1987).

Gordon, P. and Newnham, A. (1985) *Passport to Benefits? Racism and social security*, London, Child Poverty Action Group and Runnymede Trust.

Gough, I. (1979) *The Political Economy of the Welfare State*, London and Basingstoke, Macmillan.

Halsey, A. H. (ed.) (1988) *British Social Trends since 1900: a guide to the changing social structure of Britain*, (2nd edn) London and Basingstoke, Macmillan.

Harrington, M. (1962) *The Other America: poverty in the US*, Harmondsworth, Penguin.

Hayek, F. (1944) *The Road to Serfdom*, London, Routledge and Kegan Paul.

Hills, S. J. (ed.) (1990) *The State of Welfare: the welfare state in Britain since 1974*, London, Oxford University Press.

Jacobs, S. (1985) 'Race, empire and the welfare state: council housing and racism', *Critical Social Policy*, no. 13, Summer.

Kilbrandon Committee (1964) *Report of the Committee on Children and Young Persons (Scotland)*, Kilbrandon, Hon. Lord (Chair), Cmnd. 2306, Edinburgh, HMSO.

Langan, M. and Schwarz, B. (eds) (1985) *Crises in the British State, 1880–1930*, London, Hutchinson.

MacGregor, S. (1981) *The Politics of Poverty*, London, Longman.

Marshall, T.H. (1977) *Social Policy in the Twentieth Century*, London, Hutchinson (4th edn).

Morgan, K. O. (1984) *Labour in Power, 1945–1951*, London, Oxford University Press.

Panitch, L. (1976) *Social Democracy and Industrial Militancy*, Cambridge, Cambridge University Press.

Parker, H. (1983) *The Moral Hazard of Social Benefits*, London, Institute of Economic Affairs.

Parker, J. and Mirlees, C. (1988) 'Welfare' in Halsey, A.H. (ed.) op. cit., pp. 462–517.

Seebohm Committee (1968) *Report of the Committee on Local Authority and Allied Personal Social Services*, Seebohm, F. (Chair), Cmnd. 3703, London, HMSO.

Seldon, A. (1981) *Whither the Welfare State?*, London, Institute of Economic Affairs.

Sleeman, J. F. (1979) *Resources for the Welfare State: an economic introduction*, London, Longman.

Taylor-Gooby, P. (1984) 'The welfare state from the Second World War to the 1980s' in D355 *Social Policy and Social Welfare*, Block 2: *Issues in the Study of Welfare*, pp. 1–56, Milton Keynes, The Open University.

Titmuss, R. M. (1958) *Essays on 'the Welfare State'*, London, Unwin.

CHAPTER 3
RESTRUCTURING WELFARE: THE BRITISH WELFARE REGIME IN THE 1980s

JOHN CLARKE AND MARY LANGAN

INTRODUCTION

As we saw in Chapter 2, the welfare state emerged out of the post-war resolution of international and domestic social tensions and was consolidated in conditions of economic expansion and political stability. In the 1960s and early 1970s the welfare state was expanded and modernized in response to the changing demands and needs of a society that was, despite the post-war boom, vulnerable to the problems of long-term decline. Just as the welfare state was beginning to take its place as a venerable British institution, the events of the late 1970s and the 1980s threw it into a crisis which led many to ask whether it could or should survive in its familiar forms.

The oil price rise of 1973, triggering the first worldwide recession since the 1930s, brought the return of mass unemployment throughout the west, eroding what had been for the founders of the welfare state one of its supporting 'pillars'. The combination of slowing growth and rising prices – 'stagflation' – produced intense pressures to curtail public expenditure and wages at a time of growing job losses and increasing poverty. In countries with strongly organized labour movements and deep-rooted social-democratic traditions (such as Sweden and Austria), governments tried to negotiate these problems in close collaboration with unions and labour parties. Where labour organization and welfare traditions were weaker, as in the USA, which also experienced a more acute problem of relative economic decline, the tendency for direct attacks on trade-union organization and on the funding of welfare services emerged at an early stage. However, as the problems of economic recession persisted, and even intensified, through the 1980s, the pressures on public provision of welfare provoked both widespread rethinking about the state's role in welfare and the restructuring of welfare regimes throughout the advanced capitalist world.

In Britain, as we have seen, the failure of the Labour government's attempts to reconcile the conflicting demands unleashed by the crisis of the mid 1970s through the corporatist mechanism of the social contract was succeeded by the emergence of a conservative approach dominated by the 'new right'. Their programme – which advocated an enhanced role for market forces and proposed to 'roll back' state intervention in industry and welfare – developed in Britain in parallel with similar 'neo-conservative' and 'free market liberal' policies in the USA. Under Margaret

Thatcher and Ronald Reagan these policies came to dominate the 1980s. There was a concerted effort to change the balance of the mixed economy of welfare – to shift the state from its dominant role and to promote the roles of the market, voluntary and informal sectors in welfare provision.

Despite this aim, by the end of the 1980s many core services were still delivered through state institutions. There is considerable debate about how far the new right agenda of 'rolling back' the state has been achieved in the sphere of welfare. One radical commentator concluded that the quality of social citizenship afforded by the welfare state has effectively shrunk to nineteenth-century proportions (Krieger, 1987). Another commentator, also sympathetic to the social-democratic tradition, judges the performance of the welfare state over the same period as a success in that it survived while key parts even thrived (Le Grand, 1990). This chapter is concerned with assessing the scale of the shift in the mixed economy of welfare and its consequences for the British welfare regime by the early 1990s. We conclude the chapter by discussing the different assessments that have been made of the scope of the welfare reforms of the 1980s.

I SOWING THE SEEDS OF DISILLUSION: THE THREE Ds

The drive to reduce the role of the state in the provision of welfare in Britain was supported by a sustained ideological campaign which placed a heavy burden of blame on the welfare state for the nation's economic and moral decline. This campaign began in the early 1970s, but became more influential after Margaret Thatcher took over the leadership of the Conservative Party following Edward Heath's election defeat in 1974. In this section we shall be concentrating on three key themes in the new right critique of the welfare state: its claims that state welfare had contributed to *deindustrialization*, had created *disincentives* and had caused *demoralization*. These three 'Ds' link economic, political and moral evaluations of the consequences of state welfare and identify conditions which could only be remedied by reductions in public spending and a withdrawal from the state's dominant role in the welfare regime. The new right critique gained in authority in response to the failure of Labour's social contract and, after Margaret Thatcher's victory in 1979, became a guiding theme in government policy, even though its translation into practice proved more difficult than its proponents had anticipated.

The *deindustrialization* thesis (most strongly advanced by Bacon and Eltis, 1976) argued that the growth of the state was detrimental to national economic performance and was, indeed, creating the conditions for the structural decline of Britain's manufacturing base. The expansion of the state had these economic effects through a number of interlinked mechanisms. Most strikingly, the expansion of the state (or public sector) withdrew resources from the market sector and industrial production both in terms of the potential labour force (as state employment grew) and in terms of potential investment (as taxation increased to pay for the expanded state). More indirectly, although people were receiving a wider range of 'social goods' – those provided by the state rather than being purchased in the marketplace – wage- and salary-earners were reluctant to take these into account when considering the impact of both taxation and inflation on their purchasing power and thus demanded higher levels of income to increase their real (market-place) purchasing power. The expansion of state spending had resulted in manufacturing being sub-jected to a multiple squeeze – by resource competition from the public sector, rising wage demands and, finally, by rising levels of taxation of corporate profits. The result of these combined pressures was a rapidly declining level of new investment in the manufacturing sector and this created the prospect of deindustrialization.

These concerns were articulated in the agenda of the new right in the Conservative party from the mid 1970s. It focused concern about public spending on the costs which it imposed on personal, corporate and national economic development and argued for the need to free enterprise from the constraints and inhibitions imposed by what they identified as 'excessive' taxation. Public spending was thus at the forefront of the Conservative agenda for the 1980s and was paralleled in the USA by the adoption of what has been termed the 'business agenda' during the Republican presidencies of Ronald Reagan (Moody, 1987). There, too, 'big government' was identified as strangling enterprise through excessive taxation and interference in the workings of the market.

The arguments about deindustrialization and economic decline overlap with the Conservative case about disincentives and public spending. Drawing on neo-liberal (or free market) economics, the argument about *disincentives* emerged during the late 1970s and exerted a strong influence on Conservative party thinking and policy throughout the 1980s. Public spending was held to exert a disincentive effect on people's level of econ-omic activity in two very different ways. First, the high levels of personal and corporate taxation were seen as inhibiting enterprise and risk-taking because both individuals and companies failed to gain the 'just rewards' of their efforts. Thus both individuals and companies would exert themselves to less than maximum levels because of the diminishing returns due to increasing levels of taxation. If the nation's economic performance was to be improved, the enterprising instincts of both individuals and companies had to be liberated from the stifling effect of taxation.

Reducing taxation also meant that public spending would have to be reduced, at least if national debt – that is, government borrowing – was not to be increased. By contrast, under Reagan, the USA rapidly increased national debt through combining increased public spending – although not on welfare – while cutting personal and corporate tax rates. The concern about disincentives identified another result of public spend-ing which provided a justification for reducing public spending: the disin-centive effect of welfare benefits. Here, it was argued, the level of income which people received through various state benefits cushioned them from the necessity of seeking employment. The generosity of public spending undermined the will to work. Enterprise was thus being stifled by both the source and output of public spending, although through rather different mechanisms. The American economist J.K. Galbraith ironically summed up this economic theory: the rich don't work because they get too little money, while the poor don't work because they get too much.

The disincentive effects of public spending were linked, in Conservative arguments, to other inhibiting consequences of an overpowerful and over-interfering state: an excess of regulation and officialdom which prevented people and companies getting on with their own business. This critique of the state was expressed as follows by Sir Keith Joseph, one of the most influential proponents of new right Conservatism in the late 1970s:

> Our monetary problems reflect the underlying weakness of this man-made chaos, the divorce of work from production, of cost from benefit, of reward from performance, the greatest government spending spree of all time which is designed primarily to keep people busy instead of useful ...

> Monetarism is not enough. This is not intended as a counsel of despair, but a warning note. The government's intention to contract the money supply is welcome and potentially beneficial to all. But it is not enough unless there is also the essential reduction of the state sector and the essential encouragement of enterprise. We are over-governed, over-spent, over-taxed, over-borrowed and over-manned. If we shirk the cure, the after-effects of continued over-taxation will be worse than anything we have endured hitherto ...

> That is why, by itself, the strict and unflinching control of money supply though essential is not enough. We must also have substantial cuts in tax and public spending and bold incentives and encouragements to the wealth creators, without whose renewed efforts we shall all grow poorer.

> (Joseph, 1977; quoted in Clarke, Cochrane and Smart, 1987, pp. 135–6)

Although both deindustrialization and disincentive arguments focus upon the economic consequences of public spending, the new right critique of welfare was not limited to the identification of economic malaise but also pointed to the social and cultural consequences of state welfare. Linked to the inhibition of enterprise was the decline of 'independence' – the ability of people to take the responsibility for their own lives. In these terms, the result of state welfare was *'demoralization'* – the sapping of a once vital national culture through people's expectation that the state would provide. Again, there is an overlap with the arguments about disincentives, in that the expansion and accessibility of state benefits as a substitute for wages were seen as undermining the 'will to work' and as promoting a 'culture of dependency' in which individuals no longer took responsibility for their own lives (see, for example, Davies, 1987).

These criticisms of state welfare formed the basis for new right arguments about the need for change – the need, as Margaret Thatcher once put it, to 'shake off the shackles of socialism'. Proposals for achieving this centred on both reducing and changing the role of the state in providing welfare. Some argued that the welfare benefit system needed to be reformed to tighten up eligibility, to reduce the demoralizing effects of excessive benefit levels and to make the system more 'efficient' by targeting benefits on the 'most needy' (Smart, 1987). More broadly, arguments from the new right stressed the need to break up the state's 'monopoly' of welfare provision, creating enhanced roles for private and voluntary sector alternatives and thereby allowing welfare 'consumers' to exercise greater choice among different welfare providers.

In these ways the expanded role of the post-war state in the organization and provision of welfare featured as a central issue on the agenda of the new right in the late 1970s and 1980s, combining arguments from neo-liberal (or free market) economics with moral evaluations of the consequences of state intervention. The British new right shared many of these arguments with the political right in the USA associated with Reaganite Republicanism and there was extensive cross-fertilization between both political movements and the numerous think-tanks and allied institutions which developed around the Atlantic new right during this period (see, for example, Loney, 1986; Saloma, 1984; and Clarke, 1991). As a result, the Conservative governments beginning in 1979 brought with them the expectation that something would be done about the state of welfare. What they did do has been rather more complicated than the simple objective of 'rolling back the state' might have suggested.

2   ROLLING BACK THE STATE?

In discussing the 'roll-back' of the welfare state it is important, as Mishra (1990) argues, to distinguish a number of different stages in the unfolding of the offensive on welfare, or distinct levels on which it operates. There was a general ideological attack on welfare, which often had a propagandist or rhetorical character. This was important in creating an anti-welfare climate of opinion, but did not necessarily translate into practicable policy proposals. Thus, highly publicized leaks from a Conservative think-tank in 1982 suggesting government plans to privatize health and education are better understood as 'testing the water', 'kite-flying' or 'softening up public opinion' rather than as serious policies. The next stage is policy as outlined in party conferences or election manifestos: again this may fulfil other purposes (enthusing the party faithful, impressing the media, allaying public fears) than acting as a precise indication of what the party might do in government (commitments that, for example, 'the NHS is safe in our hands'). Then there is actual government policy, which may well be far removed from think-tank schemes or manifesto promises. The final stage is the practical outcome of government measures enacted in legislation or other executive actions, which again may differ from earlier plans.

Looking back at the 1980s, it is apparent that the government proceeded in a relatively cautious fashion in the welfare sphere rather than directly implementing a 'grand plan'. It implemented its agenda gradually, in a piecemeal way, carefully preparing public and professional opinion, pushing forward here, making tactical retreats there. It began where resistance was weakest – in housing – and carried on where anti-welfare prejudice was strongest – in social security. Only after three election victories did Mrs Thatcher seriously begin to extend market forces in those areas of welfare with stronger public and professional support – the NHS and education. Indeed, as Le Grand has pointed out, 'one of the striking features of the first eight years of Mrs Thatcher's government was how little it affected the welfare state' (Le Grand, 1990, p. 351). It was not until 1988 that the Conservative government began to introduce systematically its 'market reforms' into health, education and personal social services.

In this section we shall consider some of the evidence about the fortunes of the British welfare state during the 1980s. From the political agenda which the new right established and from the hostility expressed towards the inefficiencies, inequities and social and economic consequences of state welfare by senior government figures during the 1980s, it would be reasonable to expect evidence of a shrinking welfare state or declining public spending on welfare. In fact, this is not what we find when considering the patterns of public spending during the 1980s. Table 3.1 presents data on welfare spending between 1973/4 and 1987/8 which suggest that patterns of public expenditure on welfare have been remarkably stable. Indeed, the evidence is so at odds with the expectation that one commentator has written: 'Overall, what all this shows is that the welfare state, and indeed welfare itself, is very robust. Over the thirteen years from 1974 to 1987, welfare policy successfully weathered an economic hurricane in the mid 1970s and an ideological blizzard in the 1980s' (Le Grand, 1990, p. 350).

Le Grand explores a number of reasons for this 'robustness' of welfare. One is the effect of bureaucratic and professional inertia within the state, such that significantly changing policy direction is a much longer drawn-out process than might be assumed from the statements of politicians. A second explanation relates to the changing patterns of demography and need. We saw in the previous chapter that demographic shifts, in particular an increasingly older population, bring with them consequences for welfare spending, for example in relation to pensions and health costs. The long-term trend towards a growing population of older people did indeed continue during the 1980s and brought with it increased demands for welfare. Alongside this was the substantial growth of the numbers of people unemployed which rose sharply at the beginning and again at the end of the 1980s. The actual size of the unemployed population and its consequences for welfare costs are matters which are made more compli-

Table 3.1   Public expenditure on the welfare state: overall trends, United Kingdom (1987/8 prices)

	Year-on-year change (%)	% of general govern- ment expenditure	% of GDP
1973/4	–	50.5	21.6
1974/5	13.3	51.0	24.5
1975/6	2.5	52.2	25.4
1976/7	3.7	55.4	25.5
1977/8	–4.7	55.7	23.7
1978/9	1.5	53.6	23.2
1979/80	1.1	52.6	22.9
1980/1	1.0	52.1	24.0
1981/2	1.1	52.1	24.3
1982/3	1.9	51.7	24.2
1983/4	4.9	53.3	24.5
1984/5	1.2	52.5	24.3
1985/6	1.4	53.3	23.7
1986/7	4.4	54.7	24.0
1987/8	1.0	55.6	23.2

Source: Le Grand, 1990, Table 8.1

cated by changes in government definitions of unemployment and the conditions of eligibility for benefit which we will consider further in the next section. Nonetheless, in broad terms increased unemployment needs to be understood as having an impact on patterns of welfare spending during the 1980s.

The third explanation considered by Le Grand involves making distinctions within the broad patterns of welfare spending and looking at the relative fortunes of different welfare programmes. In relation to Figure 3.1, it is possible to see that the proportions of welfare spending directed to different programmes changed (Le Grand, 1990, p. 341). Even when the changing demographic patterns are taken into account, it is clear that some welfare programmes fared better than others during the 1980s. Le Grand suggests that some of these differences can be accounted for by considering the significance of these programmes used extensively by the middle classes, whose political importance as a pressure group may affect government choices about welfare spending. Drawing on research by Le Grand and Winter (1987), he argues that results 'for the Conservative government were much more robust, showing that services extensively used by the middle classes (although not necessarily those with a high proportion of middle-class employees) fared substantially better relative to need than those used primarily by the less well off' (1990, p. 346). Le Grand suggests that although this is not a complete explanation it is significant for some of the major shifts during the 1980s.

It is worth adding a couple of points to this argument. The first concerns the distinction between services *used by* and those *staffed by* the middle

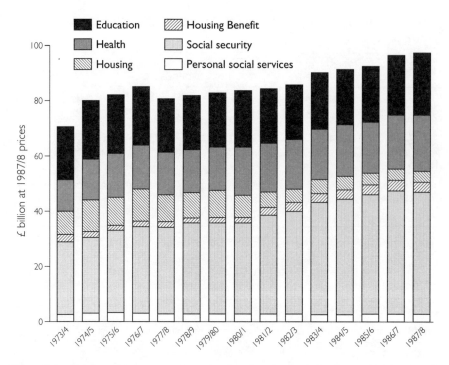

Figure 3.1   Public welfare expenditure by function, United Kingdom, 1973/4–1987/8
Source: Le Grand, 1990, Figure 8.2

classes, especially given the significant contribution which the expansion of the welfare state made to the post-war growth of the middle classes in Britain. There are grounds for thinking that some distinctions may be drawn between the 'commercial' and the 'state'-based sections of the middle classes, particularly in relation to government policy on public spending. The state-based sections, referred to by some new right voices as the 'polyocracy' or in the USA as the 'new class', who are dependent on public spending for their income, have supported the further growth of the state as the basis of social improvement and have had a greater propensity to support the Labour party or centre parties than the commercial sections of the middle classes. They were also the objects of new right critiques of the expanded state ('trendy' social workers and teachers, for example). It is perhaps not surprising that their political support or loyalty has not been a major objective of Conservative policy calculations during the 1980s.

Even so, this analysis of the different programmes of the welfare state does not capture all the significant changes which have taken place during the 1980s. The involvement of the state in welfare means more than determining the overall level of spending or its distribution within particular programmes. There are also important issues about both how – or under what conditions – welfare is provided and about the relationship between the state and the other providers of welfare. These are the subjects of the following two sections.

3   TIGHTENING THE NET: WELFARE BENEFITS IN THE 1980S

Although it was the Labour government of the mid 1970s that abandoned the full employment 'pillar' of the welfare state, it was not until the 1980s that the 'safety-net' provided by the welfare state for those out of work or otherwise unable to support themselves was significantly lowered (by reducing the value of benefits) and weakened (by reducing eligibility). Together with a series of measures to deregulate the labour market (the abolition of wages councils, anti-union legislation, significant reductions in protection against unfair dismissal etc.), these policies resulted in a sharp deterioration in the welfare rights of a substantial section of the population.

Given the concern with the claimed disincentive and demoralizing effects of welfare, it is hardly surprising that the benefits system was a major focus of Conservative policy-making during the 1980s. The initiatives taken had a number of objectives:

1   to reduce the disincentive and dependency creating effects of benefits;

2   to create a more efficient benefits system by 'targeting' benefits at the most needy; and

3   to encourage moves away from the state as the primary agency of social insurance.

In pursuing these objectives, successive governments made changes to the benefits systems ranging from changes in regulations affecting the conditions of eligibility and payment, through changes in the value of payments, to a substantial restructuring of the Supplementary Benefits programme (now named Income Support). The effects of these changes need to be considered alongside other initiatives, particularly in relation to pensions and taxation.

Perhaps the most important single contribution to reducing 'disincentives' has been the changes affecting Unemployment Benefit. Here the conditions of eligibility were revised to dissuade 'scroungers' – by requiring, for example, that those claiming benefit should prove they were 'genuinely seeking work' and, for some groups of claimants (the young unemployed), that they should attend training schemes or face loss of benefit. On top of this increased stringency affecting eligibility, unemployment benefits (whether insured or from Supplementary Benefit) were made taxable in 1982, thus reducing their value. During the 1980s the overall value of unemployment benefits declined substantially in comparison with average male earnings, as Figure 3.2 shows. The main means of accomplishing this decline were the removal of the earnings-related supplement from Unemployment Benefit in 1982 and by consistently raising benefits by less than either the earnings or inflation indexes. Despite the decline in the relative value of unemployment benefits, expenditure on such benefits rose because of the rise in the numbers of people unemployed during the first half of the 1980s, a trend repeated at the beginning of the 1990s.

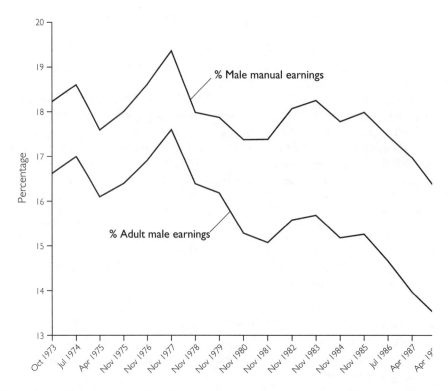

Figure 3.2   Unemployment Benefit, standard rate, as percentage of average male earnings, 1973–88

Source: Barr and Coulter, 1990, Figure 7.5

The search for greater efficiency in the benefits system focused on the principle of targeting. This meant an attempt to move away from 'universal' benefits to benefits directed at those most in need. This principle was most clearly articulated in the review of Social Security which reported in 1985 (DHSS, 1985). The resulting legislation reduced the value of SERPS-based pensions, restructured Supplementary Benefit (with particular impact on what were termed 'special needs payments'), replaced Family Income Supplement (paid to low-earning households) with Family Credit and froze the value of Child Benefit, thus moving family support increasingly away from universal benefits to means-tested ones. Figure 3.3 indicates the degree of success achieved by these measures in their objective of increasing the proportion of benefit spending channelled through means-tested rather than insurance-based or non-contributory routes.

One particular feature of the change from Supplementary Benefit to Income Support was the reorganization of the basis of 'special needs payments', available to those facing exceptional hardships or special circumstances which fell outside the normal benefit coverage. In the mid 1960s these had been codified as a set of payments for which claimants could apply and the discretionary control of them by Supplementary

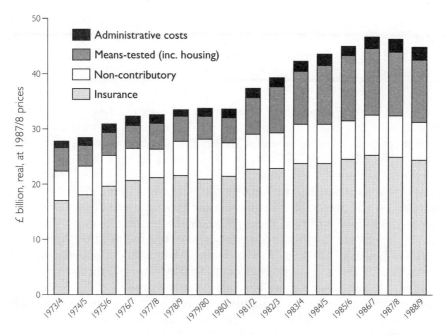

Figure 3.3   Social security spending, Great Britain (£ billion, real, at 1987/8 prices), 1973/4–1988/9

Source: Barr and Coulter, 1990, Figure 7.1

Benefit officers had been reduced. The Social Security Act 1988 reversed this trend, restoring discretion to officers, establishing a cash-limited budget for such payments and adding a further twist by requiring most payments to be made on a loan footing. As a result, the amount paid out in such exceptional payments declined rapidly – the combined effect of declining numbers applying for them, a more rigorous refusal of applications (often on the basis that claimants were deemed unable to repay such payments) and the effects of the cash-limited Social Fund itself.

The third objective of social security policy in the 1980s was to reduce dependency on the state. This was interpreted as increasing the availability of alternatives to state-based insurance systems and the government achieved rather less success here than in relation to the first two objectives. Two major initiatives aimed at transferring sickness insurance and pension insurance to the private sector collapsed in the face of considerable hostility, not least from the private insurance sector itself. The insurance companies found the prospect of establishing universal insurance schemes for both sickness and pensions less than attractive given that the requirement to insure *all* employees meant covering 'poor risks' (low-waged with low job security) as well as good risks (understood as white-collar and salaried employees). At the end of the 1980s this proposal returned in a more limited form in the encouragement to 'contract out' from SERPS and take out personal pensions. The encouragement took a characteristic double form – with tax relief available for those choosing to transfer to private pensions combined with the declining rewards promised to those staying within the state sector. Overall, though, there has been a substantial movement from the state to the private sector for pensions provision, primarily as a result of the growth of occupational pension schemes.

Assessing the consequences of benefit policy during the 1980s is a complicated issue. The first – and most notable – feature is the increase of the dependent population as a whole, that is the number of people in receipt of state benefits. Figure 3.4 shows the widening gap between actual spending on benefits and what the true level would have been if the number of people receiving benefits had stayed at the 1973/4 level. In part, this is the predictable result of trends we have considered earlier – increasing numbers of retired people and rising unemployment. But it is also the result of a further trend, sometimes referred to as the 'familialization of poverty'. The group most likely to be at risk of poverty shifted during the 1980s from single pensioners (slightly down from 59.6 per cent of all single pensioners being below the poverty-line in 1979 to 55.6 per cent by 1985) to lone-parent families (rising from 46.6 per cent of such households in 1979 to 63.9 per cent in 1985). This compares with the risk of poverty for married couples without children at 8 per cent of all such

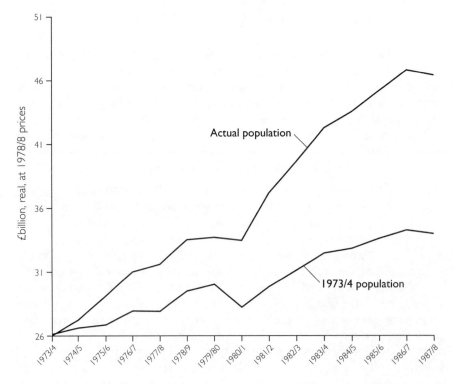

Figure 3.4   Real benefit expenditure, Great Britain (£ billion, at 1987/8 prices), 1973/4–1987/8

Source: Barr and Coulter, 1990, Figure 7.4

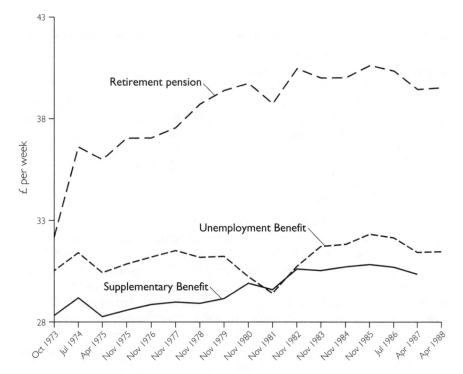

Figure 3.5   Standard rates of benefit at April 1987 prices
Source: Barr and Coulter, 1990, Figure 7.6

households in 1985 (Piachaud, 1988). Given that the vast majority of lone-parent households are headed by females, some commentators have also referred to this trend as the 'feminization of poverty', while other evidence suggests that there has also been a 'racialization of poverty' with increasing numbers of ethnic minority households in poverty (see **Cochrane, 1993**).

The impact of benefit rates on this growing population in poverty is also difficult to assess. By comparison with the Retail Price Index (RPI), most benefit rates were subjected to a sharp reduction in the early 1980s but then had their value restored or even increased in the middle of the decade (see Figure 3.5). However, there are grounds for thinking that this comparison overestimates the value of benefits for a number of reasons. Certainly, as we saw with Unemployment Benefit, there was a fall in value relative to average male earnings during the 1980s and this holds true for other benefits. From the early 1970s benefits were index-linked to average earnings or the RPI whichever grew faster. The Social Security Act 1980 cut the link with earnings with the result that there has been a widening gap (and a resulting saving in expenditure) between earnings and benefit rates.

More significantly, the RPI measure underestimates the effects of other fiscal policy changes which have borne unevenly on those on low incomes.

The changes in taxation policy (the other arm of the improving incentives strategy of 1980s Conservatism) shifted the tax burden from direct (income-related) taxation to indirect taxes (most notably the increase in VAT on purchases and the impact of the Community Charge/poll tax). Indirect taxation has a regressive effect – that is, it bears more heavily on low-income households because they spend proportionately more of their total income on purchases subject to taxation. Some estimates which take into account such taxation effects have suggested that the living standards of those in the bottom 20 per cent of incomes fell by up to 8 per cent between 1979 and 1986. The introduction of the Community Charge/poll tax worsened that situation through the insistence that all households (however poor) must make some contribution to the provision of local services.

Overall, then, Conservative policies in the 1980s must be judged a partial success *in their own terms*. The supposed disincentive effects of the benefit system have been reduced by lowering the 'replacement ratio' (the level of benefits relative to earned income). The benefits programmes have become more 'targeted', indexed by the increased use of means-tested benefits, and there has been some growth of private-sector alternatives to state benefits, at least in the field of pensions. However, at the same time both the numbers in poverty and the numbers dependent on state benefits have grown – as has the income gap between those dependent on benefits and those in employment.

4   VARIETIES OF PRIVATIZATION

We have already noted that one concern of the new right at the beginning of the 1980s was to create or encourage alternatives to state provision of welfare. This was expressed in terms of claims for the superior performance of non-state institutions in relation to two key values. First, private-sector alternatives were viewed as being more efficient than public-sector ones as a result of being 'disciplined' by market forces or competition. By comparison, public-sector institutions were viewed as excessively bureaucratic, controlled by administrative or professional interests and unresponsive to the pressures for efficiency which market-based organizations faced. Secondly, the existence of alternative sources of welfare – whether market-based or in the voluntary sector – was seen as important in promoting consumer choice and responsiveness. In state welfare provision, public-sector bodies held the position of 'monopoly suppliers'. It was argued that this had the effect of preventing welfare consumers from exercising choice about how their needs were to be met, while the absence of competition meant such public-sector monopolies were under no pressure to be responsive to consumer interests.

The break-up of such monopoly positions has thus been a constant theme of Conservative social policy during the 1980s and the creation of alternatives has taken a variety of forms. The most obvious one has been the encouragement of 'market forces' in the supply of welfare services. In some aspects of welfare, this has meant fostering private-sector competition directly, for example through tax concessions supporting private health insurance. In the decade between 1976 and 1986 the numbers of people covered by private health insurance more than doubled from 2.2 million to 5.2 million (Le Grand *et al.*, 1990, p. 106).

A more substantial policy route has been the requirement for competitive tendering for the provision of some public services. Compulsory Competitive Tendering (CCT) has been applied to both the NHS and local authority services during the 1980s, requiring that agencies put out to tender certain aspects of service provision (such as cleaning and catering in the NHS, environmental services and leisure facilities for local authorities). According to the 1991 consultative document on further CCT plans for local authorities, the government viewed these measures as having delivered significant cost savings while maintaining or even improving the standards of service quality (Department of the Environment, 1991). Allied to this has been the creation of a more extensive pattern of market relations in housing through the requirement that local authorities make available the 'right to buy' to tenants, thus moving substantial amounts of the public-sector housing stock (usually the most desirable) into private ownership.

To some extent these sorts of changes have fostered a greater involvement of the private sector in the provision of some welfare services. But in many respects they have been marginal to the core activities of welfare – education, health and personal social services – which are still primarily delivered through state institutions. However, these have not remained immune from significant changes aimed at promoting what have been termed the 'three Es': economy, efficiency and effectiveness (Audit Commission, 1988). We may identify three related initiatives which have aimed to promote a more efficient and 'business-like' approach to welfare provision:

- quasi-markets
- the separation of purchasers and providers
- decentralization and 'opt-out'.

Quasi-market is a term used to refer to the creation of internal trading systems within public-sector organizations: these are intended to mimic the behaviour of real markets, by creating internal trading between different sections. The most visible creation of quasi-markets has been in the NHS through the National Health Service and Community Care Act 1989 under which health units are required to price their services (for particular types of operations, for example) so that 'purchasers' (either District Health Authorities or GPs who are 'budget-holders') may 'shop around' for the best priced service. In this setting both purchasers and providers function as trading entities within the internal market of the NHS. Similar patterns of internal trading are being required of local authorities for many services which have not been put out to competitive tendering. Le Grand extends the term quasi-market to cover a variety of ways in which the 'purchaser' and 'provider' roles are being separated in the provision of welfare, such that the major role of the state is intended to become a purchaser rather than provider:

> ... the proposed reforms in primary and secondary education, health, housing and social services all involve the introduction of what might be termed 'quasi-markets': the separation of state finance from state provision and the introduction of competition and provision from independent agencies. If these reforms are carried through to their logical conclusion, the welfare state in the 1990s will be one where local authorities will not own and operate schools, houses and residential homes, and where health authorities will not own and operate hospitals. Instead local authorities and, increasingly, central government will be financing a growing number of private and voluntary institutions, all competing for custom: opted out and other independent schools, housing associations, private landlords, trust hospitals, private and voluntary residential homes. This shift from the state as funder and provider to the state primarily as funder with perhaps only a residual role as provider will undoubtedly create enormous changes in the way services are delivered and employees treated.
>
> (Le Grand, 1990, p. 351)

There are three significant issues to develop from these observations. The first concerns the likely 'residual' role for state provision. Even residual state provision will exist within a quasi-market, such that the 'provider' part of a local authority social services department, for example, will have to sell its services to the 'purchaser' section of its own or neighbouring authorities. More importantly, perhaps, the nature of the residual services supplied through the public sector is likely to depend on a combination of two sets of conditions: the potential profitability of the service in question (which will determine the extent of private-sector interest) and the availability of voluntary-sector alternatives (which may vary between different localities). The response of the private and voluntary sectors to such changes has been ambiguous. Private-sector competition, increased by 'quasi-private' institutions such as 'opted-out' hospitals, health services and schools, has tended to concentrate where expectations of 'profitability' are highest (such as prestigious medical centres and teaching hospitals).

The voluntary sector has been willing to enter into new partnerships with the public sector, but reluctant to take on the task of filling gaps in the network of service provision. Where voluntary alternatives are well established the new model poses few problems, but the spread of voluntary alternatives is by no means complete, either in terms of the range of services or geographically. Some voluntary bodies, particularly those based in minority ethnic communities, have expressed reservations about becoming dependent upon funding from, and subject to scrutiny by, state agencies. The likelihood is that residual public-sector provision in education, health, housing and personal social services is likely to be concentrated on the unprofitable and unattractive services for the poor.

Our second point concerns markets and customers. The stated objective of many of the 1980s' reforms has been to create greater customer responsiveness among public-sector services through the introduction of market forces. The 'quasi-market' nature of many of the changes, however, has a parallel in the creation of 'quasi-customers' – that is, service purchasers are not the direct consumers of a service but their managerial 'proxies': health authorities or GPs in health services; school governors and head teachers in education; care managers in personal social services and so on. These 'proxies' are expected to represent the best interests of the customers, but, as we shall see in the next section, this expectation is not without its problems.

Thirdly, Le Grand's discussion of the purchaser–provider split omits one further element in the division of responsibilities: that of 'regulation' or 'inspection'. In theory, the creation of an 'arms-length' relationship between purchasers and providers should also include an element of regulation or inspection to ensure that the contracted 'provider' is delivering satisfactory standards of service. This should mean an expanded inspection function for the 'purchaser' sections of the public sector to monitor the performance of providers whether they are based in the private, voluntary or public sectors. However, during the 1980s many of the existing inspectorates in the public sector (ranging from health and safety to education) have seen their funding base, staffing levels and their effectiveness shrink. At the same time, there have been suggestions that inspection services may themselves be privatized or put out to competitive tendering.

So far, we have highlighted the most visible varieties of privatization in the form of market and quasi-market forces and their impact on public-sector welfare. There is one further variant of privatization which requires attention in which a different meaning of 'private' has been at work. This is the transfer of welfare from the public realm (which includes public, voluntary and commercial sectors) to the private realm of the family. In terms of ideological commitments, this is in line with Conservative views about 'freeing' the family from the state, enabling the restoration of responsibilities to the family which had been appropriated by the state and thereby reinforcing parental responsibility and authority. In practice, it has meant the expectation that families will undertake an increased amount of the 'caring' work that is involved in the provision of welfare, particularly in relation to the 'dependent' population of children, people who are sick or have disabilities and older people (Graham, 1984).

One example may illuminate this transfer from the state to the family, although there are many. One of the proclaimed successes of the NHS during the 1980s was that hospitals were treating more patients than ever before. Leaving aside the phenomenon of lengthening waiting lists (i.e., that while hospitals were treating more patients they were failing to match increased demand), the key to the success was increased 'through-put'. The length of time being spent in hospital by patients was substantially reduced. As a result, recuperative or post-operative care that once took place within the hospital was transferred to the patient's private resources, usually the family. Given the prevailing gender distribution of care within families, this mostly hidden transfer of care responsibilities meant an increase in female domestic labour – the 'labour of love' which is embodied in women's family obligations (Finch, 1989; Graham, 1984; Ungerson, 1987).

Since these forms of welfare work are private in the strongest sense, being hidden within households and kin networks, they cannot be adequately assessed in terms of establishing the social costs of welfare. Elsewhere it is possible to measure patterns of resource inputs and outputs and the shift of resources or activities between sectors, but women's unwaged work is not measurable in this way. In terms of the national economics of welfare, then, it is not possible to estimate the size of or the shift towards this form of privatized care. Nonetheless, most studies of particular patterns of care – whether of children, people with disabilities or older people – indicate both that many welfare or care needs are fulfilled through wives, sisters and daughters and that the burdens of care have increased during the 1980s (Ungerson, 1987; Finch, 1989).

Such patterns have been given increasing official legitimacy through the idea of the importance of 'primary carers'. The 'discovery' of the amount of care provided by and within families during the late 1970s led to the work of women in providing care being dignified through the concept of 'primary carer'. Against this all other forms of care (provided by the state or other agencies) were viewed as the provision of secondary care – support for the work of primary carers (see, *inter alia*, the Barclay Committee, 1982). In a speech to the 1977 Conservative Party Conference, a future Secretary of State for Social Services, Patrick Jenkin, expressed this view of primary care in a definitive way:

> Quite frankly, I don't think that mothers have the same right to work as fathers do. If the good Lord had intended us to have equal rights to go out to work, he wouldn't have created men and women. These are biological facts ... We hear a lot today about social work – perhaps the most important social work is motherhood.
>
> (quoted in Clarke, Cochrane and Smart, 1987, p. 140)

In spite of this eloquent combination of religious, biological and legal justifications for the importance of motherhood, Conservative social and economic policy never resolved the issue of working mothers. Although rhetorically committed to the celebration of motherhood, the Conservatives nevertheless oversaw the expansion of women's paid employment during the 1980s, including a continued rise in the numbers of mothers taking on paid work. In part, this reflects the primacy of market forces over family obligations in the Conservative agenda – employers wanted an increasingly 'flexible' labour force, for which women 'returners' proved the best recruiting ground. It also reflects the growing salience of women's earnings, either as sole or joint earner, for maintaining household incomes and living standards. In part, it represents the absence of any sustained family policy – either in the form of adequate benefits for child support (what earlier generations of feminist campaigners had called the 'endowment of motherhood') or of developed childcare facilities. Instead, the pattern of women's 'double shift' (domestic work at home combined with waged labour outside the home) has developed on the assumption that their labour time is infinitely flexible and expandable – able to fill gaps in the labour market and the work of welfare wherever and whenever they appear (Langan, 1988).

In this section we have explored the changing conditions under which welfare has been – and will be – delivered, highlighting the shift away from a central role for the state. This involves expanded roles for the private, voluntary and domestic sectors of welfare and a withdrawal of the state from direct provision except for what have become increasingly residual service provisions. These changes have had significant consequences for the internal regime or character of the state itself and it is to these that we turn our attention in the next section.

5 MANAGERS AND CITIZENS: DELIVERING WELFARE

The attack on the direct provider role of the state was expressed through critiques of the power and influence exerted through two key aspects of the organization of welfare – bureaucratic systems and professional control of the content of services. The varieties of privatization discussed in the previous section were intended to undermine the influence of both bureaucratic and professional control of welfare delivery in the central and local state and to replace them with systems more responsive to the customers of those services. Competition, quasi-markets and partnerships have tried to make state provision mimic the patterns of the marketplace – which Conservative governments have argued would deliver greater efficiency, greater responsiveness to customer demand and greater accountability to those who pay for services.

In the process a new model of organizations has been developed which draws extensively on new theories of management. These theories – stressing flexibility, adaptability, a commitment to 'quality' products and services, and customer orientations – were created in the USA in the late 1970s as a response to the USA's declining economic competitiveness. Such theories were based on a critique of US enterprises as being too bureaucratic, too rigid and too inattentive to customers. (See, for example, Peters, 1989; Moss Kanter, 1990; Handy, 1990; and the commentary by Wood, 1989.)

This critical base created a strong affinity between this 'new managerialism' and the attempts to transform public-sector organizations in Britain. Its ideas played a significant role in redefining how welfare agencies are to relate to their 'customers' – a word which substantially replaced the language of 'citizens' or 'clients' in the effort to create new sorts of relationships between the state and its service recipients. The development of new managerial competences in the public sector was one of the key routes to creating those new relationships. Managers, as opposed to either professionals or bureaucrats, would embody the new commitments to efficiency, effectiveness and economy, to 'delivering value-for-money' services and to being 'customer-centred' (Flynn, 1990).

Most of the changes in welfare which we have discussed so far have carried with them a new definition of managerial roles as the means through which they can achieve success. Markets require new managerial skills in order for organizations to be able to compete successfully; quasi-markets similarly require new managerial skills to create effective trading and coordinate costs and services; decentralized or devolved services (as in the local management of schools) need new managerial skills for budgeting, resource control, contracting and planning; partnerships need new managerial skills to create and sustain new types of relationships between different organizations; and, above all, the customer relationship implies a need for new managerial skills to ensure value-for-money services.

In these ways, 'management' has come to take on a central role in the reorganization of the welfare state (McLaughlin, Cochrane and Clarke (eds), forthcoming). It carries the weight of changing the pattern of the state from a relationship of provider–user to a market or quasi-market relationship between suppliers and customers. The managers of the new pattern of state services are themselves accountable in two distinctive ways: on the one hand to customers in terms of the services they deliver, and on the other to those who pay taxes (nationally and locally) for the money spent on those services. This second version of accountability has in practice referred to the financial limits established by central government, given a declining degree of local political control over either funding or level of services. Throughout the 1980s it has been the control over resourcing of all services by central government which has been the central issue for considerations of welfare (whether it has been the funding of the NHS or education, or the control and 'capping' of local authority expenditure).

In the early 1990s, however, there was an attempt to establish a stronger basis for the accountability to customers through the proposals for a 'Citizens' Charter'. The charter initiative effectively redefined citizenship as a customer relationship and aimed to translate citizens' rights into measurable criteria for service delivery. If delivery standards (e.g. NHS waiting times) were not met, the 'customer/citizen' would be entitled to seek redress or compensation.

What is striking about these two forms of accountability is their effect on other mechanisms of accountability and control. Most public welfare services had been subject to some degree of democratically based political control, either through local authority elections or other, at least partially representative, bodies such as Community Health Councils. The combination of markets and managers renders such representative mechanisms of control and accountability increasingly marginal. During the 1980s local authorities lost much of their power to determine the nature of local services as a result of legislative and financial constraints imposed by central government; these included the abolition of some particularly 'troublesome' forms of local government (the Greater London Council and the Metropolitan County Councils). Instead, there has been an increasing stress on giving managers the 'freedom to manage' – which means freedom from 'political interference' – so that they can get on with the job of providing value-for-money services (Clarke and Newman, forthcoming).

It is not that the state has been simply replaced by the market, but that what has remained of state welfare has been reconstructed to mimic the market through the creation of quasi-markets and quasi-customers. Such state services are, of course, not markets in the full sense, since they are subjected to both legislative and financial control by central government. Similarly, most welfare 'customers' are not customers in any full sense since there are extremely limited opportunities for 'shopping around' and many are dependent on welfare services for their well-being. Nonetheless, the effect of these changes has been to modify the pattern of relationships of welfare provision by reducing the significance and power of intermediate institutions (such as local government) which previously stood between them as individual service-users and central government. The field of economic, social and political relationships has been increasingly reduced to a situation in which individual 'customers' find themselves operating in a variety of market or quasi-market relationships within a welfare system increasingly directly determined by central government policy and funding.

6 A NEW REGIME? WELFARE IN THE 1990S

We began this chapter by noting the new right critique of state welfare within the post-war settlement. The expected outcomes of that critique might have been a much reduced state welfare system, providing only residual welfare for those whose needs could not be met through private, voluntary or informal means. As we have seen, however, the real outcomes of the 1980s do not fit this view of the state being 'rolled back' in any simple way. By contrast, we have considered a range of changes which suggest that neither can it be claimed the welfare state has continued relatively unscathed and unchanged through the 1980s. How, then, are we to make sense of what has taken place? As Mishra (1990) suggests, it is more useful to contrast the reality of welfare provision in the early 1990s with the actual pattern that prevailed a decade earlier, rather than measuring the results of the Thatcher welfare reforms against some of the more extreme anti-welfare rhetoric of the new right think-tanks of the 1970s. There are conflicting interpretations of the impact of social policies and some different characterizations of the new welfare regime emerging in the early 1990s.

For Krieger, the 'roll-back' has been drastic, and its consequences close to catastrophic. He concludes from his survey of 'social policy in the age of Reagan and Thatcher' that 'there is no welfare state, only a set of welfare provisions' (1987, p. 196). Though he notes the uneven progress of the offensive against welfare on both sides of the Atlantic, he considers that the consensus politics embodied in the 'Keynesian welfare state' have been decisively rejected and that this episode of post-war history marks simply 'a transitory motif of class compromise' (ibid., p. 196).

However, in the view of Hills and his colleagues at LSE, 'reports of the death of the welfare state have, like Mark Twain's, been greatly exaggerated' (Hills, 1990, p. 1). In their survey of different sectors of welfare, they note the absence of 'simple overarching trends', but insist on the 'failure' of any overall 'roll-back' strategy (ibid., p. 10). Le Grand, as we have seen, finds the welfare state in 'robust' form. Further, he anticipates that the introduction of 'quasi-markets' in health, education and social services from 1988 onwards is unlikely to lead to a substantial fall in public spending on welfare or to a decline in standards.

In this debate it is clear that much depends on how widely or narrowly 'the welfare state' is defined. Krieger focuses on issues of employment and unemployment and income maintenance. As we have seen, the abandonment of the goal of full employment, the erosion of workers' rights and drastic reductions in both the value and availability of benefits have undoubtedly had a major impact. Permanent mass unemployment, deepening poverty and growing homelessness are inescapable features of modern life in both Britain and the USA. Le Grand, by contrast, concentrates on global levels of public expenditure on welfare and somewhat arbitrary measurements of 'outcomes'. He notes that, despite the economic upheavals of the 1970s and 1980s, the ideological shifts from Labourism to Thatcherism and the 'alleged end of consensus', state spending on welfare increased in real terms and remained steady as a proportion of GDP. Furthermore, 'virtually all measures of outcome' – in health, education, housing etc. – indicate an improvement (Le Grand, 1990, pp. 347–50).

Mishra (1990) has criticized such arguments about the 'irreversibility' of the welfare state on the grounds that looking at overall spending neglects sectoral shifts, and that focusing on state spending means ignoring both events in the labour market and taxation policy. He also maintains that Le Grand and his colleagues elevate short-term over long-term trends and that they are insensitive to the complex effects of social differentiation and ideology. It is striking that the economic gains of the Thatcher/Lawson 'economic miracle' of the later 1980s, which provide the basis for Le Grand's sanguine assessment of the prospects for the welfare state in the 1990s, were already threatened by the deepening recession which marked the end of the 1980s and the beginning of the 1990s.

If we define the welfare state as embracing full employment, a set of state social services (health, education, housing and personal social services) and a programme of basic income maintenance benefits (unemployment, sickness, disability, old age), then we can assess the 'roll-back' in each sector. Full employment was the first to go – and it is worth noting that no major political party now offers to bring it back. State social services, however, with the exception of public housing, are largely intact, though there are significant trends towards new patterns of service delivery within a largely state-financed system. The income maintenance programmes have been substantially cut back both in value and coverage, but they have not been abolished and they still guarantee a survival of sorts to millions of people. We can conclude that the welfare state has survived, though there can be little doubt that it has undergone significant changes since the late 1970s. How then can we characterize the new welfare regime of the early 1990s?

For pessimists of the Krieger school, the emerging model of British welfare is a *residual* one which approximates to the sort of liberal free market arrangements of nineteenth-century Britain, or even modern America. This means the further retreat of the state from both the provision and financing of welfare in favour of self-help and charity, while maintaining a basic level of cheap and stigmatized, means-tested services and benefits for those who cannot or will not make their own arrangements. Though there were trends in this direction in Margaret Thatcher's Britain, they were significantly slowed down by her removal from the leadership of the Conservative Party at the end of 1990. While John Major has carried on the broad policies of his predecessor, there were early signs of a softer approach towards welfare services. Major's 'Citizens' Charter', outlined in 1991, indicated both a recognition of the depth of public support for state welfare services and at least a rhetorical commitment to maintain and improve them, although not necessarily in their old forms.

Most other commentators remain uncertain about the new form of welfare. Many recognize, like Mishra, that the old welfare state, the 'neo-Keynesian post-war orthodoxy', has effectively disintegrated, but can see 'no new settlement in sight', no sign of a clear 'replacement' for the old regime. There is general acknowledgement of a decisive shift within the mixed economy of welfare, but disagreement over how this should be interpreted. Some welcome the emergence of a greater 'welfare pluralism' and greet the shift from a welfare state to a 'welfare society' (Rose (1986) in Britain; Rein and Rainwater (1986) in the USA). They regard the retreat of a bureaucratic and paternalistic state as opening up opportunities for a wider range of smaller-scale private and voluntary welfare agencies, self-help and community initiatives. They believe that individual consumers and users, as well as welfare professionals and workers, will be able to play a wider role in a more decentralized and user-sensitive welfare system. Thus, for example, the *New Statesman* argued in an editorial on community care that the

> ... purchaser–provider split might be Labour's best hope of breaking the provider dominance that so fetters service development and delivery today. The division is one that – properly exploited – could mean a questioning of health providers' priorities and practices by purchasers, and a real orientation of services around the needs of individuals and communities.
>
> (*New Statesman,* 11 October 1991)

In the same vein, Howard Glennerster (1992) conceded that, in the course of studying the first wave of GP budget-holding, he had been converted from a position of scepticism to regarding this as 'one of the most innovative parts of the NHS reforms'. He argued that 'fundholders, acting for individual patients, undermine providers' inefficiencies because they have a direct incentive to do so'.

Others envisage a shift from Britain's broadly social-democratic-inspired welfare state (though one that has always retained significant individualist/selectivist elements) towards the more conservative corporatist model that prevails in Germany, a trend that may be encouraged by Britain's ever closer relations with its EC partners (Esping-Anderson, 1990). The greater role of voluntary organizations in the emerging mixed economy of welfare, particularly in community care, anticipates a pattern that has long existed in Germany and may provide an example for Britain. However, the British government's refusal to endorse the Social Charter in 1989 or the Social Chapter of the Maastricht Treaty, signed by all other EC member-states in December 1991, reflects a chronic suspicion about 'Europeanization' which may be expected to continue into the 1990s.

There are other commentators who remain sceptical about greater welfare pluralism or social corporatist trends. Mishra (1990) emphasizes that the private, voluntary and informal sectors 'cannot be regarded as functional equivalents' of state-provided services, as they are organized on different principles and differ in scope. He argues that their growing significance is not simply a change in the form of welfare, a simple rearrangement of the mixed economy of welfare, but that the privatization of supply is likely to mean a diminished *entitlement* to any particular welfare service. He accuses enthusiasts for welfare pluralism of confusing collective responsibility for meeting social needs with the forms of delivery of welfare services. He advocates the 'democratic class struggle' model advanced by Korpi (1983), Stephens (1979) and Esping-Andersen and Korpi (1984) as the only guarantee of adequate welfare services in advanced capitalist society. These authors recommend a tripartite framework of government, employers and labour representatives within which 'societal bargaining' over welfare and other matters can proceed, allowing labour to articulate its vision of a genuinely collectivist welfare system.

By the early 1990s the British welfare regime can be viewed as being positioned by the tensions between these different welfare models. On the one hand, there has been a sustained attempt to dismantle the social-democratic features of the post-war welfare settlement and to install a more market-oriented (and quasi-market structured) pattern of welfare. Heavily influenced by US theory and practice, this has pulled the state sector towards a more residualist position in relation to both welfare benefits and the provision of welfare services. Such changes have led to an enhanced role in the mixed economy of welfare for the private, voluntary and domestic sectors combined with a sustained restructuring of the state sector towards behaviour which mimics markets.

At the same time, there has been a substantial reconstruction of the idea of the 'citizen' away from its liberal/social-democratic roots which had been a major influence on the British post-war settlement. The reconstruction has been a double one. On the one hand, national policy has stressed the citizen as customer, eligible to complain about service failures, moving away from the citizen as the focus of rights and obligations framed by the duty of the state to ensure the conditions under which all citizens can be full participating members of the society. On the other hand, European trends have seen the emergence of a racially restrictive definition of European citizenship, affecting both existing and would-be citizens from minority ethnic groups (see also Chapter 9 in this book).

With the single European market taking effect in 1993, much consideration has been given to the implications of the free movement of people within the European Community. Governmental attention (and the concern of influential extra-governmental agencies such as the Trevi Group) focused on the risks which free movement created in terms of terrorism and unwanted migration. At the core of these concerns has been an impulse to police the conditions of membership of the European Community – the status of citizenship. Free movement and the other benefits of European citizenship, it was argued, were goods which needed to be strictly limited to those who were demonstrably citizens. Not for the first time, but perhaps more powerfully than before, 'race' came to be seen as the single most visible demonstration of 'citizenship', combining the implicit racial 'test' as the basis of detecting suspected non-citizens among existing residents (and thus denying access to social benefits to black people and members of other minority ethnic groups) with racially exclusionary principles to potential migrants. This proved to be the aspect of European social policy with which British governments felt most at home, while aggressively distancing themselves from other aspects of harmonization.

As before, the emerging 'mixed economy' of the British welfare regime does not correspond precisely to any abstract 'type': it is not simply social-democratic, residual or corporatist. Both its post-war construction and its more recent reconstruction, however, show the influence in practice of those types as conflicting strategies for the organization of welfare regimes in late capitalist societies. The present regime – the effort to drag the British state into a more residual role in a new mixed economy of welfare – is marked by both the domestic political imperatives of 1980s' Conservative economic and social policies and the continued significance of both the social-democratic and corporatist strategies as alternative possible versions of 'welfare' and as political forces which have to be resisted if a more 'residual' regime is to be created.

REFERENCES

Audit Commission (1988) *The Competitive Council*, London, The Audit Commission for Local Authorities in England and Wales.

Bacon, R. and Eltis, W. (1976) *Britain's Economic Problem: too few producers*, London and Basingstoke, Macmillan.

Barclay Committee (1982) *The Future of Social Work*, London, Tavistock.

Barr, N. and Coulter, F. (1990) 'Social security: solution or problem?' in Hills, J. (ed.) op. cit., pp. 274–337.

Clarke, J. (1991) *New Times and Old Enemies: essays on cultural studies and America*, London, HarperCollins.

Clarke, J., Cochrane, A. and Smart, C. (1987) *Ideologies of Welfare*, London, Hutchinson.

Clarke, J. and Newman, J. (forthcoming) 'Managing to survive? Dilemmas of changing organizational forms in the public sector' in Deakin, N. and Page, R. (eds) *The Costs of Welfare*, Aldershot, Social Policy Association/Avebury.

Cochrane, A. (1993) 'The problem of poverty' in Dallos, R. and McLaughlin, E. (eds) *Social Problems and the Family*, London, Sage/The Open University.

Davies, S. (1987) 'Towards the remoralization of society' in Loney, M. *et al.* (eds) op. cit.

Department of the Environment (1991) *Competing for Quality*, London, DoE.

Department of Health and Social Security (1985) *Reform of Social Security*, vols 1–3, Cmnd 9517/8/9 (Green Paper), London, HMSO.

Esping-Andersen, G. (1990) *The Three Worlds of Welfare Capitalism*, Cambridge, Polity Press.

Esping-Andersen, G. and Korpi, W. (1984) 'Social policy as class politics in post-war capitalism: Scandinavia, Austria and Germany' in Goldthorpe, J. H. (ed.), *Order and Conflict in Contemporary Capitalism*, New York, Oxford University Press.

Finch, J. (1989) *Family Obligations and Social Change*, Cambridge, Polity Press.

Flynn, N. (1990) *Public Sector Management*, Hemel Hempstead, Harvester Wheatsheaf.

Glennerster, H. (1992) quoted in *British Medical Journal*, 1 February, vol. 304, p. 276.

Graham, H. (1984) *Women, Health and the Family*, Brighton, Wheat-sheaf.

Handy, C. (1990) *The Age of Unreason*, London, Arrow.

Hills, J. (ed.) (1990) *The State of Welfare: the welfare state in Britain since 1974*, London, Oxford University Press.

Joseph, K. (1977) *Monetarism is not Enough*, London, Centre for Policy Studies.

Korpi, W. (1983) *The Democratic Class Struggle*, London, Routledge and Kegan Paul.

Krieger, J (1987) 'Social policy in the age of Reagan and Thatcher' in Miliband, R. *et al*. (eds) op. cit., pp. 177–98.

Langan, M. (1988) 'Women under Thatcherism' in Alcock, P. and Lee, P. (eds) *Thatcherism and the Future of Welfare*, Papers in Social and Urban Policy, no. 1, Sheffield Polytechnic.

Le Grand, J. (1990) 'The state of welfare' in Hills, J. (ed.) op. cit., pp. 338–62.

Le Grand, J. and Winter, D. (1987) 'The middle classes and the welfare state under Conservative and Labour governments', *Journal of Public Policy*, vol. 6, pp. 399–430.

Le Grand, J., Winter, D. and Woolley, F. (1990) 'The National Health Service: safe in whose hands?' in Hills, J. (ed.) op. cit., pp. 88–134.

Loney, M. (1986) *The Politics of Greed*, London, Pluto Press.

Loney, M. *et al*. (eds) (1987) *The State or the Market: politics and welfare in contemporary Britain*, London, Sage.

McLaughlin, E., Cochrane, A. and Clarke, J. (eds) (forthcoming) *Managing Social Policy*, London, Sage.

Miliband, R. *et al*. (eds) *Socialist Register 1987*, London, Merlin.

Mishra, M. (1990) *The Welfare State in Capitalist Society: policies of retrenchment and maintenance in Europe, North America and Australia*, Hemel Hempstead, Harvester Wheatsheaf.

Moody, K. (1987) 'Reagan, the business agenda and the collapse of labour' in Miliband, R. *et al*. (eds) op. cit.

Moss Kanter, R. (1990) *When Giants Learn to Dance*, London, Unwin Hyman.

Peters. T. (1989) *Thriving on Chaos*, London, Pan.

Piachaud, D. (1988) 'Poverty in Britain', *Journal of Social Policy*, vol. 17, no. 3, pp. 335–49.

Rein, M. and Rainwater, L. (1986) 'Introduction' in Rein, M. and Rainwater, L. (eds) *Public/Private Interplay in Social Protection*, New York, Sharpe Armonk.

Rose, R. (1986) 'Common goals but different roles: the state's contribution to the welfare mix' in Rose, R. and Shiratori, R. (eds) *The Welfare State East and West*, New York, Oxford University Press.

Saloma, J. (1984) *Ominous Politics: the new conservative labyrinth*, New York, Hill and Wang.

Smart, C. (1987) 'Securing the family? Rhetoric and policy in the field of social security' in Loney, M. *et al.* (eds) op. cit.

Stephens, J.D. (1979) *The Transition from Capitalism to Socialism*, London and Basingstoke, Macmillan.

Ungerson, C. (1987) *Policy is Personal: sex, gender and informal care*, London, Tavistock.

Wood, S. (1989) 'New wave management?', *Work, Employment and Society*, vol. 3, no. 3, pp. 379–402.

CHAPTER 4
GENDER, 'RACE' AND CLASS IN BRITISH WELFARE POLICY

FIONA WILLIAMS

INTRODUCTION

The aim of this chapter is to provide an understanding of the relationship between welfare policies in Britain and existing social divisions, particularly those of class, 'race' and gender. The previous two chapters have already begun to point to the ways in which welfare policies defined women in certain ways or excluded racialized groups or reinforced class divisions. For example, in Chapter 2 it was noted that the Beveridge Report 'embodied a set of assumptions about gender relations and the family' (p. 26) where women were seen primarily as wives and mothers whose main access to National Insurance and National Assistance benefits was via their husbands' wage-earning capacities. Reference was also made to the ways in which the notion of welfare citizenship became dependent upon a test of nationality, a test which was interpreted in racial terms (p. 28). It was suggested that the post-war education system reflected and reproduced existing class and gender inequalities. It is also clear from the first three chapters that the development of welfare is not simply a story of policy-makers and policy-making, nor of a 'golden age' which began to lose its shine, but a story of the complexity of political, economic and social forces, of pressures both internal and international, all subject to conflict and change. With this in mind, we need to explore further the assumptions that British welfare policies have held about the needs and roles of particular social groups. This involves an understanding of such policies within their specific historical context, as well as an indication of the differential ways in which such policies have been constituted, experienced or challenged over time. In these terms this chapter looks at welfare policies during the post-war period in Britain and up to the 1990s. To begin with, we need to look at the ways in which the welfare experiences of different and unequal social groups have been articulated and explained.

I CHANGING ISSUES AND CHANGING EXPLANATIONS

Until relatively recently analyses of welfare policies operated with a *limited view of social divisions and inequalities*. Many of the studies of welfare in the 1950s, '60s and '70s used categories derived from the discourses of welfare professionals – 'problem families', 'children at risk', 'the old', 'the handicapped' etc. Those more concerned with social inequalities analysed social groups in terms of class-derived categories of deprivation – 'the poor', 'the unemployed', 'the homeless'. The extent to which such categories or inequalities may have reflected or cut across other social relations of power and inequality – of gender, say, or 'race' – was little considered. Such studies also operated with a *limited view of human agency*: that is, the ways in which people themselves may experience shape, challenge or change welfare policies were also overlooked. Those who used welfare provision were seen as its passive recipients and beneficiaries, while politicians, policy-makers, professionals, and to some extent pressure groups, were seen as the combined motor of welfare development.

1.1   CLASS AND CAPITAL: AGENCY AND STRUCTURE

By the end of the 1970s analyses of 'the political economy of welfare' (Gough, 1979) began to attend to, amongst other things, this question of human agency. Gough developed the concept of the welfare state as an uneasy truce between conflicting interests: the interests of capitalism in accumulating profit and in having a healthy, cared-for and appropriately skilled workforce, and the interests of the working class in improving or maintaining their social and economic conditions, as well as the interests of the state in maintaining political stability and its own legitimacy. In this way people's needs, interests and actions were defined in terms of *class* divisions and *class* conflicts in relation to the needs of capitalist production. The idea that people themselves determine the conditions of welfare was introduced through the notion of class struggle: the state and capital concedes more (wages, welfare benefits) when faced with political instability from collective class organization. In this scenario class is seen as the predominant form of power and inequality, and production its major focus. In so far as other social divisions – of gender or 'race' – are acknowledged then they are explained in terms of the needs of capitalist production: thus, woman's domestic role serves to produce and maintain the workforce; immigrant labour represents a 'reserve army' variously pulled into and pushed out of production.

So, whilst the political economy of welfare analysis develops a notion of human agency, its notion of and explanations for different social divisions are still limited. And, whilst it recognizes the role that women play in social reproduction and the role that women and black people play as low-paid labour, it does not explain *why* they play these roles. It accounts neither for the specificity of female or racial oppression, nor why or how these are either ameliorated by or reproduced in welfare policies and provision. In addition, whilst acknowledging human agency through class struggle, the analysis implies a unitariness in this and does not explain why struggles for some welfare reforms (for example, in National Insurance after 1911) resulted in policies which sometimes represented greater gains to the skilled, male working class than they did to women or so-called 'aliens'. For these sorts of explanations we need to turn to feminist and anti-racist critiques, black scholarship, as well as to work exploring disability, sexuality and age as sources of oppression.

1.2   THE DIVERSITY AND INTERRELATIONSHIP OF SOCIAL DIVISIONS

The range of critiques of welfare focusing on the particular experiences of different social groups has emerged from a combination of political developments. The first is from what are sometimes called the 'new social movements' – feminism, the struggle against black oppression, the gay and lesbian movements, the disability movement. The second is the associated development of what is called the 'user movement' – the collective organization of groups who use welfare services, for example, People First, the organization of self-advocacy groups for people with learning difficulties, or Survivors Speak Out, the organization of people who use psychiatric services. In some cases the new social movements and user movements overlap – the women's health and the disability movements, for example.

GENDER

The emergence of different feminist critiques of welfare in the 1970s and '80s in particular illustrates the ways in which there has been a greater recognition of a complexity of social relations of power and inequality as well as a development of conceptual categories to understand and explain them. Much of the feminist work that explored women's experiences of the post-war systems of social security, pensions, health care, housing, education and personal social services found that policy, provision and practice in these areas underpinned three main assumptions about women's lives: that their primary roles would be those of wife and mother; that they would be living within a heterosexual married relationship; and that they would be financially dependent upon their husbands. This means that women stand in a contradictory relation to the welfare state. On the one hand, welfare policies have provided women with material and social improvements: family allowances/Child Benefit, access to safer childbirth and more reliable forms of contraception as well as employment opportunities. On the other hand the assumptions behind welfare policies have often circumscribed women's lives, with the consequence that many women's needs have been overlooked or marginalized or existing inequalities have been reproduced. Thus, for example, the women's refuge movement from the mid '70s campaigned long and hard for the housing needs of women and children fleeing from domestic violence to be recognized by local authorities. Similarly, the development of anti-sexist teaching strategies grew out of an awareness of the ways in which the organization of schools and their curriculum narrowed girls' expectations. The assumption of financial dependence meant that over the post-war period many of those groups of women without a male breadwinner partner – lone parents, widows, divorced or separated women – were forced into poverty (Glendenning and Millar, 1987; see also **Cochrane, 1993**). And the assumption of women's destiny as wife and mother helped to marginalize and pathologize those whose lives do not fit this pattern – older women, lesbians, mothers in paid work. Furthermore, in so far as women do enter paid employment, then these assumptions contribute to gender and 'race' inequalities at work. This is nowhere better exemplified than in the public sector where women form the major part of the workforce but predominantly in the lower paid, lower grade jobs. One study quotes a *pro rata* factor of ten in pay differences in local government between senior council officers, generally men, and lowest grade employees, generally part-time women (Cockburn, 1991, p. 106).

One of the effects of the development of these analyses has been to focus more intensely and critically upon areas of *social reproduction*. This means not only the process of bearing children, but the physical, emotional, ideological and material processes involved in caring for and sustaining others. The conditions in which this takes place and the consequences and expectations flowing from it are crucial for women's lives, but also, as Chapter 2 showed, central to welfare provision. In addition, these conditions, consequences and expectations vary according to women's social class. So feminist analyses have sought to explain why women play such a major role in social reproduction, and what consequences this experience, and the way the state intervenes, has for women and for gender inequalities. In answering these questions feminist critiques of welfare have drawn on the notion of patriarchy to understand women's oppression in terms which go beyond seeing this as biologically determined (it's all natural) or economically determined (it's all down to capitalism). In this way the class production/capitalism focus provided by the political economy analysis has been broadened by feminist analysis to include a gender/reproduction/patriarchy focus.

DISABILITY

Feminist critiques of welfare have been further refined by another set of issues: how far are women's experiences of welfare modified by divisions of class, 'race', disability, age or sexuality? One example of this can be found in research and campaigns around women and disability. Jenny Morris, writing from a disabled, feminist perspective, has drawn attention to the ways in which not only social policies but also feminist writing on social policy have obscured the experiences of disabled women (Morris, 1991). In the area of work on informal care, feminist analyses have often focused on the role and needs of the female *carer* in providing unpaid care. This, she argues, marginalizes the needs and experiences of those who receive care, often women themselves. Prioritizing the needs of carers has also led too quickly to the explicit or implicit rejection of community care policies as the exploitation of women's unpaid labour in the home in favour of residential or communal forms of living (in, for example, Finch, 1984, or Dalley, 1988). This position, Morris points out, often ignores the wishes of disabled people themselves and especially their rights to family relationships and private domestic life which in the past have been denied them. The tendency to ignore the capacity of men to care is also seen as playing into the commonly held assumption of health and social services professionals that a married woman who becomes disabled should not expect to sustain her relationship with her husband (Morris, 1992, p. 37). Furthermore, many of those women who fall into the 'cared for' category are sometimes also carers themselves. Indeed, in the case of women with learning difficulties who live at home with older parents, ostensibly to be cared for, it is often they who do the caring (Williams, 1992). In these different ways, then, disability can reconstitute women's experiences, perspectives and needs for welfare provision, and research in this area illustrates the complexity of relations of social power and their relationship to welfare.

'RACE'

Work by black feminists has also sought to describe and analyse the ways in which black women's experiences of welfare are different from white women's, because of the way these are structured by 'race' as well as by gender and class (Bryan *et al.*, 1985; Carby, 1982a, 1982b; Brah, 1987; Mama, 1989). Research by black scholars and anti-racist critics has demonstrated that there are many dimensions to the relationship between 'race', racism and welfare. There is the role that black labour has played in maintaining lower social expenditure within the health service; or the historical relationship between immigration controls and welfare provision (for example, the use of welfare agencies – like the DSS and NHS – to check immigrant status and the denial of benefits to dependants). The relationship historically and today between welfare development and imperialism, and between welfare and nationality, also points to questions such as should there be a nationalist basis to welfare eligibility? What is the meaning of 'nation' and 'nationality' in welfare policy? Such work has examined the different forms of racism that exist in welfare policy, for example, where existing processes of social control become 'racialized' – the disproportionate numbers of black young people in units for disruptive children (Carby, 1982a) or facing incarceration and psychiatric detention; the pathologizing of black family life in assessment procedures within the social services; the heavier policing of black youth and black communities; the presentation of black cultures as a threat to traditional education and to national culture. A second example is where existing procedures deny the specific needs of black people or deny access to appropriate provision – where a false sense of universalism, 'treating everyone the same', serves to deny cultural differences (in the provision of food in residential homes, for example) or to deny the existence of racial harassment (by ignoring the incidence of racial attacks on housing estates). These issues are explored later.

Together these different processes mean that for black women their experiences of the way the education system treats their children, the health service treats their fertility, the social security system treats their rights to benefit, or the personal social services treat their family life, may sometimes be very different from white women's. Experiences of racism and sexism are not simply incremental forms of oppression but, as the examples later in this chapter demonstrate, a reconstitution of those experiences in specific ways.

At a conceptual level, this work on 'race' and welfare demands an under-standing of the political and economic context of racism – an understand-ing which avoids reducing racism to economic determinism (it's all down to capitalism, again), or to cultural, racial or territorial essentialism (it's all due to essential and inevitable cultural/racial differences) or merely to explanations of discriminatory behaviour (it's all irrational prejudice). Instead, it requires an understanding of the relationship between imperi-alism, racism and the international division of labour and the develop-ment of the welfare state, as well as the relationship of these to both capitalism and patriarchy. In other words in order to make sense of class, 'race' and gender divisions in welfare, we need to see the welfare state within a context of the shifting social relations of capitalism, patriarchy and imperialism.

In Britain today we might describe that context as a patriarchal and racially structured capitalism. At the same time, we need to be aware that the social divisions of class, 'race' and gender are not the only structured divisions which have a bearing on people's lives, and particularly upon their experience of and access to welfare provision. The examples referred to above, and those elaborated below suggest that disability, age and sexuality constitute in Britain sites of significant oppression which are mediated through some of the ableist, ageist and heterosexist assump-tions running through welfare policies. Again, these forms of inequality change over time, as they are both contested and subject to other forms of social, demographic and political change. The significance of particular social divisions also changes across different societies: for example, in some countries (such as Northern Ireland) religious divisions are struc-tured in inequality. In analytical terms, then, it is important to be more sensitive to the complex, contradictory and multi-faceted nature of social divisions. Take the category of 'race': we need, on the one hand, to recog-nize that there is no uniform racial or racialized experience, for this is reconstituted not only in terms of existing social divisions – class, gender, age and so on – but also by diverse ethnicities and identities (see, for example, **Baldock, 1993**). People are also more than the sum of their class, 'race', gender, disability, age or sexuality locations, for these inter-act with individual biographies and identities. Yet at the same time, whilst acknowledging this complex diversity, it is also important not to lose hold of an understanding of the broader patterns of power and racial inequalities.

A FRAMEWORK

In order to explore further the relationship of these social divisions to the development of welfare policies I want to suggest that the interconnected themes of *family, nation* and *work* provide a useful framework (see Wil-liams, 1989). Taken together these three areas incorporate much that is significant in welfare policy about the social relations of capitalism, patri-archy and imperialism, as well as the key processes of production and social reproduction and the way these are connected to the formation of social divisions in society. That is to say, particular and changing ideas and conditions about what constitutes family life, what constitutes nationhood, culture and national unity and the ways in which people are brought into (or excluded from) particular forms of production, have a major bearing on the formation and outcomes of welfare policy, provision and practice.

The remainder of this chapter looks at examples of policies or policy development in post-war Britain to the present day in terms of the shifting discourses around family, nation and work and the impact these policies have for different social groups. First, though, it is helpful to describe briefly the constitution of family, nation and work in social policies prior to 1945. Although the post-war reforms marked a major shift in social policy (described in Chapter 2), they also absorbed a welfare legacy which perceived women primarily as mothers and wives and which had already laid the basis for the restriction or exclusion of some groups of welfare-users on the basis of nationality, 'race' or their marginalization from paid work. In other words, the development of the Beveridgean welfare state with its (limited) views of universalism and citizenship premised on the white, male, heterosexual, able-bodied norm had its roots in earlier welfare reforms and their specific relationship to capitalism, imperialism and patriarchy.

2   FAMILY, NATION AND WORK: THE EARLY YEARS

The most significant expansion of the British welfare state is generally traced from 1945. However, the period from 1880 to the 1920s represents the consolidation of collectivist forms of state organization and social regulation. Amongst these were the welfare policies introduced from the first decade of the century – old-age pensions, health and national insurance, school meals, the supervision and control of 'mental deficients', maternity and child welfare, public housing and the various unemployment benefits after 1919. These were part of attempts by the state to appease, supervise and control an increasingly militant working class. They also represented an attempt to ensure the fitness of British soldiers to defend the Empire and the skills and health of a labour force to maintain British industrial supremacy in the world markets, which was increasingly under threat from competition from the United States and Japan. At the same time these policies began to consolidate particular images and conditions of family life and work life and their relation to national and imperialist interests in ways which excluded and marginalized certain social groups. So, for example, policies for women focused upon their needs as mothers over and above their needs as wage-earners. The development of, for example, maternity and child welfare services after 1918 met women's very real needs but, at the same time, served to consolidate women's place in the home. In addition such policies elevated motherhood to a new dignity. 'It was', as Anna Davin explains, 'the duty and destiny of women to be "mothers of the race", but also their great reward' (1978, p. 13). Women's role in the *family* became tied to the development of *'race' and nation* within an assumption of nation as 'race'. In addition, this elevation reinforced the restriction of women to the home and the separation of home from *paid work*, a process also reflected in the exclusion of women from some of the new insurance and unemployment benefits. In the health insurance scheme of the National Insurance Act 1911 women were only eligible for three-quarters of the rate; they were also penalized by not being able to claim for time off for childbirth (see Land, 1978).

Policies around income maintenance also marked the beginnings of a popularly accepted idea that entitlement to forms of welfare provision would be restricted by *nationality*, which in practice meant 'white', Christian and English-speaking. In addition, they illustrate how close the connection was between welfare provision and immigration control. This worked in two ways: either by using denial of access to welfare as a form of control by threatening a so-called 'alien' who turned to public funds with deportation, or by using the welfare agencies themselves to police the access of 'aliens' to benefits. The Aliens Act 1905 imposed restrictions on Jewish immigrants who had begun arriving, many as refugees from Eastern Europe and Russia, from the 1880s onwards. The campaigns for immigration control often included abusive anti-Semitism, and found support from all the major political parties as well as from trade unionists like Ben Tillet, the dockers' leader. The Aliens Act demanded that no person who could not support herself or himself, or who might need welfare provision, should be allowed in, and that anyone who, within 12 months, was homeless or living in overcrowded conditions or living off poor relief be deported. Following this, the Pensions Act 1908 denied a pension to anyone who had not been both a resident *and* a British subject for twenty years. In the health insurance scheme of the National Insurance Act 1911, non-British citizens who had not been resident for five years received lower rates of benefit (seven-ninths) even though they had paid contributions (Cohen, 1985).

3 POST-WAR BRITAIN:
THE CIVILIZING MISSION BROUGHT HOME

In the subsequent development of welfare policies appeals to notions of the family, to national unity, British culture and to the centrality of the work ethic for men continued, but how these ideals were constituted shifted. Up until the Second World War national unity and British cultural supremacy tied the development of welfare policy to imperialism abroad. At the turn of the century the three main doctrines of imperialism had been power, profit and civilization; by the Second World War power and profit had begun to decline and only civilization remained (see Chapter 2). Civilization is what the post-war welfare state seemed to represent: to some on the left, like John Strachey, there was the hope that the welfare state could replace the old imperial ideal in sustaining national cohesion. Also the welfare state appeared to represent all that was 'best and British': it was seen to stand as a fine example of good self-management to the colonies and ex-colonies.

The welfare state, then, became central to the reconstruction of post-war Britain and it represented Britain's civilizing mission brought home, built with the bricks of the family and the mortar of national unity, by the labour of low-paid women and newly arrived black workers. Ironically it was often these groups of workers to whom the benefits of the new welfare state were restricted: black male workers may have built council houses but discriminating allocation criteria meant that they weren't eligible to live in them (Jacobs, 1985); working-class white and black women may have cleaned DHSS offices, but they weren't necessarily eligible to benefits in their own right. Similarly, many people with learning difficulties may have been denied ordinary life in the community, but they were still expected to provide the manual and domestic labour to maintain institutions at low cost.

Chapter 2 began to outline the ways in which the Beveridge Report espoused the ideals in family, nation, work and welfare: once again marriage and motherhood were the white, able-bodied woman's personal and national duty, whilst the breadwinner role was assigned to her husband. This ideal captured the subordinacy of women to their husband's economic power, their limited access to paid work and the destiny of permanent heterosexual coupledom. All right for some, but definitely not all right for all. In the next section I want to look first at some of the ways in which these ideals contrasted with and reconstructed the realities of the lives of black people in Britain in the 1950s and '60s, and then at the contradictory nature of welfare provision during the post-war period.

3.1   THE IDEAL, THE REALITY AND THE PATHOLOGY

In the immediate post-war period there was a substantial labour shortage especially in the manufacturing industries and the developing welfare services. The state was faced with a number of possible solutions – to draw on married women workers or to draw on migrant labour from the colonies or the poorer parts of Europe. The first solution contradicted the ideals of motherhood and it carried the costs of socialized childcare, a provision which had been ill-organized and patchy during the war (Riley, 1983). The second solution also posed problems to the state both in terms of the costs they would incur (housing etc.) and also in terms of its own racism and nationalism. The 1949 Royal Commission on Population was concerned about the problems of 'good human stock' and the 'assimilation difficulties' of black immigrants compared with Europeans (Williams, 1989), but, on the other hand, as members of the Commonwealth there were fewer administrative problems posed by the movement of colonized migrants between countries. From the beginning, then, Commonwealth immigrants were seen as presenting a 'problem' but as necessary to fill the temporary labour shortage. They were seen primarily as units of labour rather than as people with general or specific welfare needs.

The use of migrant labour combined with an ideology stressing mothers' presence in the home thus meant that white women were not drawn as fully into the labour market as they had been during the war and as they were in many other western industrialized countries at this time (especially those countries such as Hungary and Sweden without available colonized labour). Nevertheless many working-class women needed work to supplement or, in the case of widows or lone parents, to replace a male wage. For many white working-class women the compromise was part-time work which was seen as not interfering with domestic duties (Wilson, 1977). This also suited employers as it was low-paid labour which carried no extra costs such as National Insurance or sickness benefits. In different ways, then, compromises were struck in the demand for more labour, but struck in ways which reproduced gender, class and racial inequalities.

The labour shortage during and after the war also had repercussions on other areas of welfare. For example, it added pressure to the early calls for 'community care'. Many of the more able-bodied residents of institutions and 'colonies' (as, significantly, the larger institutional complexes were called) were released at this time. J. S. Cookson, the Medical Officer of Health in Gloucester, noted in 1945 that one welfare officer was surprised to find that a 'mentally deficient' client who had, before the war, been regarded as unemployable was now earning more than she was (quoted in Jones, 1985, pp. 149–50).

As members of the Commonwealth the new migrants should have been able to exercise their rights as welfare citizens, but different processes of direct and indirect racism served to exclude black people from some of their rights, to marginalize their needs and to reveal the limited definition of welfare citizenship. One part of this process emerged, ironically, through the notion of 'universalism'. The universalist services which were part of the Beveridge plan – such as the safety-net of National Assistance, the health and education services – incorporated an apparently egalitarian philosophy of treating everyone the same regardless of origin or status. Yet, not only was this ideal premised upon a particular view of gender relations and family life, as Chapter 2 showed in relation to income maintenance, it also assumed white, Christian Britishness as the normative structure governing people's needs and expectations. Furthermore, treating people the same often meant failing to recognize the specific needs of some social groups – in the case of new migrants their needs for immediate housing, for information and translation services – or for the positive acknowledgement of differences in cultural and religious traditions. Universalism in practice often meant uniformity and, for many of those who did not conform, their differences were seen in pathological terms. In other areas of provision, the conditions of eligibility were inappropriate to black people's immediate experience: for example, in council housing the qualification condition of long-term residency within a local area immediately made such provision inaccessible to new migrants. In this situation black people were forced into the private sector of housing where, along with employment, racism was at its most overt (subsequently made illegal by the Race Relations Act 1968). In some areas, initially at least, needs were met through informal networks or voluntary groups such as the National Council for Commonwealth Immigrants. In Liverpool in 1948, for example, the Colonial People's Defence Committee organized for the subsistence needs of black seamen who had been denied access to Unemployment Benefit. Perhaps more importantly, though, black workers and their dependants stepped into a situation still heavy with a legacy of suspicion that all 'aliens' were potential scroungers and trouble-makers, and framed by a cost-benefit analysis of immigrant labour: the costs of their social and welfare needs were constantly set against the usefulness of their labour. The subsequent debate which accompanied the restriction of (unskilled) Commonwealth immigrants by the Immigration Act 1962 was about the 'drain' on welfare services by black workers and their dependants even though little empirical evidence existed for the abuse or overuse of provision. In the Immigration Act 1971 the 'sole responsibility' rule restricted the opportunity for lone parents to bring children to live with them unless they could prove they had solely maintained or visited them.

Because of limited incomes and limited access to public-sector housing, black workers and their families often sought accommodation in the declining working-class areas which were marked not only by poor housing but by lower standards of health care and educational services. In relation to schools their children entered a process which was already operating to control and select children for a hierarchically structured labour market along class and gender lines. These processes took on a racialized and racist dimension. Working-class failure at school had been explained in terms of the inadequacy of working-class culture: this became reformulated to explain black children's under-achievement in terms of the inadequacies of Asian, African or Caribbean culture or family life. One example of this process is illustrated by the situation of many Afro-Caribbean women in the 1950s and '60s. Many of these women were self-supporting and were recruited to work in full-time, often low-paid, jobs with unsocial hours (often in the developing welfare services). In some cases this meant leaving children behind in the Caribbean until there were sufficient resources and accommodation to bring them over, or it meant bringing children into a situation where there was no formal provision for working mothers and in which the separation of mothers from their children and the whole idea of full-time working mothers was antithetical to familial ideology. So, whilst such women were working under the conditions imposed upon them as migrant workers, they were seen at the same time to be failing in terms of the post-war ideals of motherhood. In this way, perceptions of the inadequacies of black family life entered the discourses of welfare professionals although often in quite contrary or ethnically specific ways: Afro-Caribbean women being stereotyped as domineering and over-assertive, Asian mothers as subjugated and withdrawn. Some evidence of the pathologizing of black families can be found in the evidence to emerge in the 1980s of the disproportionate numbers of black children taken into care (ABSWAP, 1983).

A further example of the pathologizing of black families can be seen in the treatment of black children in the education system. From the beginning of the 1960s the presence of black children in schools became defined as a 'problem', even though the 'problem' was often that they were victims of the direct and indirect racism of teachers and pupils. In 1965 a DES circular suggested schools should have no more than 30 per cent immigrant children and recommended the 'bussing' of surplus black children to other schools. In the 1960s a disproportionate number of Afro-Caribbean school-children were labelled as 'Educationally Sub-Normal' (ESN) and sent to special schools, or were labelled as 'disruptive' and sent to special units (Carby, 1982a). Such processes did not go unchallenged. By the early 1970s campaigns and research by black professionals and parents had begun to expose this situation, for example, Bernard Coard's book *How the West Indian Child is Made Educationally Sub-normal in the British School System* (1971). In their book *Black Women's Lives in Britain* Beverley Bryan, Stella Dadzie and Suzanne Scafe describe this process:

> As mothers and as workers, we came into daily contact with the institutions which compounded our experience of racism. We were the ones who had to take time off to confront teachers and the education authorities about the miseducation of our children. We were the ones who battled it out with the housing authorities, the Social Services, and the DHSS, as we demanded our right to decent homes and an income above subsistence level.
>
> (Bryan *et al.*, 1985, p. 163)

The fact that black and white women in particular found work in the growing welfare state was quite significant in two ways. First, as low-paid workers women and black people played an important role in reducing public expenditure costs. Indeed, to some extent the welfare state, especially the NHS, has continued to depend on the availability of low-cost labour. A study of a London hospital by Doyal, Hunt and Mellor (1981) found that 84 per cent of domestics and 82 per cent of catering workers were from abroad, and that, in spite of the tightening up of immigration controls, the NHS had still found ways of recruiting migrant labour. Second, women and black workers in the public sector also became an important site of resistance in terms of defending public-sector cutbacks through their unions from the mid 1970s, and by increasingly challenging the racism and sexism of welfare provision through the development of anti-racist and anti-sexist strategies especially in education and social work in the 1980s.

3.2 CONTRADICTIONS IN WELFARE

Earlier I suggested that one of the important points to emerge from studies and campaigns around women and welfare was that women stand in a contradictory relationship to welfare provision. On the one hand it can play a significant and liberating role in their lives, but on the other hand it may also serve to restrict women, to define them in certain ways and even reproduce existing divisions of class, gender, 'race', disability, age or sexuality. For example, the creation of Beveridge's 'safety-net' of National Assistance (later Supplementary Benefit and now Income Support) has provided an important and necessary alternative to financial dependency on a man for some women with children. At the same time this kind of financial dependency on the state, whilst giving women freedom from an oppressive or unreliable relationship, also throws them onto the poverty-line and reproduces existing economic inequalities between men and women (see **Cochrane (1993)** on the relationship between female lone parents and poverty). This contradictory relationship can also be seen in some aspects of health care.

The creation of a National Health Service in 1948 was marked by an improvement in both health and the availability of health care. In 1951, for example, infant mortality was half the rate it had been in 1931 and by 1971 had fallen further. Yet at the same time the *class differences* in the infant mortality rate actually widened. For example, in 1979 three times as many babies aged between 28 days and one year in Social Class V died as in Social Class I. A similar ratio of disadvantage was found in babies born to mothers whose country of origin was Pakistan (Graham, 1984, pp. 50–1). Studies into the distribution of health care also found that middle-class people benefited from health provision more than those in the working class (Le Grand, 1982). These sorts of differences can also be found in women's experiences of health care. On the one hand, the universal provision of health care is particularly important for women. Women use and need health care services more often than men; this is not only because they bear children but also because they are usually responsible for the health care of their families; in addition, as women live longer than men they are likely in their old age to experience more chronic illness. Yet the way in which health services intervene in women's lives can be restrictive and serve to reproduce existing divisions and inequalities.

Take the example of fertility control. The development and availability of contraceptive and reproductive technologies have undoubtedly provided women with greater control over their lives, but at the same time these have been used by the medical profession as forms of control over women. The Abortion Act 1967 legalizing abortion was a landmark for women. The Act represented one of a number of liberalizing reforms of the late 1960s including the legalization of homosexuality between consenting adults over the age of 21, and the easing of the divorce law. Subsequently, over the 1970s and '80s, the abortion reform was threatened by attempts to restrict its scope (as indeed were both divorce law and the freedom of gay men and lesbians) – especially on its availability to women of over 20 weeks' pregnancy. These threats became one of the focal organizing issues of the Women's Movement under the slogan 'A woman's right to choose'. However, under the Abortion Act access to abortion within the NHS is still controlled and determined by the medical profession. Through the women's campaigns to defend women's right to abortion it became clear that women experienced the issues of fertility control in different ways. By the early 1980s the development of black feminism highlighted the fact that for black women and women in the Third World (and poor, white, working-class women) the issue was one of a woman's right to *fertility*, not simply to abortion. Abortion, sterilization and long-lasting contraceptive injections were not experienced as rights by these women but often as impositions or controls by state professionals operating with a pathologizing and eugenicist view of black and poor women's fertility (Bryan, Dadzie and Scafe, 1985, p. 103). Similarly research into the experiences of disabled women suggests that welfare professionals often take for granted the assumption that disabled women are unable to take on the responsibilities of motherhood (Morris, 1991; Begum, 1992). In the case of women with learning difficulties such assumptions have led to sterilization without their consent (Williams, 1992).

The social regulation of access to motherhood is also reflected in the development and use of reproductive technologies. Research by Lesley Doyal (1987) on the availability of infertility services shows that in many areas state provision is patchy and treatment rarely free (such as incurring fees for insemination). Most *in vitro* fertilization is carried out privately without guarantee of success. However, the availability of such procedures is determined not only by ability to pay but by assessments about a woman's suitability as a mother. As Doyal explains, this poses a contradiction for the ideology of motherhood: whilst *all* women are presumed to want to find motherhood desirable, only *some* women are considered suitable for fertility treatment. The practice of only accepting women in stable heterosexual partnerships as suitable for infertility treatment – and thereby discriminating against lesbians and single heterosexual women – was formalized by the recommendations of the Warnock Report which preceded the Human Embryology and Fertilization Act 1990.

This section has selectively discussed welfare policies from the 1940s to the late 1970s. By the early 1980s a shift had begun to take place. At the beginning of the post-war period the ideologies of the traditional family, of national unity and British culture, of full male employment and the work ethic were all used in the justification of the nationalization of welfare provision, increased state intervention and a limited form of white male egalitarianism. Thirty years later, by the 1980s, traditional ideologies of family, nation and work were being called on by the new right as the justification for the re-privatization of welfare, less state intervention, the supremacy of the market and the continuation of marked inequalities. It is to these issues we now turn.

4 FAMILY, NATION AND WORK: THE NEW RIGHT AND BEYOND

The period from the beginnings of economic recession in the mid '70s and through the 1980s is marked by a restructuring of welfare (described in Chapter 3) but also – by the beginning of the '90s – by other changes and more contradictory developments. So, for example, the 1980s began with a clear commitment by Margaret Thatcher's new right government to principles of individualism, private property and the private market, the family, competition and inequality: 'There is', said Mrs Thatcher, 'no such thing as society: there are only individuals and families.' Yet, this was also a period of the continuing development of equal opportunities, of anti-discriminatory movements and of the collective organization of self-defined welfare constituents – the women's health movement, disability groups, carers' organizations, survivors' groups – organizations often influenced by the concepts of oppression and by strategies of empowerment derived from the so-called 'new social movements'. At the same time, the very conditions of family life, of the organization of work and of the concept of nationhood themselves underwent considerable change so that, by the 1990s, there was some tempering of earlier ideological commitments. Whilst, as Chapter 3 showed, the new right's critique of the welfare state was based on the three Ds – deindustrialization, disincentives and demoralization – we could suggest that its own social policy project was limited by the three Cs – *contradiction, challenge* and *change*.

I want to examine these developments in three parts: first, by looking at the contribution of new right social policies to maintaining inequalities and social relations of power; second, by exploring the new right's attempt during the 1980s to rework the themes of family, nation and work through social policies; and, third, by way of conclusion, to look at some of the limitations of the new right project in terms of changes, challenges and contradictions which became more apparent in the '90s.

4.1 THE INTENSIFICATION OF INEQUALITIES

Cuts in social expenditure relative to needs, cutbacks in local authority spending, unemployment, low pay and the failure of income maintenance benefits to mitigate poverty have together produced much sharper divisions between the quality of life experienced by poor people and the rest of society. Just taking income alone, Table 4.1 shows that the top one-tenth of earners in Britain fared much better than the lowest one-tenth of earners between 1971 and 1981, but that this was more marked between 1981 and 1989. It also shows how little, in spite of the Equal Pay Act in 1970 and the strengthening of the Sex Discrimination Act in 1986, manual women workers' pay improved both compared to men's and compared to higher-paid women in manual or non-manual work. In other words, growing income disparities are structured by gender and class both separately and together. There are further racial dimensions to these inequalities. Table 4.2, from Bruegel's (1989) analysis of gender and 'race' variations in the 1986 London Living Standards Survey, based on informants' recall of their earnings since 1981, indicates that the earnings of black men, and particularly of black women, failed to rise in keeping with their white counterparts, and that overall women's increases were less than those of men.

Table 4.1   Gross weekly earnings of full-time employees[1]: by sex and type of employment, Great Britain (£ and percentages)

	Males					Females				
	1971	1981	1986	1988	1989	1971	1981	1986	1988	1989
Manual employees										
Mean (£)	29.0	120.2	174.4	200.6	217.8	15.3	74.7	107.5	123.6	134.9
Median (£)	27.7	112.8	163.4	188.0	203.9	14.6	71.6	101.1	115.6	125.9
As percentage of median:										
Highest decile	147	151	155	157	158	143	143	150	154	156
Lowest decile	68	69	65	64	63	71	70	69	69	69
Non-manual employees										
Mean (£)	38.5	160.5	244.9	294.1	323.6	20.0	97.5	145.7	175.5	195.0
Median (£)	34.0	147.0	219.4	259.7	285.7	18.2	87.7	131.5	157.1	173.5
As percentage of median:										
Highest decile	175	167	175	180	181	169	172	167	172	174
Lowest decile	60	60	57	55	54	65	68	65	63	62
All employees										
Mean (£)	32.4	138.2	207.5	245.8	269.5	18.4	92.0	137.2	164.2	182.3
Median (£)	29.4	124.6	185.1	215.5	235.5	16.7	82.8	123.4	145.3	160.1
As percentage of median:										
Highest decile	162	168	173	178	180	165	172	170	178	181
Lowest decile	65	64	60	59	59	66	68	65	63	63

Note: [1] Figures relate to April each year and to full-time employees on adult rates whose pay for the survey pay period was not affected by absence.

Median: earnings of a group of employees. The amount at which 50% of the employees have earnings above or below this level.

Highest decile earnings: the amount at which 90% of the employees have earnings below and 10% have earnings above this level. The deciles of a distribution divide it into tenths. Thus 80% of the group have earnings between the highest and lowest deciles.

Lowest decile earnings: he amount at which 10% of the employees have earnings below and 90% have earnings above this level.

Source: table taken from Johnson, 1991; data from New Earnings Survey, Department of Employment

Table 4.2   Increase in earnings, 1981–6

	All individuals		*49%*
All men	53%	All women	45%
White men	57%	White women	53%
Black men	22%	Black women	5%

Source: Bruegel, 1989, Table 10; data from London Living Standards Survey, GLC, 1981–6

Part of this failure to maintain income levels is the detrimental effect of being unemployed: that is, employment following a period of unemployment is likely to be worse paid. Because of the rates of benefit paid, unemployment is also an important indicator of the incidence of poverty, and this is another area where class, gender and 'race' differences are more marked. Between 1979 and 1986 male unemployment rose by 143 per cent and female unemployment by 189 per cent (EOC, 1986). In fact, this hides the figures of married or cohabiting unemployed women who cannot claim benefit. In 1987 general unemployment began to decline, but then rose again from 1990 to reach 9.4 per cent in February 1992 (Department of Employment, 1992). The unemployment rate for ethnic minority women between 1986 and 1988 was 16 per cent compared with 9 per cent for white women. During these years the unemployment rate for men of Caribbean origin was 22 per cent compared with 10 per cent for white workers; for Pakistani/Bangladeshi workers it was 27 per cent; unemployment was highest for young Afro-Caribbean men aged 16–24 at 31 per cent (Department of Employment, 1990).

The gender, 'race' and class inequalities in low earnings, whilst in part due to a historical legacy, are intensified by the restructuring of the workforce which is taking place at an international level. One consequence of this is that the workforce is no longer dominated by a unionized and skilled (and white and male) workforce, but has been broken down into a smaller (usually white and mostly male) core workforce with a peripheral workforce of low-paid, part-time workers, often black and white women and black men. Furthermore, the pay levels in the public sector – a major employer of women and minority ethnic groups – have fallen behind levels in other industries, and contracting out of services has often involved a worsening of pay and conditions (Beechey and Perkins, 1987; also see Chapter 3 in this book). Added to this is the fact that various policies and strategies whose aim was to protect the low paid have been weakened or removed: the Wages Act 1986 removed the wages council minimum wage protection from workers under 21 and weakened adult protection. Eligibility for employment rights and access to social security benefits have been curtailed: for example, someone working under 16 hours and with less than 5 years continuous services has no rights in relation to sickness pay, unfair dismissal, redundancy pay or reinstatement after maternity leave. These conditions apply particularly to women workers, black workers and young workers (Land and Ward, 1986; Arnott, 1987).

Poverty due to declining levels of Income Support also has gender, 'race', disability and age dimensions, not only because of the characteristics of unemployment but because many of those on Income Support are female lone parents. In 1986 about 40 per cent of the income of lone parents (91 per cent of whom are women) came from state benefits (Johnson, 1990, p. 212). Women are also the majority of older people who depend on state pensions. The declining value of Income Support, Child Benefit, widows' benefits, losses of entitlement in Housing Benefit, free school meals, maternity grant, disablement allowance, young people's allowance and the replacement of special needs payments by the discretionary loan system of the Social Fund, all contribute to making those who are already poor through their marginalization from paid work – older people, women, disabled people, unemployed people – poorer. Furthermore the rate-capping of local authorities means that many of the services provided by local authorities and used by these groups – transport, day centres, public housing, leisure facilities – have dwindled or have increased their costs; in many areas local authorities, for example, have withdrawn the token £3 to £5 per week 'wage' given to people with learning difficulties who work in Adult Training Centres.

In so far as racial inequalities have long existed in work opportunities and access to welfare provision and benefits, they have tended to be strengthened by these developments. For example, youth training schemes reinforce rather than mitigate racial inequalities, directing black young people into less skilled work – or no work at all (de Sousa, 1987). Also, access to benefits has been more tightly linked to immigration controls. In social security offices and further education colleges, administrators have been required to act on behalf of the immigration authorities by checking the immigration status of applicants or by refusing access until eligibility is proven (Gordon, 1985). The overall effect is to deter black and non-English-speaking applicants.

4.2 THE REWORKING OF FAMILY, NATION AND WORK

The new right's social policies have also represented an ideological reworking of the place of the traditional family, of British culture and their indispensability to the supremacy of the private market. One element in this has been the attempt to elevate the family to a high position of responsibility for the welfare of its members, for exercising freedom in the selection of private and/or state welfare provision – schools, health care, housing and so on – and for responsibility for morality, discipline and the transmission of British cultural values. The move towards families exercising responsibility for their members can be seen in the extension of children's financial dependence on their parents through the removal of rights to social security from most sixteen- and seventeen-year-olds. It is also reflected in the emphasis on parental responsibility for the discipline of their children in the 1990 White Paper on crime (Langan, 1991). This notion of parental responsibility has also in some places shifted an attempt to restore specifically *paternal* responsibility. The Child Support Act 1991 on child maintenance proposes to minimize state support for female lone parents through pursuing errant fathers to accept financial responsibility for their children.

These moves are not only favoured by the new right, they also overlap with demands by some parts of the feminist movement to encourage greater involvement of men in childcare responsibilities. However, what marks a difference is that within new right discourse the shifts are associated with the identification of female lone parents as central to the growth of a 'dependency culture' described in Chapter 3 (see also **Cochrane, 1993**). This has gained particular currency from the writings of the American, Charles Murray (1990). Murray suggests that welfare benefits have created in the USA and Britain an 'underclass' character-ized by high rates of female-headed families, illegitimacy, poverty, crime and unemployment. One solution he proposes is to shift dependency of mothers away from the state onto breadwinner fathers. Like the new right he sees the ethics of male wage-earning and family responsibility as inextricably linked: 'Young men who don't work don't make good marriage material. Often they don't get married at all; when they do, they don't have the ability to fill their traditional role. In either case, too many of them remain barbarians' (1990, p. 23).

Community care policies, too, have stressed the mobilization of 'families, friends and neighbours' in providing support for older people (Griffiths, 1988). It is interesting that in these policies, as Janet Finch has pointed out, the government is working not so much with a model of an indepen-dent nuclear family as with the assumed existence of a spatially sepa-rated but nevertheless interdependent extended family where members may call on female relatives for care (Finch, 1989, p. 125). The attempt to limit the influence of non-traditional ways of living can also be seen in Section 28 of the Local Government Act 1988, which prohibits local auth-orities from promoting homosexuality as a 'pretended family relation-ship', as well as in the restrictions placed on *in vitro* fertilization mentioned earlier (Evans, 1989).

The ideological strategy of the new right in the 1980s was the attempt to make the traditional family a vital link between moral principles and cultural life on the one side, and market principles and economic life on the other. But the cultural values which the family is asked to defend are derived from its days of high imperialism and, as such, are essentially British, white and Christian. The assertion of British (or, more specifi-cally, English) culture by the new right was developed as a way of affirm-ing the national interest, and the national interest was seen by the new right to be the reassertion of the freedom of the market and the associated revival of Britain as a major competitor in the world economy. However, this assertion of British/English culture requires the minimizing, in the name of national interest, of the influence of other cultures. One conse-quence of this has been the development of a new form of cultural essen-tialism which emphasizes the inevitability of cultural differences together with the unimpeachability of 'British identity'. Although, as I describe later, this ideological project was neither as consensual nor coherent as it appeared, nevertheless it has become a key theme in some new right politicians' resistance to EC harmonization. The process was also clearly visible in the educational debate and education policy of the 1990s. In a collection of essays entitled *Anti-Racism: an assault on edu-cation and value* (Palmer, 1986), new right educationalists argued that anti-racist initiatives in schooling contributed to a lowering of standards and constitute an assault on the traditional British values in education.

Moves to reduce the influence of anti-discriminatory practice in favour of the restoration of 'British' cultural values can be seen in the Education Act 1988. This also demonstrates the way in which notions of the family are seen as holding together the values of both work and nationhood through state welfare provision. The Act introduced a core curriculum and testing and selection processes explicitly to meet the needs of industry and employers. It also emphasized the need for the teaching of traditional morality and British cultural values as against anti-racist and anti-sexist teaching. Finally, it represented the role of the family as consumers, shopping wisely in the market-place for education to fit the needs of its children. In keeping with the notion of the dependency of children, the consumers are seen here as the parents rather than the pupils. The Act also includes for parents the right to choose education appropriate to their own 'culture'. In 1990 a ruling from the Secretary of State for Education said that parental choice included the right of white parents to withdraw their children from schools with a large proportion of Asian children, and that this choice overrode the race relations law. In support of this ruling, Fred Naylor of the Parental Alliance for Choice in Education stated: 'The Secretary of State has now cleared up the matter. It has nothing to do with race but with culture' (*Observer*, 22 April 1990).

Whilst this reworking of family, nation and work can be seen as a particularly assertive ideological form of economic liberalism, it has also to be seen as a defensive strategy to weaken the perceived threats and challenges to inequalities in these three areas. For what also marks the 1980s has been a growing awareness and resistance to 'race' and gender inequalities and its expression, particularly with regard to 'race', in increasingly diverse political forms – whether through forms of rebellion (riots against racism in Brixton in 1981), through institutionalized equal opportunities and anti-racist and anti-sexist strategies, through voluntary self-help (such as black women's refuges) or through religious fundamentalism, or through opposition to fundamentalism (Southall Black Sisters, 1990).

4.3 CONCLUSION: CONTRADICTION, CHALLENGE AND CHANGE IN THE 1990S

Within the field of welfare the development of local authority equal opportunities programmes in the areas of gender, 'race', disability and sexual orientation has been significant. This is not only in terms of access to employment, training of employees and the delivery of services but also in acknowledging diversity of family and cultural experience, in revealing previously hidden areas of, for example, racism, sexism, heterosexism, ableism, and in legitimizing these as areas for concern and action. However, such initiatives have sometimes been only tokenistic or, more importantly, have developed within the context of the shifting balance of power between central and local government, the dwindling and impoverishing of particular areas of provision – for instance in public housing and inner-city schools – and an ideological counter-attack by the new right in which 'special needs' have been reinterpreted as 'special privileges' or special pleading by particular interests.

All this has weakened and in some cases distorted the outcomes of such initiatives. So, for example, in an analysis of municipal socialism in the 1980s Kathryn Harriss (1989) suggests that the growth of identity-based movements and demands (from women's groups, black groups, lesbian groups, disabled groups) provided the local state with a way of managing conflict within the community and its own conflicts with central government. They did this, first, by incorporating grassroots movements into local state structures and controlling their power through competitive and time-limited rationing of funding; and, secondly, because of its own lack of resources, by being able to meet the *specific* needs of these groups (such as for anti-discriminatory policies), while not able to meet the more general needs for improved housing, social services and education provisions.

Nevertheless, the development of movements of identity has also, as explained earlier, given rise to a better appreciation of the complex and interrelated formations of social power in society. Furthermore, this development has also been accompanied by a more thorough-going set of critiques and demands about the social relations of welfare – the hierarchical relations between the providers and users of welfare services. In particular, many groups representing people with disabilities, learning difficulties and psychological distress analyse their situation as a particular form of compounded oppression: they are marginalized and *oppressed by the institutions of society*, but this is compounded by the creation of *dependency by welfare professionals*. Their demands therefore include not only rights in relation to employment, education, marriage, sexuality, motherhood and so on, but also rights within welfare provision – access to information, accountability and representation. For example the charter of Survivors Speak Out, an organization of people who use psychiatric services, demands amongst other things:

- choice of services, including self-help alternatives
- facility for representation of users and ex-users of services on statutory bodies, including Community Health Councils, Mental Health Tribunals and the Mental Health Act Commission
- provision of resources to implement self-advocacy for all users
- full and free access to all personal records
- legal protection and means of redress for all psychiatric patients
- provision for all patients of full written and verbal information on treatments, including adverse research findings
- an end to discrimination against people who receive, or have received, psychiatric services: with particular regard to housing, employment, insurance etc.

(Survivors Speak Out, 1987)

Similar sorts of demands around the right to self-help alternatives and access to professional knowledge also emerged from the women's health movement (especially the setting up of Well Woman clinics) and the women's refuge movement for women escaping domestic violence (see also **Foreman and Dallos, 1993**). In some ways this focus on a user-led movement overlaps with new right discourses within health, education and personal social services which emphasize consumer sovereignty and consumer choice. So, too, do some of the arguments overlap, such as the critique of welfare professionals, described in Chapter 3. However, there are key differences: the user-led movement also operates within overlapping discourses of democracy and oppression; the language is of rights, representation and citizenship, and of discrimination. Furthermore, their demands usually include the provision of universally available specialist services – '[the] provision of free counselling for all; provision of refuge, planned and under the control of survivors of psychiatry, adequate funding for non-medical community services, especially crisis intervention' (Survivors Speak Out, 1987). On the other hand, consumer sovereignty and consumer choice are part of an individualistic market (or quasi-market) model advocated by the new right where the consumer's power lies in the exercise of choice from a range of services presented by welfare agencies, but where accountability is not tied to user representation, but to greater financial controls.

Optimistically, it is possible to see the introduction of concepts like consumer sovereignty, accountability and quality control as the openings in which user movements can begin to push for their demands. Pessimistically, it could be seen as a displacement of more fundamental concerns over resources, funding and structured inequalities. However, in some areas the development of user-focused groups has led to collective organization over more general funding resources. It might be that one of the key contradictions identified in the early 1980s has now been turned on its head. That is to say, in the early 1980s the left and feminist critiques of welfare as statist, authoritarian and bureaucratic were seen by some to partly create the conditions for the new right's restructuring of the welfare state (Hall and Jacques, 1983). Yet by the 1990s the new right's advocacy of consumer sovereignty, professional accountability, the identification of needs and the development of quality control can be seen to have given an impetus for the new constituencies of welfare to demand, though not necessarily to achieve, more far-reaching and radical programmes of welfare provision.

Finally, whilst the new right has sought to reinstate values of the traditional family, of traditional British culture and the work ethic, the conditions of these three areas have themselves changed, placing further limitations on the success of the new right project. Some of the changes in relation to the organization of *work* have already been outlined. In the UK there has been an increase in people working in low-paid, part-time, casual and sub-contracted work. The inequalities between this group – often women, lone parents and black and minority ethnic workers – and those in full-time, constant, skilled or professional work have widened.

This has been exacerbated by the decreasing availability of benefits or provisions (housing, transport etc.) to this group. They have been increasingly excluded from contributory benefits, while at the same time contributory benefits have themselves declined in value. The tightening of benefits, changes in social security, labour law and workforce programmes have all played a role in directing and controlling labour into the acceptance of low-paid, flexible work (Lister, 1989; Deakin and Wilkinson, 1992).

It has become increasingly evident that changes in the organization of work, in demographic change and in the role of women have exposed the inadequacies of the post-war social security and insurance system. But it is also clear that the recent reforms in social security, whilst supporting the changes in the nature of work, simply intensify inequalities in inefficient ways (see Deakin and Wilkinson, 1992). This twin failure may create a space where there is more debate about an alternative system based on a universal principle of a basic wage but incorporating a recognition of diverse needs – for example, the role of women (and men) in caring for children or older people (see, for example, Lister, 1989).

In relation to the *family*, one contradictory element has been between the reality of diversification of family forms and policies which reinforce a specific patriarchal family form which was noted in Chapter 3. This diversification is marked by a shift away from the male-breadwinner nuclear family held to be the administrative norm in the post-war social security reforms, to the increase in divorce, remarriage, lone (predominantly female) parents, older women living on their own, and wives and mothers in paid, often full-time work (Wicks, 1987; see also **Dallos and Sapsford, 1993**). It is important to say that the changes have not been uniform for all social groups – Afro-Caribbean women have commonly worked in full-time jobs throughout the post-war period, for example, and lone parents, step-parents and lone older women are not entirely new phenomena. Also they have not been accompanied by wholesale changes in attitudes, especially towards the division of labour in the home. Alongside these shifts towards diversification there has also been some acknowledgement within social work of the greater cultural diversification of family forms and its attendant ethnocentric, pathologizing and racist responses from service-providers (Dominelli, 1988). And there has also been an articulation through the gay and lesbian movements of alternatives to the heterosexism of the nuclear family in spite of government attempts to control these.

By the early 1990s the Conservative government's attitude began to display greater ambivalence towards these changes. Some government ministers welcomed women's entry into paid work as necessary for the liberalization of the free market: for example, Norman Fowler, when Secretary of State for Employment, welcomed the 1990s as the 'decade of the working woman'. Others, like Patrick Jenkin and Douglas Hurd, have seen this development as undermining the traditional family and have urged women to put their duties as mothers first. Yet others, like Edwina

Currie when Minister for Health, have acknowledged the problems these trends raise but have seen the solution in terms of individual responsibility to choose childcare in the private market, seeing public provision as limited to those children in need or at risk (see Langan, 1991). Again, new right social policies have differed in their approach to family relationships. The consequence of some policies has been, as described earlier, to reinforce female and child dependencies, yet the Children Act 1989 promoted the idea that children have the right to be consulted about their own choices in the case of divorce.

A similar ambivalence exists in relation to the increase in divorce. While the Law Commission recommended dropping the fault grounds in divorce to make divorce a less bitter and expensive process, many in the government felt uncomfortable about a proposal which was seen to make divorce easier and further undermine the traditional family. Yet again, in relation to inequalities, there has been a modification of the earlier attempts to justify inequalities as 'natural'. John Major's commitment at his election as Prime Minister in 1992 to a notion of a 'classless society' was more reminiscent of Harold Macmillan's famous description of the 1950s, 'we're all middle class now', although now, as then, this notion dramatically disregards the existence of economic inequalities.

The issue of *nation* reveals a tension similar to that of family in the opening up of borders on the one hand and the attempt to impose national and cultural border controls on the other. The breaking-up and shifting of national boundaries in Eastern Europe and the Soviet Union and unification and moves to harmonization within Europe can be contrasted with assertions within Britain about the uniqueness of British/English cultural traditions and the need to preserve them. Such assertions are made (for example, in debates over the National Curriculum, the Salman Rushdie affair or the Gulf War) both in the context of Europeanization as well as in the context of the reality of Britain as a multi-racial society. They are reflected in the tightening up over recent years of the implementation of the nationality and immigration laws. These moves have a knock-on effect on black users of welfare services because it is often through welfare agencies such as colleges, DSS offices and housing departments that such controls operate, often serving to throw suspicion indiscriminately on black users, as, for example, in the threat to deport Asian women who have migrated to the UK as dependants of their husbands but who subsequently seek help from refuges for battered women and require Income Support (*Observer*, 2 June 1991).

A second element in this tension around nation lies in the greater awareness that problems such as poverty and ill-health have international dimensions. The international flows of capital and labour, the growth of the multinationals and the internationalization of the market all limit the extent to which national welfare policies can solve their own social problems, just as Europeanization limits the legitimation of such policies. In other words, internationally based political strategies and social policies are likely to become an increasingly significant development.

At the same time any shift towards harmonization of social policies within the EC would have very uneven outcomes. For example, the development of the Social Chapter may, in the UK at least, improve prospects for some with its recognition of the rights of 'vulnerable groups' and its demands for equal treatment for men and women and gay men and lesbians. Yet it makes little reference to racism and the needs of immigrant workers. Its protective employment provisions only apply to EC nationals and any moves towards harmonization may lead to a strengthening of those policies and procedures by which Europe's racialized and migrant communities are denied rights. These include a tightening of immigration controls and restrictions on asylum-seekers, circumscribed or restricted access to social security, housing, health and education provision, denial of the right to family reunion, or to nationality (Arnott, 1990).

These examples of changes of work, family and nation serve to illustrate the ways in which discourses around these areas are subject to contradictory pressures as the social and material conditions of family life, nation and work life themselves change. While these changing conditions provide opportunities to challenge forms of inequality and power within society, they have also given rise to processes which strengthen and reinforce these forms of inequality. These changes represent, too, part of the restraining influences upon the new right's attempt to articulate a coherent and traditional model of the relationship between family, nation and work. In addition, this model has faced challenges, not only in terms of the realities of people's lives, but in terms of alternative discourses rooted in theories of oppression and liberatory and anti-discriminatory strategies. In relation to welfare policies, concepts of the individual, choice and freedom have created a space for the elaboration of concepts of democratic, civil and welfare rights by those who use welfare services. However, these developments have revealed key tensions in the formulation of welfare policy.

At the beginning of this chapter I discussed the significance of political developments, reflected also in welfare campaigns and struggles, in pointing to the complexities of social power and inequalities. People's lives and their needs and demands for welfare provision are constituted, articulated and structured by a diversity of identities and inequalities. It is these diverse identities and needs which the New Social Movements and the user movements in welfare have begun to articulate. In so doing they have exposed the 'false universalism' of the Beveridge welfare state. Yet one of the tensions that still remains unresolved is how to develop universal welfare policies which are neither monolithic nor uniform but which are able to meet the *diversity* and *difference* of people's welfare needs in forms which do not reproduce difference in unequal ways. This tension – between universalism and difference – is not just peculiar to welfare, it is one of the central issues in the development of social, political and cultural life, nationally and internationally, as we head towards the end of the twentieth century.

REFERENCES

ABSWAP (Association of Black Social Workers and Allied Professionals) (1983) *Black Children in Care*, Evidence to House of Commons Social Services Committee, London, ABSWAP.

Arnott, H. (1990) 'Fortress Europe', *Poverty*, no. 75.

Arnott, M. (1987) 'Second-class citizens' in Walker, A. and Walker, C. (eds) *A Growing Divide: a social audit 1979–87*, London, CPAG.

Baldock, J. (1993) 'Old age' in Dallos, R. and McLaughlin, E. (eds) op. cit.

Beechey, V. and Perkins, T. (1987) *A Matter of Hours: women, part-time work and the labour market*, Cambridge, Polity Press.

Begum, N. (1992) 'Disabled women and the feminist agenda', *Feminist Review*, no. 40, Spring.

Beveridge, W. (1942) *Social Insurance and Allied Services*, (The Beveridge Report) Cmnd 6404, London, HMSO.

Brah, A. (1987) 'Women of South Asian origin in Britain: issues and concerns', *South Asia Research*, vol. 7, no. 1, May.

Bruegel, I. (1989) 'Sex and race in the labour market', *Feminist Review*, no. 32.

Bryan, B., Dadzie, S. and Scafe, S. (1985) *The Heart of the Race: black women's lives in Britain*, London, Virago.

Carby, H. (1982a) 'Schooling in Babylon' in Centre for Contemporary Cultural Studies (1982) op. cit.

Carby, H. (1982b) 'White women listen: black feminism and the boundaries of sisterhood' in Centre for Contemporary Cultural Studies (1982) op. cit.

Centre for Contemporary Cultural Studies (1982) *The Empire Strikes Back*, London, Hutchinson.

Coard, B. (1971) *How the West Indian Child is made Educationally Subnormal in the British School System*, London, New Beacon Books.

Cochrane, A. (1993) 'The problem of poverty', Ch. 6 in Dallos, R. and McLaughlin, E. (eds) op. cit.

Cockburn, C. (1991) *In the Way of Women: men's resistance to sex equality in organizations*, London and Basingstoke, Macmillan.

Cohen, S. (1985) 'Anti-semitism, immigration controls and the welfare state', *Critical Social Policy*, Issue 13.

Dalley, G. (1988) *Ideologies of Caring*, London and Basingstoke, Macmillan.

Dallos, R. and McLaughlin, E. (eds) (1993) *Social Problems and the Family*, London, Sage/The Open University.

Dallos, R. and Sapsford, R. (1993) 'Patterns of diversity and lived realities' in Cochrane, A. and Muncie, J. (eds) *Politics, Policy and the Law*, Milton Keynes, The Open University.

Davin, A. (1978) 'Imperialism and motherhood' in *History Workshop Journal*, no. 5.

Deakin, S. and Wilkinson, F. (1992) 'Social policy and economic efficiency: the deregulation of the labour market in Britain', *Critical Social Policy*, Issue 33.

Department of Employment (1990) 'Ethnic origins and the labour market', *Employment Gazette*, March.

Department of Employment (1992) *Employment Gazette*, April.

de Sousa, E. (1987) 'Racism and the YTS', *Critical Social Policy*, Issue 20.

Dominelli, L. (1988) *Anti-Racist Social Work*, London and Basingstoke, Macmillan.

Doyal, L., Hunt, G. and Mellor, J. (1981) 'Your life in their hands: migrant workers in the National Health Service', *Critical Social Policy*, Issue 10.

Doyal, L. (1987) 'Infertility – a life sentence? Women and the National Health Service' in Stanworth, M. (ed.) *Reproductive Technologies: gender, motherhood and medicine*, Cambridge, Polity Press.

Equal Opportunities Commission (1986) *Annual Report*, Manchester, EOC.

Evans, D. (1989) 'Section 28: "Law, myth and paradox"', *Critical Social Policy*, Issue 27.

Finch, J. (1984) 'Community Care: developing non-sexist alternatives', *Critical Social Policy*, Issue 9.

Finch, J. (1989) *Family Obligations and Social Change*, Cambridge, Polity Press.

Foreman, S. and Dallos, R. (1993) 'Domestic violence' in Dallos, R. and McLaughlin, E. (eds) op. cit.

Glendenning, C. and Millar, J. (eds) (1987) *Women and Poverty in Britain*, Brighton, Wheatsheaf.

Gordon, P. (1985) *Policing Immigration: Britain's internal control*, London, Pluto Press.

Gough, I. (1979) *The Political Economy of the Welfare State*, London and Basingstoke, Macmillan.

Graham, H. (1984) *Women, Health and the Family*, Brighton, Wheatsheaf.

Griffiths, R. (1988) *Community Care: agenda for action, A Report to the Secretary of State for Social Services*, London, HMSO.

Hall, S. and Jacques, M. (1983) *The Politics of Thatcherism*, London, Lawrence and Wishart.

Harriss, K. (1989) 'New alliances: socialist-feminism in the eighties', *Feminist Review*, no. 31, pp. 34–54.

Jacobs, S. (1985) 'Race, empire and the welfare state: council housing and racism', *Critical Social Policy*, Issue 13.

Johnson, N. (1990) *Reconstructing the Welfare State: a decade of change, 1980–1990*, New York and London, Harvester Wheatsheaf.

Johnson, N. (1991) 'The politics of Thatcherism: social policy in retreat?', paper delivered to the 25th Annual Conference of the Social Policy Association, University of Nottingham, 9–11 July.

Jones, G. (1985) *Social Hygiene in Twentieth Century Britain*, Beckenham, Croom Helm.

Land, H. (1978) 'Who cares for the family?', *Journal of Social Policy*, vol. 7, no. 3.

Land, H. and Ward, S. (1986) *Women Won't Benefit*, London, NCCL.

Langan, M. (1991) 'Who cares: women in the mixed economy of care' in Langan, M. and Day, L. (eds) op. cit.

Langan, M. and Day, L. (eds) (1992) *Women, Oppression and Social Work*, London, Routledge.

Le Grand, J. (1982) *The Strategy of Inequality*, London, Allen and Unwin.

Lister, R. (1990) 'Social security' in McCarthy, M. (ed.) op. cit.

Mama, A. (1989) 'Violence against black women: gender, race and state responses', *Feminist Review*, no. 32.

McCarthy, M. (ed.) (1989) *The New Politics of Welfare: an agenda for the 1990s?*, London and Basingstoke, Macmillan.

Morris, J. (1991) *Pride Against Prejudice*, London, Virago.

Morris, J. (1992) 'Us and them? Feminist research, community care and disability', *Critical Social Policy*, Issue 33.

Murray, C. (1990) *The Emerging British Underclass*, London, Institute for Economic Affairs.

Palmer, F. (1986) *Anti-Racism: an assault on education and value*, Nottingham, Sherwood Press.

Riley, D. (1983) *War in the Nursery: theories of the child and the mother*, London, Virago.

Southall Black Sisters (1990) *Against the Grain*, London, Southall Black Sisters.

Survivors Speak Out (1987) *Report of the National Conference of Users of Psychiatric Services*, September.

Wicks, M. (1987) 'Family matters and public policy' in Loney, M. *et al.* (eds) *The State and the Market*, London, Sage.

Williams, F. (1989) *Social Policy: a critical introduction*, Cambridge, Polity Press.

Williams, F. (1992) 'Women with learning difficulties are women too' in Langan, M. and Day, L. (eds) op. cit.

Wilson, E. (1977) *Women and the Welfare State*, London, Tavistock.

CHAPTER 5
HONG KONG: A RESIDUAL WELFARE REGIME

EUGENE MCLAUGHLIN

1 LIBERAL APPROACHES TO WELFARE

According to liberal social theorists there are three primary systems for delivering welfare, namely, the family, the voluntary sector and the free market. These *private* welfare systems maximize freedom of choice and efficiency in the production and consumption of welfare services for individuals, while at the same time enhancing individual and community welfare obligations. As a consequence, liberal political economists – such as Friedrich von Hayek and Milton Friedman – contend that the involvement of the state in the provision of welfare should be a residual and minimal one.

While conceding that the state has a responsibility to provide a safety-net for the really destitute, liberals argue that this responsibility should be limited to means-tested minimum benefits and entitlement rules should be strict. The state has at most a minimal role in providing income maintenance for old age, unemployment or sickness. It does not have a role in delivering benefits within a universalist framework or with the purpose of redressing wealth imbalances. Liberals are also opposed to social insurance generally, because they believe that it results in the imposition of higher rates of taxation and therefore interferes with the operation of the economy. Government-provided schemes are thus deemed unacceptable because they are monopolistic, restricting the individual's freedom and choice. Nor do they believe that the state should have anything other than a minimum role to play in the provision of housing, education and health care. Any departure from these principles would undermine, first, the three primary welfare systems, second, individual incentives to work and, finally, the workings of the free market economy (Harris and Seldon, 1979; Murray, 1984).

This type of theorizing 'lapsed into academic and political obscurity – particularly in the years between 1940 and 1970' (George and Wilding, 1985, p. 19). However, as has been documented elsewhere in this book, in the late 1970s and 1980s new right governments were elected in the UK and USA which attempted to implement policies premised upon this liberal doctrine. Such has been the impact of these governments that many of the liberal ideas about the desirability of a residual welfare state seem destined to remain on the political agenda in the 1990s.

Although the USA is conventionally utilized by social policy experts as the prime example of a residual welfare regime, we have decided to focus on Hong Kong for several reasons. First, if we want to find a society which has been committed to classic liberal principles in matters of social welfare for the last one hundred and fifty years it is to the last significant British colony that we must look. In Hong Kong the family, the voluntary sector and the market have been actively encouraged to take primary responsibility for the delivery of welfare. As a consequence, we are provided with an example of the highly complex set of relationships that governs private and public welfare provision within a residualist framework.

This leads on to the second reason why we are focusing on Hong Kong. It is intended to remind the reader of a 'forgotten' colonial dimension of British and indeed European social policy. British social policy is usually understood in terms of the formation and operation of the welfare state. It is well documented, for example, how the social welfare of the British people came to occupy a central place in British politics in the course of the twentieth century and how after the Second World War all political parties pledged themselves to the creation of a welfare state. However, what has not been documented is how, over the same time-period, successive Liberal, Labour and Conservative governments presided over an imperial welfare system that was firmly based on residualist principles. As far as successive British governments were concerned, the welfare needs of British citizens took precedence over the welfare needs of British subjects.

The final reason we have chosen Hong Kong is because we believe that it is important to analyse the welfare framework of the powerhouse economies of the advanced Asian Pacific rim. These hyper-industrialized nations seem to have the capacity to deliver full employment, relatively high standards of living and highly developed social infrastructures without the trappings of western welfarism. Hong Kong (along with Japan) has led the spectacular economic advance of the Asian Pacific rim and many believe that after reunification in 1997 it may revolutionize China's competitive position in the global economic system.

2   THE CONTEXT

In 1997 the city-state of Hong Kong will become a Special Administrative Region of the People's Republic of China, thus ending one hundred and fifty years of British colonial rule. Commentators are undecided whether this will signal the end of a unique economic and social entity or in fact herald the beginning of a new one known as 'one country [China], two systems [capitalism and socialism]'. After Hong Kong was ceded to Britain in 1841 it developed from an opium emporium into a general free trade entrepôt and since 1945 has established itself as *the* free market economy. Both Hayek and Friedman view Hong Kong as being the closest that any modern society has yet come to approximating the classical liberal ideal. The stated economic philosophy of the government is one of 'positive non-intervention', meaning that:

> ... economic affairs are conducted in an environment of virtually unfettered free enterprise. Government policy has long dictated a virtually hands-off approach towards the private sector, an approach that seems well-suited to Hong Kong's exposed and dependent economic and political situation. The philosophy that underlies government in Hong Kong can be summed up in a few short phrases: law and order, minimum interference in private affairs, and the creation of an environment conducive to profitable investment. Regulatory economic controls are held to a minimum, no restrictions are placed on the movement of capital, little protection and few subsidies are given to industry, and the few direct services provided by the government are operated on a commercial basis.
>
> (Rabushka, 1979, p. 44)

There are no import tariffs or controls on the movement of capital. There is no minimum wage legislation for workers, no equal opportunities legislation and the trade union movement is numerically weak and ideologically split. Market forces and government regulations are minimal, there is no direct state ownership of strategic industries and a stable structure of very low corporate and personal taxation (15 per cent maximum effective rate of income tax) is maintained. There is no central bank, no automatic mechanism to control the money supply and no attempt to carry out an active policy of macro-economic management. The only instrument of government fiscal policy is a budget, and revenue is raised from taxation, land sales and utility charges.

The nature of the political system is viewed as being of central importance to the success of this free market system. There have been few changes in Hong Kong's system of governance since it was seized in 1841. Until the late 1980s the colony's administration replicated the classic Crown Colony pattern, with power concentrated in the hands of a Governor, advised by nominated Executive (Exco) and Legislative (Legco) Councils, comprising government officials and appointed unofficial members who represented élite interests in the colony. However, the powers invested in Exco and Legco are limited so the colony is in effect run entirely by career civil servants. Because direct democracy has been strictly checked, the government does not have to worry about upsetting the electorate and losing elections and, until very recently, there have been no political parties competing ideologically.

Despite its adherence to the principles of 'laissez-faire', a more subtle reading of the evidence suggests that the state has played a decisive role in ensuring Hong Kong's developmental process (Appelbaum and Henderson, 1992; Castells *et al.*, 1990; Schiffer, 1991). As Sir David Trench (Governor, 1964–71) put it, 'Hong Kong's generally laissez-faire economic policies have always been based on considered decisions, not mere paralysis of mind and will' (quoted in Miners, 1989, p. 47). The government provides the legal framework within which market forces operate and it also regulates the functioning of the banking sector. It has invested heavily in law and order to secure the colonial status quo: since the nineteenth century the police force has been by far the largest sector of the colonial administration. As a consequence Hong Kong has always been one of the most heavily policed and highly regulated societies in the world: in the early 1990s there was one police officer for every 174 citizens. The paramilitary structure of, and the wide-ranging powers invested in, the Royal Hong Kong Police are a reflection of the fact that traditionally its key role has been to quell challenges to colonial rule.

The state has also been periodically forced to intervene because of the economic vulnerability of Hong Kong; possibly only Singapore is as dependent on overseas trade as Hong Kong. Since the mid 1970s total exports of goods and services have averaged 92 per cent of the Gross Domestic Product whilst total imports of goods and services averaged 99 per cent. The colony imports 80 per cent of its food and nearly all of its raw materials. It has hardly any natural resources, only 12 per cent of its land is arable and its inadequate natural water supply necessitates expensive reservoirs with back-up supplies coming from China. If the principle of government non-intervention were to be strictly adhered to, the colony would cease to function in a very short period of time.

The state has also been involved in the development of a complex infrastructure which has facilitated rapid economic development since 1945. In response to the global protectionism of the 1970s and the rise of competitors, steps were taken to encourage economic diversification and technological innovation. After the financial crisis engendered by the signing of the Sino-British agreement in 1984, the decision was taken to link the Hong Kong dollar to the US dollar in order to restore fiscal stability. The government also stepped in to rescue banks that went to the wall during the 1980s and, after a corruption scandal surrounding the Hong Kong Stock Exchange in 1987–8, legislated tighter regulatory controls.

Therefore on many fronts there is evidence of 'systematic and comprehensive state intervention' (Castells, 1992, p. 34). However, in the realm of social welfare and social policy, intervention has been much more tightly constrained. This has become the key indicator of possible shifts in the ideological commitment to the policy of 'positive non-intervention'. It is in this 'taboo' area that the state has had to be particularly careful and as a result of its positioning we are seemingly provided with one of the most striking examples of a residual welfare regime – one that the new right in both Britain and the USA looked towards as proof of their theorizing on the superiority of family, voluntary and market-based welfare systems over state-provided ones:

> ... advocates of a market morality have claimed to find in Hong Kong the symbols and examples of an anti-egalitarian philosophy. Differences in income and wealth they attribute wholly to differences in

talent, energy and productivity; economic growth they attribute partly to the incentives imparted by unequal rewards – the steeper the gradient, some would say, the sharper the spur to succeed.

(Donnison, 1985, p. 2)

However, as we shall see, the state's position on welfare is much more intricate and contradictory than has traditionally been thought.

3   SOCIETY AND SOCIAL POLICY: 1945 TO THE 1960s

By the end of the Second World War Hong Kong was a colony in crisis. Because of the restructuring of the international economy and the trade embargo on the newly founded People's Republic of China, Hong Kong found itself in an economically impossible situation. The economic problems were compounded by the fact that there was a mass influx of refugees from China between 1946 and 1950. As a result, by 1966 Hong Kong's population had increased from 600,000 to 3,750,000. In the immediate post-war years unemployment rates soared to 30 per cent and it was generally believed that Hong Kong was a dying city. Despite this, the principle of minimal state intervention was adhered to.

As a result of this, Hong Kong's post-war development process differed from that of Asia's other 'little dragons' (Singapore, Taiwan and South Korea) and Japan. The major enterprises did not receive direct assistance from government. Instead part of the capital which fuelled Hong Kong's development originated with the Chinese entrepreneurs who fled to the colony in the late 1940s and 1950s in order to escape the Chinese and Indo-Chinese revolutions, with the rest coming from the colony's banking system (Riedel, 1979). By comparison, much of the capital for Taiwanese and South Korean industrial enterprises came from government-owned financial institutions. The governments in Taipei and Seoul assumed an active role in steering their respective market economies and in the post-war period did not hesitate to regulate industrial and commercial activities. Even in Singapore there was considerable intervention with the government deciding which industries to give priority to in terms of state support (Regnier, 1987).

Thus Hong Kong took a very different path to economic development and, rather than dying, 'the flexibility provided by the untrammelled operation of the free market' allowed the colony to become the most successful of the 'little dragons' (Davies, 1990, p. 4). By the late 1980s the colony was the world's eleventh largest trading economy and enjoyed a spectacular growth rate of 12 to 14 per cent per year (*Financial Times*, 10 May 1991). The colony's initial economic success was built on the emergence of small manufacturing enterprises which had the inbuilt capability of responding quickly to world demands. Of equal significance was the large reserve army of labour which could be drawn upon. By 1959 there had, therefore, been a fundamental shift in Hong Kong's economic base, from depending on 'entrepôt' trade and the export of primary products to a light manufacturing capacity and the export of manufactured goods, mainly textiles.

3.1   THE GOLDEN AGE OF VOLUNTARISM, 1945–1965

In the immediate post-war period the issue of social welfare was central to discussions about British decolonization. In 1945 the Colonial Office released a memorandum entitled 'Social Welfare in the Colonies' which viewed welfare as being crucial to social development; at a conference in 1947 it was formally recognized that social welfare should be a function of colonial government. However, there was a very different conceptualization of welfare informing these discussions to the 'from-the-cradle-to-the-grave' one underpinning debates in Britain; rather the view was: 'We should strive not to develop a system of state aid and assistance, but for a system of direction and coordination and a supplement of private effort' (quoted in Hodge, 1973, p. 217). Hence the coming of age of the British welfare state (described in Chapter 2 of this book) had little impact on the imperial social welfare infrastructure. In the course of the 1950s and '60s the majority of the colonies moved towards formal independence and those remaining were allowed to go their own way in terms of formulating their own social policies. In the case of Hong Kong this meant there was to be no dilution of the commitment to the free market – and no welfare state (Rayner, 1992).

The guiding principles and parameters of the Hong Kong government's post-war social welfare commitments were established in the period between 1945 and the mid 1960s. The government made it clear that its primary concern was to promote the economic well-being of the colony rather than the social welfare of its people. It was stressed that welfare should be provided, as it had been in the pre-war period, by the family, kin, voluntary agencies and the market. The principle of fees for welfare services was established in relation to any services that were provided and, as we shall see, this was accompanied by adherence to the Victorian distinction between the deserving and undeserving poor.

A Social Welfare Office (SWO) was established in 1947 and its primary role was to liaise with voluntary welfare agencies and to encourage the Chinese to look after themselves. Because of the scale of the crisis in the immediate post-war period and the mass influx of refugees from mainland China, Hong Kong was officially designated an area deserving of international aid. Consequently, major international relief organizations established local offices and there was a considerable injection of funds into indigenous voluntary relief agencies. These agencies took primary responsibility for the colony's destitute. In addition to acting as an intermediary the SWO made concerted efforts to reactivate the pre-war community welfare organizations and to encourage them to take responsibility for supplementing the efforts of the relief agencies. By 1951 twenty-one welfare associations had been set up, 'carrying out a considerable amount of practical social work – opening and running free schools for the poor children of the districts, providing free medical treatment, organizing sports activities and setting up women's domestic training or sewing classes [and] free maternity aid' (SWO, 1954, p. 34).

The primary contribution of the SWO was twofold: first, to institute mechanisms to screen out the undeserving poor and, second, 'to encourage self-help and defeat the insidious evils of inaction' amongst those receiving welfare (SWO, 1954, p. 22). In order to do this, able-bodied unemployed people were left to fend for themselves. For very old, severely disabled and exceptionally destitute people, the SWO provided emergency relief through Free Feeding Centres and Relief Centres. There was no cash relief, only free meals and dry rations. Hence, the government clearly limited its involvement to that of encouraging and coordinating voluntary welfare efforts and discouraging destitution and dependency. There was also a belief within government circles that if life was made as difficult as possible for the refugees, many of them would return to China.

If we analyse specific aspects of welfare we can see more clearly how the Hong Kong government conceived of its welfare role. In education, fee-paying private schools catered for the majority of children with government schools only catering for 5 per cent of the registered school population. In the 1950s the government made concerted efforts to persuade private schools to provide a primary-school place for every child by 1961. The government also encouraged voluntary health care provision through subventions while the government's immediate role was defined as providing health care for the poor, not the whole community. Little attention was paid to the quality of the provision and there was no regulation of the private sector other than to try to cajole it into providing for more of the population.

It was only in the area of housing that the state became directly involved in this period and the nature of this involvement provides important evidence concerning the dominant attitude towards welfare provision. Over 500,000 refugees came to Hong Kong in the 1950s and squatter settlements quickly sprang up, particularly in the absence of any coordinated public housing policy. Voluntary efforts were initially prioritized and a Housing Society was established in 1948 through which low-interest government loans were made available to middle-income families. 'Approved' areas and 'tolerated' areas were set aside from 1951 for squatters and the less well-off to construct their own dwellings and in 1952 a Housing Corporation was established to construct homes for the better-off.

However, the pressure for more intervention intensified because of the number of squatters who were losing their homes in fires. The breaking-point came in December 1953 when a fire in Shek Kip Mei squatter camp left 53,000 people homeless. In 1954 a Resettlement Department was established with a remit of rehousing 50,000 people per year. But this still did not keep up with the demand and by 1964 there were 550,000 squatters compared with 300,000 in 1953. A total of 31 per cent of the population was living in temporary structures. As Castells *et al.* argue, 'Although economic growth was reaching historic heights, the city was still unable to house its people. Industrial productivity and the expansion of international trade were increasing real wages, but the collective living conditions in Hong Kong were still on the edge of ecological disaster' (1990, p. 24).

The state was forced to intervene because of the sheer scale of the squatting problem, the incapability of the private sector to deliver the necessary housing and the social and economic costs if it did not. This intervention was not born out of any ideological shift but out of sheer pragmatic necessity. It was made clear that the rehousing programme was not a welfare operation:

> Squatters are not settled simply because they need, ... or deserve, hygienic and fireproof houses; they are resettled because the community can no longer afford to carry the fire risk, health risk and threat to public order and prestige which the squatter areas represent and because the community needs the land of which they are in illegal occupation. And the land is needed quickly.
>
> (Commission for Resettlement, 1955, p. 46)

The clearance of squatter settlements released valuable land for industrial and commercial development. As the 1954 Annual Report cynically stated, 'The fires [in squatter areas] freed for proper development substantial areas of valuable land which the presence of squatters had rendered unusable and whose removal had defied all ingenuity' (Hong Kong Government, 1954, pp. 131–2). The economics of squatting was thus a significant factor in the decision to intervene.

The rehousing of mass numbers of people also resulted in the geographical relocation of the workforce near to where the new factories were situated. Given this rationale it is not surprising that little attention was paid to the quality of public housing. Quantity not quality was the issue and just over 600,000 people were rehoused between 1954 and 1965. Six-storey blocks of flats were built without elevators or electricity, with communal facilities for cooking and washing and toilets on each floor. There was no garbage disposal system and no amenities were provided. The spatial criterion was fixed at 2.2 square metres per person and the average flat was 11 square metres. On the pro side, as Castells *et al.* argue, 'Rents were very low, the location of most settlements was very convenient for dwellers' activities, and, above all, admission into these estates was a guarantee of full integration into Hong Kong society' (1990, p. 24). Furthermore, the principle had been established that the Hong Kong government had a direct responsibility in the provision of public housing. By committing itself in 1972 to rehousing 1.5 million people in ten years, it eventually found itself responsible for one of the world's largest public housing programmes.

3.2   SOCIAL CRISIS AND DEMANDS FOR SOCIAL WELFARE

In the mid 1960s the Hong Kong state reassessed its role in the provision of social welfare. The immediate cause of this assessment was that the colony's economic position continued to improve and, although living standards were low, full employment had been achieved. As a consequence the international relief organizations began to withdraw from the colony. This had significant implications for the poor and the destitute – and the government. In 1964 two state committees were appointed to review the housing problems of the colony. The resultant White Paper formally acknowledged the responsibility of the government in the housing of the squatter population and proposed a new housing programme. There was also a commitment to take responsibility for providing social amenities and management services; in order to do so, a Housing Board was established in 1964. However, although the Hong Kong government was becoming directly involved in the provision of public housing, it remained a distinctly uneasy and hesitant commitment.

The hesitancy of the government was also reflected in the White Paper on social welfare. This advocated a five-year plan for the development of the colony's social services. However, the scope was limited. As far as the White Paper was concerned, the aim of social welfare was the promotion of independent living and in order to bring this about it stressed the importance of 'positive rehabilitation as opposed to the establishment of the soup kitchen'. There was therefore no fundamental change in the attitude towards social security. Neither was there a shift in the belief that the state should not have prime responsibility for social welfare: every effort had to be made to 'preserve, support and reinforce' the family and ensure that it remained a strong, caring unit. Welfare commitments were focused and limited accordingly:

> Priorities should be devised so that constructive government social welfare services are directed first and foremost towards children and young people, counselling being an integral part of such services. As for adults whose resources are limited, these services should be concentrated first upon those who are in special need, and cases where it is likely that rehabilitation, treatment or assistance will be effective within a reasonable time in enabling individuals or families to become more self-sufficient, and, if possible, self-supporting.
>
> (Hong Kong Government, 1965, p. 11)

Effectively the government was reiterating that, 'Destitution, homelessness, physical or mental handicap, family breakdown: these were private disasters not public responsibilities. If certain strangers (such as those in the employ of imported charitable institutions) were prepared to offer help, this was the victim's good fortune and/or their shame' (Jones, 1990, p. 171). This stress on family responsibility resulted in a family counselling and casework service being established. The Chinese family was to be bolstered in order to carry out its welfare functions.

Events overtook Hong Kong, however, when serious social disturbances engulfed the colony in 1966 and 1967. The colony was not prepared for the disturbances because in the post-war period there had been little trade union reaction to its policies of benign neglect. This was in marked contrast to the militancy of the Hong Kong trade unions in the period prior to the Second World War. Given the considerable disparities in wealth, manifest racial inequalities and lack of social provision, it is not surprising that there had been periodic challenges to colonial authority in Hong Kong. In 1922, for example, a dispute involving 30,000 seamen and dockers broadened into a general strike. After eight weeks the employers acceded to the workers' demands. In 1925–6 a succession of anti-imperialist strikes broke out in Shanghai and Canton and as a consequence of the British authorities killing sixty-four strikers the dispute spread to Hong Kong. The Hong Kong strike committee issued a set of wide-ranging demands including: the right to vote and freedom of speech and assembly; equality between Chinese and non-Chinese; a maximum working-day and a minimum wage; collective bargaining and the implementation of a workers' insurance scheme. The colonial authorities responded by declaring a state of emergency and implementing draconian law and order measures. To the relief of the British authorities the strike eventually collapsed as a result of political realignments in mainland China (see Young, 1981; Tsai, 1993).

Between 1951 and 1966 there had been a considerable decrease in the levels of industrial conflict and militancy with an average of only 8.75 strikes per annum. This was due to a variety of factors. First, the organized working class was weak. The union movement was internally divided between those who supported the communists and those who supported the nationalists in China. Secondly, the unions had no formal access to the decision-making processes of the colony. As a result the legislation governing the trade unions and working conditions reflected the interests of capital which enjoyed formal representation in the colonial decision-making processes. Continued economic growth also enabled employers to concede wage increases unilaterally and this was accompanied by relative price stability. In addition the flood of immigrants created a massive reserve army of labour which considerably weakened the position of the trade unions. The restructuring of the economy also affected the union movement. Over 30 per cent of the workforce was in firms employing less than fifty workers and employers used tight categories of skilled and unskilled workers. The small category of permanent skilled workers preferred to negotiate on a private basis. There was also a quick turnover of factories which militated against the development of unions amongst the unskilled workers.

The trade unions also contributed to industrial and social harmony through their role as key providers of social welfare. Many of the unions concentrated on the welfare of their members *outside* the workplace, not within it:

> Because of the inadequate education and welfare facilities in the
> colony, the provision by unions of schools, clinics, and cheap food is a
> valuable social and economic service to their members. The long
> tradition of acting as mutual aid societies means that the provision
> of welfare benefits continues to be an important function. In
> addition to the facilities already mentioned, the unions pay out cash
> benefits for unemployment, sickness and accidents, marriage and
> maternity and ... funeral and death gratuities.
>
> (England and Rear, 1975, p. 93)

Within the workplace, in order to keep their skilled workers, certain
employers offered a package of paternalistic welfare provision. Large
Cantonese factories offered free or subsidized food; large Shanghainese
and traditional British concerns offered free or subsidized food, dormitory
accommodation for single workers, medical care, loan facilities and
schools (Rear and England, 1975, pp. 254–73).

However, in the mid 1960s the government should have been more concerned that only 13 per cent of the workforce was unionized and by the
fact that the vast majority of workers had no access to the welfare services
either of the unions or paternalistic employers. Most of the workforce was
unskilled or semi-skilled and was on hourly and daily rates of pay. Hong
Kong workers had the longest urban working-day and working-week in
South East Asia, working an average of 60–70 hours, often in dangerous
and/or unhealthy conditions. They had little in the way of legal protection
or employment rights (Scott, 1989, p. 89). Legal restrictions were limited
to prohibiting fourteen- to sixteen-year-olds from working more than
eight hours a day and children under fourteen from working in industry.
Forty per cent of the population was under the age of fifteen, yet educational provision was minimal. In terms of living conditions Hong Kong
had the highest population density in the world:

> ... every stairway in Chinese areas of Victoria and Kowloon had its
> restless sleepers with their little bundle of possessions clutched to
> them through the night. Every street where pavements were wide
> enough had its clutter of lean-to shelters of cardboard, tar-paper, old
> corrugated iron, cocooned into some semblance of a dwelling where
> families were raised, and whose sanitation was the nearest public
> lavatory.
>
> (Cameron, 1991, p. 282)

Given the defining characteristics of what Frederic C. Deyo (1989) has
defined as a 'hyper-proletariat' and the social economic and political
pressures that were building up, many observers viewed Hong Kong as a
potential time-bomb. That bomb exploded in 1966 and 1967 when serious
disturbances engulfed the colony. The government had a forewarning
concerning the volatile state of the colony in 1956 when nationalist riots
broke out in one of the resettlement camps. In restoring order the police

and army killed fifty-nine people. Although it was recognized that the social conditions of the colony had been a contributory factor in these disturbances, no measures were taken to alleviate pressing social and working conditions.

In 1966 and 1967 the colony went headlong into social crisis. In April 1966 a protest against fare increases on public transport escalated into full-scale rioting which was again suppressed by the Hong Kong police. A commission was appointed to look into the causes of the rioting and it was officially acknowledged that reforms needed to be implemented. However, before the colony had time to recover from the 1966 riots, fresh disturbances broke out which posed a more fundamental challenge to the continuation of colonial rule in Hong Kong. Between March and December 1967 Hong Kong felt the effect of the Cultural Revolution and was rocked by widespread work stoppages, intermittent strikes, anti-imperialist demonstrations and a bombing campaign. Through a combination of curfew measures, mass arrests, detentions and deportations and the continuous deployment of riot police, colonial order was once more restored. Fifty-one people died in the disturbances and over five thousand arrests were made (Waldron, 1976).

4   THE CONFIGURATION OF CONTEMPORARY SOCIAL POLICY

The Hong Kong and British authorities found themselves under considerable international pressure in the aftermath of the disturbances. The world's media focused attention on the 'sweatshop' working conditions and Third World living conditions that people had to endure. The most immediate response was to implement labour legislation. In 1967 the working-week of women and young people was reduced to forty-eight hours. An Employment Ordinance was introduced bringing in basic employee rights. Subsequent amendments introduced maternity leave, paid holidays, sickness allowances, severance pay and compensation for industrial accidents. Despite the fact that much of the legislation was not enforced, the principle had been established that some fetters had to be placed on Hong Kong's form of capitalism if long-term social order was to be preserved (Chan, 1990).

However, labour legislation alone was never going to 'close the gap' between the colonial state and Hong Kong society. At the political level, although there were no moves towards democracy, a number of changes were proposed. Community consultative/advisory committees and grievance procedures were set up, concerted efforts were made to improve the image of government departments and a commitment was made to localize the civil service and to examine the viability of recognizing Cantonese as an official language. Perhaps more significant than the contemplated political reforms, were the proposed social reforms. As Scott has argued:

If the regime's claim that it had the consent of the people to govern was to have any validity whatsoever, it followed that there had to be improvements in social policies and in the delivery of public goods. In effect, government had to bringing about a limited redistribution of income through the provision of services.

(Scott, 1989, p. 105)

A new governor, Sir Murray MacLehose, appointed in 1971, argued that the future stability and prosperity of Hong Kong would be built on 'four pillars' of social policy, namely, public housing, education, medical and health care and social services. In the 1970s and '80s, for the first time, it was publicly acknowledged that the state had a role to play in the coordination and planning of social welfare and committed itself to achieving social policy targets. However, it was made clear that social welfare provision would be directly linked to the state of Hong Kong's economy and not paid for by raising taxation levels. This meant that the implementation of the various social policy White Papers would depend on continued economic growth (see Table 5.1). So, for example, following the 1974 recession a number of the proposed projects were delayed or only semi-realized. After this the return of economic prosperity ensured more resourcing of social welfare. However, the government has continually stressed that there is no unqualified right to welfare provision; in Hong Kong welfare has to be earned.

Table 5.1   Economic growth and social services development in Hong Kong in the 1970s and 1980s

	GDP (HK$m)	Relative size of public sector	Total public expenditure (HK$m)	Percentage increase over last year	Expenditure on social services (HK$m)	Percentage increase over last year	Expenditure on social services/ total public expenditure
1974/5	44,578	15.0	6,692	–	2,662	–	39.8
1975/6	46,464	14.2	6,576	-1.8	2,873	7.9	43.7
1976/7	59,339	12.4	7,355	11.8	3,059	6.5	41.6
1977/8	68,905	13.3	9,168	24.6	3,829	21.9	41.8
1978/9	81,163	14.9	12,122	32.2	5,187	35.5	42.8
1979/80	107,047	14.6	15,619	28.8	6,807	31.2	43.6
1980/1	137,209	16.1	22,057	41.2	9,721	42.8	44.1
1981/2	165,346	17.8	29,383	33.2	11,544	18.8	39.3
1982/3	186,868	19.1	35,684	21.4	14,494	25.6	40.6
1983/4	207,948	18.6	38,596	8.2	16,371	13.0	42.4
1984/5[1]	248,984	16.4	40,944	6.1	18,432	12.6	45.0
1985/6[2]	285,550	16.0	45,647	11.5	20,699	12.3	45.3

Notes: [1] Revised estimate. [2] Estimate.
Source: Chow, 1986b, p. 143

If we analyse MacLehose's 'four pillars' of social policy, we will see that the state's commitment to increasing expenditure on social services did not mean that it was going to take front-line responsibility for organizing, delivering and managing welfare. Only in the sphere of public housing was the state forced to remain directly involved. As we shall see, there were unintended consequences of one of the world's most residualist welfare regimes becoming responsible for one of the world's largest public housing programmes.

4.1   PUBLIC HOUSING

A new Housing Authority was set up in 1973 which amalgamated the functions of the previously separate housing bodies. It became the sole body responsible for planning, delivering and managing a ten-year housing programme. The stated objectives were to provide high-quality housing for 1.5 million people and to eradicate substandard housing.

The manner in which the government initially framed its involvement in the provision of public housing has resulted in a series of complex outcomes. The extent of the commitment may have been new but the ideologies underpinning official policy remain essentially unaltered. First, although the Housing Authority has had an impressive record in the construction of housing units and is now directly responsible for the housing of 47 per cent of the colony's population, it has failed in its overall objectives. At one extreme there are still 300,000 squatters in Hong Kong and a significant proportion of the population lives in substandard private accommodation and, at the other, there has been the growth of a middle class who, because of the nature of the property market, have had difficulty in accessing housing. Secondly, the allocation of the new public housing was not necessarily related to people's need. A considerable proportion of the housing was allocated to squatters because they were occupying valuable government land. So it is the land development needs of the government that has determined which sections of Hong Kong society have been given priority. Thirdly, because of continuing full employment and rising wages, many of the tenants of public housing are technically no longer entitled to such housing. This has placed the state in an invidious position because any attempt to evict residents on grounds of excessive income or to raise rents significantly, runs the very real risk of sparking disorder. Finally, because less land was available in the urban areas of the colony, nine new towns have been developed in the New Territories. However, in order to entice people to move to the new towns there has had to be a commitment to providing schools, hospitals and amenities and expanding the transport infrastructure accordingly. Critics have argued that this represents an over-commitment by the government.

The state has responded by trying to redefine its role in the housing market through gradually implementing diversification and privatization policies. In the late 1970s a Home Ownership Scheme was launched specifically aimed at the 'sandwich class' of middle-income earners who are not eligible for public housing but who cannot afford properties exorbitantly priced on the private market. This scheme provided a variety of accommodation at prices 30 per cent below market prices and with cheap mortgages and generous repayment schedules. The private sector has also been contracted to develop affordable middle-class housing estates to strengthen this sector of the Hong Kong housing market in the run-up to 1997. In late 1992 it was announced that the government intended to purchase private-sector flats which would be re-sold to middle-class families at heavily subsidized prices.

The form of state involvement in the provision of public housing has also been redefined. There have been tentative efforts to limit the public subsidy of tenants whose economic conditions have improved. Rents in newly built estates are more closely tied to income level and to the quality of accommodation provided. Efforts have also been made to entice better-off tenants to leave the public sector by making them eligible for the Home Ownership and Private Sector Participation schemes. The most recent plan is to upgrade the housing stock by demolishing all the old estates and eliminating public slums. This provides the state with the opportunity to radically restructure its responsibilities (Mosher and Taylor, 1991). The intention is for the private sector to have a considerable input and home ownership schemes will be introduced. In the 1990s 1.137 million flats will be built: the private sector will deliver 483,000 whilst the Housing Authority will construct the rest. However, 291,000 of the 654,000 Housing Authority flats will be sold off: 'From this perspective the ultimate goal of the public housing programme would thus be to ensure the transition from being a homeless immigrant to a home owning citizen ... The last stage of Hong Kong's housing policy proclaims privatization as the superior goal of the public interest' (Castells *et al.*, 1990, pp. 40–1). It also gives the state the opportunity gradually to withdraw from the direct provision of public housing whilst at the same time stimulating and diversifying the housing market in Hong Kong (Mosher and Taylor, 1991). By the late 1990s it is hoped that 60 per cent of Hong Kong families will own their own homes.

4.2   EDUCATION AND HEALTH

Commentators are agreed that, after public housing, education is Hong Kong's most sought after public provision. In the 1970s free compulsory education was introduced and a commitment was made to ensuring that all children would receive three years' secondary education. This change was prompted partly in response to international criticism about the extensive use of child labour in Hong Kong's sweatshops, and partly to meet industry's need for a better-educated labour force (Fung, 1986). However, traditional attitudes towards education still prevail so that the overwhelming majority of the new school places have been provided by private schools and government-aided voluntary schools (see Table 5.2). Until recently very little attention has been paid to the quality of this expanded system. In the 1970s for example there was no real attempt to regulate the teaching standards or to standardize educational facilities within the private sector. In addition, little attempt has been made to rethink the nature of the education provided in the colony. The government adheres to the laissez-faire principle of allowing the schools and the parents to choose which type of education children receive. This has led to the prestigious model of education provided by the Anglo-Chinese schools becoming the model of education. Consequently, an education system has evolved which is highly competitive, placing extreme pressure on children to pass exams and to conform to authoritarian standards. Critics of the system argue that little attention has been paid to anything other than results and discipline. Considerable pressure has also been placed on the schools to deliver education in quantity rather than in quality. As Youngson has noted, in order to meet official targets it was decided to 'use the school buildings like factories and to operate a two shift or even three shift system' (1982, p. 47).

More recently the government has committed itself to upgrading the quality of the education system. However there are two provisos. First, it has been made clear that if more funding has to go into education, it will have to be cut back in other areas of social services. And secondly, the private sector is going to be encouraged and strengthened.

> The aim is to provide a strong private school sector subsidized by government, in order to improve the quality and diversity of education available. It will introduce an element of differentiation to the otherwise uniform school system to give parents more choice. Under the scheme any secondary school not run by the government and meeting specified standards will receive a public subsidy for each student enrolled. It will be free to set its own curriculum, entrance examinations and fee levels with minimum government control.
>
> (Hong Kong Government, 1991b, p. 131)

Hong Kong's health policies have been successful in lowering infant mortality rates and extending life expectancy rates to the point where they are now better than those of the UK and USA. However, there have been continuing complaints about the nature of the public health system because basic medical services are provided on a first come, first served basis. Fees are charged for services other than children's care and accidents. There are currently fifteen government hospitals which provide 13,000 beds and 36 voluntary and private hospitals which provide 12,500 beds. Because of the intense pressures on the system it has 'depended on deterrents such as crowded conditions, unpleasant surroundings, lack of privacy, impersonal service, long waiting lines' (Ng, 1990, p. 400). A report at the beginning of the 1980s stated that, because of the caseload, doctors were spending an average of less than two minutes with each patient and that patients were having to queue for an average of three hours (Benton, 1983). At the other end of the colony's medical provision, the private sector advertises the fact that it is able to offer some of the most sophisticated health care in the world.

Table 5.2   Public and private educational and health provision in Hong Kong, 1988–90

	1988[1]	1989[1]	1990[1]
Registered schools (by category)			
Government	95	96	96
Grant	22	22	22
Subsidized	917	898	893
Private	1,553	1,525	1,540
Special Education	71	72	71
Total	2,658	2,613	2,622
School enrolment			
Kindergarten			
Private	214,703	201,750	196,466
Primary			
Government and aided	483,232	483,191	475,054
Private	53,279	52,945	51,666
Total	536,511	536,136	526,720
Secondary			
Government and aided	347,417	355,349	363,229
Assisted private	3,686	3,357	3,116
Other private	120,981	106,242	88,905
Total	472,084	464,948	455,250
	1988[2]	1989[2]	1990[2]
Hospital beds (by category of hospital)			
Government hospitals	12,302	12,352	12,679
Government maternity homes/ clinics	385	363	317
Government-assisted hospitals	9,577	9,537	9,464
Private hospitals	2,749	2,763	2,782
Private nursing/ maternity homes	44	44	44
Total	25,057	25,059	25,286

Notes: [1] As of September. [2] As at end of year.

Source: Hong Kong Government, 1991, Hong Kong, HK Government Printer

All four of the 'little dragons' have had to confront the problem of how to deliver health care services in the 1990s. Singapore chose Medisave, a nation-wide hospital insurance scheme; Taiwan prioritized primary health care and committed itself to introducing a national insurance scheme by 1995; and Korea tentatively opted for some form of national health service system. Hong Kong evaded the issue of insurance schemes by opting for a review of the hospital system which drew heavily on health-care developments in Britain. It is within this context that a Hospital Authority was established in 1991 in order to transfer ownership and responsibility from a central government department to an independent statutory authority. It is hoped that the Hospital Authority will achieve: better integration of government and subvented hospital services; greater flexibility; greater participation by voluntary organizations in the delivery of services; and incentives for better management through increased devolution and financial independence at the Health Authority level and decentralization and financial autonomy at the hospital level (Yuen, 1991). The government is banking on the Health Authority delivering a more efficient allocation of existing resources rather than having to commit more resources to the health service. There is also the possibility that the system will become more cost-oriented and that fees will be increased (Ng, 1990).

4.3 SOCIAL SECURITY

As has been mentioned previously, social security has been viewed within a very particular ideological framework in Hong Kong. It is argued that, because the colony has one of the lowest tax systems in the world and government policy is geared to producing an open and competitive economic environment, everyone is given the opportunity to better themselves. This means that there is very little sympathy for the poor:

> It is a widely held view that in Hong Kong enterprise and hard work are the key to success, and that the poor are those deficient in such values. Assistance should therefore be minimal and provided with the objective of developing the ethic of self-reliance and commitment to work. Implicit in this view is the belief that if the community generously subsidizes its less able members, this all important economic ethic will be weakened. The deprivation of the few should not be allowed to interfere with the prosperity of the majority.
>
> (Leung, 1990, p. 68)

Very little research has been carried out on the extent of poverty in Hong Kong. It is interesting to note, for example, that *The Other Hong Kong Report* (Wong and Cheng, 1990) – a 'critical lens' on what's happening in Hong Kong – has nothing to say about the vast disparities of wealth and poverty in the colony. Surveys indicate that it rates very low in people's priorities (Lau and Wan, 1991). A study of young workers at the beginning of the 1980s showed that 11.3 per cent believed that poverty was due to fate and 38.6 per cent believed that it was due to indolence (quoted in Leung, 1990). Over 80 per cent of these respondents believed that poverty could only be solved through the individual's own efforts whilst only 2.4 per cent thought the state should intervene.

In 1972 a White Paper on social welfare was introduced committing the government to the principle of public assistance for those who did not have adequate means of support, as well as special help for disabled and older people, the provision of special facilities for disabled people and the expansion of social and recreational facilities for young people. By the end of 1971 cash-based public assistance had reluctantly been introduced. However, a very tight definition of eligibility for such relief was used, namely those beyond the working age and those unfit for work. Given the stringent conditions of eligibility and the minimum levels of assistance it is not surprising that older people make up the large majority of public assistance recipients in Hong Kong (see Table 5.3). In 1973 there was the trial introduction of a non-means-tested Special Needs Allowance for infirm older people and those with severe disabilities, with the government promising that if the take-up was successful it would be extended to other groups such as chronically sick people and widowed mothers with young children. However, this never happened – probably because the take-up rate was too successful.

Table 5.3   Number of recipients of public assistance by category, 1972/3–1989/90

Reason for eligibility	1972/3	1983/4	1989/90
Age	10,043	35,894	44,070
Chronic sickness	3,379	7,731	7,657
Low income	2,712	1,916	1,012
Widow with children/lone parent	1,670	2,561	3,977
Unemployed	154	1,574	1,618

Source: Extracted from Director of Social Welfare Reports

It is undoubtedly true that the reforms initially introduced in the 1970s marked a considerable shift in the government's involvement in social welfare (see Table 5.4). However, there are clearly defined limits to this increased involvement. The introduction of cash-based public assistance was specifically justified on the grounds that it was inexpensive and more manageable than a social insurance scheme. Hence there has been no fundamental shift on the issue of social insurance. It has also been made clear that the rates paid will vary periodically to take account of special needs and to preserve work incentives.

Catherine Jones (1990) has noted that the introduction of demo-grants – that is, non-means-tested, non-contributory, unconditional payments to specified categories of people – is usually associated with social solidarity and welfare-mindedness. They were introduced in the west for contin-

Table 5.4   Social services expenditure figures, 1971–91

	Spending (HK$ million)	Percentage of total government spending
1971/2	50.6	1.7
1974/5	251.0	4.0
1977/8	414.6	5.0
1980/81	838.8	3.9
1988/9	3,475.5	5.8
1990/91	5,251.9	6.1

Source: Extracted from Hong Kong Budget Reports

gencies defined as being universal and deserving and therefore not justi-fying means-testing. They were also supplements to social insurance systems. Universal tax-financed benefits were easier to administer and constituted a useful symbolic statement of a government's welfare responsibilities. So does the introduction of demo-grants such as the Spe-cial Needs Allowance mean that the Hong Kong government has moved towards fully acknowledging its role in the provision of welfare for the poor and unfortunate?

The difference is that in Hong Kong demo-grants have been introduced not in the aftermath of social insurance as is the case elsewhere, but as a *substitute* for it and as an *improvement* on public assistance. In addition there was one category of demo-grants which was conspicuous by its absence – family allowance/child benefits. As we have seen elsewhere, this was one category that most Western European states acknowledged as being part of their social welfare obligation. However, in Hong Kong the introduction of such benefits was rejected on the grounds that they would undermine the traditional duties and responsibilities of the Chinese family and disrupt the relationship between parents and chil-dren.

5   THE DELIVERY OF SOCIAL WELFARE

5.1   THE FAMILY AND SOCIAL WELFARE

There are two very important pieces of research which provide an indi-cation of how the Chinese family in Hong Kong has adapted to its milieu. Janet Salaff's (1981) study, *Working Daughters of Hong Kong*, furnishes an insight into how the Chinese family in Hong Kong compares with its mainland counterpart. In China we find one of the most powerful forms of familism in the world: 'The basic building block of the stable Confucian order is the family. If that is established, other relationships begin to fall into their important but secondary places' (Redding, 1990, p. 45). The centripetal extended family has evolved to be the key social institution in

South China, having as its central objective the attainment of self-reliance:

> In the centripetal form, the family becomes a power base to manipulate other institutions. Families consequently stratify the community while endeavouring to develop their own power and wealth. A centripetal family gathers in its forces by demanding the primary loyalty of its members and mobilizing their labour power, political and psychological allegiances on behalf of kinsmen.
>
> (Salaff, 1981, p. 8)

The two main practices of the feudal Chinese family that oblige members to centre their loyalty on the family and kinship network are partible inheritance (through which all the sons hold equal claim to the property of the family) and ancestral worship. Not surprisingly, the Chinese family has all the internal features of the classic patriarchal family, most significantly a highly gendered division of labour, patrilineal descent and patrilocal residence. In its relations with the external world the efforts of this family form are geared towards ensuring its survival and advancement through the concerted efforts of all its members (Baker, 1979).

Salaff analyses the impact of Hong Kong's hyper-industrialization, urbanization and westernization upon the Chinese family. She argues that although the economic, political and social environment of Hong Kong has truncated the traditional family form, in many other respects it has enhanced its core features and value system. Free market economic policies and government non-intervention reinforced the tendency of the Chinese family to turn to itself for its economic survival and well-being:

> A combination of low wages, which forces two or more family members into the job market, and rock bottom government social service commitments frequently creates the conditions of desperation that drives families back onto their own resources. A necessity for survival, the family wage economy is also a precondition for cherished aspirations for future advancement in the class structure. Social restrictions, which in other capitalist societies might somewhat curtail the economic aggrandizement of individuals and their family units (high taxes, partial nationalization measures) are absent.
>
> (Salaff, 1981, pp. 42–3)

Salaff argues that, as a consequence, traditional gender relations were also reproduced. It was the daughters who played a pivotal role in ensuring the survival of the family. A daughter was 'trained early to contribute her talents and energies unstintingly to the kin group and to identify herself totally with its survival and aspirations' (1981, p. 289). Because of their mother's enforced participation in the economy, daughters at an early age took on domestic and family tasks. In addition they were involved in home-based 'out work' which contributed to the family budget and prepared them for working in factories. Because of how they were viewed within the patriarchal family and because of the market demand for their labour in the 'global assembly line', girls entered the workplace as soon as legally possible. The wages they brought home were used not only to ensure the family's survival but to make social advancement possible by either going towards the education of the male children in the family and/or, if there were enough family members earning, permitting a family to set up a business.

Salaff acknowledges that through their contribution to the family economy these young women did make gains. For example, marriage choices were widened, the young women enjoyed a more varied social life and their filial role within the family was enhanced. However, she argues that the need to sustain the 'family wage economy' and the religious–cultural focus on patriliny set clear limits on the new-found freedoms of the young women. As a consequence Salaff concludes that an untrammelled free market economy and minimal welfare provision create the need for a centralized family economy and, given the particular nature of the Chinese family, traditional gender divisions are structurally reproduced. Therefore, 'wage labour participation has enabled close-knit families to reintegrate their daughters of toil by incorporating their earnings and experiences as a promising means of attaining primary family goals' (p. 259). She suggests that only when state-sponsored social policies are implemented that undermine the need for a centralized family economy, will these traditional divisions be broken.

Lau Siu-kai's (1981) study into political stability in Hong Kong provides more information about the Chinese family in Hong Kong. He argues that a 'utilitarian familism' developed which was distinctive from traditional Chinese familism: 'Utilitarianistic familism is … a kind of familism wherein the family represents the major reference group with which an individual identifies and for whose material well-being he/she strives' (1981, p. 202). Within this family form there was a stress on immediate materialistic needs and satisfaction and a prioritization of family members at the expense of outsiders. He claims that this self-centred family came about because 'social and economic insecurities have been absorbed by the individual families and family groups'. Whilst Lau maintains that a Chinese family form has evolved in Hong Kong which is highly functional for its members, he also argues that it is alienated from society: '[It] does not value very much the non-material rewards which society can proffer, rather, society is considered to be largely insignificant, and the family is to "exploit" society for its utilitarian purposes' (1981, p. 202).

Government officials could take heart from these in-depth studies which showed that the family was central to people's lives and that its members were capable of looking after their own welfare. However, Salaff's and Lau's studies also showed the heavy strain that the family and family members had to bear and that there was no guarantee that the family could continue to deliver all the welfare needs of its members. Lau warned that whilst this family form had carried the older generation through the momentous changes of the post-war period, there was no guarantee that it could carry the next generations through.

The riots in the late 1960s had indicated that all was not well with this family form. An analysis of the youths who were involved in the riots, for example, showed that a significant proportion of them were single or no longer kept in contact with their families. In the 1970s women made up approximately 33 per cent of the working population which again had ramifications for the family, especially because there was no welfare provision for working mothers. Such problems were compounded by the long working hours and weeks that people had to endure. The buoyant youth employment market also gave young people a financial independence which was similar to that enjoyed by working-class youth in Britain in the nineteenth century. In addition, the extensive social and spatial disruption caused by the public housing and new town programmes put considerable strains on relationships between elderly parents and their children (Chow, 1987).

However, the government did not offer welfare benefits to relieve the pressure on the family. Instead it launched an ideological campaign to promote family obligations and duties. *Family Life Education* campaigns were initiated by the social welfare agencies. Its stated objectives were to improve the quality of family life, to prevent family breakdowns and to promote interpersonal relationships and social consciousness. There were annual consciousness-raising campaigns conducted by subvented voluntary agencies in tandem with the Social Welfare Department with slogans such as 'Building a Happy Family', 'Honour Your Parents', 'Love and Care Help Build Up a Happy Family' and 'Responsible Parenthood'.

As Catherine Jones (1990) has noted, all members of the family were targeted by these campaigns. Young couples were counselled on love and marriage as well as family planning whilst older people were advised on how 'to adapt to the changes of ageing and learn to get on with the younger generation'. Essentially the family was being modernized so that it could continue to take primary responsibility for looking after its members:

> The modern Hong Kong family was being expected (or at any rate instructed) to be as caring of its old and/or its disabled as of its young (irrespective of who was actually living in the family home); to have a care for and take a pride in its neighbours and neighbourhood; to see its well-being and future as ultimately bound up with the well-being and future of the colony itself.
>
> (Jones, 1990, p. 222)

In 1990 the government announced that it was drafting social welfare proposals for the 1990s and beyond. As a consequence the role of the Chinese family in the delivery of social welfare was debated once more. The substantive debate coalesced around the welfare of older people and childcare provision. Government statistics indicated that the number of people over the age of 65 would grow at a much faster rate than the overall population. In the 1960s they accounted for 4 per cent of the population but by 1990 this figure had risen to almost 13 per cent (Phillips, 1992). Hence there were renewed arguments that some form of financial protection should be ensured for workers when they retired. This time the idea of social insurance was not even suggested. Instead welfare pressure groups argued for a Singapore-style Central Provident Fund, that is, a form of 'forced savings' system in which each participant has his/her own account into which contributions are paid and interest earned. Although it was made clear that the intention was not to transfer wealth from taxpayers and that contributions from employers would be voluntary, the suggestion was rejected on the grounds that it would adversely affect the economy. One of the other main reasons given for the rejection was that:

> ... the twin institutions of market and family have been unusually successful at this task. The state is a latecomer in the provision of social security. Its track record as evidenced by the performance of existing schemes in so many countries is dismal indeed. Indeed savings have tended to decline in countries where state social security schemes have been introduced. Do we really want to risk weakening the market and the family as the front-line social security institutions and make way for the state?
>
> (Wong, 1988, p. 50)

The plight of Hong Kong's senior citizens was graphically illustrated by two incidents in 1990. Workers of the main public bus company went on strike to try to improve their retirement provision because under existing arrangements they were entitled to a maximum one-off payment of the equivalent of approximately £1,500 for thirty years' service. In the ensuing public debate it was disclosed that generous employers in the colony gave retiring employees between £1,500 and £2,200 and recommended that they return to mainland China where the cost of living is so much cheaper (Lau, 1990). In December 1990 a fire broke out in 'caged accommodation' in which six died and fifty were injured. Because of this fire, the Hong Kong public was once more reminded that 4,200 older men shared 126 apartments in which their beds were 'caged' to protect their meagre belongings. These incidents sparked off renewed debate about whether the contemporary Hong Kong family was capable of looking after its older members.

The extended Chinese family traditionally provided security in old age and their senior members occupied a respected and valued place in the society; status and authority increased with age (Phillips, 1992). However, the proponents of the Central Provident Fund cited research which suggested that the Hong Kong family was not capable of looking after older members because of changes in the family form and the collapse of social support networks. The trend towards the nuclear family and smaller families continued to gather pace in the 1980s. By the late 1980s almost 80 per cent of families were nuclear in form with a household size of 3.7. Divorces, so long a taboo in Chinese society, increased from just over 24,000 in the early 1980s to well over 43,000 by the end of the decade. In addition, fears about post-1997 have provoked a mass exodus of the young and able from the colony; it has been estimated that 60,000 per year will leave in the run-up to reunification (Kwong, 1990). Relatives in their old age are being left behind because many of them do not want to emigrate to Canada and Australia. The nature of the housing policies and constant and wide-reaching urban redevelopment mean that the extended kinship system cannot be maintained. As a consequence, older people make up 80 per cent of single households in the colony. Older people are also living longer: in 1971 the average life expectancy for males was 68 and 75.6 for females; by 1991 it was 74.7 and 80.3 respectively. The last relevant statistic relates to female participation in the work-force. Given that women carry out the vast majority of caring, irrespective of culture, the fact that over 80 per cent of women in Hong Kong are in employment has had considerable implications for the care of older relatives (International Project on Family and Community, 1986). Furthermore, given the shifts in the Hong Kong economy and the likely further feminization of the workforce, there is little likelihood of this trend being reversed.

In the same time period the family came under further scrutiny because of the issue of 'latch-key kids'. In 1991 this became an issue after a series of tragedies where children had been left on their own. In the ensuing debate various facts came to light concerning childcare provision in Hong Kong. Given the numbers of women in the labour market it might have been expected that childcare was highly developed. However, there are only 1,489 crèche places and 31,134 nursery places for the under-six population of 600,000. Public crèche and nursery places are only free for the deprived and there are stringent application requirements for the others. Women's groups have demanded that there should be more accessible public crèche/nursery provision (Association for the Advancement of Feminism, 1992).

However, the social welfare proposals did little to address these concerns. The Governor, in his annual policy speech, made it clear that, 'The challenge for Hong Kong is to improve our social services without creating the sort of dependency culture found in some western states' (Legco, 10 October 1990). The acting Secretary for Health and Welfare hammered home the point: 'Families which can do so will wish to continue to play their part in giving all possible support to individual members. We in Hong Kong appreciate welfare services but we must never ever forget our proud tradition of family.' The government's concession on these issues consisted of allowing senior citizens to claim old-age allowance at the age of 65 and introducing a child supplement of approximately £14 per month for families on public assistance. The government also announced that it was considering introducing legislation which would make it a criminal offence to leave children unattended.

5.2 THE VOLUNTARY SECTOR AND CONTEMPORARY SOCIAL WELFARE

As has been indicated previously, the voluntary sector has continued to play a considerable role in education and health care in Hong Kong. The same is true in the social welfare arena. Because historically the government steadfastly refused to become anything other than indirectly involved, it was left to the voluntary sector to deliver the majority of social welfare. From the mid 1960s the government officially recognized the voluntary sector for the purpose of delivering welfare services. It now provides over 60 per cent of the direct welfare services and employs approximately 80 per cent of welfare personnel.

The 1973 White Paper on the future of social welfare in the colony laid down the ideological reasons for this division of labour between the government and the voluntary sector (Kwan, 1986, p. 181):

- voluntary social services can provide a basis of comparison with government services, and stimulate improvement;
- voluntary services can be more experimental in pioneering new programmes or in raising standards of existing services;
- while the government accepts responsibility for the provision of social welfare services, there are areas where the government sees a need and is prepared to meet that need not by the direct provision of services but by providing a financial subvention to agencies so that they can deliver the service;
- non-governmental agencies have been traditionally successful in harnessing community efforts.

The exact relationship between the voluntary sector and the government is complex. The government argues that a 'partnership' exists and can cite the numerous means available to the voluntary sector to influence welfare policies by working through the non-statutory Hong Kong Council of Social Services (HKCSS) which represents 210 voluntary agencies. However, given that more than 80 per cent of their extensive budgets are met through subvention (see Figure 5.1), some commentators have argued that the voluntary agencies are no more than 'camouflaged quasi-government agencies' (Chow, 1986a, p. 409). From this perspective, the importance of Hong Kong's extensive voluntary sector lies in the fact that the state is removed from front-line accountability for the delivery of services whilst at the same time, through funding and policy formulation, it can tightly control the extent and nature of welfare provision.

Renewed attempts have also been made to involve the community in the work of the voluntary agencies. The family revitalization crusade linked into a campaign to promote a sense of community responsibility, active citizenship and public charity in Hong Kong. A policy of community-building was introduced in 1978 which aimed to foster community development, involvement and awareness amongst the people of Hong Kong. As well as being an attempt to involve people in local decision-making, it

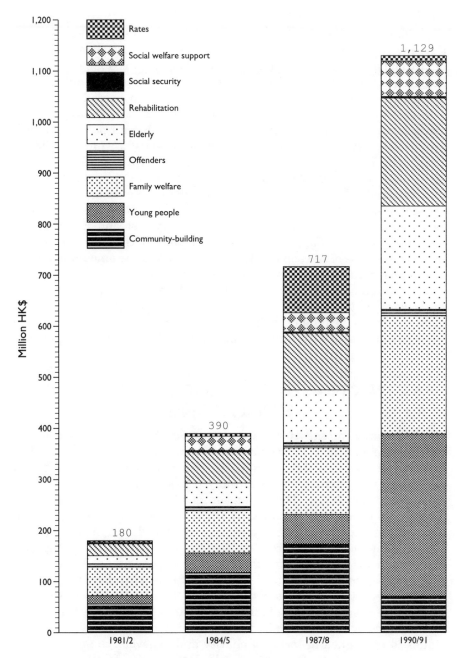

Figure 5.1   Subventions by programme, 1980/81–1990/91 (HK$)
Sources: Director of Social Welfare, *Annual Departmental Reports*

attempted to inculcate a sense of community responsibility at the level of the neighbourhood.

This sense of responsibility was linked in to a concerted effort to promote public charity in Hong Kong. A 'Community Chest' was established in

1968, made up of representatives from the voluntary welfare agencies in the colony and supported by the banks and big business. The logic behind the Chest was that instead of each agency trying to raise money independently and in competition with each other, the people of Hong Kong would be encouraged to give money to the Chest. This money would then be divided amongst the participating agencies. Chest-sponsored community activities with slogans such as 'Happiness is giving, so give now' and 'We share because we care' became a part of Hong Kong's public life with people being exhorted to give as much as they could afford (Jones, 1990, p. 222). Hong Kong people responded by donating HK$70 million in 1989. However, if we analyse the Community Chest it gives us another glimpse into how public charity is perceived in the Colony. No mechanism of public accountability was built into the Community Chest. Despite slogans such as 'The Community Chest serves our community best' and 'Every cent is well spent', it is a self-appointed committee which decides how the money is spent. Because of the popularity of the Chest and the amount of money that it raised, voluntary groups and associations could not afford to ignore it. However, any groups and associations which participated found that the government reassessed their grants accordingly to take account of money they received from the Chest (Kwan, 1986, p.184). Once again, the government was tightly controlling access to funding for welfare agencies.

6 MAKING SENSE OF SOCIAL WELFARE IN HONG KONG

As we have seen, the Hong Kong state in the post-war period has remained committed to liberal principles of non-intervention and this has determined the essential parameters of social policy. First, although expenditure has increased substantially, it has not been realized through raising taxation levels. The expansion of the social services has been directly linked to a buoyant economy and it has been made clear that such expenditure must not interfere with economic development. Second, involvement has been financed from general revenue and no attempt has been made to establish contributory or cost-sharing schemes. Third, despite substantial subvention levels, for the most part there has been no conscious effort to coordinate the various social services. Most intervention has taken the form of crisis intervention. Fourth, there has been no formal recognition of social welfare as an indisputable right. It continues to be defined in terms of charity and benevolence and it is constantly reiterated that people should look to the family, voluntary agencies and the market for their welfare needs. The state has been aided in successfully maintaining these parameters by two factors: first, immigration meant that Hong Kong has had a very young population and, second, the spectacular economic success of the colony has guaranteed full employment and rising incomes for the majority of the population. Extreme labour shortages in the late 1980s resulted in significant increases in wage levels with basic unskilled wages averaging approximately £3,500 per year with some factories offering a £200 monthly bonus to anyone staying three months. However, in the same time-period top government officials were earning over £50,000 (with perks) and stock-broker analysts were being offered signing-on fees of £200,000 and salaries of £150,000 (Rafferty, 1991).

Nevertheless, it has to be recognized that the parameters have been challenged from the 1970s onwards. Despite attempts to prevent the politicization of welfare, this is exactly what happened as a result of its increasing state involvement in the delivery of welfare provision. Although there have been no major industrial or political confrontations in Hong Kong since the late 1960s, the reforms of the 1970s combined to unleash new political and social processes in the colony. The political reforms created formal structures for the airing of grievances and channels for citizen participation (Lee, 1982).

In the course of the 1970s and '80s grassroots pressure groups, with the support of a new generation of radical social and community workers (Hong Kong's new middle class), began to organize and campaign in order to protect and promote their interests. It is no coincidence that the most serious campaigning concentrated on public housing, the area in which the state was most directly involved. There were successful colony-wide protests about the lack of facilities on housing estates, lack of consultation, forced relocation policies and waiting-lists and rent strikes against proposed rent increases. Whilst many of these protests were issue-based and involved short-lived coalitions, there is little doubt that they constituted a form of community politics not previously seen in the colony. Ironically, 'Instead of calming down social protest, it [the government's reform programme] stimulated demand, fostered community organizations, and politically enfranchised the residents at the local level. This done, violent protest receded, but it was exchanged for a greater say by the people in the running of local affairs' (Castells *et al.,* 1990, p. 150).

Many of the pressure groups that emerged out of these community-based campaigns linked into renewed demands for political changes to the colony's decision-making process. As a consequence, fully fledged political pressure groups campaigning for a more responsive and accountable form of government emerged in the second half of the 1970s. In response to renewed demands for the extension of social and political rights, the government became more intricately involved in public debates about the future of social welfare provision and political change. In 1980 the government announced that elections, based on a universal adult franchise, would take place for District Boards. Although these Boards had no real powers, the community pressure groups took the opportunity to consolidate their formal political position. At the same time trade unionists, social workers and church representatives were appointed to the Legco. Through these community representatives the contentious issues of increased social welfare and democratic reform were placed on the colony's political agenda (Cheng, 1991). In addition, as Castells *et al.* have argued, in Hong Kong a comprehensive social wage exists in the form of heavily subsidized housing. So how can we explain the presence of this significant social wage in an avowedly laissez-faire society?

Given the scale of the squatting problems caused by immigration, the government could not afford not to intervene. Because all land in Hong Kong is Crown land and because of the scarcity of land, the state could not entertain squatting in the way other developing societies have. As was noted earlier, squatting threatened the very survival of the colony. In addition, Castells *et al.* have chronicled how involvement in the provision of mass housing underpinned economic development. They argue that 'the main structural effect of the public housing programme has been its role in the reproduction of labour power' (1990, p. 114) and, as such, is the fundamental component of the social wage in Hong Kong. It has been estimated that the amount of subsidy from government to tenants of a public housing unit in the mid 1980s was equivalent to 70 per cent of that household's income (Yu and Lai, 1985). The public housing programme enabled Hong Kong workers to survive on low wages for their long working hours, without putting excessive pressure on firms. In addition it also created, through life tenure and low rents, a fundamental safety-net for families in a society without social insurance and minimum welfare provision. Finally, the programme ensured social stability and provided material expression of citizenship to a largely immigrant population, particularly after the social crisis of the late 1960s.

In the aftermath of the reforms ushered in by Sir Murray MacLehose, many political reformers and community activists hoped that the Hong Kong government would eventually move towards accepting a more institutional model of social welfare. However, in 1984 the British government – without consulting the people of Hong Kong – signed an agreement returning the colony to Chinese sovereignty on 1 July 1997. Despite the assurances that under the 'one country, two systems' formula nothing would change for fifty years after 1997, the shock-waves of this agreement reverberated throughout Hong Kong. In an effort to restabilize the colony the government immediately issued proposals for the development of representative government. In 1985 elections were held for the first time to elect twenty-four unofficial members to the Legco. The election was not by universal suffrage but through nine functional constituencies, representing various groupings in society, and an electoral college. In addition the District Board elections held in the same year provided an avenue for pro-democracy, pro-social welfare pressure groups to consolidate their political position. This politicization process intensified in the aftermath of the Tian'anmen Square massacre in Beijing in June 1989 (see Ming Pao News, 1989). In addition to the first mass demonstrations since the late 1960s taking place, pro-democracy candidates won sixteen of the eighteen contested seats in the first direct elections for Legco held in September 1991.

This rapid change set the alarm bells ringing amongst the colony's ruling élites because many of those elected in both the 1985 and 1991 elections supported the expansion of social welfare provision. Concern was expressed by representatives of the business community that the introduction of elections had led to the politicization of welfare: 'We are all aware of demagogues and their gospel of "free lunches" and the possibility of turning Hong Kong into a welfare state. These people do not hesitate to bribe the masses rather than to build for our future' (quoted in *South China Morning Post,* 26 October 1990). The government was also warned by business leaders against increasing social welfare expenditure as a means of buying off discontent and instability.

They need not have worried, as official statements and actions in the early 1990s indicated that the government had decided to take a stand against the further expansion of its welfare commitments. The 1991 review of social welfare, for example, stressed that:

> The welfare programmes of Hong Kong have been designed and developed with cognizance of the innate local values of concern for the family, commitment to self-improvement, self-reliance, mutual support and generosity, reluctance to be dependent upon 'welfare', high respect for social order and a combination of ingenuity and resourcefulness.

(Hong Kong Government, 1991b, p. 2)

Towards the end of 1991 an austerity programme was introduced to ensure that public expenditure was kept under control. It was announced – without consultation with the Hong Kong Council of Social Services – that the social welfare budget was to lose HK$370 million between 1992 and 1996 and the voluntary sector was informed where the cuts would be made. This resulted in widespread protests from social workers, trade unions and community groups, and representatives of the voluntary sector stated that the partnership had been broken by the government (*South China Morning Post*, 4 January 1992). The government refused to back down, pointing out that the cuts could have been more severe.

One group was particularly affected by the hardening of government attitudes in the late 1980s and early 1990s. Until 1982 the Hong Kong government had an 'open centre' policy which allowed Vietnamese refugees freedom of movement and employment within the colony. However, in July 1982 a 'closed camp' policy was introduced. These camps were run by the prison authorities and new arrivals were incarcerated in order to deter the Vietnamese from coming to Hong Kong. Despite this, in the mid 1980s the numbers of arrivals remained high and in 1988 a new policy was adopted. Under this revised policy Vietnamese arriving after 16 June 1988 were treated as illegal immigrants unless they could prove otherwise. 'Screening' procedures were tightened up and those defined as illegal immigrants were held pending repatriation. In doing so, Hong Kong was unilaterally renouncing the 1979 Geneva agreement on Vietnamese refugees (Cunliffe, 1990). In November 1989 the government announced the imminent introduction of mandatory repatriation. On 12 December 1990 fifty-one people were forcibly repatriated and in late 1991 a further eighty-seven were repatriated under the colony's 'Orderly Return Programme'. In May 1992 Britain finally signed an agreement with Vietnam for the compulsory return of nearly all 55,700 'boat-people' held in camps in Hong Kong.

These draconian measures have been justified on the grounds that giving the Vietnamese access to public housing, education and health would place an unacceptable burden upon the colony's social services. In May 1991 Legco agreed that further building of accommodation for the boat-people should cease. In fact, as Leonard Davis (1990) has shown, the government has deliberately left the majority of welfare provision for the boat-people to charitable organizations, saying that it is not Hong Kong's problem. The vast majority of the money that the government spends goes towards covering the security costs of maintaining the closed camps. Hence, in the course of the 1980s and 1990s the government has implemented policies which are designed to keep 'undesirables' out of 'Fortress Hong Kong'. It is determined to do nothing that could possibly act as a positive incentive for asylum-seekers to come to the colony. In doing so, it has made clear which sections of the population are eligible for welfare and which sections are not.

7 CONCLUSION

In the countdown to 1997 it seems as if there will be little dramatic change to the Hong Kong government's welfare policies. Certainly, there seems little chance that the government will become more involved in the provision of welfare. In fact, through privatization, devolved management strategies and reiterating that families should take responsibility for their members, the government seems determined to distance itself further from front-line welfare responsibilities. Turner et al. (1980), in their analysis of Hong Kong in the late 1970s, argued that there were two effective forms of restraint on the further development of social provision in the colony. The first was the lack of democracy and the second was the economic framework: 'any substantial change in taxation and government expenditure, or accelerated raising of social standards by, for example, such devices as a legal minimum wage or improved social assistance, is limited by the compulsive need to preserve the flexibility of the economy in changing world market conditions and opportunities' (Turner et al., 1980, p. 11).

The other reason why the government is unlikely to deviate from its present position is the reunification with the People's Republic of China (PRC) in 1997. The latter has always paid close attention to developments in the colony and has periodically expressed particular concern about social and political matters, especially any moves towards democratization or increased public expenditure on social welfare. It has been suggested that one additional reason why the Hong Kong government has been extremely wary in the field of welfare provision is because the PRC disapproves of anything approximating a welfare state. As Peter Hodge pointed out, 'There are remarkable comparisons to be made between China's provision for education, medical services, public assistance and housing [and that of Hong Kong] ... It is conceivable, although never discussed, that for fairly obvious reasons in light of 1997 and beyond, the social developments of the two neighbours are being kept in step' (Hodge, 1981, pp. 15–16).

The welfare regime of the PRC is an amalgam of different ideological influences – Confucianism which, as we have seen previously, stresses that the family should be the primary welfare institution and Marxism/Maoism which emphasizes a proletarian work ethic and propagates the virtues of diligence, frugality and thrift, mutual and collective responsibility and self-reliance. There is also a high degree of decentralization in the delivery of welfare services in China. Because of the emphasis on self-reliance and mutual aid, local work units are responsible for deciding on the appropriate level of welfare support for their members and for financing and distributing that support. Furthermore,

> China's welfare philosophy insists that welfare support expand only as production expands, and that there be neither a radical vertical redistribution of income nor a diversion of resources from more immediately productive uses. Welfare support, then, must be provided in a way that does not foster a sense of welfare dependency and frustrate the consolidation of socialism.
>
> (Dixon and Macrov, 1992, p.11)

The PRC has made it clear that it wants Hong Kong, in conjunction with its other Special Economic Zones, to be at the forefront of its modernization drive (Hartland-Thunberg, 1990). As a consequence, the Beijing government has entered alliance with Hong Kong's conservative business élites to ensure that the linked demands for increased democracy and more extensive welfare provision are neutralized. Ideologically, laissez-faire colonialism will be replaced by Chinese communism but it looks as if the people of Hong Kong and their families will still have to work hard for their own welfare in the twenty-first century.

REFERENCES

Appelbaum, R. and Henderson, J. (eds) (1992) *States and Development in the Asian Pacific Rim*, London, Sage.

Association for the Advancement of Feminism (1992) *Women's News Digest*, no. 25, January.

Baker, H. (1979) *Chinese Family and Kinship*, London and Basingstoke, Macmillan.

Benton, G. (1983) *The Hong Kong Crisis*, London, Pluto Press.

Cameron, N. (1991) *An Illustrated History of Hong Kong*, Hong Kong, Oxford University Press.

Castells, M. (1992) 'Four Asian tigers with a dragon head: a comparative analysis of the state, economy and society in the Asian Pacific rim' in Appelbaum, R. and Henderson, J. (eds) op. cit.

Castells, M., Goh, L. and Kwok, R. Y. W. (1990) *The Shek Kip Mei Syndrome*, London, Pion.

Chan, M. K. (1990) 'Labour vs Crown: aspects of society–state interactions in the Hong Kong labour movement before World War Two' in Sinn, E (ed.) *Between East and West: aspects of social and political development in Hong Kong*, Hong Kong, Centre for Asian Studies.

Cheng, J. Y. S (1991) 'Political modernization in Hong Kong', *Journal of Commonwealth and Comparative Studies*, vol. xxix, no. 5, pp. 294–320.

Chow, N. (1986a) 'The past and future development of social welfare in Hong Kong' in Cheng, J. Y. S. (ed.) *Hong Kong in Transition*, Hong Kong, Oxford University Press.

Chow, N. (1986b) 'A review of social policies in Hong Kong' in Kwan, A. Y. H. and Chan, D. K. K. (eds) op. cit.

Chow, N. (1987) 'Moving into New Towns: the costs of social adaptation', *Asian Journal of Public Administration*, vol. 9, no. 2, pp. 132–43.

Commission for Resettlement (1955) *Annual Report*, Hong Kong, Government Printer.

Cunliffe, S. A. (1990) 'Vietnamese refugees in Hong Kong and the lessons for the international community', *Politics*, vol. 10, no. 2, pp. 9–14.

Davies, K. (1990) *Hong Kong to 1994: a question of confidence*, London, Economist Intelligence Unit.

Davis, L. (1990) *Hong Kong and the Asylum Seekers from Vietnam*, London and Basingstoke, Macmillan.

Deyo, F. C. (1989) *Beneath the Miracle: labour subordination in the new Asian industrialism*, Berkeley, CA, University of California Press.

Dixon, J. and Macrov, D. (eds) (1992) *Social Welfare in Socialist Countries*, London, Routledge.

Donnison, D. (1985) *The Egalitarian Approach to Social Policy*, Hong Kong, Hong Kong University Press.

England, J. and Rear, J. (1975) *Chinese Labour Under British Rule*, Hong Kong, Oxford University Press.

Fung, Y. W. (1986) 'Education' in Cheng, J.Y.S. (ed.) *Hong Kong in Transition*, Hong Kong, Oxford University Press.

George, V. and Wilding, P. (1985) *Ideology and Social Welfare*, London, Routledge.

Harris, R. and Seldon, A. (1979) *Over-ruled on Welfare*, London, Institute of Economic Affairs.

Hartland-Thunberg, P. (1990) *China, Hong Kong, Taiwan and the World Trading System*, New York, St Martin's Press.

Hodge, P. (1973) 'Social policy: an historical perspective as seen in colonial policy', *Journal of Oriental Studies*, vol. xi, no. 2, pp. 207–19.

Hodge, P. (1981) 'The politics of welfare' in Jones, J. F. (ed.) *The Common Welfare: Hong Kong's social services*, Hong Kong, Chinese University Press.

Hong Kong Government (1954) *Hong Kong Annual Report*, Hong Kong, Government Printer.

Hong Kong Government (1965) *Aims and Policy for Social Welfare*, Hong Kong, Government Printer.

Hong Kong Government (1991a) *Hong Kong*, Hong Kong, HK Government Printer.

Hong Kong Government (1991b) *Five Year Plan for Social Welfare Development in Hong Kong*, Hong Kong, Government Printer.

International Project on Family and Community (1986) *High Rise Families, Hong Kong*, Victoria, Australia, Consultancy Report no. 1.

Jones, C. (1990) *Promoting Prosperity: the Hong Kong way of social policy*, Hong Kong, Chinese University Press.

Kwan, A. Y. H. (1986) 'Social welfare and services in Hong Kong' in Kwan, A. Y. H. and Chan, D. K. K. (eds) op. cit.

Kwan, A. Y. H. and Chan, D. K. K. (eds) (1986) *Hong Kong Society: a reader*, Hong Kong, Writers' and Publishers' Cooperative.

Kwong, C. K. (1990) 'Emigration and manpower shortage' in Wong, Y. C. R. and Cheng, Y. S. J. (eds) op. cit.

Lau, E. (1990) 'Old age tensions', *Far Eastern Economic Review*, no. 1 March, pp. 22–4.

Lau, S. K. (1981) 'Utilitarian familism: the basis of political stability' in King, A. Y. C. and Lee, R. P, L. (eds) *Social Life and Development in Hong Kong*, Hong Kong, Chinese University Press.

Lau, S. K. and Wan, P. S. (1991) 'Attitudes towards to social problems' in Lau, S. K., Lee, M. K., Wan, P. S. and Wong, S. L. (eds) *Hong Kong: indicators of social development*, Hong Kong, Hong Kong Institute of Asian Pacific Studies.

Lee, M. K. (1982) 'Emerging patterns of social conflict in Hong Kong society' in Cheng, J. Y. S (ed.) *Hong Kong in the 1980s*, Hong Kong, Summerson Eastern Publishers Ltd.

Leung, B. K. P. (ed.) (1990) *Social Issues in Hong Kong*, Hong Kong, Oxford University Press.

Miners, N. (1989) *The Government and Politics of Hong Kong*, Hong Kong, Oxford University Press.

Ming Pao News (1989) *June Four: a chronicle of the Chinese democratic uprising*, Fayetteville, University of Arkansas Press.

Mosher, S. and Taylor, M. (1991) 'Undeclared interests', *Far Eastern Economic Review*, no. 7, November, pp. 22–6.

Murray, C. (1984) *Losing Ground*, New York, Basic Books.

Ng, A. (1990) 'Medical and health' in Wong, R.Y.C. and Cheng, J.Y.S. (eds) op. cit.

Phillips, D. R. (ed.) (1992) *Ageing in East and South East Asia*, London, Edward Arnold.

Rabushka, A. (1979) *Hong Kong*, Chicago, IL, Chicago University Press.

Rafferty, K. (1991) *City on the Rocks*, Harmondsworth, Penguin Books.

Rayner, L. (1992) 'Hong Kong: prospects for democracy', *The Round Table: The Commonwealth Journal of International Affairs*, no. 332, pp. 229–37.

Redding, S. G. (1990) *The Spirit of Chinese Capitalism*, Berlin, Walter De Gruyter.

Regnier, P. (1987) *Singapore: city state in South East Asia*, London, Hirst and Co.

Riedel, J. (1979) *The Industrialization of Hong Kong*, Tübingen, J. C. B Mohr.

Salaff, J. (1981) *Working Daughters of Hong Kong*, Cambridge, Cambridge University Press.

Schiffer, J. (1991) 'State policy and economic growth: a note on the Hong Kong model', *International Journal of Urban and Regional Research*, vol. 15, no. 2, pp. 180–96.

Scott, I. (1989) *Political Change and the Crisis of Legitimacy in Hong Kong*, Hong Kong, Oxford University Press.

Sinn, E. (1989) *Power and Charity*, Hong Kong, Oxford University Press.

Social Welfare Office (1954) *Annual Report*, Hong Kong, Government Printer.

Tsai, J. F. (1993) *Hong Kong in Chinese History*, New York, Columbia University Press.

Turner, H. A., Fosh, P., Gardner, M., Hart, K., Morris, R., Ng Sek-hong, Painlan, M. and Yerbury, D. (1980) *The Last Colony: but whose?*, Cambridge, Cambridge Univeristy Press.

Waldron, S. (1976) 'Fire on the Rim: a study in contradictions in left-wing mobilization', unpublished PhD thesis, Syracuse University, Syracuse, NY.

Wong, Y. C. (1988) 'Symposium on Central Provident Fund' in *Hong Kong Economic Papers*, no. 18, Hong Kong, Asian Research Service.

Wong, Y. C. R. and Cheng, Y. S. J. (eds) (1990) *The Other Hong Kong Report*, Hong Kong, Chinese University Press.

Young, J. Y. S. (1981) 'Political modernization in Hong Kong', *Journal of Commonwealth and Comparative Studies*, vol. xxiv, no. 5.

Youngson, A. J. (1982) *Hong Kong: economic growth and policy*, Hong Kong, Oxford University Press.

Yu, F. L. and Lai, S. M. (1985) 'The welfare costs of Hong Kong's public housing programme', *Urban Studies*, vol. 22, pp. 133–40.

Yuen, P. P. (1991) 'The implications of the corporatization of health care delivery in Hong Kong', *Asian Journal of Public Administration*, vol. 13, no. 1, pp. 23–38.

CHAPTER 6
THE GERMAN WELFARE STATE: A CONSERVATIVE REGIME IN CRISIS

MICHAEL WILSON

1 GERMANY AS A CONSERVATIVE WELFARE REGIME

The reconstruction of West Germany after 1945 was both economic and political, with a new Federal constitution which limited the powers of the central state and gave considerable autonomy to the Federal states (the *Länder*). Besides guaranteeing individual liberties, the new constitution also reproduced many of the features of the old Bismarckian or Imperial welfare state. A conservative definition of social rights and obligations, including those relating to welfare benefits and the primacy of the family, is enshrined in the Basic Law. Although there is some variation between the *Länder* in the ways in which social services are provided, the Basic Law ensures that the key elements of the German welfare state are uniformly applied throughout the Federal Republic. This is particularly the situation with respect to the main form of income support – that of Social Security.

German Social Security is nationally administered and is based firmly on a principle of status maintenance through a system of compulsory social insurance contributions in which benefits are strictly proportional to former earnings. Claimants' welfare incomes, when claiming sickness or unemployment benefit or in retirement, reflect their work incomes. Esping-Andersen (1990) suggests that status maintenance is a defining characteristic of a *conservative* welfare regime (see page 8 in Chapter 1 of this book); in the German case, this principle must also be seen in the context of a welfare regime which has distinctively pro-family ideals and which, by law, preserves a large role for voluntary bodies in the provision of social services, particularly the churches.

The German welfare system includes another form of income support for those who do not have an adequate contributions record to qualify for Social Security. This is Social Assistance and here benefits paid are calculated according to needs rather than by relation to former earnings. Social Assistance is intended as a 'safety-net' of minimum income and is strongly demarcated from Social Security. Social Security is administered by the Federal Ministry of Labour and is paid as of right according to contributions records. Social Assistance is discretionary and is paid through Social Affairs offices of the *Länder*. Social Assistance is also subject to the principle of *subsidiarity*, which is a central aspect of the conservative German welfare regime.

In German law subsidiarity requires that claimants must show that neither their own resources nor those of their family are adequate to meet minimum needs before they are considered eligible for assistance. In practice this entails a family means-test in which partners are responsible for each other, and parents for children and vice versa. The second aspect of subsidiarity is contained in the Federal Social Assistance Act which specifies that the state and the *Länder* must collaborate with voluntary welfare organizations in the provision of services such as children's homes, residential care for old people, and some social work training. The requirement that the state (including the *Länder*) shall not assume functions which voluntary bodies or families can and should provide in caring for those in need is traced by Jarré (1991, p. 211) to the social encyclical of Pope Pius XI in 1931, itself a notably conservative document in its emphasis on the sanctity of marriage and the family and in its anti-abortion stand. Germany's Basic Law allows abortion only where the mother's life is in danger or where there is a serious risk to health (Flamm, 1983, p. 42). Subsidiarity has resulted in a large voluntary sector in the provision of welfare services (excluding cash benefits) in Germany; it was estimated in the late 1980s to involve 760,000 paid workers, assisted by 1,500,000 volunteers (Jarré, 1991, p. 216).

The characterization of Germany's welfare regime as 'conservative-corporate' (by Esping-Andersen, 1990) is based on the distinctive features of welfare programmes and social policies in West Germany (FRG, the Federal Republic of Germany, sometimes referred to here as the Federal government). The former German Democratic Republic (GDR, or East Germany) was very different both in its policy objectives (particularly for women) and in its system of social security. Above all, the GDR guaranteed a right to work for all adult citizens which was matched by the responsibility to work for most citizens – men and women. The GDR's equivalent of Social Security was confined to the long-term sick, pensioners and disabled people, while medical treatment was free. Unemployment benefit was felt to be unnecessary in a command economy which maintained full employment, even if this policy also entailed inefficiency, over-staffing and low income per head by Western standards.

The treaty of unification of October 1990 which united Germany (as an expanded Federal Republic) also extended West German laws, including welfare and social legislation, throughout the former GDR. The collapse of the Eastern economy (whose Gross Domestic Product was estimated to be 40 per cent lower within two years of the treaty of unification) produced large-scale unemployment, much of which was hidden in work creation schemes, in training programmes, and by early retirement.

The official unemployment rate (in August 1992, two years after unification) was reported as 14.4 per cent in the old GDR and 6.0 per cent in the former West Germany but the true rates were closer to 31 per cent and 8.2 per cent respectively, when account is taken of disguised unemployment.[1] Even this may have understated the true position in the East where, broadly, 45 per cent of jobs disappeared after unification (Riedmüller, 1992). Many of these 'lost' positions were those held by women who were driven back into the family and off the official count of those unemployed or into early retirement at an earlier age than men who were unemployed. This reflects the conservative aspects of German welfare programmes where care in the community, of old people and of young children, has been a task for women who are 'normally' outside the labour market. The most striking illustration of the differences in the gendering of labour-market policies in the East and the West was the provision of kindergarten places for working mothers. In the old GDR, provision of pre-school places was virtually universal and at a token cost (Heinen, 1990), whereas in West Germany kindergarten places were unsubsidized and rarely satisfied 20 per cent of demand at the best (Senftleben, 1992a, p. 85)

The Federal government attempted to deal with the employment crisis in the East by extending West German labour-market and welfare programmes, with their conservative social policy objectives, to the five new *Länder* (plus East Berlin as part of the new *Land* of Berlin) into which the old GDR was divided. This produced both a severe funding problem for the German welfare state and the German economy and a conflict of welfare values between East and West. The specific contrasts between the two welfare regimes and the strains which unification produced are discussed later in this chapter. A more detailed examination of the West German welfare regime is useful before making comparisons with the welfare regime of the GDR.

The right to welfare support (especially to income support) and access to welfare programmes such as health care and education is a fundamental part of the post-war concept of German citizenship. As indicated earlier, the West German approach to income support had two main aspects: the first (Social Security) was insurance-based while the second (Social Assistance) was paid on the basis of proven need. These two aspects of the dual system will be considered in turn in the next two sections.

2   THE DUAL SYSTEM I:
THE SOCIAL SECURITY STATE

The core of the welfare system is a mandatory scheme in which employers and workers co-insure against loss of income through sickness and unemployment, contribute to retirement pensions, and insure against the costs of medical treatment – the system of social insurance, to which both employees and employers contribute a percentage of income. Those active in the labour market are covered by the insurance-based schemes which are administered by private corporations, composed of representatives of employees and employers, except for public-sector employees whose insurance benefits are paid directly from government revenues. The funds which the private sector administers are autonomous and do not form part of public expenditure totals. Partly for this reason, political debate in Germany has not, until recently, identified the greater part of welfare spending (that is, Social Security rather than Social Assistance) as a 'burden' on the performance of the economy, although its costs are considerable. Another reason for the late emergence of a 'welfare back-lash' in Germany, along the lines of British and US arguments since the mid 1970s, has been the universalism of social insurance in Germany and its inclusion of the middle-class rather than being primarily a system for the poor. The British system of income support, in contrast, has mainly covered the lower-income groups who had limited access to occupational pensions and whose employment has either been more precarious or has been in declining 'heavy' industries with a large proportion of manual workers. Thus, although nominally universal, British income support or social security schemes have been characterized by what Titmuss (1963) termed a 'division of welfare', in which middle-class groups had much greater opportunities for private welfare and working-class groups relied almost entirely on state provision.

Le Grand and Winter (1987) argue that in the British case, those welfare programmes which serve the middle class (such as education and health) suffered far less during the new right welfare backlash of the 1980s than did programmes which (almost) exclusively served the poor (such as social security, public housing and the personal social services). (See also Chapter 3, pp. 55–6.) In Germany both social security and health care have been welfare programmes which have included the whole population (except the very rich) for a long time.

The 'middle-class' foundation of the German welfare state has a long history, dating back to the 1880s and Bismarck. The first unification of Germany in 1870 brought together a large number of disparate states with economies of greatly varying levels of economic development, particularly in the proportion of the labour force engaged in industry. The states along the north Rhine and especially the Ruhr (in contrast to eastern Germany and Prussia) were already experiencing their first industrial revolution and, in consequence, there was a growing industrial proletariat which suffered from the steep trade-cycles of the last quarter of the nineteenth century (Clapham, 1963, Ch. 11) and which supported the then Marxist Social Democratic Party (SPD). One of Bismarck's aims was to bind the new working class into the new German Empire. Negotiations with the leaders of the SPD produced the first schemes of social insurance in Europe, directed firstly at the 'labour aristocracy' and later extended to the large class of civil servants and others. By 1911 Germany had extended social insurance to cover 13.6 million men across a wide range of social classes, from agricultural workers to civil servants and white-collar workers in the private sector (Clapham, 1963, p. 333), in contrast to Britain where national (i.e. social) insurance was still in its infancy. The conservative project of contributory social security as a means of ensuring social order and incorporating the new working class was the founding principle of the Bismarckian welfare state.

The coverage of social insurance in Germany across such a wide range of employees ensured the support and legitimacy of the principle of social insurance amongst the middle class as well as the working class. Johnson's (1985) account of the ferocity of the English debate in the Edwardian period over fears that social insurance ('national insurance' in Britain) would drive out self-help and thrift, contrasts with the position in Germany twenty years earlier where the principles of state-sponsored social insurance schemes were accepted by the German labour movement and, more reluctantly, by employers (Clapham, 1963, Ch. 11). The adoption of national insurance in Britain between 1906 and 1911 for only a limited range of working-class occupations robbed the system of that 'middle-class legitimacy' which Leibfried (1989) argues is distinctive of Germany. He contrasts the 'targeting' of the early British welfare state on the relief of poverty and on the poor (what he calls a 'residual' welfare regime) with the widely-based 'social security state' which Germany had already built before the First World War and which continued in the post Second World War German Federal Republic (Leibfried, 1989, p. 16). Britain did not even approach a 'social security state' until after 1948 and the Labour government's National Insurance Acts (see Chapter 2 in this book). Even then, strong elements of the residual model of welfare continued to mark the British welfare regime, in social security and income maintenance.

The post-war German state entrenched in its Constitution the principles of universal social security for those active in the labour market. For non-economically active women the German social security state assumed that benefits 'derived' from their male partner's contributions. With increasing divorce rates in West Germany, the conflict over benefit and pension entitlements intensified, producing a strongly gendered debate over welfare rights and responsibilities. The concept of the 'woman who services her man and her children' underlies the German welfare state and its social security provisions. Flamm, commenting on the German welfare state and its basis in German constitutional law, says:

> The special biological position of women and mothers must be reflected in the law. Specific protective legislation exists applicable only to women or to mothers. The woman's equal right to participation in gainful employment cannot be divorced from the background of maternal obligations and the health of the family.
>
> (Flamm, 1983, p. 43)

and later:

> Marriage as a conjugal association intended to be for life, is an essential concept of the Basic Law (Federal Court of Justice). The [Marriage Act] emphasizes the principle of partnership and the equal rights and equal responsibilities of the spouses. They bear the same surname and run the household by mutual agreement. Both spouses are entitled to be gainfully employed. However, the choice and exercise of this employment are subject to the precept that the

interests of the other spouse and the family deserve due attention. The spouses are under an obligation to one another to support the family suitably by means of their work and their property. If the housekeeping is left to one spouse (usually the wife and mother), he or she thereby fulfils the obligation to contribute to the household by working.

(Flamm, 1983, p. 44)

That unwaged work *is* left to the wife and mother more commonly in Germany than in other European states is evidenced by the comparatively low rate of women's labour-market participation. At 50.3 per cent in 1986 it was lower than any other advanced economy in the European Community, apart from the Netherlands. Moreover, the rate scarcely increased during the twenty-year period up to 1986 in contrast to other welfare states, even in other conservative regimes such as that of France (see Table 6.1).

Table 6.1   Women's labour-market participation rates in selected European countries, 1966–1986 (per cent of women aged 15–64 years)

	1966	1970	1975	1980	1986
Germany	48.5	48.1	49.6	50.0	50.3
UK	49.9	50.7	55.1	58.3	61.0
Sweden	55.3	59.4	67.6	74.1	78.3
Denmark	55.1	58.0	63.5	–	76.5
France	46.4	48.3	51.2	54.4	55.3
Belgium	38.6	40.2	44.0	48.2	51.3
Netherlands	–	–	31.0	35.4	41.1

Source: OECD, 1988

Thus a high proportion of German women are reliant on derived benefits from their husbands. Where divorce has occurred, this brings particular problems for unemployed women and for women in retirement who rely on a share of their former husband's pension. The social security state made limited attempts to address the gender inequalities of divorce within a system in which the husband is 'normally' employed and the mother of dependent children 'normally' at home as an unwaged housewife. But this has produced only marginal changes to the dependent position of married women in West Germany. The dependency of wives on husbands through the West German social security system is one of the strongest points of contrast with social policy and its consequences in the former GDR.

The basic feature of the German system of social security is high benefits for high contributions. A German worker would typically contribute 25 per cent of his or her salary in unemployment and sickness insurance and, in addition, pay taxes on income. The benefits are proportional to contributions. The first tier of unemployment benefit pays 63 per cent of former earnings, rising to 68 per cent for those with dependent children. Similar proportions apply for those who are unemployed because of sickness.[2] Pensions are also related to contributions and therefore to former earnings. The close relationship between incomes in work and levels of income support in unemployment or retirement reproduces the same inequalities outside the labour market as occur within it. Thus Leisering (1988) characterizes the German social security system as one of 'status-maintenance' in which the same status differentials are preserved when not working as when claimants were working, albeit at a reduced level of income. Those who were low-earners when at work will have low benefits when unemployed or retired, while those on average and above-average work incomes will gain levels of income support which reflect their relative earning power in the labour market. Given that income inequalities from employment in Germany are large, it follows that there are correspondingly large inequalities in Social Security incomes.

Germany's 'status maintenance' system of social security can be contrasted with the British system of flat-rate benefits in Income Support and Unemployment Benefit, which produces an equality for the unemployed, as long as one disregards personal savings and access to resources outside the income support schemes. It can be further, and perhaps more usefully, compared to the Swedish social-democratic model (see Chapter 7 of this book). This was: '... explicitly committed to mitigating class and gender inequalities, with the result that inequalities of income and living conditions were significantly less than in most other Western countries' (Ginsburg, ibid., section 1).

In contrast to the Swedish welfare regime, the German social security state operates in such a way as to mirror the inequalities produced by a capitalist labour market without any concern to reduce income inequalities. It does, however, provide a more generous 'safety-net' of minimum income than Britain, through the rates paid for Social Assistance – the second element of the dual welfare system. This relative 'generosity' of the German welfare regime comes at a comparatively high cost to both employers and workers.

Taxes and social security contributions in Germany account for a significantly higher proportion of workers' pay and of Gross National Product than in Britain. In 1978 the combined total of taxes and social security contributions in Germany amounted to 38.7 per cent of GNP compared to 34.3 per cent in Britain (Scharpf, 1983, p. 11), putting Germany near the top of the European Community league of deductions from personal incomes. This gap widened with the reduction of direct taxes on incomes in Britain during the 1980s. As a result, the 'burden' of taxation (including social/national insurance) is higher in Germany than in Britain. Average net income in Western Germany is 67 per cent of gross income (Institut der deutschen Wirtschaft, 1992a) compared to 75 per cent in Britain (Atkinson, 1991).

The new right argument (developed from the mid 1970s in Britain and the USA), that high levels of personal taxation are detrimental to economic growth and to work incentives by discouraging extra effort, has not been tested against the German experience, where the marginal rate of taxation (including social security contributions as well as income taxes) is amongst the highest in Europe, after Sweden and the other Scandinavian countries' welfare regimes. The apparent paradox of high levels of German personal 'taxation' going hand-in-hand with the most successful economy in Europe but without a political reaction against 'excessive' welfare spending can be explained by the fact that the size of social insurance contributions in Germany is visibly and individually linked to the size of benefits, including pensions – the biggest single personal benefit in the social security system, at a projected 38.8 per cent of social expenditure in 1990 (Wienand, 1988, p. 11). As a consequence, contributions are not perceived as taxation but rather as insurance in the strict sense of the term where benefits are directly linked to the size of contributions.

Britain, in contrast, retained a graduated system of social insurance *contributions* (with a contributions ceiling somewhat above average earnings) without graduated *benefits*. The lack of a link in Britain between earnings status and benefit entitlement meant the absence of the status maintenance principle of the conservative welfare state and the likelihood that social insurance contributions would be perceived as another tax rather than as genuine insurance. This goes some way to explaining why an ideology of a 'welfare burden' more easily took root in Britain than in a conservative welfare regime such as Germany's.

3 THE DUAL SYSTEM II: SOCIAL ASSISTANCE

Social Assistance (*Sozialhilfe*) is an entirely separate system of income maintenance from Social Security, with roots in the poor relief of the nineteenth century, which in turn derived from a religious and charitable tradition of alms-giving from the middle ages onwards. Thus it has a longer pedigree than does Social Security and one which, as Leibfried says, makes the claimant an *applicant* rather than a *client* (1979, p. 74). The scale-rates for Social Assistance, to ensure a 'dignified existence' (according to the Basic Law), are those recommended by the German Association for Public and Private Relief. This Association is made up of religious and voluntary bodies, trade unions and the German Red Cross. Although the Social Assistance rates are not binding on the regional states, they are fairly uniformly applied, with small variations for differences in the cost of living. In the post-war period Ginsburg estimates that Social Assistance rates represented about 20 per cent of net average earnings, but this appears to exclude a number of linked benefits including housing benefit, sickness and health benefits and special-needs payments. If these are taken into account, the total package of benefits for the average recipient of Social Assistance is better than 50 per cent of net average earnings (Ginsburg, 1992, p. 73).

Social Assistance was largely (80 per cent) financed by the local author-ities* until, hard-pressed by the influx of asylum-seekers in the early 1990s, Federal funds bailed them out. Local authorities are still respon-sible for paying for 'local' claimants as opposed to refugees. The potential of demand-driven expenditure paid for out of local taxation, compared to the national balanced budgets of the Social Security system, means that local councils have a strong incentive to control expenditure on Social Assistance. Since local authorities have a wide discretion in determining eligibility for Social Assistance and are answerable to local electorates for their expenditure, there exists an in-built political demand to tighten up on Social Assistance payments.

Claims on Social Assistance grew throughout the period from 1970. The number of claimants doubled during the first major recession in the western economies, that of the middle 1970s, from 0.75 million claimants in 1970 to 1.4 million claimants in 1980 (Ginsburg, 1992, p. 74) and the number continued to grow as unemployment rose throughout the 1980s. There were more than 3.5 million claimants of Social Assistance in 1988 – two years before unification (Voges and Rohwer, 1992).

Social Assistance is a non-contributory benefit: it does not depend upon a contributions record in the German economy; entitlement is based solely on need rather than on citizenship (Voges and Rohwer, 1992). Non-citi-zens may claim Social Assistance unless they are adjudged to have come to Germany with the intention of claiming assistance, in which case they may be deported unless they claim refugee status. Asylum-seekers who came to Germany in great numbers after the economic collapses in East-ern Europe at the end of the 1980s were paid Social Assistance as a matter of humanitarian policy rather than because they had a legal entitlement. Their status as non-citizens (awaiting court decisions on their status as political refugees) meant that the German government was able to reduce the rates paid to them by 25 per cent of the recom-mended minimum levels of Social Assistance as the idea of a 'refugee crisis' gathered momentum in the early 1990s. Not only were the rates at which Social Assistance was paid to refugees reduced, but the criteria for refugee status were more strictly enforced, as a result of constitutional changes.

Throughout Germany (in the East particularly but also in the West) those whose Social Security entitlement is low (because of low past earnings) may choose to claim Social Assistance rather than Social Security if it means higher benefit. Social Assistance, then, represents the German *poverty-line* or minimum standard of living. It is, however, more generous in its minimum income levels than the British equivalent and, in provid-ing additional cash grants for specific needs such as winter clothing and bedding, more resembles the British system before the changes of the 1980s.

---

* Communities and districts within the *Länder*, except in Bremen, Hamburg and Berlin where the *Länder* act as local as well as regional authorities.

Like Income Support (previously National Assistance then Supplementary Benefit) in Britain, German Social Assistance was intended to be of short duration. Its scale-rates are better than Britain's and Germany has fewer individuals in poverty than does Britain. Taking the poverty-line at 50 per cent of a country's average income, Germany had 11 per cent in poverty in 1985 and Britain had 16 per cent (Atkinson, 1991, p. 16). Germany's *per capita* income was also distinctly higher than Britain's.

The minimum standard of living of Social Assistance in Germany is set not by government, but by an autonomous body – the German Association for Public and Private Relief – who provide most of the German personal social services. Social Assistance is intended to be an exceptional method of income maintenance for those who have no other means and are in need. The official description of Social Assistance is 'help towards self-help', with the implication that the recipient will re-enter the 'normal' labour market or make themselves 'available for work' after an 'exceptional' period of Social Assistance.

Such a concept is rooted in the expectation of (male) full employment, a realistic assumption in Germany until the 1970s. It also reflected a gender-blind conception of labour-market opportunities in which women's Social Security rights could be assumed to be safely derived from their male partners. With the rise of longer-term unemployment, a rise in lone parenting (mainly by women, in common with Western European patterns generally) and a disproportionate increase in unemployment amongst non-citizens, Social Assistance claims have grown, as has the length of the period for which claims are made. Increasingly, Social Assistance has come under political attack in Germany in a very similar way to welfare expenditure in Britain and in the USA. Social Security payments, although defined as a problem (particularly the 'burden' of pensions) from the later 1970s onwards, have not attracted the same hostility as has Social Assistance even though the cost of pensions far outweighed all other forms of social expenditure (Wienand, 1988, p. 11). There appears here to be the same link between welfare programmes which mainly serve the poor, and which come under attack in a market economy which has run into difficulty, and those which serve the middle-class, and which are better protected in times of economic downturn (Le Grand and Winter, 1987).

One of the responses to rising unemployment was to end the agreements covering temporary workers which had been made by the German government from the 1950s to the early 1970s, particularly with Italy, Yugoslavia and Turkey. These agreements had provided for temporary work permits which were renewable and which could be extended for longer periods, or upgraded to permanent work permits. The continued rise of unemployment in the 1980s produced a response of downgrading many permanent work permits to temporary status. This increased the risk to non-citizens of deportation if they claimed Social Assistance since non-citizens on temporary work permits could be deported if they drew Social Assistance for a protracted time. The numbers of potential Social Assist-

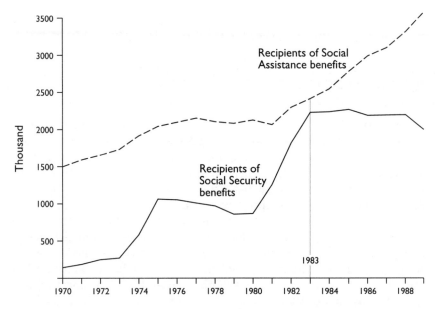

Figure 6.1   Number of recipients of Social Assistance benefits and Social Security benefits, 1970–89
Source: Voges and Rohwer, 1992, p. 178

ance claimants may well have been understated for a number of reasons, one of which was the risks which non-citizens ran when making claims.

Nevertheless, claims for Social Assistance continued to rise throughout the 1970s and '80s as labour-market conditions became more difficult. There was a common pattern of rising numbers of welfare claimants throughout the advanced economies from the 1970s onwards and Germany was not unusual. The point to note in the German case, however, is the way in which the rise in Social Security claims was contained after 1983, whilst Social Assistance claims continued to grow (see Figure 6.1). The visible difference here owed more to the way in which initiatives in the labour market and in work creation schemes transferred potential claimants from the ranks of the 'open' unemployed to those hidden in re-training schemes, temporary work programmes (ABM) and in further education which, in Germany, covers people of all ages below retirement age who are undergoing some form of job-related training.

Not surprisingly, Social Assistance is a system of benefit in Germany which has never carried the legitimacy of Social Security whose benefits have been 'earned'. Furthermore, according to Voges and Rohwer (1992), those most liable to become claimants for Social Assistance are single mothers, non-citizens and those caring for a dependent relative. In other words, labour-market opportunities and with them Social Security status and its protection are strongly conditioned by gender and by the citizen/ foreigner distinction. A disproportionate number of Social Assistance claimants were not 'available for work' and thus ineligible for Social Security benefits even had they qualified for them by a minimum of a year's insured employment in the preceding three years.

Although Voges and Rohwer's analysis is probably correct for West Germany, a different pattern emerged in the former East Germany, according to a small-scale study of Social Assistance claimants. In a comparison of one West Berlin district with an East Berlin district, Grossmann and Huth (1992) found that Eastern claimants of Social Assistance were much more likely to be those who were available for work but were unemployed.

As already stated, Social Assistance is the responsibility of the individual districts in Germany rather than the Federal state. Social Security, however, is sectorally based and, through the system of autonomous corporations, is immune to quarrelling between the *Länder* and the Federal government about who should bear the costs. In the system of Social Assistance the local authorities and the *Länder* are responsible for a needs-led system of income support over which they have little control (Senftleben, 1992a, p. 45). This was tolerable to the individual *Länder* as long as the rate at which Social Assistance claims rose was modest, along with the costs of work creation programmes and further education (that is, the total costs of unemployment, both open and hidden) and this was broadly the position until the mid 1970s. From this point onwards, however, claims for Social Assistance rose steadily throughout West Germany even before unification produced a marked acceleration in the total costs of unemployment.

4 SOCIAL ASSISTANCE AND THE PRINCIPLE OF COMPENSATION

The post-war German welfare state also operated a principle of compensation for those excluded from the labour market because of disability. As labour-market conditions became more difficult in the 1970s, this principle was further extended to 'compensate' certain groups such as older workers and mothers for leaving the labour market.

Compensation to 'victims' was a considerable expenditure throughout the history of the modern German welfare state. Until 1980 compensation payments from tax revenues exceeded the total of Social Assistance payments. By 1985 the ratio of 'victim compensation' payments to Social Assistance was 65 per cent even after the rapid increase in Social Assistance claims. If compensation to those leaving the labour market on grounds other than disability (early retirement, for example) is included, then compensation as a whole was broadly equal to Social Assistance expenditure.

Although both compensation and Social Assistance are non-insurance benefits, they are carefully distinguished in welfare legislation and in their social policy basis:

> Social Security is founded on the joint insurance of the insured ...
> Caring support (i.e. compensation) rests on the moral claims of vic-

tims. Social assistance, on the other hand, is not based on any [criterion] of achievement.
(Senftleben, 1992b, p. 1)

Thus the first two systems of income support are defined as legitimate claims and Social Assistance (by implication) as 'charity'. The ideological exposure of Social Assistance in Germany led to an increasing pressure towards labour-market solutions for Social Assistance claimants as their numbers rose. For women claimants of Social Assistance, particularly, this has highlighted certain tensions within the German conservative welfare regime.

Although Germany does not maintain specialized anti-fraud personnel in the administration of Social Assistance (unlike Britain and the USA in welfare claims), fraudulent claims are investigated in the case of specific suspicions such as undeclared cohabitation. Claims are assessed individually through interviews at local Social Affairs Offices and suspected fraud is investigated by local officials. Thus a 'case-work' approach is developed towards Social Assistance claimants which further distinguishes them from claimants of insurance benefits. Social Assistance fraud is prosecuted and benefits may also be withdrawn, although not where there are dependent children. Even so, control of the rising numbers of Social Assistance claims in the 1980s laid less emphasis on fraud control and more emphasis on reskilling and remotivating claimants to enter the labour force.

Increased funds were made available to the *Länder* for work creation projects specifically to employ Social Assistance claimants and to give them insured, if low-paid, work. The *maximum* salary allowed was 60 per cent of average individual incomes and was only slightly higher than Social Assistance rates after deductions for social insurance and taxes were made. Policies towards Social Assistance claimants served to marginalize them further, although it is doubtful if work creation projects had more than a limited effect on the total number of claimants. The bigger effect was produced by policies to restructure the labour force generally.

5   FAMILY, WELFARE AND THE LABOUR MARKET

The labour market, both in the East and in the West, was marked by labour shortages until the 1970s. West Germany signed a number of agreements with foreign countries from the 1950s onwards which recruited 'guestworkers' (*Gastarbeiter*) on temporary work contracts. These agreements were all ended by the mid 1970s as unemployment increased. East Germany recruited considerable numbers of migrant workers from Africa and the Far East until shortly before unification, reflecting its insulation from world recessions until the collapse of the Soviet trading bloc in the late 1980s. In both parts of Germany, foreign workers were recruited under the same conditions of employment as Germans but were concentrated in lower-paid work and, in West Germany, their Social Security entitlements were low, reflecting their low wages.

The tightening labour-market conditions from the later 1970s onwards in West Germany led to a growth in longer-term unemployment (Paterson and Southern, 1991, p. 245). Although they had been recruited as a 'temporary' workforce to meet the labour shortages of the 1950s and 1960s, many guestworkers did not return home despite financial incentives to do so (Braham and Mayor, 1992).[3] They continued to work (although experiencing higher unemployment rates than did German citizens), reflecting the segmentation of the labour market and a continued shortage of labour in those jobs which indigenous workers preferred to avoid.

West Germany's other major response to difficult labour-market conditions was to extend education and training so that, in effect, entry to the labour market was deferred for many young people. Somewhat later, early retirement schemes were encouraged, using Federal money (and thus weakening the principle of autonomous pension and unemployment funds) to compensate older workers for leaving the labour force. At the other end of the age scale, youth unemployment was not so easily compensated. Without having worked for at least a year in the preceding three years, young people were ineligible for Social Security. They could not always claim Social Assistance because of means-testing of parents – the principle of subsidiarity, in which parents could be expected to support unemployed adult children financially.

The response to growing unemployment amongst young people was major changes to the system of education and training. These reforms of the education system which were aimed at both improving the quality of training and deferring 'normal' employment had the effect, as Wallace (1991) points out, of producing a long period of 'post-adolescence' in which young people '... are living on training allowances, grants and part-time jobs, and young adults are often dependent upon parents for lengthy periods of time.'

Young Germans who enter higher education 'cannot expect to leave until they are twenty-five at the earliest' and, apprenticeships, which in 1980 started on average at sixteen and a half years, do not now start until eighteen or older (Wallace, 1991). Deferring labour-market entry for the young has not lessened class and gender inequalities in West Germany. German qualifications are closely tied to job opportunities (even at manual levels) and salary. The level of qualification obtainable depends on which of the three types of school children have attended, even though education or training or a mixture of the two (sandwich-type courses) is now compulsory for all up to the age of eighteen.

In the German tripartite education system[*], only the grammar schools (28 per cent of the school population in 1985) offer the *Abitur* which is

---

[*] A small proportion – 6 per cent – attend comprehensive schools.

essential for entry to university. Technical schools (with 27 per cent of the school population) offer a leaving certificate which is essential for technician training and formal apprenticeships, and high schools (39 per cent) offer only a school-leaving certificate. The connections between parental social class and education level, on the one hand, and their children's educational opportunities, on the other, are probably as closely correlated as they are in Britain and lead to a similar reproduction of class inequalities between generations. Wallace argues that:

> Despite the widespread belief in meritocracy in Germany, the children of the poorly paid and mostly unskilled guestworkers are most likely to leave school unqualified, fail to find apprenticeships and do the less satisfying jobs. Further, divisions of gender mean that girls are concentrated in a very small number of the less prestigious apprenticeships leading to less good jobs in the catering and service sectors.
>
> (Wallace, 1991)

Statistics for Berlin school-leavers in 1989/90 show that school-leavers who were non-citizens (because their parents were not citizens) were three times more likely to leave school without even the lowest qualification, and four times less likely to have the university entrance qualification (Braham and Mayor, 1992).

Unification has added a further complexity to the German linkage between schooling and qualifications. The GDR had a different system of qualifications which, except at university level, were unlike those in the West and which used different terminology. The treaty of unification accepted (and assimilated) GDR qualifications at face value, but there is some evidence that private-sector employers discounted East German qualifications and that there has been an effective 'deskilling' of the East German labour force in the labour market. Occupational segregation of men and women was strong in both the former West Germany and in East Germany. In the West, women were concentrated in the public sector and in services, and at the lower levels within these categories. Thus, for example, women are more likely to be primary-school teachers or high-school teachers, than grammar- or technical-school teachers – with a distinct wage differential in favour of the more prestigious schools (Blau and Ferber, 1986). Women were also excluded from building work and many manual jobs in engineering, both legally and by custom. The proportion of workers in industry in Germany remained the highest in the European Community (Pearson *et al.*, 1990) and in Germany it is in industry that the highest salaries are paid. Women in employment are more likely to be in lower-paid, service-sector jobs. This results in lower entitlements to Social Security income support, whether unemployed or when retired, for women who have no 'derived' benefits from marriage. For those who fall outside the Social Security system, Social Assistance at comparatively low rates is the income safety-net.

Certain categories of women – notably single mothers – are more likely to lose eligibility for Social Security than men. Entitlement to Social Security depends on availability for work and thus on having adequate (and affordable) childcare facilities. In West Germany such facilities were both scarce and unsubsidized and therefore expensive. This made it difficult for women to take proportionate advantage of jobs in work creation schemes or in the normal labour market. Claimants of Social Assistance (excluding retired households) were 65 per cent female in Grossmann and Huth's small-scale study (op. cit., 1992, p. 18). The relative disadvantage of women is not surprising in a welfare regime which has conservative social policy objectives and which, in particular, constructs women as the normal 'carers' whether for children or for elderly relatives.

Before the problems which unification and the collapse of the East German economy brought, two major concerns were expressed within the conservative German welfare regime: the problem of paying for retirement pensions and the problem of caring for old people.

Germany has an ageing population, in common with Western Europe generally and with most of the developed world. The 'dependency ratio' of those of working age to those in retirement was predicted to rise sharply by the year 2000 with a consequent problem of funding old-age pensions and in fact many of the autonomous pension funds were already running into deficit (Wienand, 1988, p. 49). The price for bailing out pension funds with Federal assistance from tax revenue was a limited cut-back in Social Security entitlement in 1982. This took the form of recalculating unemployment rates on basic work-incomes rather than on full work-incomes, such that overtime pay, bonuses and special responsibility allowances were disregarded when assessing entitlement. Clearly, the rise in the number of Social Security claimants was also influential in this reduction in benefit, the effect of which was to reduce the first tier of unemployment benefit to an effective mid 50 per cent of former earnings rather than the mid 60 per cent. This limited retrenchment was *not* accompanied by a neo-liberal debate about the dangers of too high an earnings-replacement ratio for unemployed people, unlike in Britain and the USA where the ratio was constructed as the primary problem (see, for example, Minford, 1987, p. 77). The central principles of the German social security regime – those of status maintenance and of full male employment – were unaffected by these changes. The rigid divide between insurance and assistance, with on the one hand Social Security protection for those in secure employment (predominantly men) and on the other hand Social Assistance for those in precarious employment or without employment (predominantly single women, foreigners and a growing number of the low-achieving school-leavers) was defended by the coalition government, led by the conservative Christian Democrats, as the correct and individualized solution to welfare needs. The right's solution was to 'lift major sections out of assistance altogether' (Chamberlayne, 1991/92, p. 9) by a number of schemes which were then extended to the former GDR, particularly by early retirement and by work creation programmes but at a great and growing cost. The 'normal' form of Social Security has been maintained as a market-produced one of unequal benefits produced by unequal 'contributions'. Social Assistance remains as a stigmatized form of welfare.

Attempts were made by the Social Democrats to propose alternative solutions, in response to the growth of the 'dual labour market' in the 1970s and '80s and the increase in precarious employment of many claimants. They proposed a 'basic social insurance' which would not be funded by individual contributions but by the existing unemployment and pension funds, ignoring past contributions or the lack of them entirely (Chamberlayne, 1991/92, p. 9). This would have largely ended Social Assistance with the fiction that everyone had paid insurance premiums whether they had or not. Habermas attacked such proposals as 'conservative' because they still linked welfare-outcomes with the capitalist market and particularly because they would have continued to undervalue 'invisible' unpaid work by women mainly carried out in the home (Habermas, 1985). The labour movement (the trade unions and social democratic parties) was 'clinging to a concept of full employment in terms of life-long, full-time and well-secured labour ...' (Evers et al., 1990, p. 202). It is just such a concept that the German conservative coalition has applied in the East, employing a number of fictions about past employment and salary levels in the GDR, together with a drastic programme of early retirement of those no longer 'economically active'.

The conservative response to the perception of a growing burden of 'caring' for older people in the early 1980s was to restate the traditional role of women as the carers of first resort and to argue for a de-professionalization of care combined with self-help within a conservative concept of subsidiarity: 'Conservative concepts of self-help argue within the logic of substitution. Much of the work done by highly paid professionals (in hospitals, kindergartens and nursing homes, for example) is supposed to be shifted easily to the working place of the family' (Evers et al., 1990, p. 212, summarizing the views of Norbert Blüm in 1983, later Federal Minister of Labour in the conservative coalition).

The personal social services in Germany are provided by a mixture of professionally qualified, paid staff and unpaid volunteers. In Berlin, for example, with a population of 1.85 million people, there were 33,000 volunteer care workers in the mid 1980s (Evers et al., 1990, p. 212), most of whom were women – or young men choosing an alternative to military service. Services such as children's homes and old people's homes are organized mainly by religious bodies, the Red Cross and trade unions. The largest voluntary organizations are those of the churches: *Caritas* (Catholic) and *Diakonisches Werk* (Protestant). This form of subsidiarity in the provision of personal social services has two consequences in the German system. Firstly, it introduces a large number of volunteers into the caring services (broadly, two volunteers for each paid carer) who have had no professional training. 'Care' within institutions is thus perceived as an extension of the familial 'caring roles'. This *normalized* care within the family, both for children and old people. Secondly, the effect of the dominance by religious bodies (and by the Red Cross and some trade unions) of the provision of social work has been to institutionalize conservative ideas of obligations and responsibilities. This particularly meant in the German welfare state the primacy of the family as the first resort when care is needed, following the principle of subsidiarity in the German Basic Law and the special legal status given to the family.

The charitable and religious foundation of much German social work remained evident throughout the history of the welfare state. Thus patriarchal ideas about gender roles in caring are strongly embedded in German social work practice. The conservative argument in Germany for substituting 'care in the family' for care in institutions (which required some public funding) had a stronger resonance in a conservative welfare regime than did, perhaps, the neo-liberal arguments in Britain for 'care in the community' precisely because the German model drew upon traditional and conservative ideas about women's roles which are found throughout the German welfare system.

The conception of substituting care by women in the family for institutional care came in a period when rising welfare costs became defined as a problem, and linked with the position of women in the labour market:

> Envisaging increasing needs for services already provided through public institutions, conservative planners opposed very early the vision of a high rate of women's labour-market participation attained at the price of an enlarged share of public services. Instead, it would be less expensive for the state to give allowances to women occupied with care at home.

(Evers *et al.*, 1990, p. 203)

This was the solution proposed by the Federal conservative government: to raise care-allowances for those in need, and proportionately more for those at home than in institutional care, thus making it financially attractive for family carers to look after those in need, particularly old people. The effect of the reform, if it were carried through, would be to withdraw more women from the labour market and to reinforce the conservative welfare regime's reaction to rising unemployment by 'compensating' certain categories of potential workers for leaving the labour force, in this case by enhanced payments for caring within the family.

Probably the most gender-specific policy of compensation for leaving the labour market was the Upbringing Allowance for new parents. It was in principle payable to either parent, enabling them to leave their job for up to two years, although in practice it was overwhelmingly the mother who left the labour force. At 23 per cent of individual net average earnings it was a considerable inducement to new mothers to give up their jobs, especially given the cost and lack of provision of childcare.

Overall, the response of the German social security state to the problems which affected the industrialized world in general from the mid 1970s onwards, has been to discourage labour-market participation by certain groups and to do so by reasonably generous levels of 'compensation'. Rising unemployment has been met by a greater emphasis on education and training, and by adult retraining schemes for unemployed people and a willingness to fund work creation programmes on a growing scale. Feminist arguments against the linkage of work records to welfare outcomes were overwhelmed by the enormous costs of unification and the need to provide income support to unemployed people in the East, as were challenges from the left to the insurance–assistance divide. The German welfare state remained strongly conservative in its basic principles concerning gender roles within the family and the primacy of the labour market as the primary determiner of incomes, through both employment and social security.

The high costs of maintaining such a welfare system were felt as unemployment rose throughout the 1980s. The ageing population led to funding problems with insurance-based pensions, and there were also problems with health-care costs which rose faster than welfare expenditure generally through the 1980s. In addition to these pre-unification strains came the further increase in unemployment which followed unification.

6   THE STRAINS OF UNIFICATION

The Federal state, before unification, promoted an inter-*Länder* system of revenue-transfer through which the more affluent *Länder* in the south (Bavaria and Baden-Württemberg, for example) subsidized the relatively declining *Länder* in the north (Niedersachsen, for example). The transfer of wealth between states was mainly directed at sharing the costs of unemployment and restructuring between south and north. This Federal system of income equalization between *Länder* came under severe strain as the result of unification and the need to transfer a significant part of West Germany's Gross National Product to the East. A recent estimate (Institut der deutschen Wirtschaft, 1992a) is that for each West German, 3,000 Deutschmarks were transferred each year to the former GDR and similar sums were projected until at least the year 2000 (see Figure 6.2). The average gross income in western Germany two years after unification was 3,900 DM per month (2,600 DM net).

As the East German economy collapsed, the strain on the German systems of Social Assistance, Social Security and work creation grew enormously. As noted above, it was estimated that the East German economy had a 40 per cent lower GNP in the first quarter of 1992 than at the time of unification in 1990, reflecting its relative 'backwardness' in the face of western capital and the collapse of Eastern European bloc organizations. As an illustration of the size of the need for reconstruction, one estimate

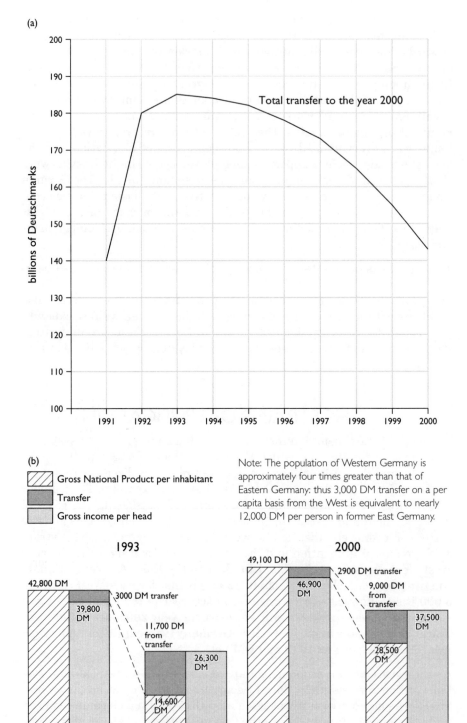

Figure 6.2   West–East transfer

Source: German Economic Institute, Cologne, in *Welt am Sonntag*, 6 September 1992

was that a total of 185.8 billion DM would be transferred from West to East Germany in 1993; this was 7 per cent of West Germany's GNP (Institut der deutschen Wirtschaft, 1992a). Even by the year 2000, the same source estimated that 5 per cent of German GNP would have to be transferred eastwards to maintain the social costs of economic reconstruction and of income transfers (i.e. Social Security, Social Assistance and pensions).

Coming on top of the strains of funding West German unemployment which had shown a steady rise since the 1970s, the costs of unification appeared to produce a belated 'fiscal crisis' of the German welfare state in which the demand for public expenditure outran the ability of the state to satisfy it. In most western countries (certainly in the USA and in Britain) the 'fiscal crisis' of public expenditure in general, and of welfare spending in particular, occurred earlier than in Germany, almost certainly because of the relatively poor economic performance of Britain and the USA (where demands to 'roll back the state' were first articulated politically in the 1970s). Although delayed, the costs of unification meant that a 'fiscal crisis' in public expenditure now faced a unified Germany.

From an East German perspective, the problems appeared differently. Firstly, the extent of unemployment was largely hidden by the different schemes which West Germany extended to the East. This was in addition to early retirements brought in by the caretaker government in the GDR which negotiated the treaty of unification. Early retirement became the norm for most people over 45. Many of the young were in temporary work creation programmes (ABM) which were funded for a maximum of two years (with one year more normal than two) and although unemployment after such ABM employment brought entitlement to insurance benefits rather than Social Assistance, it was based on low earnings. Even so, a much higher proportion of Easterners than Westerners were only eligible for Social Assistance rather than Social Security because the extent of unemployment was much greater in the East and many young people were unable to qualify for insurance benefits. Pensioners' entitlements were calculated in such a way that their former earnings in the GDR were undervalued and their pension in Deutschmarks left them relatively poor.

The differences in unemployment rates and in job security between East and West can be seen in the figures for the new *Land* of Berlin (shown as two parts still in the table) and for the new *Land* of Brandenburg in August 1992, almost two years after reunification (see Table 6.2).

The official unemployment rate for West Berlin, at 11.3 per cent, was close to the real unemployment rate of 12.9 per cent (taking account of short-time working, early retirement schemes and retraining programmes). In East Berlin the real unemployment rate was 32.1 per cent when taking into account the same programmes, despite an official unemployment rate of 13.8 per cent. A similar gross understatement of unemployment occurred for the state of Brandenburg.

Table 6.2   Open and hidden unemployment, economically active only (percentages and absolute figures)

	West Berlin	East Berlin	Brandenburg
Official unemployment rates	11.3%	13.8%	14.7%
of which:			
Men	12.1%	12.2%	19.6%
Women	10.4%	15.5%	10.2%
Hidden unemployment of which:			
Short-time working	3194	7739	38,274
Retraining	5796	36,946	86,666
Early retirement 1[1]	–	21,563	43,877
Early retirement 2[1]	110	30,876	91,185
Work creation schemes	6351	28,205	n/a
True unemployment rate	12.9%	32.1%	27.0%
Total economically active	977,796	683,623	11,882,000

Note: [1] See Note 1 at end of chapter.

Source: Information der Landesarbeitsamtes, Berlin-Brandenburg, 3 September 1992; recalculated from the original data

These figures certainly understated the true levels of unemployment in the East. Social Assistance claimants are reported entirely separately by the districts of each *Länder* and are not included here. Many potential claimants of Social Assistance will be deterred by the subsidiarity rules which mean that they are expected to turn first to partners, parents or adult children if these are working and have a sufficient income.

The 'cost' to East Germans was not simply widespread unemployment but the potential loss of independence which subsidiarity meant, particularly to women and young people. No such principle operated in the GDR which stressed the obligation to work, actively encouraged mothers to work and provided a variety of social supports, including state-subsidized childcare. An early effect of the treaty of unification was to dismantle many of those supports and to replace them with West German 'conservative' social policies, notably the 'availability for work' rules if women wished to claim unemployment benefit. To be eligible, women had to show that they had adequate childcare arrangements. But many kindergartens had closed because of 'lack of demand', resulting from the withdrawal of state subsidies which had been universal in the old GDR.

Perree and Young argue that one of the main effects of unification was that women in the former GDR bore a disproportionate share of the costs of unification, not only in the labour market but socially and culturally as well. As they put it: '... shortly after the unification treaty was signed and its practical consequences began to be felt, the observation became commonplace that "women were the losers" in this' (Perree and Young, 1992, pp. 1–2).

7   THE IMPACT OF UNIFICATION ON WOMEN IN THE EAST

The Stalinist regime imposed upon East Germany after the Second World War included the principle that paid work was obligatory for all adults – both for men and for most women. Like all communist regimes the GDR maintained full employment throughout its history. In fact, for most of its 45-year history it was faced with problems of labour shortages and recruited foreign workers until shortly before the Communist government fell. It is difficult in such regimes to isolate a 'social security' system of income support in anything like a western sense because unemployment as such was legally and in practice impossible. However, social policy (including specifically welfare legislation) could be distinguished, in particular pensions and pensionable age, parental leave, subsidies for childcare, no-fault divorce and freely available abortion. All of these shaped the position of women in the GDR in different ways from their West German equivalents and led to very different patterns of labour-market participation, household formation and motherhood.

Firstly, labour-market participation: 91 per cent of women of working age had paid jobs in the GDR compared to 50 per cent in the FRG for all women of working age, where only 35 per cent with children aged under six were in the labour force, much lower than in the East (Perree and Young, 1992, p. 4). This high labour-market participation was made possible by a system of work-place and district kindergartens which were heavily subsidized and by longer school-hours and after-school facilities (such as youth clubs) which were either free or at token cost.

The GDR encouraged a 'dual role' for women, combining motherhood and paid work, partly as a policy to overcome labour shortages but also as part of an official ideology of gender equality. Reforms in the 1970s considerably extended maternity leave and further increased the provision of pre-school and after-school facilities as an inducement to women to remain in the labour force (this was another response to labour shortages). While maternity leave in the Federal Republic is better than the EC average, one major contrast with the East is the lack of subsidized childcare facilities.

Although the Federal Republic's constitution gives equal status to men and women, the constitutional court has allowed sex discrimination against women, notably in the construction industries because of their 'dangers' (Perree and Young, op. cit., p. 6). This was not the case in the GDR where women worked in 'traditionally' male industries such as building, engineering and manufacturing. Wider labour-market opportunities for women in the East allowed a limited access to (relatively) higher wages because communist ideology favoured higher wages in heavy industry than in traditional white-collar jobs. Nevertheless there was considerable, if unacknowledged, gender segregation of occupations in the GDR which disadvantaged women. There is also no evidence that household tasks were more fairly shared in East Germany than in the Federal Republic despite the much higher proportion of working mothers.

Family patterns were also very different in the East: 38 per cent of marriages ended in divorce and 29 per cent of women aged 18–40 chose not to marry at all though many were mothers:

> Because the GDR facilitated combining paid work and motherhood and subsidized motherhood regardless of marital status, a substantial proportion of women chose to raise their children alone or with live-in male friends rather husbands (in 1989, 33.6 per cent of all births were to unmarried women).
>
> (Perree and Young, 1992, p. 4)

The Federal Republic, in contrast, heavily subsidizes marriage through its tax system and, as noted earlier, ties many women's pension entitlements and other social security benefits to their husband's earnings. This pressure on women for conventional marriage is unsurprising in a conservative welfare regime but, because of the terms on which unification was agreed, considerable ideological pressure was brought to bear on East German women.

When the old political regime in the GDR fell in November 1989, it was widely expected that a separate East German state would continue in some form or other. The Women's Movement (the UVF) was very active in the Round Table discussions which took place between the fall of the Wall and the conservative election victory in the first free elections in the East. As Perree and Young argue:

> Because the UVF, like other participants in the Round Table, believed at first that the GDR would continue as an independent state, they assumed that many of the benefits they had taken for granted would continue – subsidized child-care, legal abortion, affirmative action for women entering male jobs, paid maternity leave – and so focussed on making them more gender fair.
>
> (Perree and Young, 1992, p. 3)

The consequence of the Christian-Democratic-led conservative victory in 1990 in the East was that the GDR was incorporated into the Federal Republic as simply five new *Länder*. West German laws and institutions were applied to the East with transitional arrangements to phase out GDR laws on parental leave and subsidies for childcare. Divorce became possible only under Federal laws and the abortion issue is to be decided by the (West German) constitutional court and it is unlikely that it will be anything like as liberal as the old East German law. The Social Charter, a charter of social rights and benefits which had been proposed by the UVF to preserve women's rights as established in the old GDR system and which had commanded wide support in the Round Table discussions, was lost in the conservative victory.

The dismantling of Eastern support systems to families and individuals proceeded very rapidly. Youth clubs closed, subsidies to kindergartens were withdrawn and many closed through lack of 'demand'. In West Germany the personal social services – such as home helps, care for old people and children's homes – were provided, where they were at all, by voluntary bodies such as *Caritas*. Much of the caring support in the GDR was provided by People's Solidarity on a 'volunteer' basis usually organized through the Communist Party (the SED) and its youth organizations; it was demanded by the state as part of East German citizenship. Such support was free to recipients in the GDR; West German support is charged according to means (Karger, 1992).

The dismantling of the social support system to families went hand in hand with a collapse of the East German economy which, Perree and Young argue, had a specially damaging effect on women's employment opportunities:

> ... the (unacknowledged) gender segregation of the GDR has concentrated women workers in areas particularly prone to economic collapse: agriculture, food processing, textile manufacturing, and social services were all especially vulnerable industries. Moreover, women were more likely than men to be in lower level jobs in many occupations, and those at the bottom were least able to defend their jobs or convert their positions as government managers into owner/manager roles.

> (Perree and Young, 1992, p. 5)

Heinen (1990) has argued that, despite the greater independence of women and their higher rate of economic activity in the GDR, traditional gender-role segregation remained strong in the household with women carrying a 'double burden' (*Doppelbelastung*) of paid work and housework. The greater impact of unemployment upon women in the East following reunification meant that traditional gender roles re-emerged, this time applied to women's labour-market participation. The expectation now is that the man should have priority in finding employment and that a woman's place is in the home (Karger, 1992). The Federal Republic has very weak sex discrimination laws and the article in the constitution declaring formal equality between men and women 'has a history of judicial interpretation that permits differential treatment, including exclusion of women from entire industries ... and allows explicit preference for male workers' (Perree and Young, 1992, p. 6).

This is not the place to attempt a full evaluation of the gains and losses which have accompanied the unification of Germany. Our focus on the position of women, however, has highlighted the role which assumptions about gender played in two very different welfare regimes and how significant such assumptions have been in the transition to unification. Both regimes revealed patterns of gender segregation and inequality in both paid employment and domestic responsibilities, although they took rather different shapes. In the GDR, the combination of the requirement to work with forms of social support such as state-subsidized childcare placed a premium on women's 'dual role' as workers both in the home and in the labour market. By contrast, the Federal Republic places greater formal emphasis on women's domestic obligations and does little to support their participation in the labour market. In their different ways, both systems show how significant the relationships between the family, gender assumptions and labour markets are for the organization of social welfare.

8   CONCLUSION: THE FUTURE OF THE GERMAN WELFARE REGIME

The German social security system has always been relatively expensive for both employees and employers given the high rates of contributions needed to maintain it. However, until the 1970s it was self-financing without transfers from tax revenues. Germany's competitive position in world markets appeared secure, despite the pressures on wage costs which such a system contained. Growing productivity and high levels of capital investment in the long post-war boom meant that upward pressures on wage costs and prices could be contained. The funding problems of an ageing population, in pensions and in care costs, which emerged in the 1970s were assimilated by means of tax transfers and by marginal reductions in some social security benefits. However, as a system it was less well adapted to rising and long-term unemployment in which the insurance/assistance division stigmatizes those unable to get secure employment and where demands on the insurance budgets from those who had been in insured employment pushed the budgets into deficit. This is precisely what happened in the 1920s when the original system of Social Insurance collapsed under the impact of mass unemployment.

Rising unemployment in West Germany from the 1970s onwards (and particularly following the 1981 recession) raised political challenges to the conservative insurance/assistance divide, as noted above. These challenges were unsuccessful because of the domination of the Federal government throughout the 1980s by conservative coalitions who responded to rising unemployment with work creation programmes and by inducing whole groups to leave the labour market, particularly mothers and foreigners, or to defer their entry to it. Deficits began to emerge in several insurance and sickness budgets which had to be met from tax revenues. This was in addition to the earlier rescue of pension funds. From the 1970s onwards, there was an increasing division between those in secure (and social insurance protected) employment and those in precarious and low-paid jobs. As Ginsburg puts it:

> ... the winners in the welfare state being workers and their families within the primary labour market; pensioners with a full contri-

butions record and above average pre-retirement incomes; and those with unearned income from private wealth. The losers are the households of the unemployed; people with intermittent and/or low income from work, often in the secondary (casual) labour market; pensioners and widows with poor contributions records; lone mothers; and the 'post-materialists' or drop-outs, including the homeless …

(Ginsburg, 1992, p. 72)

But he goes on to cite Schmidt's estimate that the 'winners' in the West German welfare state are a substantial majority of the population and the 'losers' are less likely to vote and, by implication, being weakly organized politically, do not represent a challenge to the social security state. However, the rise in Social Assistance claimants from the 1960s to the 1980s – from 0.75 million claimants in 1970 to 2.4 million claimants in 1987 (Ginsburg, 1992, p. 74) – represents another fiscal strain on the German welfare state and this, coupled with deficits in health, pension and social insurance budgets, existed before the additional pressures resulting from unification.

The mass unemployment in the East which followed unification must raise considerable doubts as to whether a system, already under strain, can continue to fund the very large transfers which are required. The conservative-led government used a number of fictions to extend the insurance/assistance system to the East where the GDR's non-contributory welfare system meant that there never had been contributions to independent insurance or sickness budgets. Eastern pensions, for example, are now calculated on years of service in East Germany at the 'average' level of pay for the job, ignoring the impossibility of translating former pay in East German currency into West German marks when there had never existed a market rate of exchange between the two currencies.

Net real income in the East two years after unification, taking into account cost of living differences, was 80 per cent of the average in the West. Much of this was income transfers from the Federal government in the form of work creation, pensions and unemployment benefits. Output per head in the East was only 34 per cent of the average in the West (calculated from data from the Institut der deutschen Wirtschaft, 1992b), indicating the size of the subsidy which was needed to maintain East German incomes.

The German economy's ability to maintain East German incomes at a level probably higher, on average, than before unification has not meant the avoidance of political and social disorder. The extension of the West German rules of subsidiarity has meant that many young Easterners are now dependent on their parents for support or are in temporary work programmes rather than being assured of secure employment as in the former GDR. The rise of the right-wing Republikaner party throughout Germany (with 20 per cent of the vote in some states) and repeated attacks on foreigners, particularly in the East, followed the far right's identification of the unemployment problem with the presence of foreigners and the demand to expel them – both asylum-seekers and Turks, Yugoslavs and others who had been settled and working in Germany for many years. The rise of xenophobia in Germany is linked with the problem of unemployment rather than with poverty as such. The imposition of the conservative West German welfare regime on the East has disadvantaged not only women but older people and youth as well, who have either been driven out of the labour market or cannot get into it.

Leibfried (1989) argued, before the problems of unification, that the high costs of the German (and some other European) welfare models might well lead to a European harmonization of welfare which introduced a 'residual' welfare regime along the lines of the British and US models. In a residual welfare regime, he argued, categories of claimants are segregated into the deserving and the undeserving. The latter are harshly treated in terms of eligibility tests and incomes, thus producing an 'underclass', as has emerged in the United States (Leibfried, 1989, p. 16). The enormous rise in costs which the West German welfare system experienced as a result of unification with the East came on top of its own endogenous strains, making a move towards residualization more possible. The obvious category of the 'undeserving' poor in the conservative German welfare regime are the Social Assistance claimants whose benefits are 'unearned' and have always been stigmatized. Claimants of Social Assistance were already being faced with tighter tests of availability for work in Germany and could be threatened under the existing law with suspension of benefit for non-cooperation (unless there were dependent children).

The fiscal strains on the German welfare regime will be heavily exacerbated if recession continues to produce more unemployment, as has been the case since the late 1980s. What Leibfried calls the 'universalism' of the German model, by which he means a relative lack of differentiation between 'deserving' and 'undeserving' claimants (he was comparing Germany with the USA), may give way to a welfare regime which targets lone parents and those who have been unemployed long-term as agents of their own poverty rather than as victims. The socially conservative features of the German welfare regime would aid such a development, particularly the insurance/assistance divide and the construction of women as dependent on men as the primary earners.

NOTES

1   The 'true' rates are calculated as the total of (a) the number of unemployed people under social security regulations (*Arbeitslose*), (b) those in work creation programmes – ABM schemes (*Arbeitsbeschaffungsmassnahmen*), (c) those in further training (*Weiterausbildung*), (d) those on short-time working (*Kurtzarbeiter*) and (e) those in early retirement of which there were two schemes (the first dating from the final year of the GDR (*Altersübergangsgeld*); the second is the West German *Vorruhestand*, now applied throughout the whole of the Federal Republic). Short-time working was much more significant in the old GDR than in Western Germany, at 4 per cent of the economically active in the Eastern states in August 1992. The position of short-time workers was particularly precarious at that time.

2   The first tier of unemployment benefit (*Arbeitslosengeld*) may last between one and three years, depending on the individual's contributions record. It may also be extended if the claimant accepts an offer of further training from the Ministry of Employment (*Arbeitsamt*). It is not subject to a household means-test. The second tier of benefit (*Arbeitslosenhilfe*) is means-tested: parents may have to pay for adult children and vice versa, and partners for each other. At 56 per cent of former earnings (58 per cent if dependent children are members of the family), it is lower than the first tier but still related to former earnings status. Sickness insurance (*Krankengeld*) is paid at similar rates to the first tier of unemployment benefit. Time spent on sickness insurance does not count against time spent on unemployment insurance.

3   Approximately 14 million 'guestworkers' spent some time in Germany, of which 11 million returned to their country of origin, propelled (partly) by the inducements which the West German government offered. The largest remaining group was the Turks, who were joined by dependants (wives and children) and who now form the biggest single group of 'foreigners' in Germany. The Turks are unlikely to return to their 'homeland'; most are non-citizens (including their children).

REFERENCES

Atkinson, A. (1991) *Poverty, Statistics, and Progress in Europe*, The Welfare State Programme, Discussion Paper no. 60, London, London School of Economics.

Blau, F. and Ferber, M. (1986) *The Economics of Women, Men and Work*, Englewood Cliffs, NJ, Prentice-Hall.

Braham, P. and Mayor, B. (1992) *Race, Education, and Society*, Notes to TV Programme 7, Milton Keynes, The Open University.

Chamberlayne, P. (1991/92) 'New directions in welfare? France, West Germany, Italy and Britain in the 1980s', *Critical Social Policy*, no. 33, Winter.

Clapham, J. H. (1963) *The Economic Development of France and Germany, 1815–1914*, Cambridge, Cambridge University Press.

Esping-Andersen, G. (1990) *The Three Worlds of Welfare Capitalism*, Cambridge, Polity Press.

Evers, A., Ostner, I., and Wiesenthal, W. (1990) 'Cash and care: different conceptions of work and employment and their impact on innovations in the field of care' in Evers, A. and Wintersberger, H. (eds) *Shifts in the Welfare Mix: their impact on work, social services and welfare policies*, Boulder, CO, Westview Press.

Flamm, F. (1983) *The Social System and Welfare Work in the Federal Republic of Germany*, (2nd English edn), Frankfurt am Main, Deutsche Verein für öffentliche und private Fürsorge.

Ginsburg, N. (1992) 'The Federal Republic of Germany: the welfare state in the social market economy', Chapter 3 in *Divisions of Welfare: a critical introduction to comparative social policy*, London, Sage.

Grossmann, H. and Huth, S. (1992) *Zur Sozialhilfesituation in Berlin: Pilotstudie in einem Ost-und einem Westberliner Bezirk*, unpublished manuscript, Berlin, Freie Universität.

Habermas, J. (1985) 'Die neue Unübersichlichkeit die Krise des Wohl-fahrstaates und die Erschöpfung utopischer Energien', *Merkur*, vol. 1.

Heinen, J. (1990) 'The impact of social policy on the behaviour of women workers in Poland and East Germany', *Critical Social Policy*, no. 29.

Institut der deutschen Wirtschaft (1992a) in *Die Welt am Sonntag*, p. 25, 6 September.

Institut der deutschen Wirtschaft (1992b) in *Die Welt am Sonntag*, p. 45, 4 October.

Jarré, D. (1991) 'Subsidiarity in social services provision in Germany', *Social Policy and Administration*, vol. 25, no. 3.

Johnson, P. (1985) *The Historical Dimensions of the Welfare State Crisis*, Discussion Paper no. 3, The Welfare State Programme, London, London School of Economics.

Karger, C. (1992) Interview with Carmen Karger, psychologist-counsellor, InkoZentrum, Arbeitslosenverband Deutschland e.V., Hellersdorf, East Berlin, 8 September.

Le Grand, J. and Winter, D. (1987) *The Middle Classes and the Welfare State*, The Welfare State Programme, Discussion Paper no. 14, London, London School of Economics.

Leibfried, S. (1979) 'The United States and West German welfare systems: a comparative analysis', *Grundrisse sozialpolitischer Forschung*, no. 3, University of Bremen, FRG.

Leibfried, S. (1989) *Income Transfers and Poverty Policy in EEC Perspective: on Europe's slipping into Anglo-American welfare models*, paper prepared for the EC Poverty Seminar, Florence, September.

Leisering, L. (1988) Recorded interview, 2 December, University of Bremen.

Minford, P. (1987) 'The role of the social services: a view from the New Right' in Loney, M. *et al.* (eds) *The State or the Market: politics and welfare in contemporary Britain*, London, Sage.

OECD (1988) *Labour Force Statistics, 1966–86*, Paris, Organisation for Economic Cooperation and Development.

Paterson, W. and Southern, D. (1991) *Governing Germany*, Oxford, Basil Blackwell.

Pearson, R., Andreutti, F. and Holly, S. (1990) *The European Labour Market Review: the key indicators*, Institute of Manpower Studies Report no. 193, Brighton, University of Sussex.

Perree, M. and Young, B. (1992) *Two Steps Back for Women: German unification, gender, and university 'reform'*, unpublished draft paper, Berlin, Freie Universität.

Presse-Informationen des Landesarbeitsamtes Berlin-Brandenburg (1992) *Arbeitsmarktstatistik*, Friedrichstrasse 34, 1000 Berlin 61, 3 September.

Riedmüller, Senator Professor B. (1992) former Minister of Science, Land Berlin. Recorded interview, 8 September.

Scharpf, F. (1983) 'Strukturen der post-industriellen Gesellschaft', *Soziale Welt,* no. 1.

Senftleben, P. (1992a) 'Bericht zur Abteilung für Sozialwesen (pp. 44–87)', *Geschäftsbericht 1990–1991*, Bezirksamt Tiergarten von Berlin.

Senftleben, P. (1992b) unpublished (no title), Report to the Senatsrat, Land Berlin.

Titmuss, R. M. (1963) 'The social division of welfare' in *Essays on the Welfare State* (2nd edn), London, Unwin.

Voges, W. and Rohwer, G. (1992) 'Receiving Social Assistance in Germany: risk and duration', *Journal of European Social Policy*, vol. 2, no. 3.

Wallace, C. (1991) 'Education and training in Britain and Germany: past trends and future prospects', *Social Studies Review*, vol. 6, no. 4, pp. 143–8.

Wienand, M. (1988) *The Social System and Social Work in the Federal Republic of Germany*, Frankfurt am Main, FRG, Deutsche Verein für öffentliche und private Fürsorge.

CHAPTER 7
SWEDEN: THE SOCIAL-DEMOCRATIC CASE

NORMAN GINSBURG

I WHY SOCIAL-DEMOCRATIC?

For supporters and critics alike, Sweden has almost invariably been portrayed as having the most developed and most extensive form of the welfare state under capitalism. It is frequently used as the clearest example of what has been called the social-democratic model or welfare regime (Esping-Andersen, 1990; see also page 9 in Chapter 1 of this book). The reasons for this are readily apparent. At the start of the 1990s Sweden spent a greater proportion of its national income on welfare benefits and services than almost any other nation-state, with a strong emphasis on direct public provision of benefits and services that were universally accessible to all citizens. The welfare state in Sweden was explicitly committed to mitigating class and gender inequalities, with the result that inequalities of income and living conditions were significantly less than in most other western countries. Labour-market, industrial and economic policies had been geared to maintaining 'full employment', so that Sweden has maintained exceptionally low levels of official unemployment even during the recessions of the past two decades.

There is, nevertheless, some controversy about the precise way in which this welfare system should be characterized. Some authors have argued very strongly that its development was the historical outcome of working-class political struggle over the last century, led by the trade union movement and the Social Democratic Party (SAP). In other words, according to this argument, the Swedish system was not only social-democratic in terms of outcomes, but also in terms of its class base and its relationship to a social-democratic political party. This argument appears to be supported by the extent to which the SAP dominated Swedish national governments throughout the period in which the welfare state was constructed – indeed from 1932 to 1991 with only brief exceptions in 1936 and 1976–82 (see, for example, Esping-Andersen, 1985).

Others have taken rather a different (more pluralist) view, stressing the extent to which a social-democratic gloss has frequently been placed on more incremental changes resulting from a more diffuse set of political pressures. According to Heclo and Madsen, for example, 'retrospective rationalizations of critical choices in different policy areas frequently

This chapter is substantially drawn from Chapter 2 of *Divisions of Welfare: a critical introduction to comparative social policy* by Norman Ginsburg (Sage, 1992). It has been revised and edited for inclusion in this book by Norman Ginsburg and Allan Cochrane.

transform instances of muddling through into part of a grand design for Swedish social solidarity' (Heclo and Madsen, 1987, p. 44). Instead of identifying a class basis for the Swedish welfare state, emphasis is placed on the importance of other interest groups and popular movements (for example by Therborn, 1989), and some have gone further to argue that welfare policies have been shaped by the demands of Sweden's middle class as much as those of the working class. Baldwin suggests that 'the ability of the Scandinavian welfare states to cater to the middle classes as successfully as to workers has been the secret of their success' (1990, p. 30).

These are important debates which allow for rather different interpretations of the political basis of Sweden's welfare system, although both sides share a similar understanding both of the (universalistic) nature of the system itself and an emphasis on the importance of the historical roots of the settlements which underlie it. Curiously neither interpretation deals entirely convincingly with the actual pattern of welfare expenditure growth in Sweden.

Until the 1960s levels of welfare expenditure in Sweden lagged far behind what one might have expected after thirty years of social-democratic hegemony. In 1960 'real social expenditure' in Sweden was around 16 per cent of Gross Domestic Product – only just above the average for the OECD countries (OECD, 1985b, Table 4). (The OECD is made up of the world's twenty-four most prosperous – or 'advanced' – capitalist countries.) It was not until the end of the 1970s that Sweden could claim to have one of the highest levels of public expenditure on social welfare (as a share of its national income) amongst the capitalist states. In 1981 'real social expenditure' accounted for almost 34 per cent of GDP, a proportion only exceeded by Belgium and the Netherlands. The biggest expansion of welfare expenditure took place in the 1960s and 1970s, particularly in the late 1970s.

The growth of welfare spending as a proportion of GDP growth in Sweden in the years 1960–75 was not far above the OECD average, but in the years 1975–81 real social welfare spending increased four times as fast as the economy as a whole, and twice as fast as the OECD average in that period (OECD, 1985b, Table 4). In other words, unlike most other capitalist welfare states, Swedish governments protected and expanded the welfare state during the recession of the 1970s. Ironically, for all but one year of the 1975–81 period the SAP were in opposition, but the centre-right coalition then in government did not deviate significantly on welfare spending policy. Neither pluralist nor class-based approaches offer much explanation for this, and it is tempting to resort to a more economistic interpretation according to which the growth of welfare expenditure may be attributed to the boom in the Swedish economy, particularly in the 1960s. This certainly made much higher levels of individual and corporate taxation more acceptable.

As well as changes in the fiscal culture, renewed social pressures for welfare state expansion emerged during the 1960s. In particular, pressure built up on the leadership of the SAP to renew the socialist commitment to equality of outcome in terms of both class and gender. This was inspired by the student movement, the rediscovery of poverty within the welfare state, the rebirth of feminism and other radical, new social movements. A turning-point was reached in 1969 with the party's adoption of a policy document calling for increased social equality, arguing that this was the primary issue faced by the labour movement.

The report highlighted wage and salary differentials, poverty, unemployment and gender inequalities as issues which should be tackled more energetically, arguing that the welfare state should build upon universalism 'through "targeted" reforms for groups with special difficulties' (Heclo and Madsen, 1987, p. 178), that is those who had been left behind in the post-war economic boom. This 'equality movement' had considerable impact on SAP ideology and policy-making in the 1970s, above all, perhaps, with the introduction of sharply progressive income tax in 1971. It led to a great expansion of services and staffing within the welfare state with some modest success in improving equality of outcome.

The Swedish welfare state has been financed by very high levels of personal and corporate taxation compared with most other western states. The proportion of income paid in tax rises sharply as incomes rise, but a skilled industrial worker on an average wage in the late 1970s incurred local and national income tax at about 50 per cent of gross income, although this has gradually come down to around 40 per cent in the late 1980s (Swedish Institute, 1988). Employers also pay a substantial payroll tax for social welfare contributions (over 40 per cent in the late 1980s). The welfare state in Sweden is thus financed largely from direct central government, local government and payroll taxes, although a shift towards indirect and wealth taxes began in the early 1990s (Olsson, 1989, Graphs 2 and 3). Social insurance contributions by employees are only significant in financing unemployment benefit.

The next three sections of this chapter will focus on a series of key aspects of the Swedish welfare system at its high point in the 1980s, highlighting its distinctive features, as well as those it shares with other capitalist welfare states. They will look first at the impact of income maintenance policies, considering the ways in which they have affected levels of inequality and poverty, not only in terms of aggregate statistics, but also for particular groups such as pensioners. The consequences of these policies for women will also be considered. The following section – section 3 – will focus on the position of minority ethnic groups within the Swedish system, as part of the process of assessing the extent to which they are included within the universal framework. And section 4 will look more closely at policies for women and the family, considering the extent to which an avowed universalism may nevertheless have impacts on women which leave them excluded from all its benefits. The concluding section of the chapter will look at some of the pressures now faced by the Swedish system in the harsher economic climate of the late 1980s and 1990s.

2 INCOME MAINTENANCE POLICIES AND OUTCOMES

2.1 INCOME INEQUALITY AND POVERTY

Table 7.1 gives an indication of the comparatively high significance of cash benefits from the welfare state as an element of gross incomes in Sweden at the start of the 1980s.

Table 7.1   Relative importance of household income sources, taxes and benefits, 1980 measured by their average value as a percentage of average gross household income

Incomes, pensions, benefits and taxes	FRG[1]	Sweden	UK
Wages and salaries	63.1	64.5	72.0
Self-employment income	16.7	3.7	4.5
Property income	1.1	2.7	2.7
Occupational pensions	2.3	0.0[2]	2.5
Market incomes (total above)	83.3	70.8	81.7
Child benefits	1.4	1.3	2.2
Means-tested benefits	0.6	4.4	2.1
Other public cash benefits	14.5	23.6	12.9
Total public cash benefits	16.5	29.2	17.2
Other cash income	0.2	0.0	1.1
Gross income	100.0	100.0	100.0
Income tax	14.8	28.5	13.6
Payroll tax (employees)	7.7	1.2	3.3
Net cash income	77.5	70.2	83.1

Notes: [1] FRG is Federal Republic of Germany (i.e. until 1990, West Germany). [2] For technical reasons, Swedish occupational pensions are included in the public cash benefits.
Source: O'Higgins, Schmaus and Stevenson, 1990, Table 2.1

In 1980 cash benefits contributed 23.6 per cent of average gross income, compared to 12.9 per cent in the UK and 16.5 per cent in the FRG. To pay for this, income tax took 28.5 per cent of average gross income (which includes benefit and pension income from public and private sources, income from property and so on, as well as income from employment), compared to between 14 and 15 per cent in the other two states. Evidence for the comparatively progressive effects of this income taxation and income maintenance regime in Sweden comes from statistics on the distribution of disposable household income, adjusted for household size (see Tables 7.2 and 7.3).

Table 7.2   Percentage distribution of household disposable income, adjusted for household size, 1972/3

Quintile groups of households	FRG	Sweden	UK
Lowest twenty per cent	6.5	7.3	6.1
Fourth twenty per cent	10.3	14.1	12.2
Third twenty per cent	14.9	19.0	18.4
Second twenty per cent	21.9	24.7	24.0
Top twenty per cent	46.3	35.0	39.3

Source: Sawyer, 1976, Table 10

Table 7.3   Distribution of family equivalent (i.e. adjusted for family size) net income among quintiles of persons, 1980

Quintile groups of persons	FRG	Sweden	UK
Lowest twenty per cent	7.5	10.6	9.0
Fourth twenty per cent	12.7	16.1	13.5
Third twenty per cent	16.1	19.1	18.0
Second twenty per cent	20.7	23.1	23.4
Top twenty per cent	43.0	31.1	36.1

Source: O'Higgins, Schmaus and Stevenson, 1990, Table 2.2

In 1972/3 and 1980 the bottom 20 and 40 per cent of the distribution had very much higher proportions of total disposable/net incomes than in either the FRG or the UK, while the top 20 per cent had significantly smaller proportions. At least up to the early 1980s, the Swedish welfare state continued to redistribute incomes on a relatively progressive basis. Åberg *et al.* (1987, p. 140) conclude that 'the tax and transfer systems seem to have a more redistributive effect in 1980 than was the case in 1967', but most of the change occurred in the late 1960s and early 1970s in the wake of tax reform in 1971 and the development of the state earnings-related pension. From the mid 1970s to the early 1980s (and probably since then) there was little significant change in income distribution (Olsson, 1986, p. 58; Åberg *et al.*, 1987, p. 151). The professional and managerial classes have been able to maintain their position, in part because of the large and increasing proportion of women in this class who are in full-time paid employment compared to the other occupational social classes (Åberg *et al.*, 1987, p. 136). Åberg *et al.* use an indicator they call 'the household consumption surplus': this 'indicates how much money households have available after deducting from disposable income those expenditures required to maintain a certain basic standard' of welfare including housing. Using this, Åberg *et al.* show that the distribution of consumption has become less equal since the 1960s. The professional and managerial class has benefited increasingly and differentially from various tax reliefs, particularly on mortgages, to enhance its living standards relative to the lower classes, over and above the basic necessities. When wealth and consumption are taken into account, the professional and managerial class 'despite a long term income equalization, has succeeded in holding on to its solid lead in economic resources ... probably mostly due to the use of tax relief and the high level of inflation during the 1970s' (Åberg *et al.*, 1987, p. 150). The same is likely to be true for the 1980s and the gap may even have increased.

Table 7.4   Pre- and post-transfer[1] poverty rates[2], 1980 (percentage of people who are poor in the specified categories)

	FRG			Sweden			UK		
	Pre-transfer	Post-transfer	% Reduction	Pre-transfer	Post-transfer	% Reduction	Pre-transfer	Post-transfer	% Reduction
Elderly families	80.3	9.3	88.4	98.4	0.1	99.9	78.6	18.1	77.0
Lone-parent families	34.8	18.1	47.1	55.0	9.2	88.3	56.3	29.1	48.3
Two-parent families	12.9	3.9	69.8	21.3	5.0	76.5	17.6	6.5	63.1
Other families	20.1	5.4	73.1	30.5	7.0	77.0	12.1	4.1	68.1
Total	28.3	6.0	78.8	41.0	5.0	87.8	27.9	8.8	68.5

Notes: [1] That is, before and after the payment of benefits through the social security and income maintenance systems.

[2] These poverty rates are based on the outcome of a cross-national survey of incomes. Within this survey the following definition was used: 'Equivalent disposable income is calculated for all families, and then, attributing that income to each person in the family, the median equivalent income of all the persons in the sample is established. The poverty-line is defined as half of that median' (Smeeding *et al.*, 1990a, p. 58). The important point here is that an attempt is being made to measure the poverty of people and *not* just households, even if the assumption that household income is shared reasonably equally within households is difficult to sustain (see, for example, Pahl, 1989).
Source: Smeeding *et al.*, 1990a, Table 3.5

Table 7.4 indicates that, in 1980, 5 per cent of the Swedish population were poor. Not surprisingly this was the lowest proportion in poverty of the states considered in the table, though not much lower than the FRG at 6 per cent. There are apparently few other data on poverty in Sweden. Unlike the situation in many other welfare states, most lone mothers and low-income old people in Sweden do not have to resort to social assistance because of the development of the pensions and benefits systems. Nevertheless these groups together with those who are unemployed long-term are in relative poverty in modern Sweden. Here we shall examine the position of old people, social assistance claimants, unemployed people and women in the income maintenance system to analyse the position of those who are relatively poor within the welfare state.

2.2 OLD-AGE PENSIONS

The statutory old-age pension schemes accounted for 85.5 per cent of old-age pension payments in 1980 in Sweden, which is, unsurprisingly, a much higher proportion than in the UK (67.3 per cent) and other capitalist states (Esping-Andersen, 1990, Table 4.3). As well as the statutory pension, about half of Sweden's old-age pensioners receive payments from an occupational or private insurance pension. However, the social insurance schemes dominate pensions provision much more completely in Sweden than in most other welfare states, with private pensions accounting for less than 5 per cent of total pensions expenditure in 1980.

There are two statutory pension schemes – a basic flat-rate payment supplemented by an earnings-related scheme (called ATP) for higher earners. All Swedish citizens and foreigners settled on a long-term basis are entitled to the basic flat-rate pension which was introduced in 1948 (although a much lower, universal statutory pension had been in existence since 1913). The flat-rate pension was annually indexed to prices as early as 1951, but its real value against retail prices actually increased by 350 per cent between 1949 and 1984 (Olsson, 1986, Table 8). In this important respect, Sweden contrasts vividly with the UK in having a universal payment to old people which lifts them out of primary poverty. This has been of particular significance for women with their greater longevity and – until recently – less likelihood of having their own occupational pension. Perhaps the single most striking achievement of the Swedish benefits system is that only 0.1 per cent of older people are poor, after transfers are taken into account (see Table 7.4), compared to 9.3 per cent in the FRG, 18.1 per cent in the UK and 20.5 per cent in the USA. Compared to the UK and the USA, old people in Sweden, as in the FRG, derive relatively little (11.1 per cent) of their income from paid employment.

The movement for the ATP helped to forge the integration of the white-collar unions into Swedish Social Democracy during the 1950s. Thus the SAP managed to extend its support amongst the growing ranks of 'the new middle strata' and give them a material stake in the welfare state (Stephens, 1979, p. 179). The earnings-related statutory pension (ATP) was passed by a single parliamentary vote in 1959, after a long and furious conflict, still perhaps the most significant debate in the history of the modern welfare state in Sweden. It was a victory for the notion of a universal, state earnings-related pension as advocated by the Social Democrats and the trade union movement, and against the notion of state-regulated occupational and/or private pensions, as advocated by the centre-right parties.

The ATP gives an index-linked payment of 60 per cent of the average amount earned in the worker's fifteen most lucrative years (up to a certain ceiling), provided there have been thirty years' pensionable earnings. This level of payment and the eligibility conditions are much more generous than most statutory pension schemes. A supplement to the basic pension was added in 1969 to help those with low or no ATP. The ATP only started to make a significant contribution to old people's incomes in the 1970s and by the mid 1980s 59 per cent of pensioners were receiving an ATP pension. By the early 1990s over 90 per cent of men and 65 per cent of women should be receiving the full ATP.

Notwithstanding the universality and generosity of the statutory pension schemes, there are still significant structural inequalities in incomes amongst old-age pensioners in Sweden. The most affluent are those private-sector, white-collar employees covered by occupational or private pensions, followed by public-sector employees with occupational pensions, and then by skilled workers with occupational pensions. On the lower rungs are the pensioners solely dependent on the statutory schemes, with those at the bottom on just the basic pension. These latter include a number of self-employed people, farmers and others who have not fulfilled the eligibility conditions for ATP.

Not surprisingly, with the development of ATP and occupational pensions, income inequality amongst older people has increased in recent years, particularly between men and women. As Åberg *et al.* (1987, p. 130) explain, many 'women in particular receive lower pensions as a rule because they have often been housewives ... [and] do not reach the maximum 30-year gainful employment rule'. Even so, the relatively high level of women's earnings compared to men's in Sweden and the relative generosity of the pension eligibility rules put women in a comparatively much better position in Sweden than in most other countries. Åberg *et al.* (1987, Table 8.7) compared the incomes of Swedish pensioners by gender and occupational social class in the years 1967 and 1980. The class differentials in pension income amongst women remained largely unchanged in the period. Amongst men the pension gap between blue-collar and white-collar workers narrowed, but the gap between these two classes and the professional and managerial class remained more or less the same. Clearly, as long as wage and salary differentials are structured along class and gender lines, and while pensions are paid on an earnings-related basis, structural differences in income in old age will remain. Hence the Swedish pensions system reflects and maintains class and gender inequalities to a considerable extent, but blue-collar male pensioners have improved their relative position in the last twenty years.

2.3   SOCIAL ASSISTANCE

In contrast to the position in the UK, means-tested social assistance is administered by local authority social services departments as part of the social work system. Rates of payment are determined locally and benefit is frequently part of a casework package. It has not always proved easy for central government to control spending under this category, since local authorities are able to levy their own taxes and make their own decisions (within some constraints). The scheme was known as poor relief until 1956 when it was reformed and renamed Social Assistance; in 1982 it was reformed once again and renamed 'Socialbidrag' (Social Benefit or SB). In

1963 the proportion of the population claiming Social Assistance fell to an all-time low of 3.5 per cent, since when it has fluctuated between 4 and 7 per cent. Average levels of benefit are modest at between 3 and 4 per cent of the average gross industrial wage, a quarter of the basic pension level, though supplemented by child and housing allowances (Olsson, 1987, Table 4). Until the last twenty years most claimants were elderly or poor families, but by the 1980s claimants were predominantly single, young and often childless. At 7 per cent the poverty rate amongst non-elderly households without children is higher in Sweden than in the UK or the FRG. Amongst the factors prompting claims for SB, social workers cite unemployment, mental and/or physical illness and alcohol/drug problems. According to Gould, another

> ... factor associated with the increase in SB claimants [between 1981 and 1985] was that of refugees and immigrants from outside the Nordic area. While some of the local authorities reported around ten per cent of all households in this group, in Stockholm it was claimed that it accounted for forty per cent of the actual growth in numbers.
>
> (Gould, 1988, p. 104)

Members of minority ethnic groups (whose position in the Swedish welfare system is discussed more fully in section 5.3 below) are likely to be more dependent on SB because of their differential vulnerability to unemployment and their failure sometimes to fulfil eligibility criteria for mainstream benefits covering sickness, old age, unemployment and disability. The social assistance system in contemporary Sweden functions both to police and maintain an underclass, apparently of quite a disparate social composition – young post-materialists or drop-outs, older long-term unemployed single people, members of minority ethnic groups and others who have slipped through the statutory income maintenance system.

2.4   UNEMPLOYMENT AND LABOUR-MARKET POLICIES

At first glance, unemployment in post-war Sweden has been exceptionally low, and by any measure has been consistently lower than in other OECD countries. The official or 'open' unemployment figures are based on the number of insured unemployed as a proportion of the workforce insured against unemployment, but does not include either the insured or the uninsured on training, job creation and other labour-market schemes. 'Open' unemployment in the post-war period has fluctuated between 1 and 2.5 per cent except in the years 1982–4 when it reached an all-time peak of 3.5 per cent. The world economic downturns in the mid 1970s and early 1980s produced comparatively modest and short-lived increases in 'open' unemployment in Sweden.

This is a remarkably narrow definition of registered unemployment, however, for it excludes young people, women and others who have not worked in insured employment long enough to qualify, or not worked at all. If workers covered by the various state labour-market schemes are included, the unemployment rate is more than tripled: in 1988 the 'open' unemployment rate was 1.6 per cent, but if those on labour-market schemes are included, the unemployment rate rises to 5 per cent (OECD, 1989b, Diagram 22). This still does not include those who are seeking or are available for paid employment but ineligible for the benefits and not catered for by the labour-market schemes. If one includes early retirees, 'discouraged workers' who do not register and 'reluctantly part-time' employees, the OECD (1989b, pp. 62–3) suggests that 'the pool of under-utilized labour, was about fourteen per cent of the labour force in 1984', though it has declined significantly since then.

Until recently at least, a key component of Swedish employment policy has been the 'solidaristic wages policy' adopted in the 1930s by the trade unions in their national, centralized bargaining with the employers. The principle is one of 'equal pay for equal work' regardless of the profitability of a firm or an industry. This approach was not only justified in terms which stressed its benefits to workers, but also because of its value to employers and the Swedish economy as a whole. There were two main sides to this argument. First, it was suggested that maintaining an agreed wage level for different jobs across the economy would undermine the strategies of those firms which sought to compete solely on the basis that they could force wages down. Such firms used lower wages as a means of avoiding the need to raise labour productivity or making necess-ary structural adjustments. A high wage policy would penalize inefficient and marginal enterprises while encouraging the growth of innovative and productive companies able to compete in world markets. Secondly, and equally importantly, it was argued that the arrangements would ensure that efficient and profitable firms would not be under constant trade-union pressure to pay higher wages pushed above those of their competi-tors and thus reducing their competitive edge. With more than 80 per cent of the labour force organized in trade unions, the annual wages bargain has played a central role in employment policy. During the 1980s the solidaristic wages principle fell by the wayside to some extent, in a con-text of increased unemployment, faltering real wages and more aggress-ive strategies from employers and trade unions.

One consequence of wages solidarity is that the redundant workers from inefficient firms should be retrained or redeployed with the assistance of the state. Hence in the 1940s the state Labour Market Board (AMS) was established, an agency which helped smooth the way for the dynamic restructuring of Swedish industry by private capital, particularly in the 1950s and '60s. The AMS has presided over a range of measures. First, the employment service matches unemployed people to vacancies on a national basis. All vacancies and lay-offs have to be notified by law to the AMS which pays substantial mobility and relocation grants. The latter increasingly took the form of serious financial inducements until being cut back in 1987. A substantial proportion of unemployed people has been encouraged to migrate to the boom areas in the south of the country, often quite reluctantly, with the consequent break-up of established communities. Secondly, there are AMS training schemes (beyond the in-house training by employers) organized in training centres and schools. Thirdly, AMS oversees job creation measures including relief-work projects, temporary employment subsidies and recruitment subsidies. Finally, there are extensive special measures for the occupationally impaired, often involving the subsidy of wages in the open labour market. The expenditure on these 'active' labour-market programmes is more than double the expenditure on unemployment benefit and amounts to nearly 2 per cent of GDP, the highest level of such spending in the OECD. A very substantial proportion of the expenditure on active labour-market measures, fluctuating between 30 and 50 per cent during the 1980s, has been devoted to the occupationally impaired. Another unique result of these measures in comparative terms is that only 8 per cent of those unemployed in 1988 were jobless for more than a year, compared to about 50 per cent on average in the European Community.

The Unemployment Insurance Benefit (UIB) system is a clear exception to the universalism and direct public-sector provision generally characteristic of the Swedish welfare state. UIB is administered by voluntary societies under the control of the trade unions, and financed by government, trade union and employer contributions. In 1950 only a third of the labour force was thus covered, but this has risen to over 80 per cent in the 1980s. Benefits are paid for up to twelve months under fairly tight eligibility conditions; contribution and benefit levels vary considerably from one UIB society to another, so that members more likely to experience unemployment pay higher contributions. With increased government subsidy of the societies inaugurated in 1974, eligibility rules have become less severe, UIB society provisions more uniform and membership of a society became compulsory for all trade-union members. Although UIB is both taxable and earnings-related, Sweden is only surpassed in its generosity to the insured unemployed by Luxembourg and Denmark according to the OECD (1989b). Hence disposable income for UIB recipients is only reduced by between 12 and 29 per cent by unemployment (OECD,1989b, p. 82).

UIB remains under voluntary administration by the unions for a number of reasons. First, the generally low levels of unemployment combined with the high levels of union membership mean that pressure for a government takeover of the societies is not significant. Reflecting this, secondly, the UIB societies have been seen by the unions since the nineteenth century as an important means of recruiting and keeping members. Heclo (1974) describes the central role played by the Swedish trade unions in the development of support for unemployed people over the last century in comparison with the relative negligence of the British unions. The trade unions continue to defend the system because 'in a country with no tradition of a closed shop, services to members are very important for the maintenance of union support and identification' (Kerans et al., 1988, p. 138).

In 1974 an unemployment assistance benefit was introduced for the uninsured; with certain eligibility conditions, it is only payable for up to six months and the flat-rate payment is very modest. Nevertheless by the 1980s the number of beneficiaries was more than double the number of those on UIB, the great majority of these being young people. As Vogel (1987, p. 266) suggests, there is a growing number of young people in their twenties and of women of all ages who are in and out of paid unemployment, and ineligible for UIB, though they may claim unemployment assistance benefit.

Over the last twenty years Swedish governments have built up large public-sector deficits to finance the 'full employment' commitment by direct subsidies to industry, expansion of employment in the welfare state and the active labour-market policies, all of which absorbed a great deal of unemployment. By the late 1980s, with rising inflation and industrial militancy, the commitment to 'full employment' through measures such as we have described has been questioned more confidently by the 'new realists'. The OECD (1989b, p. 55) attributes Sweden's higher than average inflation to the low level of unemployment and the tight labour market, which gives the trade unions enhanced wage-bargaining power. They suggest that an increase of one percentage point in the official level of unemployment (a massive 67 per cent increase in terms of people) would reduce inflation in Sweden to the OECD average (OECD, 1989b, p. 71). Woodall (1990, p. 9) concludes that, 'to anyone else but the Swedes, that would seem a small price to pay', but it is not yet clear whether this trade-off of unemployment and inflation is so precise and, even if it is, what interpretation will be put on it by Swedish governments in the 1990s.

2.5   WOMEN, THE LABOUR MARKET AND INCOME MAINTENANCE

The position of women in the Swedish labour market is distinct in several respects (as documented, for example, in OECD, 1985a). The female proportion of the paid labour force, from being below the average amongst the capitalist states after the war (26.3 per cent in 1950), by 1987 rose to be at 48 per cent the second highest (after Finland) (see Table 7.5). By 1987, 79.4 per cent of adult women below retirement age were 'economically active' in paid employment or training, a ratio approaching that of men. Since the 1960s women have been keenly recruited into paid employment, not least through the active labour-market measures. In 1970 married women constituted 46 per cent of those on AMS training schemes, compared to 14 per cent ten years earlier (Wilson, 1979, p. 79). Since the early 1970s women have had parity with men (though no more than that) in terms of participation in and support from the various AMS training schemes described above.

Table 7.5   Women and paid employment: the female labour force as a percentage of the total labour force, 1950–87

	1950	1960	1968	1974	1980	1987	Increase 1950–1987
FRG	35.1	37.3	36.1	37.2	37.8	39.3	4.2
Sweden	26.3	33.6	38.1	41.8	45.2	48.0	21.7
UK	30.7	32.7	34.7	37.4	39.2	41.4	10.7
OECD average	n/a	33.7	34.8	36.5	38.7	40.7	n/a

Sources: OECD, 1989a, Table 2.3 and OECD, 1985a, Table 1–2

Women's hourly earnings as a proportion of men's have risen steadily in the post-war period to reach 90 per cent in 1981, by far the highest in the OECD states. These data, however, come from the LO, the blue-collar trade union federation, and do not by any means cover all sectors of women's paid employment. According to Ruggie (1988, p. 183), 'using samples of full-time, full-year workers in all unions, women's pay as a proportion of men's appears to be lower than previously thought – in 1981 it was 80.5 per cent overall'. In 1981, 46.4 per cent of women employees worked part-time, the second highest proportion of female part-time employment among the OECD states (OECD, 1985a, Table 1.3). Social benefits and employment protection are reduced significantly for those who work less than 22 hours a week, but it is not clear what proportion of women part-time workers are affected by this. With the growth of part-time employment women's weekly earnings in comparable occupations may be as much as 30 per cent less than men's, before taking occupational segregation into account.

Registered unemployment has been considerably higher amongst women than men, a gap that increased in the 1970s and narrowed in the 1980s, as women benefited from labour-market measures and unemployment hit male-dominated industries. Comparison of unemployment levels between men and women is problematic, as hidden unemployment is much higher amongst women. Nevertheless even on the OECD basis, female unemployment has been consistently higher than male unemployment throughout the post-war period (OECD, 1989a, Tables 2.16, 2.17). An official survey found that 90 per cent of women aged 20 to 59 wanted paid employment, but only 80 per cent had achieved it (Vogel, 1987, p. 270).

The final important feature of women's position in the Swedish labour market is vertical and horizontal occupational segregation, that is women are predominantly in lower grades than men, and are also in different occupations. Sweden thus follows a pattern in some respects similar to that of other western countries – 89 per cent of secretaries, 94 per cent of nursing auxiliaries, 78 per cent of shop assistants and 90 per cent of cleaners are women (Scriven, 1984). Compared to other states, however, women are much less prominent in 'unskilled' factory work in the private sector and extremely prominent in public-sector employment in the welfare state. According to Esping-Andersen (1990, p. 202), in the period 1965–85 'women accounted for 87 per cent of total health–education–welfare employment growth in Sweden'. He concludes that the 1970s and '80s saw, on the one hand, the upgrading of women's employment from 'junk-jobs' in private industry to higher status and better-paid jobs in the welfare state; on the other hand, this has resulted in increased horizontal occupational segregation by gender with women increasingly concentrated in clerical work and welfare work.

In this respect, when Esping-Andersen compares Sweden to the USA and FRG, it emerges as the most gender-segregated: 'More than half of the women are locked into typical female jobs, while very few women have penetrated the sanctuaries of male dominance. Post-industrialization in Sweden only augments the sex-segregation problem' (Esping-Andersen, 1990, p. 212). It would therefore seem that women in Sweden have not principally been used as substitutes for male workers in industry. They have rather been the beneficiaries (in paid employment terms) of the expansion of welfare services in the 1960s and 1970s as part of counter-cyclical Keynesian economic policies. It is, perhaps, above all as an employer that the Swedish welfare state has affected women's welfare over the past two or three decades. Positive discrimination in the active labour-market measures, sex equality legislation and belated trade-union pressure have had some success in improving women's wages and salaries relative to men's, but such pressures have had little positive effect on horizontal and vertical occupational segregation. The increase in part-time paid employment of women, much of it in low-paid service-sector jobs, seems to reflect a growing marginalization of women workers who are 'functioning once again as an industrial reserve army ... and this fact is being masked by the rhetoric of family values' (Ruggie, 1988, p. 185) which is discussed further below.

The extent of paid leave (for sickness, holidays, parenting etc.) is an outstanding achievement, with women taking two to three times as much paid leave as men. Esping-Andersen (1990) refers to this rather pejoratively as 'paid absenteeism'. On any given day 20 per cent of women workers are on paid leave of one kind or another, reaching a level of 30 per cent in the public sector. For mothers with children under three, the proportion was 47.5 per cent, four times the national average for all workers. On this basis Esping-Andersen (1990, p. 156) suggests that in Sweden, 'a very large share of what normally is regarded as labour time is in fact "welfare time"' illustrating that 'the employer's control of the purchased labour-commodity is heavily circumscribed'. The levels of sickness leave amongst both men and women are much higher that in most other capitalist states, possibly reflecting a relatively generous and open-ended sick pay scheme. In 1990 the Social Democrat government announced a reform to make employers responsible for the first two weeks of sickness to cut down alleged abuse, despite strong opposition from the trade unions.

Unravelling the links between women's position in the labour market and their eligibility for income maintenance benefits is never easy. But it seems safe to conclude that the access of Swedish women to these benefits is likely to be greater than it is for women in countries where levels of female paid employment are signifcantly lower, if only because participation in paid employment also implies eligibility for pension, sickness, unemployment and other welfare benefits. The relatively advantageous position of Swedish women compared to their sisters in other countries is still limited of course by their lower earnings and higher levels of unemployment compared to Swedish men and the high level of part-time paid employment amongst women.

3 MINORITY ETHNIC GROUPS AND THE WELFARE STATE

3.1 MIGRATION

The Swedish people are widely described as having one language, a single Lutheran religious tradition and a common culture and history, without recently being colonialists or being colonized. Native Finns, Lapps, Jews and Gypsies form long-established, relatively small minority ethnic communities. Prior to the 1930s, however, Sweden experienced large-scale emigration, especially from poorer, rural areas, to countries such as the United States. The fear of national population decline mingled with 'a mild sort of nationalism', according to Gunnar Myrdal (1938, p. 204), the influential social-democratic sociologist. The social-democratic commitment to expansionary socio-economic policies was legitimated in part by their intention to reverse the falling birth rate and the building of the welfare state was clearly linked to the recovery of national identity and purpose.

Myrdal also wrote that, 'We are just as much, and even more, interested in the physical, intellectual and moral quality of the population as in its quantity. Now at least in Sweden with its homogeneous population, quality does not depend on racial differences' (1940, p. 203). Myrdal later became an advocate of liberal race relations reform in the USA, but here, in the Swedish context, he was hinting at a social eugenic attitude to race and immigration which was then, and is still today, a significant element of social-democratic ideology both in Sweden and elsewhere, even if it is rarely made explicit. This can be seen in the history of the migrant labour force in Sweden.

Labour shortages in some industries and in some parts of the country were met by the recruitment of migrant workers in the 1950s and '60s. From the mid 1950s migrant workers arrived, mostly from Finland but also from Yugoslavia, Greece, Turkey and Italy. Finnish workers gained the right of unhindered entry to Sweden in 1954, when Iceland, Denmark, Norway, Finland and Sweden established the Nordic free labour market.

Swedish offices for the collective recruitment of workers were established in Ankara, Athens, Rome and Belgrade.

However, from 1967 onwards the government used existing immigration laws to limit, increasingly severely, the number of non-Nordic immigrants. The recruitment offices were all closed down by the end of the 1960s, except the Yugoslav one which closed in 1977. The result is that, 'since 1974 there has been practically no immigration in Sweden of non-Nordic workers' (Widgren, 1982, p. 153). Also in the early 1970s immigration from Finland was put on a much more controlled basis, which in effect means that a Finnish migrant worker has to have a job in Sweden fixed through the state employment service before being allowed entry.

By the mid 1970s, as elsewhere in northern Europe, a formidable immigration control system had been established, allowing entry to a regulated number of Finns, relatives of established immigrants and political refugees, but nobody else. This policy was subsequently consolidated into the Immigration Policy Acts of 1975 and 1976. According to Hammar (1984, p. 29), in the day-to-day practice of immigration control at the borders, immigration officers have been instructed since 1976 to identify non-Nordic people by their physical appearance – clearly an explicit form of institutional racism. The legitimation of immigration control is presented in terms of enabling 'underemployed national groups to have access to the labour market' (Widgren, 1982, p. 151) and 'the protection of the Swedish labour market' (Hammar, 1984, p. 28). Yet these considerations emerged well before the modest increases in open unemployment in the 1970s, and could equally well have applied in the 1950s, for example to the recruitment of women. Another official argument for immigration control made in the late 1960s was that 'if the number of resident immigrants became too large it would become impossible to guarantee them a reasonable standard of living' (Hammar, 1984, p. 41) with the implication that this might overburden the welfare state.

Non-Nordic immigration since 1974 has consisted of the families of already settled immigrant workers and political refugees (defined more liberally than in most states) from many parts of the world, including Latin America and South Africa. The regulations on admitting relatives of foreign residents are also much more liberal than those of the UK and the FRG.

3.2   THE STATUS OF MINORITY ETHNIC GROUPS

In 1981 about 12 per cent of the Swedish population were of migrant origin, of whom about half were Finns, and projections suggested that 'by the year 2000, 20 to 25 per cent of the Swedish population will consist of people closely linked by origin to other countries' (Castles, 1984, p. 64). With a residence permit, the status of the migrant worker and his/her family is fairly secure. The number of migrants without legal status is probably small because all residents have to have an identity number, and the extent of the informal economy is limited by the efficiency of the tax-gathering system. The police, however, have been criticized for stopping people of non-Nordic appearance for identity checks. After five years' residence in Sweden, a foreigner can apply for and obtain Swedish citizenship (two years for Nordic citizens). Naturalization policy is much more liberal than most other states, though few of the non-Nordic residents apply for it, perhaps because they feel reasonably secure without it and because dual citizenship is not allowed.

Up to the mid 1960s there were no positive social policy measures specifically directed towards migrant workers and their families, who, it was assumed, would assimilate with the support of the welfare state. Between 1964 and 1974 a long process of public discussion and consultation took place on whether the assimilationist ideology should continue or whether multiculturalism should be adopted. Eventually the Immigration Policy Act of 1975, which closed the door to non-Nordic workers, embraced a liberal, multiculturalist ideology towards Sweden's immigrant and minority ethnic communities. The policy has three goals – equality of living standards, cultural freedom of choice and political solidarity between the indigenous Swedish and ethnic minorities. Thus the state has promoted ethnic minority political, social and cultural organizations and activities, including, on a limited scale, bilingualism in schools, and in 1976 foreigners with at least three years' residence were given the vote in local and regional elections.

In terms of equality in the labour market, in living standards and in welfare, however, it is extremely hard to assess the relative position of the ethnic minorities in Sweden. Survey evidence cited by Widgren (1982, Table 9) shows that foreign workers experienced much more dangerous and unpleasant working conditions and in the 1980s the open unemployment rate amongst foreign workers was double the rate for the labour force as a whole. There is little evidence of effective measures to achieve equality of access to and use of the welfare state in relation to the needs of the minority ethnic communities. There is no equivalent to the Commission for Racial Equality in Britain, although racial discrimination was explicitly outlawed in the new constitution of 1976. However, ethnic minority trade-union representatives and local politicians are becoming increasingly numerous and vocal in pressing forward such issues. At the same time, in recent years there has been a marked increase in overt racism and racist politics in Swedish society (documented and described by Larsson, 1991), including racial attacks and harassment as well as discriminatory behaviour by the police, public officials and landlords.

There is therefore some evidence that the new ethnic minorities in Sweden, particularly the southern Europeans, mostly originating from the migration of workers in the 1950s and '60s, do constitute a racialized underclass in Sweden. The extent to which the welfare state has furthered or undermined this process is unclear, although they do seem more ' likely to be dependent on means-tested social assistance (SB) than other groups. Certainly immigration control policies developed since the late 1960s, while being more liberal vis-à-vis those already settled, are institutionally racist in discrimination against non-Nordic and, to a lesser extent, Finnish migrants and also in only requiring visas for entrants from Asia, Africa and Eastern Europe. The pressures of migration from Eastern Europe in the wake of the collapse of communism at the end of the 1980s seem likely both to reinforce labour-market and welfare divisions based on ethnicity and to put new strains on Sweden's asylum and immigration rules which at the start of the 1990s were still relatively liberal by the standards of other European countries.

4 WOMEN AND FAMILY POLICIES

4.1 IDEOLOGY AND FAMILY POLICY REFORM

Swedish social policy is famous for its relative 'liberalism' (as opposed to conservatism) vis-à-vis some of the key aspects of family policy, reflecting widely held, long-established values amongst the population. For example, the legal status of illegitimacy was abolished in 1917, liberal divorce reform was introduced in 1920, homosexuality was decriminalized in 1944 and compulsory sex and birth control education was introduced in schools in 1956. Historically, public support for lone mothers and their children has been relatively generous, and cohabitation has been treated relatively tolerantly. Compared to most other western states, defenders of a traditional patriarchal view of marriage and the family as an almost sacrosanct private institution have had much less influence. By the 1980s over 35 per cent of children were born to unmarried parents, 30 per cent of families with children under eighteen were lone-parent families (90 per cent being lone-mother families) and over one in two marriages ended in divorce, twice the rate in Britain.

Swedish family policies have also been shaped by a mixture of other ideological traditions, similar to those which have shaped policy in other states. These include the advocacy of birth control, particularly for the working class, as a means of combating poverty associated with large families. Such neo-Malthusian ideas had enormous influence around the turn of the century in establishing widespread use of modern birth control techniques by the early 1920s. The mixture also includes different variants of the feminist tradition which have had two great waves of political influence in Sweden as elsewhere. The first wave peaked with the achievement of women's suffrage in 1919, and the second wave emerged in the 1960s.

In the inter-war years, pro-natalist thinking came to prominence as Sweden's birth rate became the lowest in Europe. As discussed above, the declining population size in these years was a major political issue linked directly to fears of national decline. Swedish pro-natalism does not embrace a rejection of birth control, but alongside the notion that 'every child should be a wanted child' the view was widely accepted that the state should try to encourage people to have a modest number of children.

After coming to power in 1932 the Social Democrats began to integrate aspects of these various ideologies into their own response to the 'population question', as it was called. This ideological synthesis was performed by Alva and Gunnar Myrdal in 1934 in their book *Crisis in the Population Question* (later published in an expanded English version as Myrdal, 1945).

The Myrdals argued that population policy and socialist socio-economic policies should be inextricably entwined so that the nation and the family would protect each other and thrive. The fall in the birth rate was attributed by the Myrdals to improved birth control, the decline of child labour and, above all, the increased and unjust financial burden of child-rearing on parents. The latter were portrayed as contributors to the upkeep of the nation who were impoverished by that contribution. The goals of social policy should be to increase fertility by 25 per cent, to encourage 'medium-sized families', to improve the 'quality' of the next generation by radical improvements in child welfare, to reduce illegitimacy and to encourage marriage, while at the same time emphasizing the voluntary nature of parenthood in a democratic society. These goals were planned to be achieved by a very wide range of collectivized services and benefits in all areas of human welfare.

The Myrdals' programme unquestionably put a strong emphasis on universal social welfare measures, not just to be directed at the working class or the poor alone, yet they also expressed a strong commitment to using family welfare benefits and services to break down class inequalities, particularly amongst children. Their approach to family policy is predominantly child-centred and resembles the view of children as valuable human capital in which the state should invest heavily to secure its future. The programme was certainly not feminist in orientation and the consequences of family policy for women's position in society are not directly confronted. Nevertheless Myrdal acknowledged that,

> ... defending the right of the working woman to marry and have children becomes a protection of, and not a threat against, family values ... The forced celibacy or sterility among wage-earning women is a sign of society's incapacity to adjust itself to modern conditions. A population policy of democratic vision thus creates a new stronghold for married women's fight for their right to work.
>
> (Myrdal, 1945, p. 121)

Thus the Myrdal programme of reform included parental leave and benefits, socialized daycare and encouragement for men to take a greater share of domestic labour. Many elements in the programme thus went way beyond the confines of the Social Democrats' actual policy-making in the 1930s and '40s. The importance of the Myrdals' book was that 'population policy suddenly became a lever for socialists for far-reaching socio-political reforms in collaboration with the conservatives, who were prepared to bank on the preservation of the Swedish national stock' (Liljeström, quoted by Scott, 1982, p. 13). Population policy together with Keynesian counter-cyclical public expenditure policies became the legitimation for the expansion of the welfare state – and to a large extent that remains true today.

Family policy reforms in the 1930s in the wake of the Myrdals' report included free maternity care in public clinics, special public housing schemes for large families, rent rebates according to family size, child tax allowances, marriage loans, guaranteed maintenance for lone mothers and employment protection for mothers. In 1948 universal child benefit was introduced to replace the inegalitarian child tax allowances. Child benefit is not statutorily indexed to inflation, but it has largely kept pace with retail prices, adding about 5 per cent per child to the gross earnings of an industrial worker. In the 1950s statutory provision of birth control and family planning advice by the health service and statutory maternity leave were introduced. Notably absent from this list are liberal abortion reform, and daycare/nursery education for the under-sevens (the school-starting age), both of which represented too much of a challenge to traditional ideology. The effects of the reform on the birth rate are debatable; it stabilized as elsewhere during the mid 1930s, probably linked more to economic recovery and the fall in unemployment.

A second wave of discussion of family policy reform began in the mid 1960s. Pro-natalism remained on the agenda, particularly amongst conservatives concerned that most parents were increasingly limiting themselves to having one child. Family poverty was also of growing concern, with the rediscovery of family poverty particularly amongst lone mothers. Of much greater significance than these two factors, and in contrast to the 1930s, the emergence of the women's movement and the new feminism and also concern about the implications of and needs created by the growth of women's paid employment were both firmly on the political agenda. These two pressures – which are, of course, closely linked – contributed to what is called the 'sex-role equality' movement, an element of the wider movement for social equality of outcome in the welfare state that radicalized the Social Democrats in the 1960s.

Beginning in the early 1960s a largely female group of sociologists, economists and psychologists documented the effect of women's paid employment on the family and on children, and also the impact of patriarchy in the home and in paid employment on women's job opportunities. They advocated the break-up of the sexual division of labour in the home and equal opportunities and affirmative action policies outside the home in the welfare state and in employment. The Social Democrats' women's organization took up these ideas in 1964, and they were eventually incorporated into the party's 'Programme for Equality' adopted in 1969. The document was by no means a feminist manifesto, however, for as Scott explains:

> Just as Sweden's early social measures were accepted because they were presented as the solution to a 'population crisis' ... so the sex-

role equality program was assimilated because it was part of an 'equality program' that had something for everybody ... Thus some of the more fiercely debated measures relating to the status of women (or the status of men) were packaged so that the inclusion of women was only implicit.

(Scott, 1982, p. 7)

Among the many policy reforms ensuing from the sex-role equality movement have been liberal abortion law reform, extensive statutory parental leave and a great expansion of daycare, all of which are examined in detail below. Also unemployment benefit was extended to some non-contributory women and, possibly most significant of all, in 1971 the introduction of independent taxation rules for men and women made it 'more profitable for a wife to work even at a part-time job than for her husband to take on a few extra hours' (Scott, 1982, p. 72).

4.2   LONE MOTHERS

The position of lone mothers provides a good illustration of both the achievements and the limits of family policy in contemporary Sweden. In 1983, 19 per cent of families with children under eighteen were lone-parent families, around 90 per cent being lone-mother families. The proportion of lone-parent families is much higher than in Britain and the FRG, but somewhat less than that in the USA (Millar, 1989, Table 1.5). Only 9.2 per cent of lone-parent families in Sweden are poor, which is a very much lower proportion than in other welfare states. 86 per cent of Swedish lone mothers have paid employment, a very much higher proportion than in most other capitalist economies, and much higher than the proportion of married mothers in paid employment (Millar, 1989, Table 7.2). The net income of lone-parent families in Sweden in 1989 was as much as 87 per cent of that of two-parent families (when household size is corrected for), which is a much higher proportion than in the UK (where it was 76 per cent).

Yet it would be quite mistaken to assume that the welfare state in any way encourages the establishment of lone-parent families, since lone parents continue to face significant economic disadvantage. In 1981, 20 per cent of lone-mother families were dependent on social assistance, compared to 9 per cent of lone-father families and 3 per cent of two-parent families. There is no guaranteed minimum income for lone parents, but Advanced Maintenance payments were introduced in 1937 and subsequently considerably improved. The index-linked, flat-rate payment is about one and a half times the rate of child benefit but 'payment is conditional on the custodial parent assisting in efforts to establish paternity' (Kindlund, 1988, p. 89), so that by no means all lone-mother families receive it. About 14 per cent of Swedish children in both lone-parent and reconstituted families benefit from maintenance advances, which are paid with child benefit; the government recovers about a third of the expenditure from fathers. Lone-mother families in Sweden are thus probably more generously supported by the welfare state than in any other country in the world, yet they are far from having achieved equality with two-parent families. The welfare state merely succeeds in lifting most of them out of dependence on means-tested assistance.

4.3   DAYCARE AND PARENTAL LEAVE

The growth of women's paid employment from the 1960s onwards and the concomitant rise of the sex-role equality and women's movements have made a striking impact on social policy concerning the parenting and care of children, particularly pre-school children, that is those under seven years old. By 1983 the great majority (82 per cent) of mothers of pre-school children had paid employment. Policy has developed in two directions: with greatly increased public investment in daycare and by giving parents very substantial statutory rights to paid parental leave to care for children. These two obviously complement each other, the one supporting out-of-home care particularly for parents in paid employment, while the other supports parental care in the home. It is noticeable that both policies are designed primarily to benefit parents in paid employment and their children, rather than being universally of benefit to all, whether the parents are in paid employment or not. This no doubt reflects the very high proportion of women in paid employment in Sweden, though it is perhaps surprising that the childcare debate has not been more child-centred.

The Parental Insurance scheme was introduced in 1974 and has been improved regularly since. The basic entitlement is now eighteen months leave at 90 per cent of gross earnings, a period which can be shared between the parents as they wish. In order to qualify, the parent has to have worked six months for the same employer, or twelve of the preceding twenty-four months. Parents cannot take leave simultaneously but it can be divided up into intermittent blocks. According to Rapaport and Moss (1989, p. 10), 'in practice most parents took leave in a full-time block immediately after the birth of their child'. The government would like parents to spread leave over a longer period and/or use it on a part-time basis.

Other leave entitlements at 90 per cent of gross earnings at the end of the 1980s were:

> Fifty days pregnancy leave, ten days paternity leave, ninety days per year per child under twelve to care for a sick child or to care for a child if his/her normal caregiver is ill (average leave in 1985 was seven days per sick child), and two days leave per year to visit a child's nursery or school.

> (Rapaport and Moss, 1989, p. 11)

All these other leaves are funded by social insurance and are available to all employees without qualifying restrictions. Parents also have the right to work a six-hour day in paid employment until the child is eight.

Although there are no official statistics on the take-up rates of parental leaves, they can be assumed to be high, as reflected in the 'absenteeism' figures discussed in section 2.5 above. In 1986 over 80 per cent of fathers took paternity leave, but paternal usage of the other leaves is modest. Figures for 1984 suggest that in the first six months of a child's life, only 1.9 per cent of days taken are used by fathers, although this rises to 9 per cent in the period after the first six months. Between 1974 and 1980 fathers' usage of parental leaves increased relative to mothers', but since then there has been a modest decrease. Role reversal in Swedish famil-ies is clearly very unusual. Rapaport and Moss gained the impression that 'fathers in Sweden take a greater share of family responsibility than ... in the UK ... [but] there is insufficient evidence to confirm this' (1989, p. 38).

Public provision and funding of daycare for children, both after school for older children and pre-school for children under seven, has probably been the most significant new service development in the Swedish welfare state over the past two decades. As usual with daycare, changing defi-nitions and parameters make precise quantitative measures of the expan-sion impossible. In 1967, according to Berfenstam and William-Olsson (1973, Table 13), children under seven *with parents in paid employment* were overwhelmingly cared for privately, mostly at home by nannies, relatives or partners, but also by private childminders; only 16 per cent of them attended full-time or part-time nurseries or nursery pre-schools. By 1987 of *all* children under seven, 53 per cent were still cared for privately, again largely at home, but the other 47 per cent were cared for by salaried childminders or municipal daycare (Broberg and Hwang, 1991, Table 5.6). In 1987 34 per cent of the under-threes received care in municipal nurseries or from salaried childminders.

Behind these figures lie the two major developments of the 1970s and '80s, the development and expansion of both an administratively integrated municipal daycare service and a municipally salaried child-minder service. The daycare service includes nurseries, mothers' clubs and part-time kindergartens. At the start of the 1990s provisions varied widely amongst local authorities, some of whom provide few or no places for the under-threes. Most local authorities also organized salaried child-minding schemes:

> Childminders get a fixed monthly salary, but on condition they look after at least four children full-time or provide the equivalent hours of care for children attending part-time; many have to look after 8–10 part-time children to get their salary. One reason so many chil-dren attend organized childminding schemes on a part-time basis is that many municipalities only admit children needing full-time care to nurseries, arguing that nursery places are too costly only to be used part-time.

(Broberg and Hwang, 1991, p. 78)

This account certainly gives the impression that municipal childminding is extremely hard work, done (almost exclusively by women) for a very modest salary. Fees paid by parents cover between 10 and 15 per cent of the cost of municipal nurseries and salaried childminders, and are usually income-related. Lone-parent families are prioritized for nursery places, but children of immigrant parents are under-represented in municipal daycare (Broberg and Hwang, 1991, p. 90).

The dual provision of salaried childminding and municipal daycare reflects a long-established political division of opinion, which has remained prominent on the political agenda over the last two decades. On the political right both the Conservative and Centre parties have opposed the expansion of municipal daycare, regarding the public investment in it as discriminating against parents who stay at home with their children. These parties have argued that the state should encourage more parents to stay at home with a universal childcare allowance. Parents could then make a choice between staying at home or buying daycare, only modestly if at all supported by public subsidy. Non-socialist local authorities have tended to favour salaried childminding as a more flexible and familial form of daycare. There has been considerable tension between more tra-ditionally-minded local authorities and the central government over the expansion of municipal daycare. The non-socialist parties have focused on the class inequalities which have emerged in the use of municipal day-care. According to Broberg and Hwang (1990, p. 13), 'the higher the parents' educational and occupational status, the earlier they place their children in daycare outside the home.' The blue-collar trade union feder-ation (LO) considers this is due to the limited opening hours (6.30 am to 7 pm) and have long argued for twenty-four-hour municipal daycare to be available. In fact, however, these class differences in usage probably reflect more a difference in cultural attitudes towards parenting, to which the non-socialist parties have appealed with some success. On the other hand, middle-class parents in rural and/or traditional local authority areas complain about shortage of nursery places, where priority for places goes to lone parents and poorer children.

The expansion of publicly funded daycare in Sweden, like any develop-ment of the welfare state, has thus brought into focus a number of class and gender issues. Publicly funded daycare is by no means universally available to all who want or need it; much of it is on a part-time basis and it is not clear whether this is what mothers want or whether it is deter-mined by employers' demand for part-time workers and the limited public resources for daycare.

4.4 THE NEW PATRIARCHY?

A number of contrasting analyses of Swedish family policy have been put forward. Most analysts agree that the reforms since the 1960s are linked directly with the demand and opportunities for women's paid employ-ment. Ruggie (1984, p. 299), for example, explains the expansion of daycare in Sweden compared with its stagnation in Britain in terms of 'the differences in the role of the state toward women workers' linked to 'the respective status of labour and its relation with the state'. Ruggie stresses the significance of Swedish corporatism – the partnership of the labour movement, the employers and the state – in the promotion of employment opportunities for women. As a result, 'perhaps the most significant development concerning women workers in Sweden is the tendency toward "universalization" of the category of worker ... the distinctions among workers based on class, occupation and sex, are breaking down and becoming less determinant of workers' opportunities and rewards' (Ruggie, 1984, p. 340). This scenario is perhaps somewhat over-optimistic in the light of the evidence on gendered segmentation of the labour force, but it reflects a widely held view that the forward march of women in Sweden has been closely intertwined with the forward march of socialism and the labour movement. Ruggie dismisses feminist interpretations, which she says cannot 'adequately account for the differences that are evident in policies for women in Britain and Sweden' (1984, p. 24).

Adams and Winston (1980), however, explain such differences between the USA and Sweden in terms of different feminist strategies in the two countries. They describe Swedish women as having pursued 'social feminism' through social policy reform, while women in the USA have pursued 'equal rights feminism' through legal and constitutional reform. Adams and Winston suggest that Swedish women have chosen to advance their cause from within established political and social organizations rather than through more autonomous forms of organization. Social feminism in Sweden has thus played a significant role throughout Swedish civil society, not just in the social-democratic and labour movements. As Adams and Winston (1980, p. 157) point out, 'It can hardly be argued that the welfare state is a response to the needs of working women because most of the Social Democrats' welfare programmes were introduced before women entered the labour force in significant numbers.' Women's activism in shaping the population policies of the 1930s, so that they were implemented without a strong ideology of domesticity, has been a feature of Swedish family policy, which distinguishes it significantly from the Stalinist and Nazi variants being implemented at the same time.

The successful incorporation of social feminism into mainstream politics may have held back the development of a more critical and more radical feminist movement. Scott (1982, p. 158) suggests that self-organized, autonomous feminist initiatives such as rape crisis centres, shelters for battered women and self-help women's health clinics are rare in Sweden. The word 'feminism' is more widely associated with a revolutionary, 'separatist' view than in most other western countries. Yet the need for such organizations appears to be just as strong, and they have begun to emerge in the 1980s. As Scott says:

> It is a paradox of the Swedish welfare state that it has absorbed so many feminist demands, and yet women in Sweden appear to find it

> even more difficult than they do elsewhere to keep 'from being devoured by equality under the terms of a male value system' ... [since] they expect it all to be done in the framework of existing male institutions.
>
> (Scott, 1982, pp.147–8)

Such analysis of the limits of the Swedish welfare state in undermining patriarchy has been extended recently by a number of Scandinavian women writers. Hernes (1987) sees Scandinavian welfare corporatism as a reconstitution of patriarchy in male-dominated corporate institutions, upon which women are particularly dependent. Women are much more reliant on the welfare state for paid employment than men, and their daily lives depend much more directly on the services and benefits of the welfare state than do men's lives, because women still carry the greater burden of unpaid domestic and caring work. Yet real power in the upper reaches of welfare administration and in the corporate institutions of the private sector is predominantly in the hands of men. Hernes suggests therefore that 'one can describe the Scandinavian state form as a tutelary state for women, since they have had a minimal role in the actual decision-making process concerning distribution' (1987, p. 76). Borchorst and Siim (1987, p. 154) also suggest that, as a result of the substantial gains for women from the development of the welfare state, patriarchal power is now maintained by 'the institutionalization of women's dual roles as mothers and workers', which has left men free to consolidate their power in public and private corporate institutions. Women remain in a secondary capacity – disproportionately employed in the public sector – while men dominate in the private sector as well as in senior positions in the public sector. In other words there is a segmented (dual) labour market to which men and women have differential access. According to this argument, therefore, the Scandinavian welfare state has had a contradictory impact for women, sweeping away some of the traditional patriarchal assumptions about the primacy of women's unpaid domestic work, but establishing a new form of patriarchal citizenship for women in partnership with the welfare state as both employer and provider (Siim, 1987).

5 CONCLUSION: THE END OF AN ERA?

Since the 1930s the social-democratic hegemony and Swedish pluralist politics have shaped the Swedish welfare state in ways which have made it significantly different from the other capitalist welfare states discussed in this book. The social-democratic hegemony has been based on a degree of collaboration between organized labour, capital and the state which has not existed in other welfare states. In this partnership, however, it is still important to note that private capital continues to exercise control over industry, finance and commerce without much threat of political interference. The Swedish economy is owned and controlled by private interests to an astonishing extent, when one considers how frequently

Sweden is described as a socialist country. As Therborn points out in relation to its size (a population of just under 8.5 million), 'the number of large private industrial corporations ... in Sweden is quite impressive' (1989, p. 194). One family, the Wallenbergs, has effective control of more than a third of the total value of the Stockholm stock exchange. Yet this extremely dynamic capitalist economy has thrived alongside the development of an extensive welfare state.

Over the years since the 1930s the welfare state, as we have seen, has succeeded in ameliorating class and gender inequalities in welfare, though also reconstructing and even sustaining forms of class, gender and racial inequalities and oppression. The social-democratic hegemony would suggest that the successful development of the welfare state and of the capitalist economy may have been a symbiotic process, but this is impossible to prove.

Since the 1970s, as in other countries, representations of business and even some Social Democrats have come to believe that the welfare state is a serious drag on further economic growth. Unquestionably in the 1990s the social-democratic hegemony is going to face its greatest pressures since the 1930s. This became clear in February 1990 when the Social Democrat government resigned after failing to get an austerity package through parliament; this included a two-year wage freeze and a ban on strikes in exchange for continued support for the welfare state. The election of a Conservative government in 1991 committed to 'rolling back' key aspects of the welfare state and to substantially reducing taxation levels suggests that it is no longer possible to assume (as it was even under centre-right rule in the late 1970s) that the Swedish system will remain unscathed. In the 1991 election the Social Democrats received a lower proportion of the votes than in any election since 1928. Sweden is also committed to seeking membership of the EC and this may place other strains on its particular welfare regime, implying direct competition with countries with rather more limited forms of welfare provision.

Even without such political changes, a number of questions – similar to those raised in other welfare states – were increasingly being posed in Sweden. First, there is the question of the impact of the welfare state on the working class. There seems to be a growing perception within the Swedish working class that the welfare state may differentially benefit the professional and managerial groups and that the working class may pay in taxes a disproportionate contribution towards the costs of the welfare state. This argument is, of course, commonly made about welfare states. An understandable reaction is to call for wage increases and tax cuts to put money into workers' pockets with which they can buy the welfare services and goods that they need without having the state dictate to them how their needs should be fulfilled. Such an argument has come to the fore in the daycare debate, for example. Another related issue is the question of the remoteness and authoritarianism of the welfare state. This has come to prominence around questions such as the rights of social assistance claimants, drug addicts and parents of children taken into care (Gould, 1988), where the Swedish welfare state has tended to adopt fairly authoritarian practices. There are increasing pressures for more effective welfare rights, better advocacy for clients and more consumer participation. This again is related to a third aspect – the emergence of the new social movements over the past twenty years. To some extent the strength of the social-democratic hegemony may have held back some of these movements, such as the autonomous women's movement. Nevertheless, the anti-nuclear power movement and the peace movement have had an increasing impact on the political scene in recent years. In 1988 the Green Party exceeded the threshold of 4 per cent of the vote for the first time and thereby achieved parliamentary representation. Their philosophy of decentralization and consumer power may have an impact on the Social Democrats. Finally, it is apparent that Swedish corporations are investing more and more overseas, as a reaction to the very high levels of corporate taxation at home and also in order to be established players inside the single European market of the EC. This helps to explain Sweden's desire to join the EC.

In the 1980s Social Democrat governments attempted to respond to these pressures, while at the same time trying to counter inflation and to protect the welfare state, which is unquestionably still popular in its present form. It may be premature to talk of the crumbling of the social-democratic hegemony, though clearly a significant adaptation has already taken place, since the 1980s has seen an end to the growth of the welfare state: public expenditure as a share of GDP fell from a peak of 68 per cent in 1982 to 61 per cent in 1989 and 56 per cent in 1991. Further cuts are promised for the 1990s. Already experiments are taking place which imply the increased use of market-style methods in the health-care sector (Garpenby, 1992) and there are some signs that state ambitions to ensure equalization (for example, through pensions and services for older people) are fading (Daatland, 1992). The electoral success of the centre-right parties may not immediately lead to wholesale and radical change, since the inertia of existing 'structures may at present be the best defence against a shift away from solidaristic and egalitarian values' (Daatland, 1992, p. 46), but the pressures towards change are clear enough, with the emphasis shifting from a social-democratic towards a more liberal, social market model.

REFERENCES

Åberg, R., Selén, J. and Tham, H. (1987) 'Economic resources' in Erikson, E. and Åberg, R. (eds) *Welfare in Transition*, Oxford, Oxford University Press.

Adams, C. and Winston, K. (1980) *Mothers at Work: public policies in the United States, Sweden and China*, New York, Longman.

Baldwin, P. (1990) *The Politics of Social Solidarity*, Cambridge, Cambridge University Press.

Berfenstam, R. and William-Olsson, I. (1973) *Early Child Care in Sweden*, London, Gordon and Breach.

Borchorst, A. and Siim, B. (1987) 'Women and the advanced welfare state – a new kind of patriarchal power?' in Sassoon, A. Showstack (ed.) *Women and The State*, London, Hutchinson.

Broberg, A. and Hwang, P. (1991) 'Day care for young children in Sweden' in Melhuish, E. and Moss, P. (eds) *Day Care for Young Children*, London, Routledge.

Castles, S. (1984) *Here for Good: Western Europe's new ethnic minorities*, London, Pluto Press.

Daatland, S.V. (1992) 'Ideals lost? Current trends in Scandinavian welfare policies on aging', *Journal of European Social Policy*, vol. 2, no. 1, pp. 33–47.

Esping-Andersen, G. (1985) *Politics against the Market: the social democratic road to power*, Princeton, NJ, Princeton University Press.

Esping-Andersen, G. (1990) *The Three Worlds of Welfare Capitalism*, Cambridge, Polity Press.

Garpenby, P. (1992) 'The transformation of the Swedish health care system, or the hasty rejection of the rational planning model', *Journal of European Social Policy*, vol. 2, no. 1, pp. 17–31.

Gould, A. (1988) *Control and Conflict in Welfare Policy: the Swedish experience*, Harlow, Longman.

Hammar, T. (1984) 'Sweden' in Hammar, T. (ed.) (1984) *European Immigration Policy*, Cambridge, Cambridge University Press.

Heclo, H. (1974) *Modern Social Politics in Britain and Sweden*, New Haven, Yale University Press.

Heclo, H. and Madsen, H. (1987) *Policy and Politics in Sweden*, Philadelphia, Temple University Press.

Hernes, H. (1987) 'Women and the welfare state: the transition from private to public dependence' in Sassoon, A. Showstack (ed.) *Women and The State*, London, Hutchinson.

Kerans, P., Drover, G. and Williams, D. (1988) *Welfare and Worker Participation*, London and Basingstoke, Macmillan.

Kindlund, S. (1988) 'Sweden' in Kahn, A. and Kamerman, S. (eds) *Child Support: cross-cultural studies*, Newbury Park, CA, Sage.

Larsson, S. (1991) 'Swedish racism: the democratic way', *Race and Class*, vol. 32, no. 3.

Millar, J. (1989) *Poverty and the Lone-parent Family*, Aldershot, Avebury.

Myrdal, A. (1945) *Nation and Family: the Swedish experiment in democratic family and population policy*, London, Kegan Paul.

Myrdal, G. (1938) 'Population problems and policies', *Annals of the American Academy of Political and Social Science*, vol. 197, March.

Myrdal, G. (1940) *Population and Democracy*, Cambridge, MA, Harvard University Press.

OECD (1985a) *The Integration of Women into the Economy*, Paris, Organisation for Economic Cooperation and Development.

OECD (1985b) *Social Expenditure 1960–1990,* Paris, Organisation for Economic Cooperation and Development.

OECD (1989a) *Historical statistics: 1960–1987*, Paris, Organisation for Economic Cooperation and Development.

OECD (1989b) *Sweden: OECD Economic Survey 1988/1989*, Paris, Organisation for Economic Cooperation and Development.

O'Higgins, M, Schmaus, G. and Stevenson, G. (1990) 'Income distribution and redistribution: a microdata analysis for seven countries' in Smeeding *et al.* (eds) op. cit.

Olsson, S. (1986) 'Sweden' in Flora, P. (ed.) *Growth to Limits: Volume 1*, Berlin, De Gruyter.

Olsson, S. (1987) 'Towards a transformation of the Swedish welfare state?' in Friedman, R., Gilbert, N. and Sherer, M. (eds) *Modern Welfare States*, Brighton, Wheatsheaf.

Olsson, S. (1989) 'Sweden' in Dixon, J. and Scheurell, R. (eds) *Social Welfare in Developed Market Countries*, London, Routledge.

Pahl, J. (1989) *Money and Marriage*, London and Basingstoke, Macmillan.

Rapaport, R. and Moss, P. (1989) *Exploring Ways of Integrating Men and Women as Equals at Work*, unpublished Report to the Ford Foundation.

Ruggie, M. (1984) *The State and Working Women*, Princeton, NJ, Princeton University Press.

Ruggie, M. (1988) 'Gender, work and social progress' in Jenson, J. and Hagen, E. (eds) *The Feminization of the Labour Force*, Cambridge, Polity Press.

Sawyer, M. (1976) *Income Distribution in OECD Countries,* Paris, Organisation for Economic Cooperation and Development.

Scott, H. (1982) *Sweden's Right to be Human*, London, Allison and Busby.

Scriven, J. (1984) 'Women at work in Sweden' in Davidson, M. and Cooper, C. (eds) *Women at Work*, Chichester, John Wiley.

Siim, B. (1987) 'The Scandinavian welfare states: towards sexual equality or a new kind of male domination', *Acta Sociologica*, vol. 30, no. 3/4, pp. 255–70.

Smeeding, T., Rainwater, L., Rein, M., Hauser, R. and Schäler, G. (1990a) 'Income, poverty in seven countries: initial estimates from the LIS database' in Smeeding *et al.* (eds) op. cit.

Smeeding, T., O'Higgins, Y. and Rainwater, L. (eds) (1990b) *Poverty, Inequality and Income Distribution in Comparative Perspective*, Hemel Hempstead, Harvester Wheatsheaf.

Stephens, J. (1979) *The Transition from Capitalism to Socialism*, London and Basingstoke, Macmillan.

Swedish Institute (1988) 'General facts on Sweden', *Fact Sheets on Sweden*, Stockholm, Swedish Institute.

Therborn, G. (1989) '"Pillarization" and "popular movements"' in Castles, F. (ed.) *The Comparative History of Public Policy*, Cambridge, Polity Press.

Vogel, J. (1987) 'The victims of unemployment: labour market policy and the burden of unemployment' in Ferge, Z. and Miller, S. (eds) *The Dynamics of Deprivation*, Aldershot, Gower Press.

Widgren, J. (1982) 'The status of immigrant workers in Sweden' in Thomas, E. J. (ed.) *Immigrant Workers in Europe: their legal status*, Paris, The UNESCO Press.

Wilson, D. (1979) *The Welfare State in Sweden*, London, Heinemann.

Woodall, P. (1990) 'Survey: the Swedish economy', *The Economist*, 3 March.

CHAPTER 8
IRELAND: CATHOLIC CORPORATISM

EUGENE MCLAUGHLIN

I   CATHOLIC CORPORATISM

This chapter examines the extent to which the Republic of Ireland embodies the characteristics of a Catholic corporatist welfare regime. Until recently, this particular variant of Esping-Andersen's conservative corporatist welfare regime (see page 8 of Chapter 1) has been largely ignored, possibly because it was viewed by social policy theorists as being only applicable to 'underdeveloped' and peripheral 'Latin rim' European countries (such as Portugal, Spain and Italy) and Ireland. However, because of increasing disillusionment with the social-democratic welfare regime and the need for EC-wide 'cohesion' on social legislation, much more attention is being paid to the defining characteristics of Catholic corporatism.

This chapter begins by briefly exploring the historical evolution of social policy in the Republic of Ireland (hereafter referred to as Ireland) between 1922 (when independence was gained) and the end of the Second World War. This period witnessed the construction of an integral Catholic nation-state with the teachings of the Catholic Church governing most aspects of state policy, including social policy. As a consequence, the state viewed social welfare as being primarily the responsibility of the family and voluntary – that is, church – organizations. The chapter then examines the shifts in the post-war period towards an institutional form of welfare. The exact nature of the state's involvement and social security and expenditure outcomes are examined. It is argued that despite the dramatic increases in state welfare expenditure Catholic social teaching still has a considerable role to play in ideologically shaping the contours of social policy in Ireland. By examining how social policies operate in Ireland we are also provided with one of the clearest examples of how Catholic corporatism severely restricts women's economic, social and reproductive rights. However, before discussing the Irish case it is necessary to relate the general features of this welfare regime.

In the late nineteenth century and first decades of the twentieth century the Catholic Church enunciated a set of corporatist principles which it believed should guide social and political matters in Catholic countries. Catholic corporatism was a conservative response to 'a world that was growing more liberal and democratic, more urban and industrial, and more secular and scientific' (Hynes, 1990, p. 55). It was also propagated as a 'third way' between the extremes of free market capitalism and communism. Catholic social thinkers favoured a social and moral order based on small-scale capitalism, family property, small businesses and farms. These social thinkers wanted to ensure that the political and civic culture of Catholic nations was also imbued with a Catholic ethos. Central to their vision of the world were the principles of subsidiarity, family solidarity and social consensus.

In response to the emergence of strong nation-states, a 1931 Papal Encyclical *Quadragesimo Anno* espoused the principle of subsidiarity (also discussed in Chapter 6, pp. 141–2) as a means of circumscribing state encroachment on voluntary welfare and charity arrangements (Grogan, 1978). The state was viewed as a functional necessity – an integrating force in society which had the important role of ensuring social order. However, it should refrain from intervening in economic and social affairs unless the national interest or social equilibrium was threatened. The Encyclical stated that: 'It is an injustice and at the same time a great evil and disturbance of right order to assign to a greater and higher association what lesser and subordinate organizations can do' (quoted in Whyte, 1980, p. 67). Welfare services should be delivered by voluntary organizations and their internal affairs should be regulated through vocationalist arrangements. The appropriate role for the state was overseeing and facilitating the activities of the various subsidiary organizations.

Catholic social teaching stressed that the family was the 'first and vital cell of society'. It 'knitted' society together and the institution of marriage 'knitted' families and communities together. The family was the carrier of Catholic social values and the link between past, present and future (Coman, 1977). Since it predated the state, the latter had no right to interfere with it as long as it fulfilled its responsibilities and cared for the welfare of its members. The function of the state and voluntary organizations was to protect the family so that it could carry out its reproductive, socialization and welfare obligations. And, as Peillon has noted:

> In defending the family unit and independence of voluntary organizations, the Church was seeking to consolidate its own authority and influence. By means of voluntary associations the Church can dominate such spheres of activity as health and social services. Further, it is in a position to exercise greater influence on a family which has not been integrated into a state-controlled, welfare framework, and is therefore dependent on the state. Thus, the bitter opposition between Church and state can be seen as the clash of rival notions of the place of the family in society, and an expression of the Church's determination, by keeping the state at bay, to hold its ground in those areas where it has always maintained a preponderant influence.
>
> (Peillon, 1982, p. 95)

As we will see in this chapter, the centrality of the family within Catholic corporatism has considerable implications for women.

Peter Williamson argues that Catholic social teaching conceived of the social order 'in terms of a natural, and therefore immutable, hierarchy of status, with different privileges, rights and duties being granted to those of different status' (1989, p. 23). This patrimonial hierarchical society offered the possibility of realizing social consensus in a manner that individualistic free market liberalism and totalitarian communism could not. In order to reproduce harmonious social relations Catholic social teaching believed in the necessity of a corporatist approach to social and economic affairs. There should be institutional structures linking different interest and status groups together and these structures should have formal representation within the state. And, finally, this corporatist approach stressed that there should be a common set of moral values – provided by Catholicism – which would bond society together. Corporatism also dovetailed neatly with the principles of subsidiarity and family solidarity because 'the collective solidarity of a guild, fraternity or mutuality was clearly closer to the family unit, and hence more capable of serving its needs than was the more remote central state' (Esping-Andersen, 1990, p. 61).

Thus, Catholic social teaching argued for:

> ... a society in which socio-professional groups organize themselves into corporations and collaborate in decision making, and in which the independence of the family and voluntary organizations from the state is guaranteed. This Catholic corporatist organization ensures [in principle] that all voices are heard and that institutionalized dialogue is geared towards producing class harmony.
>
> (Peillon, 1982, p. 96)

Although, ideally, Catholic corporatism believes that the state should have a minimal role to play in the provision and delivery of welfare, there is not the liberal – and neo-liberal – obsession with strictly adhering to free market principles. Subsidiarity allows the state to intervene if the family's capacity to care for its members is exhausted and/or when it is socially necessary. Furthermore, Catholic corporatism does not necessarily preclude state expenditure on welfare so long as subsidiary organizations retain responsibility for the actual delivery of services and it is geared towards the 'social good' and support of the family. Although there is no commitment to redistributive or egalitarian social policies or full employment, the state should not preside over extreme inequalities or manifest social injustice. Thus, Catholic corporatist welfare regimes can embody both liberal and social-democratic welfare principles.

2   HISTORICAL LEGACIES

2.1   CHURCH AND STATE

The political order established in Ireland in the aftermath of the war of independence (1919–21), partition (1920) and civil war (1922–23) embodied both liberal democratic and authoritarian features (Prager, 1986). The ideologies of Catholicism and nationalism fused to shape both the nature of the state and the relationship between the state and Irish society. In no other European state, with the exception of Poland, was such a close relationship established between the Catholic Church and national identity and it played the pivotal role of bestowing legitimacy and authority on the new nation-state (Schmitt, 1973). Organizationally, the Church provided the institutional links between the new political, economic and social elites and the masses. It was able to perform such a hegemonic role in the shaping of the new state because: first, the aspirations for Irish nationhood were inextricably linked to the Church; second, in the course of the nineteenth century it was allowed by the British colonial administration to broaden its influence throughout the social infrastructure; and, thirdly, over 90 per cent of the country was Catholic. The Church was able, as both 'a state-in-waiting' and the moral guardian of constitutional nationalism, to ensure that post-colonial Ireland made the transition to Catholic nationhood (see Whyte, 1980). As a consequence, 'the Catholic hierarchy assumed a major role in determining the social and moral climate within which the Free State was to be governed' (Cooney, 1986, p. 42).

Nationalism played a double role in the shaping of post-colonial Irish society. First, the divisions created by the civil war shaped the core of Irish politics and society. The two main political parties that emerged – Fine Gael and Fianna Fail – represented the different sides in the civil war. The enduring legacy of the civil war, therefore, was the virtually unbridgeable gap between the victors who accepted the partition of the country (Fine Gael) and those who opposed it (Fianna Fail). The bitter debate about the 'unfinished' nationalist project came to dominate all others and even today two of the main political parties do not divide on a right/left basis on political, economic and social issues. Both are essentially centre-right in the mould of European Christian Democratic parties (see Dooney and O'Toole, 1992). An electoral system based upon proportional representation has reinforced the need for both parties to project themselves as representing the national as opposed to class interests. Fianna Fail has been more successful in this respect, appealing to a coalition of the small farmers, significant sections of the working class and the lower middle class. Fine Gael, by contrast, has had difficulty in securing electoral support outside of the large farming class and professional middle classes. Thus partition, the resultant civil war and the electoral system adversely affected the significance of class politics and, as Whyte (1974) has argued, a 'politics without social bases' was created.

The labour movement failed to win a leading role in the shaping of the Irish state. Its political influence was directly affected by partition because the industrial heartland of the country was located within the six counties of Northern Ireland (O'Connor, 1992). In the late 1920s as few as five per cent of the population in southern Ireland was engaged in manufacturing. As a consequence, it was the economic interests of the conservative farming class that initially took precedence within the new state. In addition, the idea was promulgated that because British rule and the

Protestant Establishment had been overthrown, Ireland was somehow a classless society. This linked into a wider social acceptance of a hierarchical society where deferential social relations were ordained by the Church as being natural.

The integrative ideologies of Catholicism and nationalism shaped the Irish state and the national identity into an inclusive, culturally homogeneous, conservative one. A concerted attempt was made to subordinate all social interests to the national-populist project of constructing and consolidating a Catholic, Gaelic and pastoral cultural identity. Both ideologies stressed the importance of national consensus, and social movements which were deemed to threaten this project, particularly ones espousing secularist ideologies, were neutralized (Girvin, 1984). The state, for example, in the immediate years after independence dealt with its enemies in a ruthless manner – for example, trade unions, the rural 'soviets' and farm labourers' organizations, the fascist 'Blueshirts' and the IRA. Thus, the divisions caused by the civil war and partition left deep scars on the national psyche and deeply reactionary political and social entities rapidly unfolded, both north and south of the border (see Munck, 1985).

So how did this ideological framework impact upon Irish social policy? After gaining independence Ireland was faced with a series of possible pathways in relation to social welfare and social legislation. The new state was bequeathed a variety of British welfare policies and institutional arrangements, ranging from the Poor Law to public health, housing and educational provision. Irish citizens had experience of state provision of old-age pensions and compulsory social insurance for manual workers and low-paid white-collar employees (Powell, 1992). In theory, therefore, the new state could have committed itself to building upon the existing welfare infrastructure. However, there was also considerable opposition in the 'new' Ireland to the whole idea of state involvement in social policy. First, middle-class nationalists had consistently complained about excessive taxation under the British and argued that they could run a more efficient administration. Secondly, there was a shift towards laissez-faire economic policies with the result that severe restrictions were imposed on public expenditure and taxes were lowered. Thirdly, there was the emergence of the powerful Catholic Social Movement in the 1920s and '30s which argued that the state should limit itself to overseeing the activities of the various subsidiary welfare organizations. Hence, 'Catholic social philosophy, economic exigencies, and the nationalist tradition, all argued for a state whose role would be less substantial than in most European nations' (Lyons, 1979, p. 476).

The Church took the lead role in the provision and management of the education and health services and in organizing public charity and assistance for the poor. As a consequence, the social policy changes that did take place were primarily administrative in nature. Although some progress was made during the 1930s and early 1940s, the social services which existed at the end of the Second World War differed little in their essential residual characteristics from those of the early 1920s (Maguire, 1986).

2.2 MOTHER IRELAND

The ideologies governing social policy determined that the family should take primary welfare responsibilities. In order to make sure that this happened, women were allocated a 'special' role by the Irish state and Catholic Church. The welfare of the family, Church and nation and the renewal of the post-colonial Irish race were directly linked to the position of women in Irish society.

There were general improvements in the status of women in Irish society in the early twentieth century and the Irish suffragette movement pressed Irish nationalists on the question of women's rights in the new Ireland (see Cullen Owens, 1984). Women played a central role in the war of independence and the Irish electorate enabled Constance Markiewicz, a leading Republican, to become the first woman ever elected to Westminster. However, as Kelly and Nic Giolla Choille have argued, 'independence for Ireland did not mean independence for women' (1990, p. 11). In the 1930s the Fianna Fail government, under Eamon de Valera, and the Catholic Church decided to confront these 'unmanageable revolutionaries' and to clarify once and for all the role and rights of women in Irish society (see Ward, 1983).

In the 1930s the Land Commission, which was set up to implement the government's land redistribution policies, refused women the right to inherit land. In 1932 a marriage bar (similar to that which then operated in Britain) was instituted when the government banned the employment of married women as civil service employees. This policy of compulsory retirement upon marriage was subsequently adopted by many sectors of the Irish economy, particularly after the passing of the 1933 Conditions of Employment Act which allowed the government to prohibit female employment in any form of industrial work and to set quotas for particular sectors. Women's groups opposed this legislation arguing, unsuccessfully, that it contradicted the 1922 constitution which had given equal rights and opportunities to all citizens of the new republic (Owens, 1983).

Women's fears that the state and the Catholic Church were determined to push through enforced domestication were confirmed when de Valera unveiled the 1937 constitution. The new constitution created a theocratic state by legislating a set of principles that ensured state activities remained within the parameters set by Catholic social teaching (Inglis, 1985). It gave formal recognition to the 'holy trinity' of the family, Church and nation and outlined a series of social policy principles which were intended to re-establish and reinforce traditional gender relations by removing women from public life. Article 40 qualified the commitment to equality before the law by allowing the state to have 'due regard to difference of capacity, physical and moral and social function'. De Valera argued that,

> In regard to labour and in regard to work, our aim ought to be that the breadwinner, who is normally and naturally in these cases, when alive, the father of the family, should be able by his work to bring in enough to maintain the whole household and that women ought not to be forced by economic necessity to go out and either supplement his wages or become breadwinners themselves.
>
> (quoted in Moynihan, 1980, p. 324)

Women's groups fought against the 'sinister and retrogressive' provisions of the constitution. They demanded restoration of clauses of the old constitution which guaranteed the equality of all citizens of the republic. Although women won back the clause which guaranteed political participation 'without distinction of sex', they failed to reverse the economic and social policy clauses. The constitution made it clear that women's primary role in Irish society was looking after the welfare of the family (Daly, 1981). Thus, Article 41 on 'The Family' stated:

41.1.1 The state recognizes the Family as the natural, primary and fundamental unit group of Society, and as a moral institution possessing inalienable and imprescriptible rights antecedent and superior to all positive law.

2. The State, therefore, guarantees to protect the Family in its constitution and authority, as the necessary basis of social order and as indispensable to the welfare of the Nation and the State.

41.2.1 In particular, the State recognizes that by her life within the family home, woman gives to the state a support without which the common good cannot be achieved.

2. The State shall, therefore, endeavour to ensure that mothers shall not be obliged by economic necessity to engage in labour to the neglect of their duties in the home.

The constitution legally established that the family was the principal institution in Irish society and that women were mothers, carers and dependants whose lives lay in the home. As a result,

> For almost thirty years after the constitution was adopted, the position of women in Irish society hardly changed at all. The common law regulation of women to domesticity and powerlessness continued. Laws based on the premise that women's rights were inferior to those of men survived in, and indeed even appeared on, the statute books.
>
> (Scannell, 1988, p. 127)

The state and the Church were at one in ensuring that family law and reproductive rights legislation reinforced the position of women in the family. The constitution banned divorce, and the sale, advertising and importation of contraceptives were legally prohibited under Section 17 of the Criminal Law Amendment Act 1935. As Pyle has pointed out,

> Males were granted the right of sexual access to their wives, which, combined with the difficulty in obtaining contraceptives, reinforced female subordination in the household by precluding female control over reproduction and via the increased work load for women that the resultant higher fertility rates involved.
>
> (Pyle, 1990a, p. 95)

Women were denied access to legal aid; no welfare was available as of right to unmarried mothers, deserted wives or prisoners' wives. A battered wife could not exclude her violent husband from the home. There was no divorce: if a wife left home, her husband had the right to claim damages from anyone who 'enticed' her away, or who harboured her or who committed adultery with her. And until the 1965 Succession Act her husband could legally disinherit her (see Scannell, 1988). Irish women were left with stark 'choices': either accept their allocated position in Irish society or emigrate. Many thousands chose to emigrate to work in low-paid sectors of the UK and US economies. They also played a crucial welfare role by sending money back to their relatives.

The legislative changes of the 1930s had considerable implications for the eight per cent of the population who were non-Catholics because, in addition to the above-mentioned restrictions, the constitution also forbade 'the publication or utterance of blasphemous, seditious or indecent material' and qualified freedom of speech and assembly if the authorities thought it would undermine public order and morality. Furthermore, the state's acceptance of the *Ne Temere* decree meant that children of mixed marriages were brought up as Catholics. As Joseph Lee has argued, 'It was difficult to avoid the impression that the state considered it a duty to impose specifically Catholic doctrine on all citizens, irrespective of their personal convictions' (1988, p. 203).

3   THE POST-WAR TRANSFORMATION OF THE IRISH STATE

Ireland missed out on the first period of economic prosperity experienced by western societies in the 1950s and early '60s (Kennedy, 1989). Such was the depth of the economic crisis that, between 1956 and 1961, 43,000 people emigrated every year. Ireland, alone of all the Western European countries, experienced a dramatic population decline. In the period 1950–59 national income expanded at less than 1 per cent per annum. Net industrial output expanded by a meagre 1.3 per cent, whereas, for example, in Denmark it expanded by 3.5 per cent, in Spain by 8.5 per cent and in West Germany by 9.3 per cent. Industrial employment actually fell by 14 per cent in this period. These were startling statistics given that the international economy was expanding. In comparative terms, the wage levels of those who remained were low: in the late 1950s nearly six out of ten industrial workers earned less than £10 per week, while in Britain the equivalent figure was less than one in ten (Cassells, 1986, p. 72).

The depth of the economic crisis and the nature of the post-war economic order resulted in a radical rethink of the Irish state's involvement in the economy. The state subsequently acquired considerable interests in the energy, steel, transport and communication sectors of the economy as well as the ownership of banking and insurance companies. However, in order not to transgress the sacred principle of private property, state and semi-state ownership was achieved not through nationalization but by creating new enterprises (Chubb, 1982, pp. 270–86).

Economic planning was adopted as part of a modernization strategy in 1958. National economic policy was re-oriented and between 1959 and 1972 three programmes for economic expansion were implemented. Protectionism was abandoned and the principles of free trade were embraced. The Anglo-Irish Free Trade Agreement was signed in 1965. This was followed by accession to GATT in 1967 and membership of the EC was finally achieved in 1973. Entry into this competitive economic arena demanded the creation of an internal environment advantageous for industrial development. Since indigenous industry was not capable of generating the necessary employment or success-fully competing in the export market, this meant enhancing Ireland's position as a base for foreign investment. The shift to an export-dominated strategy for growth was achieved by offering a generous package to persuade multi-national corporations (MNCs) to relocate in Ireland. The state, through the Irish Development Authority (IDA), announced to international capital that Ireland was the country 'where private enterprise is public policy' and administered the world's first free trade zone.

As Wickham (1980) has noted, because of the restructuring of inter-national capitalism after the Second World War, Ireland quickly accessed the global economy. A major inflow of foreign investment occurred, especially in the latter half of the 1960s, and was maintained throughout the 1970s because of accession to the EC. With agricultural exports also benefiting from higher prices and unrestricted access to the European Community market, the annual growth of Irish exports was 8.2 per cent in the late 1960s and 8 per cent in the 1970s. It has been estimated that between 1960 and 1974 the change in government economic policy generated an additional 75,000 jobs. The major politi-cal parties committed themselves to producing full employment and, as a consequence, Ireland actually became a country of net in-migration in the 1970s.

Economic neo-corporatist tendencies emerged in Ireland, as elsewhere in Western Europe, in the post-war period. Successive governments agreed that the future economic well-being (and indeed the economic survival) of the nation depended on cooperation between private enterprise, the trade unions and the state. The 1946 Trade Union Act licensed unions for the purposes of collective bargaining. In the same year an Industrial Relations Act established an industrial tribunal, the Labour Court, on which employers and employees had equal representation. In the 1960s Fianna Fail governments attempted to incorporate the trade union movement into their economic strategy. A number of tripartite and bipartite consultative bodies were established to stabilize relations between the state, the unions and the employers. A National Pay Agreement was reached in 1964 and between 1972 and 1976 four bipartite wage agreements were reached. In the second half of the 1970s there was a shift to formal government involvement in tripartite discussions which culminated in the National Understandings for Economic and Social Development in 1979 and 1980. These represented the most serious attempt to develop a neo-corporatist relationship between the state and producer groups, involving very complex trade-offs between union commitments to pay restraint and state action on a wide range of economic and social issues (Roche, 1982; Hardiman, 1988).

4   TOWARDS A WELFARE STATE

It is in this context that the Irish state also re-oriented itself in relation to social welfare and social policy and the reasons why are still debated by economists and political scientists. Coughlan has argued that,

> The Republic's welfare state could not be said to have been moulded by the pressures of a politically powerful social democratic movement, as in Britain, Scandinavia or West Germany ... Nor did the Republic, in contrast to Britain and several other countries, pass through a war time period when the requirements of a national war effort and the need to build social solidarity in face of a common enemy encouraged radically redistributive social policies.
>
> (Coughlan, 1984, p. 39)

From this perspective the Irish state took the lead role as part of its programme to promote economic development. However, it is also important to recognize that the state's shift in attitude towards welfare was a response to wider demands for change in Irish society. Politicians had always argued that increased social expenditure depended on a period of sustained economic growth. In the 1970s that growth was achieved and the rejuvenated labour movement was in a position to make renewed demands for improvements in social welfare. This demand for reform was fuelled by comparison with developments in Britain and Northern Ireland. As Garrett Fitzgerald bemoaned,

> We have the problem ... of a republic faced with the demand for imperial standards, because we were part of the UK at one time. The

demonstration effect, because of the transparency of our economy with that of Britain remains, and our people have come to expect the living standards, the social service standards and the standards of every kind of service and facility they see in neighbouring Britain.

(quoted in Bew *et al.*, 1989, pp.110–11)

The health services were criticized because of their continuing association with the public welfare system. Housing statistics indicated that there was still considerable overcrowding and substandard conditions. There was also pressure for broadening the range of the social insurance system to cover more risks and to include sections of the population excluded from the existing system. In addition the social strain resultant from a major change in demographic patterns forced the state to become involved. The censuses of 1971 and 1981 registered population increases of 5.5 and 14.4 per cent respectively and the 1981 census recorded a net in-migration of 100,000. By the beginning of the 1980s the birth rate was 21 per 1000 compared with the EC average of 12 and the rate of natural increases in the 1970s was six times that of the EC average. There was thus considerable political pressure for change and the main political parties began to view welfare expenditure as a form of 'largesse' with which to secure votes from an increasingly critical and demanding populace.

Of crucial importance was the shift in the attitude of the Catholic Church. In the immediate post-war period the Irish Church, more than anywhere else in Western Europe, retained its dominance at all levels of society and Catholic social teaching remained a powerful ideology: 'It was conditioning the language of public discourse, and concepts such as vocationalism, the principle of subsidiarity and the danger of excessive State control were current to an increasing degree' (Whyte, 1980, p. 163).

In the 1940s and '50s the Church remained wary of state intervention and encroachment and, for example, reacted unfavourably to calls for a comprehensive social insurance system, stressing that it would undermine the voluntary sector, result in higher taxation and violate Catholic social teaching because 'it aimed at doing away with poverty and consequently the opportunity of practising Christian charity' (Kaim-Caudle, 1967, p. 43). Because of the opposition of the Church the reforms that were introduced in the form of the 1952 Social Welfare Act were much more limited. However, in the course of the 1960s and '70s, in the aftermath of Vatican II, the Church moved left of centre on issues of poverty and inequality. As a consequence it was willing to sanction state expenditure on welfare on grounds of social justice. How far this constituted a departure from 'classic' Catholic corporatist principles we shall examine in the next section.

Thus a social and political consensus emerged which pushed Ireland towards a welfare state and a more expansive notion of social and economic citizenship.

In the 1970s comprehensive social insurance schemes were introduced, including invalidity and retirement pensions. The philosophy underpinning income maintenance payments also changed. From the 1960s the practice of pegging payments to subsistence levels was abandoned and more groups were deemed to be deserving of assistance. In 1977 a Supplementary Welfare Allowance scheme was introduced and the remaining traces of the Poor Law were removed from social welfare legislation. A standard basic minimum income, payable as of right, was provided in place of arbitrary and variable payments made under the 'Home Assistance' scheme. The state also committed itself to increased expenditure in housing provision, education and health services.

As a consequence of this modernization programme, by the 1980s the share of the national output designated to welfare in Ireland was comparable with the European norm, despite the fact that per capita GDP was well below the European average: in 1981 social expenditure was 23 per cent of GDP (11.7 per cent in 1960) compared with an OECD average of 25.6 per cent (13.1 per cent). By this time Ireland ranked twentieth in the OECD in terms of per capita GDP but eighth in terms of GDP share of social expenditure (Maguire, 1986, pp. 286–7, 345).

5   THE IMPACT OF THE SHIFTS IN SOCIAL EXPENDITURE

But what of the consequences of the state's economic and social modernization projects? There are three interrelated dimensions that need to be considered if we are to understand the outcomes of the Irish state's strategy: first, whether the economic policies delivered full employment; second, the repercussions for the taxation system; and, finally, the impact of social welfare expenditure.

5.1   EMPLOYMENT

Ireland depended heavily on multi-national corporations and, as they became increasingly capital-intensive, could not deliver sufficient employment opportunities for the available labour force. Furthermore, as a result of changing global economic conditions, in the 1980s MNCs began to withdraw from Ireland (Barry, 1991). The state, through the IDA, was

Table 8.1   Unemployment rates in Ireland and the EC (10), selected years (percentages)

		1974	1977	1980	1983
Males:	Ireland	6.6	10.1	8.8	16.1
	EC	–	4.8	5.2	9.8
Females:	Ireland	4.4	6.9	7.0	13.1
	EC	–	5.7	7.0	11.2
Total	Ireland	6.0	9.2	8.3	15.2
	EC	2.8	5.1	5.9	10.3

Source: Eurostat, 1984, p.17

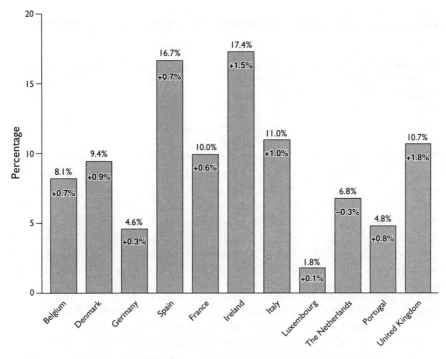

Figure 8.1   EC unemployment rates for May 1992 (seasonally adjusted)

Note: Figures in columns relate to change over the previous 12 months.

Source: *The Irish Times*, 4 September 1992

forced to spend all its efforts recruiting new MNCs to keep pace with the redundancies and relocation decisions of the MNCs (*The Independent*, 16 March 1991). Hence, despite the dramatic improvements in the economy in the 1960s and '70s, full employment was never obtained and in the late 1970s and early '80s unemployment levels began to increase dramatically (see Table 8.1). Ireland now has the highest levels of unemployment in the EC (see Figure 8.1). These levels would have been considerably higher

Table 8.2   Recipients and beneficiaries of weekly social welfare payments, 1983–90

	Number of recipients	Number of beneficiaries
1983	673,957	1,239,082
1984	701,474	1,270,539
1985	725,518	1,319,511
1986	742,885	1,326,899
1987	739,538	1,365,509
1988	726,410	1,327,260
1989	715,540	1,298,827
1990	733,297	1,318,455

Source: Institute of Public Administration, 1992

had not 240,000 people emigrated between 1980 and 1990. *The Economist* (1988) survey of Ireland documents how even before the record increases in employment had been reached, Ireland's social security expenditure had surpassed Japan's and the USA's. In the early 1990s state welfare payments were the only source of income for a significant percentage of the population (see Table 8.2).

5.2   TAXATION

The income distribution implications of the move to a welfare state depend on how the expansion is financed. In the 1970s and '80s the structure of Irish taxation differed considerably from that in other Western European countries. Taxes on expenditure provided a significant share of total tax revenue and in comparison with elsewhere there was a marked decline in the revenue share from tax on property, inheritance tax and corporation income tax. Property tax declined through a series of electoral promises, most notably in 1978 when there was a removal of all taxes on domestic dwellings.

Until 1973 estate duties were the only form of capital taxation in Ireland and the government became increasingly concerned that they were being evaded. A series of reforms was attempted. Capital Acquisition Tax (1974) and a Wealth Tax (1975) were introduced to replace the old estates duties, and a Capital Gains Tax (1975) focused on profits from speculative activities. The stated aim of these changes was to introduce a greater degree of fairness into the tax system. However, such was the opposition to the proposal for a wealth tax that the reforms were rendered ineffectual and the Wealth Tax was finally abolished in 1978. Other forms of capital taxation were also nullified by generous exemptions, tapered relief and provisions for indexation with inflation. Such was their ineffectiveness that in 1980 capital taxes represented 0.5 per cent of total taxation, a drop of 50 per cent on 1970.

Similarly with Corporation Tax. In order to attract MNCs, export earnings were effectively protected from taxation after 1958. In 1978 this was replaced by a policy of a general tax on all profits from manufacturing at the low rate of 10 per cent. The Irish state's attitude to corporation and profit taxes means that employers' contributions to Pay Related Social Insurance (PRSI) was the only contribution made by many companies to the exchequer and this contribution was the second lowest in Europe:

> This reluctance to tax the profits from enterprise, whether directly or through shareholders, along with the sacrosanct status of wealth in the form of capital, confers enormous advantages on proprietorial households relative to others with the same income level and facilitates the inheritance of wealth and its concentration among a small number of families.

(Breen *et al.*, 1990, p. 82)

Little research has been carried out on the exact distribution of wealth in Ireland. In the 1960s it was estimated that 5 per cent of the population owned 80 per cent of the wealth – a greater concentration of wealth than in Britain. We can only surmise that changes to the tax system have done little to affect this situation (see Byrne, 1989).

Whilst every effort was made to limit taxation on capital and corporate income there was a considerable rise in personal income tax revenue and social insurance contributions. In real terms, the yield from personal income tax grew more than fivefold between 1965 and 1980. This occurred because of a lack of a coherent policy in a period of ever-increasing inflation. Tax allowances and the starting-points of tax bands were not indexed to inflation. Consequently the proportion of personal income being taxed increased, as did the proportion being taxed at higher than the standard rate. Despite a protest by one million PAYE workers in 1979 against the glaring inequalities of the punitive tax system, tax payments by the PAYE sector actually increased in the 1980s.

In the early 1980s Ireland's PAYE taxpayers were shouldering 87 per cent of the income tax burden. At 35 per cent a single person started to pay tax at the developed world's highest starting-rate. Because of the steep progressiveness of the tax code, almost half of taxpayers were incurring higher rates of 58 per cent which took effect below the average male wage. No account was taken of the considerable difference in levels of income encompassed by the tax band. When 7.7 per cent for various social security deductions was added on, economists were agreed that Ireland had 'the industrial world's poorest super-taxpayers' (*The Economist*, 1988, p. 13).

The situation was compounded by the fact that, through preferential treatment and non-payment, the self-employed and farmers avoided this crippling tax system. All PAYE workers had to pay tax, and have tax deducted at source, whereas farmers and the self-employed were billed for tax in arrears if their estimated incomes exceeded a certain level. In 1984 only 127,000 farmers out of a total of 194,000 were deemed eligible for tax and, of these, 17,500 actually paid the tax which they owed. At the same time, farmers also owed approximately £24 million in uncollected levies and health charges which were deducted automatically from PAYE workers.

Thus, the evidence suggests that the burden of increased taxation underpinning the move to a welfare state was unevenly distributed among the various social classes, with the employee class in general bearing a relatively large share, while the tax burden of employers and proprietors has remained relatively light. As Wickham has argued: 'The Irish tax system, with its historic bias against the manual worker and white-collar employee, derives from the need to maintain the political support of the farming classes and to provide lavish relief to private and especially foreign industry' (1981, p. 86).

5.3   WELFARE EXPENDITURE OUTCOMES

There was considerable investment in the fields of education, health and housing. However, this did not challenge Catholic corporatist principles because the state limited its role to the provision of resources. As a consequence, private and voluntary institutions, under the tutelage of the Catholic Church, retained the strategic role of delivering these social goods. And as Breen *et al.* argue, this meant that the middle-class interests embedded in the existing infrastructure were not challenged by increased state expenditure.

Core sectors of education and health care remained under the control of the Catholic Church and were imbued with Catholic social principles. The state's role in secondary education was limited to one of funding. Two-thirds of secondary schools were privately owned and managed, mostly by religious orders. Such is the degree of autonomy enjoyed by these schools that the OECD has argued that by international standards it is 'privatized to an extraordinary degree' (OECD, 1991, p. 36). Although compulsory schooling is free, parents are still charged for all textbooks and materials (Mulcahy and O'Sullivan, 1989).

The state also became heavily involved in expenditure on health and by the early 1980s Ireland was spending a higher proportion of its GNP than many richer OECD countries. However, provision of a free national health service has never been an objective of state policy (Rafferty, 1985). Only medical card holders are entitled to free services which effectively means only social welfare recipients and their dependants have access to comprehensive health care. The rest of the population is encouraged to insure themselves under the state-regulated Voluntary Health Insurance Scheme (McDowell, 1990). The Church still has a considerable role to play in the provision of health care. Approximately half of hospital beds in Ireland are provided by the non-state sector. In addition Irish doctors 'have long considered themselves as guardians not only of the physical but also of the moral health of Irish society' (Peillon, 1982, p. 84). They have also jealously guarded the balance of private and public health care and the independence of the non-state sector.

A series of Housing Acts and budgets affirmed the government's belief in free market forces and owner-occupancy as the preferred form of tenancy. If we look at the consequences of the state's preferred housing policies, we find that inequities within the housing market have widened. Rates on domestic dwellings were abolished, grants for first-time buyers were introduced and mortgage interest subsidies were subsequently added. In 1987 the government subsidy to owner-occupiers was £218 million whereas the subsidy to local authority housing programmes was £194 million. It is not surprising, given the level of subsidies and the ideological orientation, that in the period between 1966 and 1987 the owner-occupier sector increased from 59.8 per cent to 78 per cent with 47 per cent of homes owned outright. Ireland now has the highest percentage of owner-occupied housing in Western Europe (see McCashin and Morrisey, 1985; Daly, 1989).

Although there is a commitment to maintaining local authority housing to meet the needs of lower-income groups, it is not a government priority. Expenditure on public housing fell from 8.42 per cent to 5.8 per cent between 1971 and 1981 and between 1982 and 1987 capital expenditure on local authority housing was halved. Commentators have identified a situation where a large underclass lives outside the property-owning democracy on inferior local authority housing estates:

> Despite the general increase in housing standards, certain groups have benefited little, or not at all, from the general improvement in housing conditions over the past decade or so. This is indicated by the stagnation or even the deterioration in housing conditions which has occurred amongst those with the lowest quality of dwellings or with none at all. There has been an increasing disparity between the quality of house services enjoyed by most households, and those obtained by those at the bottom end of the housing market.
>
> (NESC, 1986, p. 112)

Low-income, lone-parent families, for example, have particular problems because they are given low-priority status by local authorities. As a consequence they have the choice of accepting accommodation in unwanted estates or competing in the minuscule private sector where rents are largely uncontrolled. The travelling people have also found themselves adversely affected by the state's housing policies. Despite the fact that their numbers have increased from 11,000 families in 1972 to 50,000 in 1992, their right to serviced sites is not being met and they are deemed not to be deserving of local authority housing.

Increased state intervention was justified on the grounds that economic development would result in a more equitable sharing of the substantially augmented national wealth. As indicated, a massive increase did take place in the state's commitment to income maintenance programmes and to social services. However, Maguire argues that:

> [T]he extent to which social programmes have contributed to a more equal sharing out of the fruits of economic progress must be questioned. Inequality of income and opportunity remained pronounced in Ireland. Although the net redistributive impact of direct taxes and cash benefits increased slightly between 1973 and 1980, the redistribution of disposable income was still very unequal in the latter year. With the exception of medical services, non-cash benefits fail to contribute to the redistributive process and indirect taxes are regressive. Such evidence as is available indicates that the redistributive process operates unevenly from a social class perspective, treating the property owning classes in a relatively favourable fashion.
>
> (Maguire, 1986, p. 320)

Breen *et al.* reached similar conclusions claiming that: 'despite the enormously bloated role of the state as an economic intermediary, it has been monumentally unsuccessful either in ensuring sustained economic growth or in moderating inegalitarian tendencies in the class system' (1990, p. 209). They argue that the main beneficiaries of economic modernization and the increases in state expenditure on welfare are those classes which have paid the least in taxation. Thus, existing inequalities were compounded and new ones generated by Ireland's particular mix of welfare.

6 WELFARE IN CRISIS AND THE QUEST FOR CONSENSUS

The tensions and contradictions generated by state policies resulted in economic and political crisis. Governments in the 1970s were forced to expand public-sector employment as a compensatory measure and by the early 1980s this accounted for almost 30 per cent of the employment total (see Bew *et al.*, 1989, Ch. 3). This compensatory public employment programme worked with the increased social expenditure and spiralling unemployment to push public expenditure levels to record levels (see Figure 8.2). Government expenditure was being financed by foreign borrowing and the crippling taxation system. Political commentators began to notice the similarities between Ireland's increasing debt problem and that of Third World countries (Walsh, 1991). By the end of the decade concern was being expressed about the 'costly welfare state' and there was increasing demand for action to remedy the crisis. Thus, the consensus about the desirability of a welfare state fell apart in the course of the 1980s.

When Fianna Fail regained power in 1987 it announced that it was essential to reduce the national debt and that there would be public service redundancies, privatization, commercialization and public expenditure cutbacks. However, the then Taoiseach (Prime Minister), Charles Haughey, made it clear that this retrenchment agenda would be carried out by agreement rather than conflict. There was not the same ideological commitment to neo-liberalism as that manifested by successive Conservative governments in the UK in this period.

In 1987 Haughey constructed a national consensus by negotiating a Programme for National Recovery with the 'social partners' of the state – that is, the trade unions, the employers and the farmers. The key to this complex agreement was a public-sector pay deal to secure minimal wage increases of 2.2 per cent for three years. It was hoped that a corporatist approach and an appeal to the national interests would hold the country together. Haughey's strategy worked and borrowing was brought down to 3.3 per cent – the lowest rate for more than twenty years. In January 1991 the coalition government of Fianna Fail and the Progressive Democrats (a 'radical right' party formed in the mid 1980s) negotiated a new deal with

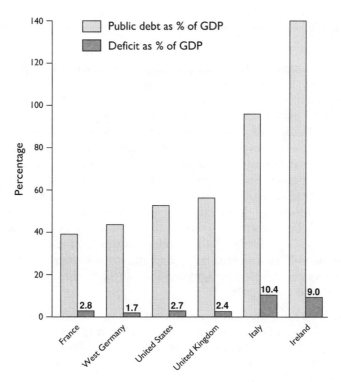

Figure 8.2   In the big league: government borrowing, 1987 estimates

Source: *The Economist*, 1988

its 'social partners' and continued with its retrenchment, tax reform and privatization programmes (see Collins, 1992; Bew *et al.*, 1989).

The government committed itself to mobilizing a 'triple consensus', consisting of: an agreement between employers and employees regarding pay and working conditions; agreement between the government and the 'social partners' over economic and social policies; and a national consensus to put the good of country above sectional interests (*Irish Times*, 27 April 1992). The first problem to be confronted was the spiralling unemployment rates. A series of government committees with representation from all the 'social partners' and groups representing the interests of unemployed people was set up to produce a coordinated approach to the problem. From the initial discussions and proposals it seems as if a fundamental shake-up of the economy and social welfare is planned in the 1990s in order to bring unemployment down to the European Community average and close the gap in living standards (see Tansey, 1991).

The influential Culliton Report, which was published in January 1992, recommended a radical approach to the formulation and implementation of industrial policy. It argued for government policies to produce a competitive, flexible regional and local economy with a 'thriving enterprise culture' and 'spirit of self-reliance' in order to bring about convergence between Ireland and the rest of Europe and to break the dependence on MNCs. The key targets of reform were the taxation and welfare systems which, it was argued, had created work disincentives, a dependency culture and an unacceptable state burden. Government attempts to reform the tax system began to take effect when the 1992 budget lowered the top tax rate from 52 per cent to 48 per cent and the standard tax rate from 29 per cent to 27 per cent. In May 1992 the Irish Minister for Social Welfare told the Fifth European Conference of Social Security Ministers that the present levels of unemployment benefits and eligibility could not be sustained and that Ireland would not have the resources to look after old people, sick people and others who may be deserving of support. He announced that proposals would be implemented to tighten eligibility criteria, to remove work disincentives and to integrate the tax and welfare systems. The government also stated that annual emigration rates of 25,000 per year to Britain, the United States and Europe until 1996 would be useful. To this end, a media campaign was orchestrated in the early 1990s to stress that emigration is a positive experience both for the individual and the country.

However, this hard approach has limitations in the Irish context because the state has been forced to realize that high levels of unemployment will remain the norm for the foreseeable future. The sheer numbers dependent on welfare benefits thus limits the state's scope for drastic cutbacks. As Breen *et al.* argue, the state's economic policies have produced 'a problem without an apparent solution'. The only option is to maintain the most disadvantaged sections of the community in their marginality. The normality of unemployment for many communities has forced the state to think about reorganizing the employment exchanges. The intention is to turn them into 'one-stop shops', supplying all welfare benefits, information and advice, make them more 'user-friendly' and incorporate them into the community (see O'Shea, 1991). The Catholic Church has also taken a lead role in demanding that the state should protect the ever-increasing numbers of the poor, by committing itself to delivering decent levels of welfare benefits and including them in the negotiations with 'the social partners'. Such a shift in state policy seems likely in the aftermath of the 1992 election. The centre-left Fianna Fail–Labour party coalition government, which was formed in early 1993, is ideologically committed to protecting both recipients of welfare and the Irish welfare state. This does not mean that all the proposed welfare and taxation reforms of the previous government will be jettisoned, because the coalition partners are also committed to adhering to the tight fiscal framework of the Maastricht treaty. However, the Progressive Democrats' demands for radical Thatcherite cuts in public expenditure have been removed, for the time-being, from the political agenda. As an indication of 'good faith', the 1993 budget increased social welfare payments in line with inflation, raised child benefits, injected funds into the public health service and levied an extra 1 per cent on incomes over £9,000 in order to meet the extra welfare expenditure.

In the 1980s it looked as if the strains and pressures caused by the manifest inequalities, the economic downturn and the public expenditure crisis would finally break the Irish political system. Commentators warned that the country was heading towards chronic political instability. However, the exact opposite happened because in spite of the bitter debates and opposing interests, its underlying Catholic corporatist ideologies and institutional structures pushed it towards seeking a broad social and political consensus. It was stressed that the survival of the nation-state needed to be prioritized over sectional interests. 'Radical right' solutions were embraced but within a framework of negotiation with the other political parties and the 'social partners'. This quest for social consensus looks likely to be widened and strengthened considerably now that a centre-left coalition is in power. As a consequence, in the first years of the 1990s, despite mass unemployment, escalating poverty and exceptional levels of emigration, the Irish state survived its worst crisis since independence.

7   WOMEN, FAMILY LIFE AND THE IRISH STATE

It has not been so easy, however, to achieve any form of consensus over the relationship between Irish women, the Church and the state. It is this relationship rather than mass unemployment, increasing poverty or the proposed restructuring of social welfare that has threatened to traumatize Irish society and destabilize the Irish state. While the Church has given its blessing to state efforts to resolve economic problems by applying modified neo-liberal economic principles, it has been less prepared to condone any liberalization of state policies which it views as threatening family life (Hannigan, 1990). As a consequence, conservative and liberal social forces, and increasingly Church and state have clashed over the status of women in Irish society. As we shall see in this section, women's groups have increasingly looked to EC institutions and legislation in their struggle to reform discriminatory state policies and practices. In turn, traditional forces in Irish society look to the nation-state to 'copperfasten' the Irish constitution against further liberalization.

7.1   DISCRIMINATION

Jean Pyle (1990a) has documented how in the post-war period the state's economic policies were consciously geared towards the twin objectives of promoting economic development and the reproduction of traditional familial relations. Given that the state opted for export-led development, a strategy that usually involves increases in the use of female labour, it could be assumed that the participation of Irish women in the labour force would have increased in the post-war period. However, this did not happen. Initially women did gain new employment opportunities but the state responded by formulating a set of economic and social criteria for evaluating proposed industrial projects and for awarding financial incentives. Specifically included in the criteria was an explicit statement regarding the preferred gender composition of the workforce. IDA reports in the early 1970s stressed that they wanted proposals which would have a workforce composed of 75 per cent men.

There was a range of other practices and social policies which remained in force until the 1970s that reinforced women's dependent status. The marriage bar, instituted in the 1930s, continued to operate. In addition there was a 'baby bar' which dictated that female employees who remained at work after marriage were dismissed when they required maternity leave. There were no legal provisions for ensuring that women had the right to adequate leave of absence for maternity and guaranteed right to reinstatement in their original employment. 'Protective' legislation, in the form of a ban on night work for women, was also implemented, restricting women's access to industrial work.

The income tax code discriminated against the participation of married women in waged work. According to the Finance Acts, the income of a married woman was considered for taxation purposes as the income of her husband, therefore added to his income and taxed according to the schedule for married couples which moved them rapidly into higher bands. When combined with the lower rates of pay for women, the financial incentive to participate in the economy was offset by the crippling taxation rates. In addition, provision for childcare was lacking. In the early 1980s only 3 per cent of pre-school children of working parents were cared for in daycare centres or pre-schools; the rest were cared for by relatives and neighbours:

> The lack of provision by state personnel of this social service was as constraining on women's options as protective legislation or the marriage bar. The absence of child-care facilities co-ordinated well with the general tenor of state policy, which was still rooted in the belief that mothers belonged in the home and which reinforced traditional gender roles.
>
> (Pyle, 1990b, p. 97)

The regulation of women also extended into health matters. In 1947 and 1950 proposals were introduced to provide universal maternity and child health services free of charge, a compulsory school medical health inspection service and measures to combat infectious diseases. This scheme ran into outright opposition from the Irish Medical Association in conjunction with the Catholic Church on the grounds that it was bureaucratic, centralizing and infringing on the rights of the family. One of the most sensitive areas in the 'mother and child scheme' was the proposal to 'make arrangements for safeguarding the health of women in respect of motherhood and for their education in that respect'. Such a proposal was completely unacceptable to Catholic social teaching and the proposals were not implemented (see Whyte, 1980).

7.2   REFORM AND REACTION

In the 1970s and '80s there were significant changes in the position of women in Irish society. In 1969 the National Commission on the Status of Women was set up and it condemned the extent of the discriminatory treatment of Irish women (see Brennan, 1979; Beale, 1986). In its deliberations it drew upon the views of the emergent women's movement. In addition, membership of the EC also required that Ireland conform with Community directives on equal pay and equal treatment with regard to access to employment (Laffan, 1991). As a consequence, a series of wide-ranging reforms was implemented in the 1970s and 1980s. The marriage bar was removed, employment equality legislation was introduced and maternity allowance was finally introduced in 1981. In the late 1970s the policy of subsidizing male employment opportunities came under renewed pressure. Given the intense competition for multi-national relocation, it became evident that in order to attract MNCs countries would have to accede to their demands to have freedom in hiring their workforce. As Pyle shows, although the Irish government did persevere with attempts to 'fix' the composition of the workforce by offering higher incentives to those companies who would adjust their labour requirements, it did effectively have to abandon this policy. The significance of these shifts cannot be underestimated. The labour force participation of married women increased from 7.5 per cent in 1971 to 19.5 per cent in 1984 and the rates for young married women aged 25–34 increased from 8.8 per cent to 26.9 per cent in the same period (Fine-Davis, 1988).

Welfare reforms were also implemented. The disqualification of women upon marriage from being entitled to short-term social welfare benefits was removed as were the discriminatory tax laws. Social assistance for unmarried mothers, prisoners' wives, deserted wives and a single woman's allowance (for elderly single women) was introduced. The Family Home Protection Act of 1976 also established that the permission of both spouses is required before a family home can be sold.

In response to an EC directive (79/7/EC) on equal treatment of men and women in social policy, the state finally implemented further reforms in the mid 1980s. Under the terms of the directive the Irish government had to implement changes in four areas affecting married women: reduced rates of benefit; duration of entitlement to unemployment benefit; admission of married women to the unemployment assistance scheme; and payments of increases in benefits to married women for adult and child dependants. Whyte (1992, p. 134) argues that the change 'was one of the most controversial and far reaching reforms our welfare system had ever undertaken' because, prior to this directive, the core value underlying the social welfare code was that the husband was the breadwinner and consequently the person to whom increases of benefit for his dependent wife and children should be paid. Married women could only receive increases in benefits for husbands who were incapable of self-support through mental or physical infirmity. Similarly, child dependant increases were not payable to a married woman except where the husband was an invalid or where she was living apart from and not supported by her husband. A married man, on the other hand, could receive increases for his wife and children regardless of her employment or financial status.

Thus the position of Irish women improved significantly in the 1970s and '80s. It is true, as Jackson and Barry argue, that women are still 'segregated in the least paid, least skilled occupations in a narrow range of branches of economic activity' (1988, p. 44; see also Hoskyns, 1988). Maternity leave is still minimal in comparison with other countries with women being entitled to only 14 weeks as compared with 26 weeks in the UK (Beale, 1986, p. 155; see also Cousins, 1992) and Ireland still has the fewest married women participating in the labour force of any EC country. Less than 30 per cent of mothers are in employment in Ireland as opposed to between 30 per cent and 40 per cent in Spain, Greece and Portugal and 70 per cent in Denmark (Pillinger, 1992, p. 23). Crèche facilities are virtually non-existent in many parts of the country and women also take primary responsibility for looking after elderly relatives because of the state's commitment to care in the community. However, women's groups, with the help of the EC, have successfully challenged the all-pervasive ideology that Irish women's only role was caring for the family.

Women's groups also realized that until Irish women obtained full reproductive rights (that is, having information about, access to and control over technologies which regulate fertility) and the right to divorce, they would not be able to obtain further substantive social rights. They looked to the courts in their campaigns to liberalize Ireland's prohibitive contraception, abortion and divorce laws. In 1979 the European Court of Human Rights ruled that the Irish government was in breach of two articles of the Convention on Human Rights – Article 6 which allows all citizens access to the courts and Article 8 which protects family life. Mrs Josie Airey claimed that the Irish courts would not protect her from her violent estranged husband. The courts would only issue an injunction against him if a judicial separation was in force. The cost of procuring a judicial separation was beyond her means and she was not eligible for legal aid. Her case, therefore, was that she was unable to obtain justice because the Irish High Court was only accessible to the wealthy. As a result of her successful appeal, the Irish government was forced to revise its rules on injunctions (Higgins, 1981, p. 82).

Supreme Court interpretations of the constitution also seemed to be supporting this tentative liberalization process. In the early 1970s it declared that the right to marital privacy included the right to import contraceptives for personal use. This resulted in the 1979 Health (Family Planning) Act which decreed that contraceptives could be supplied on *bona fide* family planning purposes. This was described by Charles Haughey as 'an Irish solution to an Irish question'. In 1985 legislation was further amended to permit the sale of non-medical contraceptives without prescription for those aged 18 or over (Healey, 1988).

There were also indications that women were increasingly prepared to travel to Britain to terminate unwanted pregnancies. The official figure for 1977 was 2,183 and by the mid 1980s it had risen to almost 4,000 per annum. Pro-choice groups were also able to point to the wide-ranging implications of the Irish state's position on abortion:

> The presence of a total ban on abortion in the 26 counties of Ireland has led to a definite gap in the health services in other gynaecological and maternity areas. Family planning advice is not available to women in all maternity hospitals. Only one hospital in the country is equipped to respond to women victims of rape, and abortion referral is not offered. For fertile women there is no genetic counselling service. One of the consequences of this underdevelopment is greater difficulties for many women in dealing with miscarriage and spontaneous abortion.
>
> (Jackson, 1986, p. 159)

In 1980 the Women's Right to Choose Group was launched and it opened a pregnancy counselling service, offering information to pregnant women, including, if requested, information about abortion services in Britain.

Powerful conservative Catholic organizations complained vociferously about the 'radical' changes that were 'afflicting' Irish society, warning of the threat to the traditional Irish family and familial relations. As far as they were concerned, such changes had to be challenged. Constitutional referendums on abortion in 1983 and divorce in 1986 witnessed a reversal of this liberalization (Jackson, 1986; Mahon, 1987). Under the 1861 Offences Against the Persons Act abortion was (and is) illegal. But it was not explicitly prohibited in the constitution. Anti-abortionist groups expressed concern that a court decision, particularly a European Court decision, could legalize abortion even if the country was hostile to such legislation. In a bitter campaign the Catholic bishops called for a 'yes' vote on the grounds that it would finally guarantee every 'unborn human life the full constitutional protection guaranteed to every citizen'. In September 1983 the electorate voted for a constitutional amendment which stated that: 'the state acknowledges the right to life of the unborn and, with due regard to the equal right of the mother, guarantees in its laws to protect, and as far as practicable, by its laws, to defend and vindicate that right.'

In 1986 the Fine Gael government attempted to amend the constitution to allow for divorce. Although opinion polls had demonstrated clear majorities in favour of removing the ban, the government was defeated in a referendum with a result which was almost an exact replica of the abortion vote. The Church was even more actively involved in this referendum than the 1983 one and during the campaign the issue of the future of the Irish family was centre-stage. Anti-divorce groups such as 'Family Solidarity' used statistics about the poverty of families headed by lone parents in the USA as an example of what could befall Irish women if divorce was introduced. Nell McCafferty, sardonically, made the connection between women's legal and economic position and their attitude towards the divorce referendum:

> What else could we do in a country where children are totally dependent on full-time mothering, and mother's function as unpaid dependent wives? It was open to Messrs Fitzgerald, Spring and Dukes [government ministers] ... when they proposed divorce, to offer a proper package that would have included an increase in children's allowance, vigorous enforcement of equal pay and enhanced job prospects for women. A nod in the direction of crèche facilities for civil servant females ... would have indicated an understanding of the difficulties that a divorced mother could face. It did not occur to them. They still have not understood that child care and money are an essential feature of a free woman's life.

(McCafferty, 1988, p. 40)

In the aftermath of the election in 1990 of a leading feminist lawyer, Mary Robinson, as President, the coalition government outlined its vision of a liberal, pluralist, 'open and compassionate' Ireland taking its proper place in a united Europe and promised to introduce a White Paper on marital breakdown and divorce and proposals for the decriminalization of homosexuality. That vision ran into immediate difficulties. In March 1991 a fresh row broke out concerning contraception. The government proposed to make contraceptives more widely available and to reduce the age at which one could buy them from eighteen to sixteen. The bishops attacked the proposals saying that it would lead to familial and social disaster by encouraging promiscuity and AIDS. The Fianna Fail government retreated by ruling out contraceptive dispensing machines and setting the age limit at seventeen.

In November 1991 the Irish government, in order to pacify the vociferous anti-abortion lobby, requested that a protocol be inserted into the Maastricht treaty to provide that nothing in the treaty should affect Ireland's constitutional ban on abortion. However, the whole issue was put back on the political agenda in February 1992 when an Irish High Court ruling prevented a 14-year-old rape victim from travelling to Britain for an abortion. The Attorney General attempted to use the 1983 amendment to prevent someone travelling to an EC country to avail themselves of a legal medical service. When the Supreme Court subsequently lifted the ban, the issue of abortion had once more displaced all others on the political agenda (Smyth, 1992).

Two issues were raised. First, the court determined that abortion was constitutionally permissible if it was established that there was a real and substantial risk to the life of the mother. And in this case, given that the girl was suicidal, the court decided that this requirement had been met. The message was clear – abortion was legal in Ireland in certain limited circumstances. Second, it affirmed the right of EC citizens to travel and avail themselves of services, including medical ones. The anti-abortion groups were appalled by the reasoning that the Supreme Court used to overrule the Attorney General. Given that there was to be a referendum on the Maastricht treaty and that it seemed as if EC law guaranteeing the right to travel could be used to overrule the Irish constitution, the anti-abortion groups committed themselves to making abortion *the* issue in the referendum. Irish and European politicians realized that the furore over the case could lead to a rejection of the treaty.

The Irish government successfully disentangled the ratification of Maastricht from the abortion issue by promising to hold a referendum on abortion after the Maastricht referendum. An all-party consensus was constructed around the economic and social need to vote 'yes' for Maastricht. It was made clear to voters that the nation's economic future was at stake in the referendum and a concerted effort was made to sideline the conservative Catholic pressure groups by defining them as a sectional interest. The government was helped by the fact that the Catholic Church supported Maastricht. The perennial concern with 'the national interest' was raised and the Church would have found it difficult to challenge the political party consensus that had been created. Allied to this was the fact that the major socio-economic classes who had solidly supported the Church desired a 'yes' vote. Furthermore, it became apparent in the course of this referendum that the Church has a wider political agenda. The Irish bishops conveyed their vision of a united Europe in which Ireland could 'give witness in the Councils of Europe to Christian values, which themselves help to form a society of justice and peace'. Hence, the Church agreed that the ratification of Maastricht should be separated from the constitutional debate on abortion.

The issue of women's reproductive rights did not disappear from the political agenda in the aftermath of the Maastricht referendum because of the government's commitment to hold a referendum on abortion in December 1992. The Church made it clear that it would not countenance abortion in Ireland under any circumstances and the Catholic pressure groups are opposed to the liberal social legislation announced by Fianna Fail in 1991. In September 1992 the anti-abortion lobby received a considerable boost in their anti-liberal campaign when the Pope personally intervened to remind Irish Catholics that,

> ... the malaise of contemporary society revolves around family life and family values ... Where the family is weakened, society descends into confusion and conflict. Neither society nor the state can substitute for the family's educational and formative influence. To defend the family, that is, the institution based on human nature and the deepest needs of the human person ... and the bulwark of civilization, is an imperative task for society's political representatives.

(quoted in *The Irish Times*, 26 September 1992)

However, Patricia Redlich, commenting in a Dublin newspaper, pointed out the consequences for women if the anti-abortion lobby succeeded in their constitutional campaign to ban abortion in Ireland once and for all:

> As always the poor, vulnerable and less informed will pay the heaviest price, this time to keep Ireland cosmetically clean. Families will cripple themselves to help a daughter in distress, young girls will walk the streets of London alone, and abortions will take place later rather than sooner. It's hard not to feel that a great hatred of women stalks the streets of Ireland today.
>
> (*Sunday Independent*, 11 October 1992)

Thus Irish society is likely to remain polarized over shifts in social policy reforms which supposedly destabilize Irish family life. As we have seen, through the constitutional referendums of the 1980s and the campaigns of the 1990s, conservative Catholic groups have attempted to force state and society into defining Irish women, first and foremost, as mothers in order to bolster the stability of the conventional Catholic family. However, despite the set-backs in the referendums, women's groups have made significant advances in a relatively short period of time and they have been able to use EC directives and the courts to challenge the constitutional 'settlement' on the position of women in Irish society. And, as the Maastricht referendum indicated, there is the distinct possibility that in the course of the 1990s the Irish state will come under continued external pressure to liberalize its position on contraception, abortion and divorce as part of the price to be paid for continuing EC membership.

8 CONCLUSION

Until the 1960s Catholic teaching largely determined the nature of Irish social policies. Strict adherence to the subsidiarity principle ensured that the austere state had a limited welfare role. It was the Church that provided a rudimentary social welfare infrastructure. The rarefied role allocated to the family in the delivery of the nation's welfare had considerable implications for Irish women. The constitution gave women two choices – stay in Ireland to rear and look after families or emigrate to work in low-paid sectors of the British and US economies.

From the 1960s onwards Ireland, as part of its development strategy, invested heavily in welfare. Although adherence to Catholic corporatist principles meant that the role of the state in the delivery of social services was not as extensive as in other countries, the investment programme marked a dramatic change in attitude towards welfare issues. The state committed itself to providing increased welfare as a fundamental right of citizenship in modern Ireland. However, core principles of Catholic corporatism determined the manner in which state welfare was delivered and this had a considerable impact on the outcome of this increased expenditure. During this period there were also shifts in the position of women in Irish society. Women's groups, with the help of EC directives, began to successfully challenge discriminatory state policies and practices.

However, in the 1980s both welfare and women suffered set-backs. Economic crisis, mass unemployment, record levels of emigration and spiralling public expenditure prompted a fundamental rethink of the state's social and economic policies. The Irish state, through a precarious balancing act with the 'social partners', was able to mobilize a national consensus in favour of modified neo-liberal solutions. It was able to do so on the grounds that Ireland needed to have a competitive economy, low levels of inflation and tight control of public expenditure in order to meet EC convergence criteria. This, it was argued, would guarantee further structural and regional funding which could be channelled into job creation projects. However, the same could not be said for the renewed debate over the rights of Irish women. The referendums and campaigns of conservative Catholic pressure groups in the 1980s and early 1990s split Irish society as they tried to block efforts to liberalize the divorce, contraception and abortion laws. This has posed a fundamental problem for the Irish state as it has linked the future prosperity of the country with the European union and there are indications that it will have to reconsider its position on traditional family policies. When faced with such dilemmas the Irish state usually opts for a compromise, but in the 1990s this may not be possible. As a consequence, it looks as if we may be heading towards a situation where there is an historic divorce between the state and Church in the wider national interest. If this happens, we will have to radically redefine the Catholic corporatist welfare regime as it operates in Ireland.

REFERENCES

Barry, F. (1991) 'Industrialization strategies: lessons from the Irish experience', *Development Policy Review*, vol. 9, no. 1, March, pp. 85–99.

Beale, J. (1986) *Women in Ireland*, London and Basingstoke, Macmillan.

Bew, P, Hazelkorn, E. and Patterson, H. (1989) *The Dynamics of Irish Politics*, London, Lawrence and Wishart.

Breen, R., Hannan, D. F., Rottman, D. B. and Whelan, C. T. (1990) *Understanding Contemporary Ireland*, Dublin, Gill and MacMillan.

Brennan, P. (1979) 'Women in revolt', *Magill*, vol. 2, no. 7 April, pp. 34–6.

Byrne, S. (1989) *Wealth and the Wealthy in Ireland*, Research Report no. 5, Dublin, Combat Poverty Agency.

Cassells, P. (1986) 'Living standards' in Kennedy, K. A. (ed.) *Ireland in Transition*, Dublin, Gill and MacMillan.

Chubb, B. (1982) *The Government and Politics of Ireland*, London, Longman.

Collins, S. (1992) *The Haughey File*, Dublin, The O'Brien Press.

Coman, P. (1977) *Catholics and the Welfare State*, London, Longman.

Cooney, J. (1986) *The Crozier and the Dail*, Dublin, Mercier Press.

Coughlan, A. (1984) 'Ireland's welfare state in crisis', *Administration*, vol. 32, no.1, pp. 31–41.

Cousins, M. (1992) 'Pregnancy and maternity benefits: a case study of Irish social welfare provision', *Administration*, vol. 40, no. 3, pp. 220–34.

Cullen Owens, R. (1984) *Smashing Times: a history of the Irish women's suffrage movement*, Dublin, Attic Press.

Daly, M.E. (1981) 'Women in the Irish workforce from pre-industrial to modern times', *SAOTHAR*, no. 9, pp. 74–83.

Daly, M. (1989) *Women and Poverty*, Dublin, Attic Press.

Dooney, S. and O'Toole, J. (1992) *Irish Government Today*, Dublin, Gill and MacMillan.

Economist, The (1988) 'Poorest of the rich: an Economist survey of the Republic of Ireland', 16 January.

Esping-Andersen, G. (1990) *The Three Worlds of Welfare Capitalism*, Cambridge, Polity Press.

Eurostat (1984) *Social Indicators for the European Community*, Brussels, European Commission.

Fine-Davis, M. (1988) 'Changing attitudes to the role of women in Ireland' in *First Report of Second Joint Committee on Women's Rights*, Dublin, Government Stationery Office.

Girvin, B. (1984) 'Industrialization and the Irish working class since 1922', *SAOTHAR*, no. 10.

Grogan, V. (1978) 'Towards the new constitution' in MacManus, F. (ed.) *The Years of the Great Test, 1926–39*, Dublin, Mercier Press.

Hannigan, J.A. (1990) 'Containing the Luciferine spark: the Catholic Church and recent movements for social change in the Republic of Ireland' in O'Toole, R. (ed.) op.cit.

Hardiman, N. (1988) *Pay, Politics and Economic Performance in Ireland, 1970–87*, Oxford, Clarendon Press.

Healey, G. (1988) 'Body politics', *Fortnight*, no. 259, February, pp. 14–15.

Higgins, J. (1981) *States of Welfare*, Oxford, Blackwell.

Hoskyns, C. (1988) '"Give us equal pay and we'll open our own doors"' in Buckley, M. and Andersen, M. (eds) *Women, Equality and Europe*, London and Basingstoke, Macmillan.

Hynes, E. (1990) 'Nineteenth-century Irish Catholicism, farmers' ideology, and national religion: exploration in cultural explanation' in O'Toole, R. (ed.) op. cit.

Inglis, T. (1985) 'Sacred and secular in Catholic Ireland', *Studies: An Irish Quarterly Review*, vol. 7, no. 4.

Institute of Public Administration (1992) *Ireland 1992*, Dublin, IPA.

Jackson, P. (1986) 'The women's movement and abortion: the criminalization of Irish women' in Dahlerup, D. (ed.) *The New Women's Movement: feminism and political power in Europe and USA*, London, Sage.

Jackson, P. and Barry, U. (1988) 'Women's employment and multinationals in the Republic of Ireland: the creation of a new female labour force' in Elson, D. and Pearson, R. (eds) *Women's Employment and Multinationals in Europe*, London and Basingstoke, Macmillan.

Kaim-Caudle, P. (1967) *Social Policy in the Irish Republic*, New York, Humanities Press.

Kelly, K. and Nic Giolla Choille, T. (1990) *Emigration Matters For Women*, Dublin, Attic Press.

Kelly, M., O'Dowd, L. and Wickham, J. (eds) (1982) *Power, Conflict and Inequality*, Dublin, Turoe.

Kennedy, L. (1989) *The Modern Industrialization of Ireland, 1940–1988*, Dublin, Economic and Social History Society of Ireland.

Laffan, B. (1991) 'Women' in Keatinge, P. (ed.) *Ireland and EC Membership Evaluated*, London, Pinter.

Lee, J. J. (1988) *Ireland 1912–1985*, Cambridge, Cambridge University Press.

Lyons, F. S. L. (1979) *Ireland Since the Famine*, London, Fontana.

McCafferty, N. (1988) *Goodnight Sisters*, Dublin, Attic Press.

McCashin, A. and Morrisey, M. (1985) 'Housing policy: north and south', *Administration*, vol. 33, no. 3, pp. 291–326.

McDowell, M. (1990) 'Competitive health insurance: the implications of removing the VHI monopoly', *Administration*, vol. 38, no. 2, pp. 138–56.

Maguire, M. (1986) 'Ireland' in Flora, P. (ed.) *Growth to Limits: the West European states since World War Two*, Berlin and New York, de Gruyter.

Mahon, E. (1987) 'Women's rights and Catholicism in Ireland', *New Left Review*, no. 166, pp. 53–79.

Moynihan, M. (1980) (ed.) *Speeches and Statements by Eamon de Valera, 1917–73*, Dublin, Gill and MacMillan.

Mulcahy, D.G. and O'Sullivan D. (eds) (1989) *Irish Educational Policy*, Dublin, Institute of Public Administration.

Munck, R. (1985) *Ireland: nation, state and class struggle,* Boulder, CO, Westview Press.

NESC (1986) *A Strategy for Development*, Dublin, NESC.

O'Connor, E. (1992) *A Labour History of Ireland, 1824–1960*, Dublin, Gill and MacMillan.

OECD (1991) *Review of National Policies for Education: Ireland*, Paris, Organisation for Economic Cooperation and Development.

O'Reilly, E. (1992) *Masterminds of the Right*, Dublin, Attic Press.

O'Shea, R. (1991) 'The management of social services A1', Social Security, Copenhagen, International Institute of Administrative Sciences Round Table, 2–5 July.

O'Toole, R. (ed.) *Sociological Studies in Roman Catholicism*, Leviston, NY, Edwin Meller Press.

Owens, R. (1983) 'Votes for ladies, votes for women: organized labour and the suffragette movement, 1876–1922', *SAOTHAR*, no. 9, pp. 32–47.

Peillon, M. (1982) *Contemporary Irish Society*, Dublin, Gill and MacMillan.

Pillinger, J. (1992) *Feminising the Market: women's pay and employment in the European Community*, London and Basingstoke, Macmillan.

Powell, F. W. (1992) *The Politics of Irish Social Policy, 1600–1900*, Leviston, NY, Edwin Meller Press

Prager, J. (1986) *Building Democracy in Ireland*, Cambridge, Cambridge Univeristy Press.

Pringle, D. (1989) 'Partition, politics and social conflict' in Carter, R.W.G. and Parker, A.J. (eds) *Ireland*, London, Routledge.

Pyle, J. (1990a) *The State and Women in the Economy*, New York, SUNY Press.

Pyle, J. (1990b) 'Export led development and the under employment of women: the impact of discriminatory development policy in the Republic of Ireland' in Ward, K. (ed.) *Women Workers and Global Restructuring*, Cornell University, Ithaca, NY, ILR Press.

Rafferty, J. (1985) 'Health services: north and south', *Administration*, vol. 33, no. 3, pp. 274–91.

Roche, B. (1982) 'Social partnership and political controls: state strategy and industrial relations in Ireland' in Kelly, M., O'Dowd, L. and Wickham, J. (eds) op. cit.

Scannell, Y. (1988) 'The constitution and the role of women' in Farrell, B. (ed.) *De Valera's Constitution and Ours*, Dublin, Gill and MacMillan.

Schmitt, D. E. (1973) *The Irony of Irish Democracy*, Lexington, MA, Lexington Books.

Smyth, A. (ed.) (1992) *The Abortion Papers, Ireland*, Dublin, Attic Press.

Tansey, P. (1991) *Making the Irish Labour Market Work*, Dublin, Gill and MacMillan.

Walsh, B. (1991) 'Interpreting modern Ireland', *Studies: An Irish Quarterly Review*, vol. 80, no. 320, Winter, pp. 400–11.

Ward, M. (1983) *Unmanageable Revolutionaries*, London, Pluto Press.

Whyte, G. (1992) 'Report of the review group on the treatment of households in the social welfare code: a legal perspective', *Administration*, vol. 40, no. 2, pp. 134–50.

Whyte, J.H. (1974) 'Ireland: politics without social bases' in Rose, R. (ed.) *Electoral Behaviour: a comparative handbook*, New York, The Free Press.

Whyte, J.H. (1980) *Church and State in Modern Ireland, 1923–1979*, Dublin, Gill and MacMillan.

Wickham, J. (1980) 'The politics of dependant capitalism: international capitalism and nation state' in Morgan, A. and Purdie, B. (eds) *Ireland: divided nation, divided class*, London, Ink Links.

Wickham, J. (1981) 'The new Irish working class?', *SAOTHAR*, no. 6, pp. 81–7.

Williamson, P. (1989) *Corporatism in Perspective*, London, Sage.

CHAPTER 9
LOOKING FOR A EUROPEAN
WELFARE STATE

ALLAN COCHRANE

INTRODUCTION

Earlier chapters have concentrated on the experience of particular countries, with shared and contrasting features being drawn out from the discussion of individual cases. We started out – in Chapter 1 – by focusing on types of welfare regime drawn from the work of Esping-Andersen (1990) and used this to provide some justification for the choice of cases to be looked at more closely in the chapters which followed, beginning with the 'hybrid' British welfare regime (in Chapters 2–4). Hong Kong (Chapter 5) was introduced as an example of the liberal market regime; Germany (Chapter 6) and Ireland (Chapter 8) were considered as rather different variants of the conservative regime; and Sweden (Chapter 7) was chosen as the prime example of Esping-Andersen's socialist or social-democratic regime.

Some of the general weaknesses of the typology were acknowledged even at this stage (particularly because of the difficulty it had in dealing with matters of gender and 'race'). All typologies tend to emphasize some features at the expense of others and in this case, too, vital aspects of welfare were marginalized. But, in broad terms, the differences between the types of welfare regimes identified by Esping-Andersen are significant, and the notion of welfare regimes is helpful in promoting comparative study because it opens up the possibility of identifying a range of different features and processes which come together to form particular national regimes.

The earlier chapters of this book have highlighted the extent of diversity between welfare regimes, even where they can loosely be placed within the same broad regime type. Esping-Andersen's typology provided a useful starting-point on the basis of which it was possible to explore the greater complexity of welfare state formation and development at national level; but the diversity of welfare regimes between individual countries can only be understood by acknowledging and exploring the ways in which already existing national institutional, political and social arrangements respond to and generate pressures for welfare (see, for example, Flora, 1986a, pp. xvi–xvii). However helpful a generalizing typology may be in drawing attention to key differences between broad categories of welfare regime and to overarching issues of importance, it cannot explain the detailed processes of interaction which lead to the formation of particular welfare regimes.

Nor, however, should the recognition of national diversity stop us from acknowledging the importance of wider changes which take place across national boundaries. In this chapter we shall be asking, first, whether common trends are encouraging a process of convergence between European welfare states (or welfare regimes) and, secondly, whether it is possible to identify moves which are leading to a cross-national or supranational welfare state, based around the structures of the European Community. Although it is tempting to see these two aspects of change as closely related, in principle policy convergence between different countries might be taking place without that necessarily implying moves towards any set of supranational institutional arrangements. Similarly, although this is more difficult to imagine, new institutional (welfare) arrangements might be developing at European level even if convergence were not taking place between the different national welfare regimes within Europe.

This chapter is divided into three main parts to take account of these analytical distinctions. The first part sets out the global context for developments at European and national levels, identifying wider trends and pressures. The second sets out to explore the extent to which there has been convergence between countries within Europe, particularly Western Europe, and explicitly refers back to the arguments of earlier chapters. It asks whether it is possible to identify a 'European model' of welfare and sets out to explore what the main features of such a model might be. The third part follows a rather different path and seeks to assess whether there have been moves towards an EC-based European welfare state and, if so, how it relates to and differs from the welfare state models discussed earlier. Finally, the chapter looks beyond the current boundaries of the EC to consider the implications of taking a wider view of Europe, both as a consequence of the promised enlargement of the EC with the absorption of countries such as Sweden and Austria and the uncertain outcomes of political and economic change in central and Eastern Europe.

I   THE GLOBAL CONTEXT

The comparative analysis of welfare states generally starts from an implicit assumption that (whatever the differences between them) they are more or less universal phenomena of advanced capitalism or even of 'modernization' (Flora and Heidenheimer, 1981a, p. 23). The implication of this is that – before any process of convergence – substantial similarities between the welfare regimes of these countries already exist. In broad terms the existence of any set of political arrangements which provides 'for citizens who are not able to cover basic needs' (Øyen, 1986, p. 2) tends to be used as a starting-point in defining welfare states for these purposes, although the definition of basic needs and the means of meeting them are likely to vary significantly between countries, even if those countries are at a similar economic level.

It is also widely accepted that in the first twenty-five years after 1945 the advanced capitalist countries (conventionally taken to be the members of the Organisation for Economic Co-operation and Development) could gen-

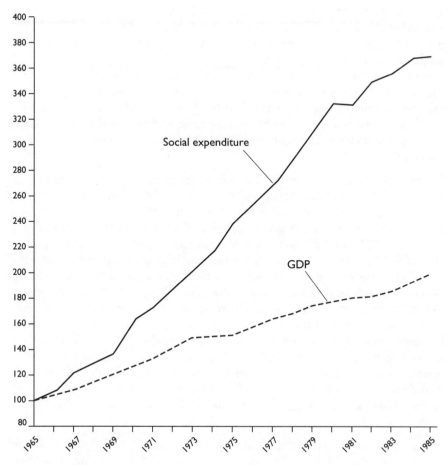

Figure 9.1   Real social expenditure and real GDP, 1965–1985 (1965 = 100)

Note: Unweighted average of 21 OECD countries.

Source: OECD, 1988; data from *National Accounts* and Social Data Bank

erally be described as Keynesian welfare states because of the ways in which the aim of full employment was linked to the provision of welfare services. Outside the OECD – in the newly industrializing or 'under-dedeveloped' countries of the world – matters were, of course, arranged rather differently, since they could not afford the costs of these forms of welfare. The precise form of such welfare regimes varied significantly between countries but the main underlying principles linking economic prosperity and welfare spending were widely shared to the extent that some have argued that they amounted to a 'post-war consensus around the mixed economy and the welfare state, to which almost all advanced Western countries subscribed to a greater or lesser extent' (Mishra, 1990, p. 1). In one version of this argument the Keynesian welfare state is seen to be an essential part of a wider set of arrangements where production, consumption, social relations and political processes are linked – in a system termed 'Fordism' (see also page 2 of Chapter 1). According to this analysis, until the mid 1970s national welfare regimes helped to under-pin a global system of interacting national economies which was charac-terized by mass production/mass consumption economies and extensive world trade, largely regulated at international level through a financial system of relatively stable exchange rates dominated by the dollar and the power of the US economy. At national level the Keynesian welfare state was said to maintain the levels of consumption and production which were necessary to maintain economic and political stability (see, for example, Harris, 1989; Jessop, 1991; Lipietz, 1986; and Chapter 1 in this book).

Others, like Esping-Andersen, have been more sceptical of the notion of 'consensus' and of generalizing welfare state models, pointing to continu-ing political differences within and between states, but few would dis-agree that there was a general expansion of welfare states in this period (Pierson, 1991, pp. 125–34). The clearest expression of a shared expan-sion of welfare can be seen simply in the continuing (and generalized) rise of social spending as a share of national income until the mid 1970s. Although levels and shares varied, the general trend was similar: social expenditure grew in real terms throughout the period. It grew only slightly as a share of national incomes through the 1950s (while those incomes were themselves growing dramatically) before a period – between 1960 and 1975 – when social expenditure grew significantly as a share of national income as well as in real terms (see Tables 9.1 and 9.2 and Figure 9.1). Not surprisingly, Flora describes the period between the early 1960s and the mid 1970s as the 'golden age of the welfare state' (1986a, p. xii).

It is possible to identify other shared features, too. One of these relates to the assumptions such welfare states made about the position of women within them and the gender division of labour within the societies of which they were part. This is less easy to extract from the overall stat-istics of 'social expenditure' but there is little doubt that Keynesian wel-fare states were patriarchal in the sense that, whatever the differences between them, each was constructed around assumptions which in their different ways ensured a secondary and dependent position for women, incorporated not as social citizens but as family members (Pateman, 1989, p. 182). Pateman argues that the development of welfare states was based on two key assumptions: first, that some aspects of welfare (such as childcare and care for disabled or infirm relatives) should generally be provided by women in the private sphere of the home; and, secondly, that women were dependent on men. She notes the paradox that: 'Women must provide welfare, and care for themselves, and so must be assumed to have the capacities necessary for those tasks. Yet the development of the welfare state has also presupposed that women necessarily are in need of protection by and are dependent on men' (Pateman, 1989, p. 193). Dominelli's (1991) analysis of welfare states, which includes countries of the old 'socialist' bloc and China as well as advanced capitalist countries, draws similar conclusions.

Table 9.1   Social expenditure as a proportion of GDP (percentage)

	1960	1975	1980	1985
Australia	9.5	17.6	17.3	18.4
Austria	17.4	23.4	26.0	28.8
Belgium	n.a.	28.7	33.9	35.8
Canada	11.2	20.1	19.5	22.6
Denmark	9.0	27.1	35.1	33.9
Finland	14.9	21.9	22.9	22.8
France	14.4	26.3	30.9	34.2
Germany	17.1	27.8	26.6	25.8
Greece	n.a.	10.0	12.6	19.5
Ireland	11.3	22.0	23.8	25.6
Italy	13.7	20.6	23.7	26.7
Japan	7.6	13.7	16.1	16.2
Netherlands	12.8	29.3	31.8	30.7
New Zealand	12.7	19.0	22.4	19.8
Norway	11.0	23.2	24.2	23.5
Portugal	n.a.	n.a.	17.3	n.a.
Spain	n.a.	n.a.	15.6	15.2
Sweden	15.6	27.4	33.2	32.0[1]
Switzerland	8.2	19.0	19.1	20.5[1]
United Kingdom	12.4	19.6	20.0	20.9
United States	9.9	18.7	18.0	18.2
OECD average[2]	12.3	21.9	23.3	24.6

Note: [1] 1984. [2] The OECD average figures are the unweighted averages excluding Portugal and Spain for all years and Belgium and Greece for 1960.
Source: OECD, 1988; data from OECD Social Data Bank

Noting these structural similarities, of course, does not imply either that all welfare states are organized in the same way or that they generate the same outcomes for women. On the contrary – as earlier chapters have indicated – those outcomes are likely to vary significantly between countries. Thane and Bock (1991, p. 15) argue that the experience of European welfare states after 1945 has been ambiguous for women because, although these states were largely constructed by men, the active intervention of women's movements ensured that at least some of the issues they wanted to raise were placed on the political agenda (even if their demands were not met). Whilst remaining highly sceptical about the extent to which women can rely on traditional (male-dominated) politics for delivering welfare citizenship to women, Lewis (1992) nevertheless points to important differences in outcomes for women in France, Britain, Ireland and Sweden. Britain and Ireland share what she calls a 'strong male breadwinner' approach to welfare in which women's independent access to benefit and other sources of income is severely limited. The underlying principles of the French and Swedish models are substantially different from each other as well as from the 'strong male breadwinner' model. The French system emphasizes support for women as mothers in the context of high levels of paid employment for women, while in Sweden the assumption is that women (as well as men) are breadwinners with reasonable (if not equal) access to the labour market. Both ensure rather better financial outcomes for women than is the case in Britain and Ireland. Earlier chapters in this book on Britain, Ireland and Sweden highlight some of the ways in which these different outcomes were achieved (see also **Cochrane, 1993**).

Table 9.2   The growth of real social expenditure (per cent per year)[1]

	1960–75	1975–80	1980–85
Australia	8.1	1.9	3.9
Austria	3.5	4.8	2.9
Belgium	n.a.	5.0	2.2
Canada	7.6	2.0	4.0
Denmark	8.8	8.4	1.8
Finland	5.6	4.1	1.4
France	7.3	5.5	3.2
Germany	4.8	2.0	0.7
Greece	n.a.	7.6	8.2
Ireland	7.2	5.1	3.5
Italy	5.5	3.9	2.8
Japan	8.5	8.2	3.2
Netherlands	6.4	4.0	2.2
New Zealand	4.0	2.0	1.0
Norway	8.3	6.8	3.8
Spain	n.a.	n.a.	1.1
Sweden	5.9	3.3	0.1[2]
Switzerland	8.1	1.4	1.8[2]
United Kingdom	3.9	2.0	1.9
United States	6.5	2.0	2.7
OECD average	6.5[3]	4.2	2.6

Notes: [1] Expenditures in constant prices were obtained by deflating current price data by the GDP deflator. [2] The '1985' data for Sweden and Switzerland refer to 1984. [3] Belgium, Greece and Spain are not included in the average.
Source: OECD, 1988; data from OECD Social Data Bank[*]

[*] Comparative statistics on levels of social spending can be confusing, because the definitions used by different agencies vary. The OECD's 'social expenditure' includes education and health as well as social security (i.e. pensions, income support, child benefits etc.); the International Labour Office's 'social expenditure' includes health but not education; and the EC's 'social protection' is largely social security. This means that the figures are not strictly comparable between the different statistical series, so in this chapter comparisons across time are only made within each series.

Generally, too, in different ways and to different extents the Keynesian welfare states were organized around ways of including and – possibly more important – excluding particular groups in society. They were defined by and have helped to define nationhood and citizenship. Even where welfare citizenship was taken for granted, not all welfare citizens were equal: 'Not all those living within a given national territory have counted equally as "members of the nation" or as citizens, and not everybody has enjoyed the same right of access to the welfare state' (Pierson, 1991, p. 80). In the welfare states of the advanced capitalist countries, access to welfare benefits was easier for some groups than for others, frequently reinforcing existing forms of inequality and helping to stigmatize those defined as residual or marginal. The most obvious way in which this was achieved was through the plethora of rules affecting migrant-workers: they were generally only eligible for a narrow range of benefits and often at risk of losing their rights of abode if they lost their jobs. Yet it was frequently these groups who were employed directly in the low-paid and casualized sectors of the welfare state itself, a situation which helped to reinforce inequalities still further. These points come out particularly clearly in Fiona Williams' discussion of post-colonial Britain in Chapter 4, but similar experiences are also apparent in the discussion of Germany (Chapter 6). In practice the operation of welfare states in most advanced capitalist countries has not only helped to exclude migrant (or 'guest') workers from some forms of welfare provision, but has helped to legitimate approaches which question the right to income support of all those who can be defined as (in some sense) non-national, even where their legal claims to citizenship are clear. 'Race', as well as gender, always provided additional divisions within the welfare state.

Just as the rise of welfare states can be seen as part of a more generalized trend for the first twenty-five years after 1945, so it is difficult to avoid drawing similar conclusions from the experience since then, even if the direction of change is rather different. If Tables 9.1 and 9.2 highlight a general trend upwards until the mid 1970s, then their message for the 1980s is equally clear: social expenditure as a share of spending has begun to fall, or at least remained stagnant, in most countries, while rates of real growth in levels of social spending have also generally fallen (see also Flora, 1986a and b). A similar and continuing trend can be seen in the figures for social protection as a proportion of the Gross Domestic Product of EC countries over the 1980s (Table 9.3). Glennerster argues that, 'Every country has gone through a period of social policy retrenchment' (1991, p. 168). Whilst it would be misleading to point to dramatic cuts in spending over these years, the contrast with the previous decades is nevertheless a stark one. It certainly looks as if the direction of pressures has changed, to the extent that it may be appropriate to speak of moves towards an 'austerity consensus' (a phrase borrowed from Offe and used by Chamberlayne, 1992, p. 299) or what Heidenheimer (1981, p. 398) described as a 'new pessimism' in most advanced capitalist countries.

This is consistent with the arguments of Pfaller *et al.* (1991a, p. 11) who suggest that welfare states are under pressure in an increasingly com-

Table 9.3   Current expenditure on social protection as percentage of Gross Domestic Product at market prices

	1980	1981	1982	1983	1984	1985	1986	1987	1988	1989
EC 12	–	–	–	–	–	–	25.8	25.7	25.3	–
Belgium	28.0	30.1	30.2	30.8	29.4	–	29.5	29.0	27.7	26.7
Denmark	28.7	30.1	30.5	30.2	28.7	27.5	26.7	27.5	29.3	29.6
Federal Republic of Germany	28.6	29.4	29.4	29.1	28.7	28.1	28.0	28.3	28.3	27.3
Greece	–	–	–	–	–	–	15.5	16.0	16.5	–
Spain	–	–	17.0	–	–	–	17.5	17.2	17.2	17.3
France	25.5	27.0	28.0	28.5	–	–	28.5	28.2	28.1	27.8
Ireland	20.6	21.3	23.0	23.9	23.3	23.9	24.3	23.6	22.4	20.6
Italy	19.8	21.7	22.4	23.7	23.3	23.4	22.5	23.0	23.1	23.2
Luxembourg	26.4	28.2	27.0	26.5	22.8	–	24.8	26.1	26.2	25.6
Netherlands	30.4	31.4	33.2	33.7	–	–	30.9	31.4	30.9	30.2
Portugal	14.4	16.0	15.7	–	–	–	16.4	16.7	17.0	–
United Kingdom	21.6	23.7	23.9	24.1	–	–	24.4	23.6	22.1	–

Source: Eurostat, 1988 and 1991, Table 3.31, p. 135

petitive world, whether because they are under attack as governments seek to reduce public expenditure, or because national economic competitiveness is threatened by successful resistance to such reductions. Pfaller points to some evidence that states with higher levels of welfare statism (those with relatively high levels of social spending and which have remained closer to full employment than others) may have been less competitive in the late 1970s and early 1980s, but the evidence is limited and he is reluctant to draw conclusions which are too definite (Pfaller with Gough, 1991). The European welfare states may be under particularly severe pressure in the face of competition from the countries of East Asia and the Pacific rim where – as the case of Hong Kong, discussed in Chapter 5, illustrates – the basic principles fit uneasily with Esping-Andersen's types and there is a greater emphasis on the linkages between economic success and welfare provision. Although the general trends are relatively easy to identify, it is less easy to find simple causal processes. This implies that there may be scope for significant differences in emphasis in different countries, each of which may define 'austerity' rather differently, just as each experienced the Keynesian welfare state rather differently.

If the dominant global consensus in the advanced capitalist countries about welfare in the years between 1945 and 1975 was one which started with notions of the Keynesian welfare state, it is also clear that there are signs of a different sort of ideological shift since the 1980s. This is reflected in arguments which stress the widespread rise of influence of the 'radical right' (or 'new' right) as an alternative source of ideas about welfare. Glennerster argues that we have seen the rise of a changed agenda on welfare, so that, even if levels of spending have remained roughly the same, ways of spending the welfare budget have changed. Such changes include the increased use of direct cash benefits, the contracting out of services to independent service-providers competing between themselves for contracts, the creation of semi-independent government agencies (see also Hood and Schuppert, 1988) and the levying of charges for services (Glennerster, 1991, pp. 170–71). It is frequently argued that there has been a widespread move away from universalist forms of service provision from 'above' towards more individualized and privatized provision allowing for greater 'choice' and a more extensive welfare mix or 'welfare pluralism', in which the state licenses or 'enables' other agencies to act (see, for example, Glennerster 1991, p. 174; Johnson, 1987; Sherer, 1987, pp. 297–8). This process started well before the final collapse of communism in the Soviet Union, Eastern and central Europe, but the political and economic failure of those regimes and their embracing of the market at the end of the 1980s reinforced the feeling that market-based economic liberalism was setting the international social policy agenda.

Although it is difficult to challenge the view that here has been a shift in the welfare agenda, it is less clear that an alternative has been created which has achieved quite the same dominance as that of the Keynesian welfare state. Mishra (1990, pp. 116–7) acknowledges that the 'ideological spectrum has shifted to the right rather than to the left' but suggests that a choice remains between what he calls 'social corporatism' (which he sees as characteristic of countries such as Sweden) and 'neo-conservatism' (which he sees as characteristic of policy developments in countries such as Britain). Both may be electorally (and economically) sustainable, but the former is more likely to defend existing levels of social provision and seek to maintain something close to full employment, while the latter is more explicitly committed to reductions in welfare spending as an end in itself. Although retrenchment was a universal phenomenon, the precise form it took varied between countries in the 1970s and '80s. Pfaller *et al.*'s summary of some of the differences in five different countries is shown in Table 9.4.

Table 9.4   Retrenchments in welfare statism in five industrialized countries in the 1970s and 1980s

	USA	Britain	France	Germany	Sweden
Tax cuts	*	*	(*)	(*)	
Regressive shifts in the tax load	*	*	(*)	*	(*)
Reduced benefits for recipients of state transfers	*	(*)	(*)	(*)	(*)[1]
Reduced eligibility for state transfers	*	*	(*)		
Reduced social services		*			
Residualization of benefits and services to the poor	(*)	*		(*)	
Reduced formation of social capital		*	*	(*)	
Reduced coverage of occupational benefits	*				
Reduction of public in favour of private provision		*			
Rising unemployment		*	*	*	
Rising inequality	*	*	(*)	(*)	

Notes: * indicates a policy shift. (*) indicates a policy move of minor importance. A blank space indicates that the policy did not apply *or* that the opposite policy was carried out. [1] Temporary measure
Source: Pfaller, A. with Gough, I. and Therborn, G., 1991b, Table 8.2, p. 275

The period since the mid 1970s has seen major changes taking place in the welfare states of the advanced capitalist countries. In part these changes can be summarized in terms which emphasize retrenchment and 'austerity' arising from the wider economic difficulties of those countries. But some aspects of the changes suggest that what has been happening goes beyond stagnation in levels of spending. It looks as if a wider process of restructuring or reshaping may be taking place. Esping-Andersen suggests that:

> Ours is an epoch in which it is almost universally agreed that a profound realignment, if not revolution, is underway in our economy and society. The proliferation of labels, such as 'post-modernist', 'post-materialist', 'post-Fordist' or 'post-industrial', often substitutes for analysis. But it mirrors the recognition that we are leaving behind us a social order that was pretty much understood, and entering another the contours of which can be only dimly recognized.
>
> (Esping-Andersen, 1990, p. 222)

Despite a marked scepticism about the possibility of developing a clear model of restructuring and his dismissal of those looking for a 'crisis' of the welfare state in the 1970s, Pierson, too, argues that it is necessary to look 'beyond the welfare state' (1991, Ch. 6).

Although the precise form of the new arrangements is not yet clear, some aspects can be identified. It is possible to point to three main features of the new world of welfare, some of which have been hinted at in previous chapters. First – and most importantly – it is necessary to acknowledge that welfare states are now more accurately understood as 'mixed economies' rather than welfare states in the traditional sense which implied a unified bureaucratic system of state-based provision. In retrospect it may be appropriate to analyse all welfare states as mixed economies of welfare (since they always relied heavily on informal care), but the nature of the 'mix' is changing to such an extent that it seems reasonable to suggest there has been a significant shift in emphasis. The role of the state seems to be moving towards forms of regulation and licensing as much as – if not more than – funding and direct provision.

Secondly, there has also been a move towards an interpretation of welfare policy as an important element in economic competition between countries. In its earliest form this found expression in the argument that particular national economies could not afford to sustain existing levels of welfare spending and remain competitive. More recently there has been explicit discussion both of the extent to which countries may compete for investment by presenting themselves as having low welfare costs for investors and the extent to which particular forms of welfare expenditure may be more or less attractive in offering social infrastructure for investment and the encouragement of economic innovation (see, for example, Jessop, 1991).

Thirdly, welfare may no longer simply be the responsibility of national governments. This is a more speculative interpretation of changes at the global level, but if in the past welfare regimes were explicitly national, it may now be that it is possible to find examples of transnational or supranational aspects of those regimes. Deacon argues, for example, that agencies such as the International Monetary Fund, the International Labour Organization and the European Community may be having a direct and significant impact on the reshaping of social policy in central and Eastern

Europe in the wake of the overthrow of the communist regimes at the start of the 1990s (Deacon, 1992b). Since the world is increasingly dominated by three major economic (and political) blocs in Europe, North America and East Asia, it is perhaps also reasonable to expect that welfare systems are also being reorganized at that level.

The first two of these possibilities suggest the existence of similar pressures which may be absorbed differently in different countries, because of the ways in which they are reinterpreted through their existing welfare regimes. But if the pressures are strong enough, they might also lead to a process of convergence between those welfare regimes. The next section of this chapter considers these issues more carefully in the context of developments in Western Europe. The third possibility goes beyond individual welfare states to suggest ways in which they might be superseded by emerging supranational state forms. That issue is taken up again in section 3 of the chapter where attention is focused on the extent to which the European Community is developing any of the characteristics of a welfare state.

2   EUROPEAN WELFARE STATES

So far in this chapter we have tended to concentrate on welfare states in advanced capitalist countries, without worrying too much about whether they are European or not, although – of course – many of those countries *are* European. So what about Europe? First, is it possible to find anything specifically European? And secondly, if it is, to what extent are changing institutional arrangements within Europe encouraging further convergence?

When viewed from outside, the general assumption seems to be that the welfare states of Western Europe take similar forms. Flora argues that 'the modern welfare state is a European invention' (1986a, p. xii). And in developing their analysis of the American welfare state Weir *et al.* emphasize that it is 'not a Western European-style welfare state' (1988, p. 9). In such broad terms, the claim seems to be little more than that the more prosperous Western European states have traditionally taken it for granted that in some sense they have a responsibility for the provision of welfare and as a result spend broadly similar levels of their national income on social welfare – and rather more than countries such as the USA and Japan. An implicit contrast is drawn between the way in which it is taken for granted in most Western European countries that the state plays an active part in shaping welfare and the opposite assumption which tends to dominate in the USA, where there is what Stoesz and Midgley describe as a 'cultural antipathy to state welfarism' (1991, p. 26). In the mid 1980s most of the EC member-states spent between 21 per cent and 33 per cent of their GDP on activities defined by the OECD as 'social expenditure'. Only Greece, Portugal and Spain spent a lower proportion, with levels more like those of the USA and Japan, whose levels of social expenditure as shares of GDP were 18 per cent and 16 per cent respectively (see Table 9.2 above on p. 244).

Such a distinction, however, is *too* broad to produce an adequate working definition likely to help us understand the ways in which European welfare states operate, even if it does emphasize (possibly rather too sharply) a difference between the situations in Europe and the USA. There is a real danger of failing to acknowledge the equally significant differences between European welfare states, some of which have been explored in earlier chapters of this book. Some shared features do run through the different chapters, however. All of the European countries considered are recognizably welfare states and in each the continued role of the state in the provision, funding and regulation of welfare is not in question. All of them, too, have clearly had to cope with the increased pressures of 'austerity': all have gone through some process of retrenchment, although to varying extents. Some other key features have remained consistent over time, since each has remained committed to a mixed economy based on capitalism, and, despite some rhetorical flourishes, welfare has continued to be delivered on the basis of a set of patriarchal assumptions and a set of more or less clear assumptions about who is eligible for welfare citizenship. But these are still very broad principles, which do little more than provide parameters within which – as we have seen – a wide range of social policy practices may exist.

The experience of Western European countries since 1945 has been characterized by shared patterns of political change and policy development existing alongside what Kastandiek calls 'an equally striking persistence of national diversity' (1990, p. 69). Using the cases of Britain, Italy and West Germany he divides the post-1945 period into five stages of development. The first (brief) stage – from 1945 to 1947/8 – he characterizes as one in which labour movements were relatively strong and social-democratic initiatives were developed. The second stage – 1947/8 to the early 1960s – was a long period of 'conservative and entrepreneurial dominance, supported by economic prosperity and the domestic impact of the Cold War' (Kastandiek, 1990, p. 70). Although Kastandiek does not explore this aspect of the period, it was also the time when in Europe (if not in the USA) the mixed economy was defined in ways which allowed the ideological dominance of the market but also retained a crucial and taken-for-granted role for the state in welfare (as well as in forms of industrial policy). The third stage – from the early 1960s to the early 1970s – saw the end of post-war reconstruction in the context of economic boom. It was the period in which welfare state spending began to grow dramatically and in which institutional reform and 'modernization' (generally led by social-democratic parties) were seen to offer the key to renewed upturn and national competitiveness. The failure of these attempts (with the partial exception of Germany) led to substantial social conflict which itself laid the basis for the fourth stage – from the early 1970s to the late '70s/early '80s – in which emphasis was placed on 'the politics of co-operation and concertation', often described as corporatism (Kastandiek, 1990, p. 72). Welfare policies as well as industrial and economic policies were the subject of negotiation between major economic interests. The fifth stage – from the late 1970s/early '80s to the start of the 1990s – was characterized by the end of corporatist arrangements at national level and the rise of neo-liberal and neo-conservative approaches in many countries. But, concludes Kastandiek, in practice 'Thatcherism has not been the vanguard of a radical reversion of post-war politics in Western Europe'. Instead he suggests that 'the diversity of national patterns has continued again' (p. 73).

But that diversity does not mean that individual welfare states can exist completely autonomously with little reference to global economic changes or political changes in other countries. Some aspects of change already discussed in the wider context of global change are particularly apparent in the European context. Even the strongest bastions of social-democratic welfarism such as Sweden and Denmark have been forced belatedly to acknowledge the pressures of financial constraint, reducing their abilities to maintain high levels of state spending. Others, such as Britain, have more or less consciously presented themselves as offering low-cost welfare, with guarantees of minimum regulatory interference by the state. Austerity welfare certainly dominates throughout Europe, and within the EC this may be reinforced by the need to compete with the relatively cheap labour and low welfare costs of southern European (what Leibfried calls 'Latin rim') member-states. Leibfried (1992b, p. 255) suggests that the model most likely to come to dominate in this process is the liberal (or 'Anglo-Saxon') one in which welfare tends to be residual and targeted, and not based on clear entitlements to benefit or commitments to the maintenance of full employment. Similar pressures are likely to exist if the previously communist countries of Eastern and central Europe are absorbed into the European economy with highly residual (or low-cost conservative) welfare regimes. (See Deacon (1992a) for a discussion of possible futures in central and Eastern Europe.)

Similarly, it is possible to see a general trend away from direct state provision towards other forms of welfare and different mixed economies of welfare. It would, however, be misleading to see these solely as moves to market mechanisms in the British-style model of Thatcherism. On the contrary, the borrowing may be rather more eclectic, with each national welfare regime drawing on elements from several others in the process of restructuring. Using a typology developed by Titmuss (1974), Chamberlayne (1992, p. 301) charts moves within four European countries in response to similar pressures since 1945. She suggests that the UK moved from a universalist approach (providing services on the basis of need) in 1950 to a residual one (in which the role of the state is minimized in favour of the market and the family) in 1985, passing through an industrial achievement phase in 1970 (that is, one in which the state's main welfare role is to reinforce economic success by providing appropriate incentives). Over the same period Italy moved from being firmly in the residual category to being more modestly in the universalist category in 1970. France moved from industrial-achievement to universalist, and West Germany remained firmly in the indus-trial-achievement category.

The point here is not to introduce yet another typology, but to highlight some of the different ways in which welfare regimes may change over time without achieving convergence. Leibfried argues strongly that the basic structures of the existing European welfare regimes are so distinc-tive that it would be a mistake to look for ways in which they might – organically – grow together. He is highly sceptical of the possibility of convergence without some form of intervention from above. Leibfried believes that 'The common ground is missing on which a European wel-fare regime could be built' (1992b, p. 255). It is difficult to disagree with that conclusion. Leibfried suggests, however, that the EC may offer one route through which such a regime might be constructed.

3 A EUROPEAN WELFARE STATE?

If a distinctive European welfare regime is unlikely to be created as the result of an incremental process of convergence between existing Euro-pean welfare states, the rise of the European Community (EC) as a supra-national political initiative at European level might encourage the parallel development of a European welfare state, linking together mem-ber-states in a single framework and possibly even providing its own forms of welfare throughout the Community. Such a welfare state is unlikely to look much like existing national welfare regimes, both because it will be reluctant to undertake tasks already performed at national level and because the EC has few powers to operate indepen-dently of its member-states. The politics of the EC combine intergovern-mental bargaining and negotiation with a degree of autonomy for the European Commission and the European Court of Justice. Although the EC's institutions and those who run them are 'European', they are also 'simultaneously linked to the national' through a complex web of appoint-ments, meetings and other networks (Sbragia, 1992a, p. 4).

Much of what is usually referred to as EC social policy bears little relationship to welfare as it is generally understood in the welfare regimes of the Community's member-states. This point is often missed in popular discussions of the EC, in part because frequent references to 'the social dimension' suggest the existence of a developed European social policy. The Protocol on Social Policy (frequently referred to as the Social Chapter) attached to the Treaty of European Union (Maastricht treaty) is often assumed to promise a fully rounded welfare state although its provisions concentrate on defining the rights of workers. Its objectives are general, focusing on the promotion of employment, the improvement of living and working conditions, and the provision of (nationally defined) adequate forms of social protection. The Protocol seeks to encourage dia-logue between management and labour, with effective consultation of workforces, as well as improved health and safety at work, equal employ-ment opportunities for men and women and equal pay for equal work.

Such an explicitly labour-market oriented package clearly takes a different starting-point from most welfare states, although its provisions fit uneasily with welfare regimes which are close to the liberal model. (The UK government refused to sign this part of the Treaty when it was first agreed by the other eleven member-states in 1991.) Leibfried (1992a, p. 17) suggests that the earlier Social Charter (Fundamental Social Rights of Workers, again agreed by eleven of the states excluding the UK in 1989), on which the Social Protocol was based, reflected a 'negative' view of social policy which stressed rights and above all the right to freedom of movement (labour mobility) for workers. Its main purpose was to remove obstacles to the operation of a single market within Europe rather than to provide a positive statement of citizenship.

There are, however, ways in which it is possible to talk of moves towards something which would look more like a European welfare state. The first involves looking more carefully at forms of income transfer to particular groups; the second implies a rather different way of looking at welfare, concentrating on the regulation of social policy from above and the promotion of shared goals across the member-states.

Some of the EC's existing expenditure could be defined as welfare spending, if the definition is drawn broadly enough. The main elements of EC spending are on the so-called structural funds, that is spending under the European Social Fund, the European Regional Development Fund and the Common Agricultural Policy. Despite its title (which to a British audience might imply the payment of welfare benefits), the first of these is oriented towards the retraining and relocation of the European unemployed. It provides support for training in areas of high unemployment with an emphasis on removing rigidities in labour markets rather than providing welfare. It is part of a package of policies intended to smooth the operations of the market or to enable 'adaptation to market-induced changes' as some industrial and employment sectors decline while others rise (Cutler *et al.*, 1989, p. 148). So, insofar as it is welfare, it is welfare-oriented towards servicing the needs of innovation and market-led economic change and restructuring. Welfare is defined here in terms of contribution to economic success.

The European Regional Development Fund (ERDF) aims to encourage infrastructural development in the poorest regions of the EC and those in industrial decline. The bulk of spending goes to Ireland and the southern countries of the EC. As a result, its operation implies a redistribution of resources from the north to the south. It could, therefore, be seen as a form of welfare policy, but – again – if it is, then this implies a changed notion of welfare in which the generation of economic growth and restructuring to fit into a wider European market is itself defined as welfare. It is not intended to provide financial support to people living in the countries of the periphery, but to integrate those countries into a single market with the help of necessary infrastructural spending. Any increase in prosperity for local residents will be incidental to the process of economic integration. The governments of the EC's southern member-states and

Ireland are resistant to suggestions that the Community's spending should be explicitly redefined as welfare spending (for example, as income support to people in poorer countries) because they want to encourage self-sustaining economic growth as a basis for prosperity (which may ultimately provide a base for improvements in nationally provided welfare). Because their main competitive edge within the EC lies in their low labour costs, the governments of these countries see social policies which might increase costs as threats to economic growth. As a result the governments of poorer countries prefer programmes which transfer resources 'in a way that improves infrastructure and enhances productivity without dramatically affecting wages' (Leibfried and Pierson, 1992, p. 346). In other words, they wish to retain and strengthen their competitiveness and scope for innovation.

The Common Agricultural Policy (through the Common Agricultural Guidance and Guarantee Fund) – involving some 60 per cent of EC spending at the start of the 1990s – incorporates welfare principles rather more clearly. It is the most supranationally organized system within the EC and regulates some 90 per cent of agricultural production and almost all the incomes of EC farmers. Unlike the other structural funds, the dominant driving force of agricultural policy *is* the maintenance of the incomes of one section of the population, rather than a process of economic restructuring. Unlike expenditure under the ERDF, most agricultural spending remains in the more prosperous northern European states, although some poorer countries (such as Ireland) do benefit from it. It is, however, not based on a set of agreed social or citizen rights for farmers, but on an economic rationale – a response to the economic restructuring of European agriculture. The income transfers are hidden behind guaranteed sales for some products and payment for withdrawing land from the active production of others. Leibfried (1992a) argues that if income transfers were to be decoupled from levels of output, then the Community's agricultural policy would more clearly be seen for what it is, namely a rather complicated social policy mechanism for providing a basic income to European farmers. If this interpretation were accepted, however, Leibfried goes on to argue, it would then be difficult to justify shutting out other claimants. It would be logically consistent to develop a more comprehensive system of benefits, related to the risks of falling income, following from European integration.

Another way into more direct involvement in the provision of social security might be to develop a scheme which involved EC employees, employees on trans-European schemes and internal EC migrants. Pieters (1991) has suggested that it would be possible to build on existing responsibilities (to coordinate rights to social security for internal migrants) to encourage the growth of what he calls the thirteenth state (which would exist alongside the other twelve EC states). This 'state' would be responsible for a European Social Security System, of which intra-European migrants could choose to be members. Such a scheme, while initially limited to a small group of employees, might become a model towards whose provisions others in individual member-states could aim. Its influence would be greater than its membership might suggest, particularly if it built on the strengths of the different national schemes (Leibfried, 1992a, pp. 47–8). In practice, however, there is little evidence that moves in this direction are taking place, not least because, if generalized, any move towards best levels of provision (which such a scheme would almost certainly require if migrants were to opt for inclusion) would imply increased costs not only at European but also at member-state levels. It seems more likely that a degree of 'harmonization' will take place around what might be called 'moderate minimum standards' of income support in the different systems, but this would not imply the creation of any new European state form to protect it (Vobruba, 1991, p. 62).

The EC's role in developing social policy takes on rather different forms, through the identification of key issues and programmes which have a high profile, even if they do not have large budgets. The EC has, for example, funded three anti-poverty programmes between the mid 1970s and the 1990s. The most recent of these (launched in 1989) is intended to build from 'small-scale, grassroots projects towards larger "prototype" projects operating at the level of mainstream agencies' (Baine *et al.*, 1992, p. 81). Although spending on programmes such as these is small by the standards of the welfare states that they are intended to influence, it represents significantly increased resources to individual projects and the partners involved in running them. It has also encouraged research into the incidence of poverty across Europe which, it might be argued, helps to raise the profile of the EC in social policy and to influence the policies of national governments. A similar strategy seems likely to be on offer in the field of urban poverty in particular, where it has been suggested that 'It may ... seem appropriate that the Community should take more responsibility for problems of urban poverty and deprivation' (Commission of the European Communities, 1991, p. 202).

Although it is possible to point to aspects of the EC's activities that are welfare-state-like, it is important not to exaggerate their significance. Most of these activities are not perceived as having much to do with social policy or welfare, either by the EC itself or – possibly more important – by the governments of its member-states. However optimistically one views the possibility of a supranational European welfare state, it is unlikely to operate in ways which look much like the individual welfare states which constitute the EC. EC expenditure represents only 1.2 per cent of Community national income and less than 4 per cent of central government spending of the EC member-states. Since the structural funds account for around 80 per cent of EC expenditure, there is not much scope for developing a significant budget earmarked for welfare spending (Leibfried and Pierson, 1992, p. 348). The difficulties of reaching agreement between the countries of the European Community at the start of the 1990s, even on the relatively modest political union proposed in the Maastricht treaty, suggest that any more far-reaching moves towards building a supranational welfare state are unlikely to be realized in the near future. At best it is possible to identify the seeds of welfarism in the operation of programmes with other ambitions and in the form of rather minor welfare programmes. It does not seem likely that the EC will be able to transform itself into a fully fledged welfare state with trans-European income support programmes and funding, operated from Brussels or any other European centre. If, however, it is Utopian to expect too much in these terms, perhaps other aspects of the EC's operation, particularly those connected with ways of regulating the operation of national systems within a single market, raise the possibility of alternative welfare developments.

It was argued by many of the supporters of the European Community in the early 1990s that it was necessary for the move towards a single European market to be accompanied by a recognition of the importance of the 'social dimension'. This social dimension was to be 'directed towards protecting and improving the rights and quality of life of workers throughout the Community as the integration process moves ahead. Social policy also works to ensure the widespread availability of the skilled and flexible workforce necessary for' European industry to maintain and improve its competitive position (Lange, 1992, p. 228). The key point about the social dimension, therefore, was that it was explicitly linked to the EC's strategy for economic integration. Majone (1991) points to the EC's own ambitions 'to increase its influence' and the difficulties of doing so through its limited spending options, but also stresses the interest of multinational export-oriented companies in Europe-wide regulation as a means of 'avoiding inconsistent and progressively more stringent regulations in various EC and non-EC countries' (pp. 96–7). One of the arguments for the social dimension, therefore, was the need to maintain consistency to make longer-term planning and investment easier for companies such as these.

Two opposing positions can be identified in debates about the forms of social policy regulation which should be developed through the EC (Lange, 1992, pp. 230–1). The first (minimalist) approach expects no more than basic rules (minimum rights on health and safety at work, gender equality at work, the access of disabled people to employment, the transferability of social security rights for internal migrants) to be delivered on a decentralized basis at member-state level, leaving individual countries to determine rights and how to protect them. The second (social-protectionist) approach seeks to raise standards of provision where they are low and to maintain them where high through a process of 'harmonization'. It argues for the EC to work against 'social dumping' or the reduction of provision to the lowest common denominator through competitive bidding between states over labour costs. Supporters of this approach argue that, 'by fostering a trained, protected, and therefore flexible work force, while at the same time gradually raising labour costs for firms, EC-level social policy would provide both carrots and sticks for firms to upgrade their technology and to compete in markets in which European firms have the most favourable prospects in the coming decade' (Lange, 1992, p. 231).

Although she acknowledges the currently limited scope of EC social policy, Cram argues that,

> ... the use of regulatory policy increasingly allows the European Commission to take on the role of 'calling the tune without paying the piper' in the field of social policy ... [B]y making use of regulatory policies in the area of social policy, rather than those involving direct Community expenditure, EC social policy, in a number of specific areas, increasingly sets the standards to be adhered to in the member states while incurring minimum Community costs.

(Cram, 1993, p. 136)

The advantage to the EC of such an approach is twofold: first it avoids the necessity of having directly to confront powerful member-states and, secondly, it ensures that the costs are borne by national taxes and individual employers rather than the EC itself. Policy-making through regulation and rule-making also tends to mask the extent of any potentially embarrassing redistribution between states and regions, instead of highlighting them as the structural funds do. Cram suggests that the creation of an effective and extensive regulatory framework for social policy is a gradual process characterized by 'the incremental development of marginal, relatively innocuous measures in order to establish precedent and competence' (Spicker, 1991, p. 9, quoted in Cram, 1993). She emphasizes the importance of non-binding 'soft law' at the European level being created outside the high controversy surrounding the signing of major treaties, and points to the ways in which the declaration of political commitment to general goals (for example, on basic levels of income support or on employment rights) may help to encourage changes, as may EC-sponsored research, such as that organized around the poverty programmes discussed above.

Key aspects of a regulatory framework are already present in provisions within treaties, Community directives and regulations (as well as the Social Chapter) even if – as noted earlier – the emphasis of these documents is on the position of people at work or in the labour market – on health and safety at work, equal treatment of men and women, protection and social security for EC migrant-workers. A relatively modest European welfare state building on labour-market policies is easier to envisage than more grandiose structures which use a vision of a United States of Europe as a starting-point. It may nevertheless have significant impact on how the national welfare states operate. Here some rules which were initially oriented towards labour markets have already had clear social policy impacts, particularly in the field of equal opportunities for women. The European Court of Justice has ruled that individuals can bring cases under Article 119 of the Treaty of Rome which relate to equal pay, and the EC has used sex discrimination as an issue on which to challenge member-states 'as an entering wedge for expanded activity' (Leibfried and Pierson, 1992, p. 338). It is one of the few areas in which the EC has felt able to enforce social policy harmonization – in the case of the UK forcing the government to prepare proposals to make men and women eligible for the basic old-age pension at the same age. Nevertheless, the outcomes of EC intervention have tended to be equivocal in this sphere, too, precisely because of their employment focus. One EC directive (agreed by the Council of Ministers in 1979 and implemented in 1984) promised equal treatment for men and women in the field of social security and led to changes to the benefits system in the UK. In practice, however, since most women do not have the same employment patterns as men, their access to national insurance benefits is limited and the dependence of other (effectively privatized) benefits – such as sick pay, maternity pay and occupational pensions – on being in the right sorts of employment (full-time and long-term) similarly reduces access while retaining 'equality' (Millar, 1989, pp. 315–7). Part-time workers (overwhelmingly women) are still not entitled to the same levels of private or public welfare support, despite EC directives and European Court decisions on equality.

Regulation of the European labour market has also given the European Commission and the European Court the responsibility of ensuring that internal (EC national) migrants did not lose out – that is, to ensure that there was no discrimination against citizens of other member-states on 'social security' issues; to determine which state would decide legally contested cases; to protect the accumulation and transfer of insurance entitlement arising from spells of employment in different countries; and to protect the right to take social entitlements to any member-state (Leibfried, 1992a, p. 35). The Commission was also able to exempt European civil servants from national schemes when they became part of (better) European schemes and made similar exemptions for workers on a number of other Europe-wide initiatives, for example those working for the Airbus consortium (Leibfried, 1992a, p. 21). In other words, the EC had a clear responsibility for co-ordination in this sphere. It was this which led Pieters to develop his notion of a European Social Security System which is discussed above.

This responsibility is, however, of limited significance for two reasons. First, it affects only a very small number of EC citizens (and there is no similar arrangement for non-EC migrant-workers whose numbers are more than twice as great). Only some 1.4 per cent of EC employees fit into this category (covering around 1.5 per cent of people, if families are taken into account). Secondly, and more significantly, in this model 'national systems are "co-ordinated" rather than harmonized' (Leibfried and Pierson, 1992, p. 338) in the sense that there is no attempt to bring the different systems to the same level, only to ensure that nationals of one EC state working in another EC state have access to the same entitlements as nationals of the state in which they are working. Again the entitlement to welfare comes from a stress on the free movement of labour, rather than a commitment to wider welfare ambitions. The European Court of Justice has ruled that what it defines as 'welfare rights' (that is, benefits which are not employment-related) may be limited to a country's nationals, even if in practice welfare is defined so narrowly by the Court that few benefits are actually excluded. The benefit systems remain national and the EC and the European Court only regulate access to them.

Despite the EC's limited scope for practical intervention, there are nevertheless some features of these responsibilities which may influence the shape of welfare at member-state and European level. The first is simply that EC requirements may encourage changes in national systems in unintended ways. Those requirements stress the portability of many benefits between countries because they are defined as employment-related (this extends to benefits such as child allowances) and this may encourage national governments to move away from universal benefits towards contributory benefits (whether state-provided or – more likely – provided through insurance or employment, for example in the form of occupational pensions) or ones which can be more easily targeted and less easily transported (such as housing benefit) (Leibfried and Pierson, 1992). The second is a more important aspect of the emerging system, which echoes some of the early experience of welfare state development at national level. A great deal of EC-wide policy is concerned with the defining of rights for citizens of EC member-states within a single market. It explicitly avoids providing similar rights for migrants who are not citizens of member-states. Their 'rights' are directly employment-related: while employed on limited-term contracts with appropriate entry certificates and visas they may call on some nationally provided benefits, but as soon as those contracts come to an end, they have no EC-guaranteed welfare rights. Their position is governed by national laws which differ from member-state to member-state. Migrant women from outside the EC without work permits who have entered as dependants of their husbands are unable to register as unemployed, to receive unemployment benefit or many other benefits (Prondzynski, 1989, p. 351). In other words the most developed aspect of European social policy is one which reinforces the notion of 'Fortress Europe' (discussed in Chapter 1), aiming to protect relatively high levels of welfare provision within the Community, while excluding all of those who may be defined as 'outsiders' (see also, for example, Gordon, 1989, and Baldwin-Edwards, 1991).

More positively, Leibfried and Pierson (1992) point to the possibility of a European welfare state that would be a 'state of courts and technocrats'; integration might be carried through with the help of the law with a 'legalistic, regulatory bias' with a 'rights based conception of a social citizenship' (p. 355). They suggest that some aspects of the EC's regulatory and legally based approach may imply moves towards forms of European social citizenship, which imply 'individualized, entitlement-based benefits rather than largesse' or charitable payments to the poor through the state (ibid., p. 335). This, they argue, fits in well with the political basis and institutional structure of the EC and would help to provide 'mandates for national action'. While Leibfried and Pierson acknowledge that moves in this direction cannot be taken for granted, such developments are, they suggest, likely to accelerate if there are renewed pressures and failures at national level: 'This would by no means signal the arrival of a European welfare state, but it would mean that social affairs had joined the growing list of policy domains in which the community had become a factor of central importance' (ibid., p. 357).

While it is possible to see how these initiatives could lead to a more developed form of welfare state – or what Leibfried possibly more accurately describes as a 'social' state to highlight the difference between the welfare regimes of the EC's member-states and what might grow out of the EC – moves in this direction are still relatively limited. They are either only apparent in cases which are strictly labour-market oriented (for example, equal pay cases, health and safety at work cases) or in the limited case of women's pension rights. The legalistic emphasis on entitlement developed by Leibfried and Pierson so far only relates to those in the labour market and substantial trans-European pressure would be required for its extension to other sections of the population (for example, in the form of a guaranteed basic income). The notion of entitlement itself still fits more easily with some countries (such as Germany) than with others (such as the UK and Ireland) where 'largesse' is still the main welfare principle. Leibfried (1992a, p. 53) himself talks of a time-scale of fifty years before the changes he points to are likely to come to fruition, even on a modest scale.

Social citizenship remains a national rather than a European responsibility despite attempts to make reference to it in the Maastricht treaty. For the foreseeable future 'social Europe' is likely to focus on specific limited proposals for intervention on which agreement is reached between governments and European interests while most other social issues are left to member-states.[†]

4   A WIDER EUROPE

Most of the discussion so far has concentrated rather narrowly on the experience of the European Community, the extent to which the welfare states of its members may be converging and the extent to which the EC itself may be transforming itself into a European welfare state. Although similarities and tendencies towards convergence were identified, stress was also placed on the importance of acknowledging continuing differences. And, again, although some signs of moves towards EC-wide structures were identified, it was stressed that the extent of such moves should not be exaggerated. They were possibilities rather than certainties, or even likelihoods. In any case, the EC is part of a wider Europe and some of the changes there may make any predictions based solely on the experience of those that were member-states of the EC at the start of the 1990s look rather unconvincing.

There are two main changes at European level which seem certain substantially to influence the future of welfare states within the continent.

[†] Much of the argument in this section of the chapter draws on the work of Stephan Leibfried, although I draw rather different conclusions than he does. I am grateful to him for both discussion and the sight of important published and unpublished papers.

The first is the likely expansion of the EC to take in many of the countries which were previously members of the European Free Trade Association (that is, including Sweden and Austria). The main impact of this possibility of expansion seems likely to be on the countries seeking to enter the EC. As Chapter 7 argued, one source of pressure for change in the Swedish welfare state has been the need to come closer to the models more dominant in existing EC countries – and in particular to move away from what are seen to be the high costs of more extensive (if not universal) welfare and sustaining a welfare state which also provides high levels of employment for women. It seems likely that one result of membership will also be higher levels of unemployment for these countries. In addition, as prosperous countries they will be expected to pay a significant 'entry fee' which may encourage a growth in structural funds and a larger budget for these aspects of the EC's embryonic welfare state (Leibfried, 1992a, pp. 26–28). Sweden would certainly be a net financial contributor to the EC's budgets (Sbragia, 1992a, p. 16). The move of the EFTA states towards the EC suggests that for the wealthier states of Europe little alternative is seen to membership of the EC. And few doubts have been raised by existing members about bringing them into membership, even if practical problems have been raised in the process of negotiation. So, at least for the countries of Western Europe, looking at the EC is a useful basis on which to approach questions of European welfare.

Matters are rather different for the countries of central Europe. In one case – that of the German Democratic Republic (GDR), as we saw in Chapter 6 – the issue was resolved by absorption into a Western European welfare regime. Even in Germany the costs of integration have been high and a final balance sheet on their social policy impact is still to be drawn up. The shock of the move from a very basic, highly regimented and inefficient universalism, promising (indeed requiring) full employment for women as well as men, to one which promises greater benefits based on high wages and a clear division of labour between men and women – but starts out by offering no more than Social Assistance and high unemployment – has been a dramatic one. Women have faced the removal of abortion rights and an end to widespread nursery provision. Although it is those who were citizens of the old GDR who have faced the most extensive changes to their welfare system as it has been replaced by one which fits with (West) German and EC norms, the impact of German unification on the EC as a whole at a time of world recession also seems to have reduced the confident progress towards Europeanization which characterized the late 1980s.

The old GDR disappeared and was absorbed into an existing system, imposing new strains on Social Assistance budgets originally only intended to deal with relatively brief breaks in employment or people excluded from the labour market for reasons of disability or childcare. But the difficulties faced by the other countries of Eastern and central Europe have been still greater without equivalent support from what remains the strongest economy in Europe. Their welfare base has been substantially undermined as all of them have faced mass unemployment and collapsing state budgets. Many have also faced substantial conflict between ethnic groups, sometimes leading to the break-up of existing state boundaries. State welfare is distrusted and other forms of provision are rudimentary. Notions of basic incomes and income support have little purchase in them. And, even if they did, the difficulties faced by Germany (discussed in Chapter 6) in attempting to spread its welfare approach to the east show the extent of the task they face. It is currently difficult to identify any clear trends in the post-communist development of welfare in the countries of central and Eastern Europe. Elements of liberal market-based residual welfare systems seem to be combining with conservative forms designed to protect powerful groups (such as some members of the former state bureaucracies and some sections of the working class), and there are also signs of what might be called an authoritarian populism developing in some countries (Deacon, 1992a, pp. 178–83). But, however the changes are characterized, it is clear that state funding for social protection is not viewed as a high priority in any of these states, for whom economic development is paramount. The argument that welfare is dependent on economic success (or indeed survival) underlies social policy developments still more sharply in all these countries than in the rest of Europe.

There are proposals to expand the EC to include many of these countries, and these proposals are supported by the governments of the central European states. The implications of such expansion for the EC and its social policy would be dramatic if realized. The EC as currently constituted is basically what Leibfried calls a Western European 'closed shop' with a reasonably manageable periphery (1992a, p. 28). The implications of this are clear from some of the current debates about excluding non-EC nationals from its borders except on a clearly licensed basis. The moves towards 'Fortress Europe' are moves to make Western Europe a secure area within which the benefits of social citizenship can be guaranteed to EC nationals, whilst others remain excluded – including, and specifically, those from Europe's old communist states who will only be welcome as guestworkers working on contracts (Morokvasic, 1991). One social policy spreading through the states of the EC like wildfire is that which restricts asylum to those with clear and narrowly restricted political grounds for claiming it. Since the fall of communism, of course, few of those from central Europe would be eligible, as they would be defined as 'economic' migrants.

If expansion of the EC took place to include these countries, it would almost certainly have to be on a different basis. The countries of central and Eastern Europe could not begin to think of meeting the existing regulatory standards on employment or social protection. One way of allowing expansion would be to move away from any pretensions to developing a social policy, so that an expanded EC would simply be a customs union (that is, a free trade area surrounded by a protective tariff wall designed to restrict lower-cost imports from elsewhere), and even then it is difficult to believe that some distinction might not have to be made between the different parts with an explicitly 'two track' Europe

(Leibfried, 1992a, p. 28). Some EC members would only be members in a strictly limited sense, for example having access to markets on preferential terms, while others continued to seek closer integration (through social policy as well as economic policy and monetary union). At the start of the 1990s the main emphasis of the EC's policies towards Eastern Europe was on assisting with the building of economic infrastructure capable of working in markets, but the scale of assistance was very small in comparison with the schemes already operating within the EC. Moves towards greater integration between existing members and expansion through the accession of the EFTA states are likely to make a 'united' Europe across the old 'iron curtain' boundaries with a shared social policy less rather than more likely, since it would impose an increased cost of membership for new members (Sbragia, 1992a, p. 17).

5 CONCLUSION

In the last decade of the twentieth century the differences between the welfare states of Europe remain as important as the similarities between them. Despite the similar pressures they have faced since the late 1970s, they have tended to respond in ways which are based on past arrangements rather than choosing to make dramatic new departures based on templates drawn from any particular existing (or theoretical) system. Although the influence of market-based ideas was strong in the 1980s, that did not mean that each country transformed its welfare state along neo-liberal lines. Even the changes which took place in the UK – whose politics are generally presented as the prime example of new right ideology in practice – cannot just be understood in this way. There was a shift in the overall social policy agenda, but the way in which that changed agenda was interpreted varied significantly between different countries.

Europe has become a more important focus for social policy debate than ever before, both in the sense that lessons (and ideas) are increasingly drawn from the experience of other European countries and in the sense that Europe itself (through the EC) is understood to have a role in the development of social policy. Although the argument of this chapter has suggested that the extent of this should not be exaggerated, it is nevertheless possible to identify ways in which the EC has begun to influence developments at member-state level and begun to set its own agenda for welfare. The most important aspects of this have been the increasingly explicit moves towards defining social policy in terms of the labour market and employment-based rights, and the extent to which legal forms of regulation and definitions of entitlement have become universally accepted aspects of social policy throughout the EC. The first of these fits in with and reinforces a more general shift towards an emphasis on the necessary relationships between economic and social policy. In this argument social policy is seen to have a key role in reshaping labour markets to fit with the needs of economic competitiveness, so that social policy becomes a form of infrastructure underpinning that competitiveness. The increased emphasis on regulation fits in with moves away from direct state welfare provision and is likely to be of particular importance in the longer term for countries such as the UK in which notions of entitlement and legal rights have in the past played little part in the distribution of welfare.

Some aspects of change at the European level tend to be lost in the language of legal regulation. So, for example, the stress on employment-based rights helps to marginalize those who are not fully involved in paid employment, and leaves decisions on their benefit 'entitlements' to the member-states. In practice this continues to leave many women in a clear position of dependence on men within families or suffering the consequences of not being so dependent in lone-parent families. The assumption remains that the norm around which social policy should be constructed is that of families constructed around a single 'breadwinner' which in many – although not all – EC countries is assumed to be the man. Women generally only gain access to benefits through their role within the family. The emphasis of European regulation on internal EC migrant-workers also – as we have seen – helps to marginalize and exclude those who are not EC citizens. It helps to create another (and much larger) category of migrant-workers whose position is precarious and much less protected, except by national legislation.

It is increasingly clear that welfare states are not hermetically sealed from each other, and within Europe the creation of a single market means that most national governments have to look over their shoulders at what is happening in other countries. At the European level there are some signs of supranational initiatives being taken. But the direction of change across countries remains uncertain and even the shifts which have taken place might be difficult to sustain in the context of wider changes within Europe outside the existing boundaries of the EC. Dealing with the consequences of the collapse of communism may turn out to be even more difficult than the crab-like progression from Coal and Steel Community to the European Community of the twelve has already proved. Meanwhile the main source of social policy development is likely to remain at the level of national welfare states for some time to come.

REFERENCES

Baine, S., Benington, J. and Russell, J. (1992) *Changing Europe: challenges facing the voluntary and community sectors in the 1990s*, London, NCVO Publications and Community Development Foundation.

Baldwin-Edwards, M. (1991) 'The socio-political rights of the migrant in the European community' in Room, G. (ed.) *Towards a European Welfare State?*, Bristol, School for Advanced Urban Studies.

Chamberlayne, P. (1992) 'Income maintenance and institutional forms: a comparison of France, West Germany, Italy and Britain 1945-90', *Policy and Politics*, vol. 20, no. 4, pp. 299–318.

Cochrane, A. (1993) 'The problem of poverty' in Dallos, R. and McLaughlin, E. (eds) *Social Problems and the Family*, Family Life and Social Policy Series, London, Sage/The Open University.

Commission of the European Communities (1991) *Europe 2000: outlook for the development of the Community's territory*, Communication from the Commission to the Council and the European Parliament, Directorate-General for Regional Policy, Luxembourg, Office for Official Publications of the European Communities.

Cram, L. (1993) 'Calling the tune without paying the piper? Social policy regulation: the role of the Commission in European Community social policy', *Policy and Politics*, vol. 21, no. 2, pp. 135–46.

Cutler, T., Haslam, C., Williams, J. and Williams, K. (1989) *1992 – The Struggle for Europe*, Oxford, Berg.

Deacon, B. (1992a) 'The future of social policy in Eastern Europe' in Deacon, B. *et al.*, *The New Eastern Europe: social policy past, present and future*, London, Sage.

Deacon, B. (1992b) 'The impact of supranational and global agencies on Central European national social policy', paper presented to First European Conference of Sociology, Vienna, Austria, August.

Dominelli, L. (1991) *Women Across Continents: feminist comparative social policy*, Hemel Hempstead, Harvester Wheatsheaf.

Esping-Andersen, G. (1990) *The Three Worlds of Welfare Capitalism*, Cambridge, Polity Press.

Eurostat (1988 and 1991) *Basic Statistics of the Community*, Brussels, European Commission.

Flora, P. (ed.) (1986a) *Growth to Limits: Volume 1*, Berlin, de Gruyter.

Flora, P. (ed.) (1986b) *Growth to Limits: Volume 2*, Berlin, de Gruyter.

Flora, P. and Heidenheimer, A. (1981a) 'The historical core and changing boundaries of the welfare state' in Flora, P. and Heidenheimer, A. (eds) op. cit.

Flora, P. and Heidenheimer, A. (eds) (1981b) *The Development of Welfare States in Europe*, New Brunswick, Transaction Books.

Glennerster, H. (1991) 'The radical right and the future of the welfare state' in Glennerster, H. and Midgley, J. (eds) op. cit.

Glennerster, H. and Midgley, J. (eds) (1991) *The Radical Right and the Welfare State: an international assessment*, Hemel Hempstead, Harvester Wheatsheaf.

Gordon, P. (1989) *Fortress Europe? The Meaning of 1992*, London, Runnymede Trust.

Harris, L. (1989) 'The UK economy at a crossroads' in Allen, J. and Massey, D. (eds) *The Economy in Question*, London, Sage/The Open University.

Heidenheimer, A. (1981) 'Towards a new welfare state' in Flora, P. and Heidenheimer, A. (eds) op. cit.

Hood, C. and Schuppert, G. F. (eds) (1988) *Delivering Public Services in Western Europe: sharing Western European experience of para-government organization,* London, Sage.

Jessop, B. (1991) 'The welfare state in the transition from Fordism to post-Fordism' in Jessop, B., Kastandiek, H., Nielsen, K. and Pedersen, O. (eds) *The Politics of Flexibility: restructuring state and industry in Britain, Germany and Scandinavia,* Aldershot, Edward Elgar.

Johnson, N. (1987) *The Welfare State in Transition: the theory and practice of welfare pluralism,* Brighton, Wheatsheaf.

Kastandiek, H. (1990) 'Convergence or a persistent diversity of national politics?' in Crouch, C. and Marquand, D. (eds) *The Politics of 1992: beyond the single European market,* Oxford, Political Quarterly/Basil Blackwell.

Lange, S. (1992) 'The politics of the social dimension' in Sbragia, A. (ed.) op. cit.

Leibfried, S. (1992a) 'Social Europe: welfare state trajectories of the European community' in Otto, H.-U. and Flösser, G. (eds) *How to Organize Prevention: political, organizational, and professional challenges to social Services,* Berlin, de Gruyter.

Leibfried, S. (1992b) 'Towards a European welfare state? On integrating poverty regimes into the European Community' in Ferge, Z. and Kolberg, J. (eds) *Social Policy in a Changing Europe,* Frankfurt, Campus Verlag, and Boulder, CO, Westview Press.

Leibfried, S. and Pierson, P. (1992) 'Prospects for social Europe', *Politics and Society,* vol. 20, no. 3, pp. 333–66.

Lewis, J. (1992) 'Gender and the development of welfare regimes', *Journal of European Social Policy,* vol. 2, no. 3, pp. 159–73.

Lipietz, A. (1986) *Mirages and Miracles: the crises of global Fordism,* London, Verso.

Majone, G. (1991) 'Cross-national sources of regulatory policymaking in Europe and the United States', *Journal of Public Policy,* vol. 11, no. 1, pp. 79–106.

Millar, J. (1989) 'Social security, equality and women in the UK', *Policy and Politics,* vol. 17, no. 4, pp. 311–9.

Mishra, R. (1990) *The Welfare State in Capitalist Society: policies of retrenchment and maintenance in Europe, North America and Australia,* Hemel Hempstead, Harvester Wheatsheaf.

Morokvasic, M. (1991) 'Fortress Europe and migrant women', *Feminist Review,* no. 39, pp. 69–84.

OECD (1988) *The Future of Social Protection,* OECD Social Policy studies, no. 6, Paris, Organisation for Economic Cooperation and Development.

Øyen, E. (1986) 'Identifying the future of the welfare state' in Øyen, E. (ed.) *Comparing Welfare States and their Futures,* Aldershot, Gower.

Pateman, C. (1989) *The Disorder of Women*, Cambridge, Polity Press.

Pfaller, A. with Gough, I. (1991) 'The competiveness of industrialised welfare states: a cross-country survey' in Pfaller, A. *et al.* (eds) op. cit.

Pfaller, A., Gough, I., Therborn, G. (1991a) 'The issue' in Pfaller, A. *et al.* (eds) op. cit.

Pfaller, A., with Gough, I. and Therborn, G. (1991b) 'Welfare statism and international competition: the lesson of the case studies' in Pfaller, A. *et al.* (eds) op. cit.

Pfaller, A., Gough, I. and Therborn, G. (eds) (1991) *Can the Welfare State Compete? A comparative study of five advanced capitalist countries*, London and Basingstoke, Macmillan.

Pierson, C. (1991) *Beyond the Welfare State?: the new political economy of welfare*, Cambridge, Polity Press.

Pieters, D. (1991) 'Europäisches und nationales Recht der sozialen Sicherheit – Zukunftsperspektiven', *Zeitschrift für ausländisches und internationales Arbeits– und Sozialrecht*, no. 1, pp. 72–94.

Prondzynski, I. (1989) 'The social situation and employment of migrant women in the European Community', *Policy and Politics*, vol. 17, no. 4, pp. 347–54.

Sbragia, A. (1992a) 'Introduction' in Sbragia, A. (ed.) op. cit.

Sbragia, A. (ed.) (1992b) *Euro-politics*, Washington, D.C., Brookings Institution.

Sherer, M. (1987) 'Welfare states: an overview of problems and prospects' in Friedmann, R., Gilbert, N., and Shere, M. (eds) *Modern Welfare States: a comparative view of trends and prospects*, Brighton, Wheatsheaf.

Spicker, P. 'The principle of subsidiarity and the social policy of the European Community', *Journal of European Social Policy*, vol. 1, no. 1, pp. 3–14.

Stoesz, D. and Midgley, J. (1991) 'The radical right and the welfare state' in Glennerster, H. and Midgley, J. (eds) op. cit.

Thane, P. and Bock, G. (eds) (1991) *Maternity and Gender Policies: women and the rise of the European welfare state, 1850s–1950s*, London, Routledge.

Titmuss, R. (1974) *Social Policy: an introduction*, London, Allen and Unwin.

Vobruba, G. (1991) 'Futures of work and security: trends in the development of wage-work and three scenarios of social security in Europe' in Room, G. (ed.) *Towards a European Welfare State?*, Bristol, School for Advanced Urban Studies.

Weir, M., Orloff, A. S. and Skocpol, T. (eds) (1988) *The Politics of Social Policy in the United States*, Princeton, NJ, Princeton University Press.

INDEX

abortion 89–90
  Germany 142, 164
  Ireland 229, 230–1
accountability 68–9
'austerity consensus' 245

Basic Law, German 6, 141, 142, 158
benefits
  comparison, Sweden, Britain and FRG, table 176
  as disincentive 9, 51, 57
  eligibility reduced 1980s 57
  expenditure 1973/88, table 60
  limited in early days 83–4
  numbers in receipt increased 60
  rates 1973/88, table 61
  value reduced 1980s 57
Beveridge, William 1, 21, 25–6
  and citizenship 28
  and gender 26–7, 77
  universalism 86
Britain
  economic growth 1960s 30
  economic policies 22
  and Hong Kong 106
  market economy 49–50
  relations with USA 21, 22, 23
  women working, table 146
British welfare system 9, 12–13, 251, 252
  charges imposed 22
  comparison, Sweden and FRG, tables 176, 177
  development 29–47
  expansion 30–5
  foundation and modernization 19–48
  gender, 'race' and class 77–104
  mixed economy 23–4
  moral aspects 21–2
  restructuring 1980s 49–76
  world role 2–3
  1945, significance of 29
  1980s 49–76

capitalism
  Britain 20, 82
  Ireland 213
  and patriarchy 82
  Sweden 198–9

and welfare 78
carers, informal 16, 46, 80
  payments for 99, 158
Catholic Church, Ireland 205–7, 207–10, 220, 224
  and abortion 231
  changes in attitudes 215
  and contraception 229
  health care 220, 226
  and women 210–12
Catholic corporatism, Ireland 205–7
centralization, feature of 1960s–70s 43–4
child allowances, table 1950/58 38
child benefit 39, 58, 79, 93, 124, 176, 192, 193, 224
Child Support Act 1991 94
childcare, 99
  Hong Kong 127, 129
  Ireland 226, 228, 230
  Sweden 194–6
Children Act 1989 100
China and Hong Kong 106, 108, 109, 134
  attitude to welfare state 136–7
churches, and social work, Germany 157–8
Citizens' Charter 68, 71
citizenship 34, 245
  Britain 27–8, 73
  Europe 73, 261
  Germany 149
class
  and British welfare 23, 24, 78
  democratic class struggle 17, 72
  and infant mortality 89
  Ireland 209, 221
  Swedish welfare 173, 174
  working 78, 114, 208, 219, 199
compensation, aspect of German Social Assistance 152–3, 159
competition see market forces
Conservative Party, and welfare state 49, 50–1; see also new right
conservative welfare regimes 8; see also Germany; Ireland
contraception

Ireland 212, 228, 229, 230
  Sweden 190
corporatism
  Ireland 205, 207
  Sweden 197, 198
Culliton report, Ireland 223–4

deindustrialization, Britain 50–1
demoralization, alleged result of welfare state 52
Denmark
  unemployment benefit 183
  welfare state 252
  women at work, table 1966/86 146
'dependency culture' 95
  see also underclass
dependants of migrants 45, 81, 87
disability
  and citizenship 28
  critique of welfare 80–1
  disability movement 79, 97
  German Social Assistance 152
  Hong Kong 123
  and motherhood 90
disincentives, created by welfare 51–2, 224
divorce 44, 89, 100
  GDR 164
  Germany 146, 164
  Hong Kong 129
  Ireland 212, 228, 229–30
  Sweden 190

earnings 91, 93
  tables 58, 92
  see also wages
earnings-related pensions
  Sweden (ATP) 179
  Britain (SERPS) 41, 58, 59–60
earnings-related supplements 57
education
  and black children 88
  Britain, table 1973/88 56
  expenditure rising 39
  Germany 154–5
  Hong Kong 119–20, table 121
  Ireland 220
  private 24–5, 30, table 31
  quasi-market 64

and traditional values 95
emigration from Ireland 218, 224
employment
  and Beveridge 25–6
  deregulation of labour market 57
  full, and welfare state 3–4, 71
  GDR 162, 163
  FRG 150
  Germany, shortages 153–4
  Hong Kong 132
  Ireland 213, 216–18
  Sweden 173, 187–8
equality see social equality
Esping-Andersen, G. 7, 8–9, 10, 12, 13, 16, 17, 21, 73, 74, 141, 142, 173, 179, 186, 205, 207, 239, 242, 248–9
Europe (non-EC) 261–4
  comparison of countries 250–3
European Community (EC)
  and Britain 72
  expansion possible 263
  expenditure 254–5
  free movement within 73
  and Ireland 205, 213, 227, 230–2
  social policy 256–7, 264–5
  social policy, harmonization 17, 101, 168, 253, 256, 258
  and Sweden 199, 200
  unemployment rates 217; table 1974/83 216
  and welfare state 249
European Court of Justice 258, 259
European Regional Development Fund 254
European Social Fund 254
European Social Security System 255–6

familialization of poverty 60–1
family
  and caring 11, 65–6
  change 99
  encouraged by government 127, 129, 130
  Germany 141, 142, 157, 130
  Hong Kong 110, 113, 124–9
  Ireland 205, 206, 210–12, 231
  new right policies 94–5
  role in welfare, Britain 19, 23, 24

and state 44–6
  Sweden 190–3
family allowances 27, 39
Family Credit 58
Family Income Supplement 58
family, nation and work, framework for study 82–3
family policies 4, 5
feminism
  and disability 80–1
  involvement of fathers with children 94
  Ireland 227
  and 'race' 81
  Sweden 192, 197
  United States 197
  and welfare services 79–80, 97
fertility control 89–90
Fianna Fail 208, 210, 214, 222
Fine Gael 208, 229
Fordism, global 2, 241–2
'Fortress Europe' 16, 260, 263
France
  welfare regime 8
  welfare state 252
  and women 244
  women at work, table 1966/88 146
free enterprise, Hong Kong 107, 109–10; see also market
free trade, Ireland 213

gay men 89, 95, 99, 190, 230
gender
  British welfare 24
  and citizenship 28
  and earnings 91, 93, table 92
  equality, GDR 163
  and EC 259
  German social insurance 146
  German social work 158
  Hong Kong Chinese 125–6
  Ireland 210–11, 225–6, 227
  role in welfare arrangements 5, 10–11, 79–80, 242, 243–4
  Sweden 185–6, 195
Germany
  conservative corporatist model 72, 141–3
  fiscal crisis 161
  future 166–8
  welfare regime 8, 14, 141–71
  women at work, table 1966/86 146
  xenophobia 168
Germany, Democratic Republic of (GDR), East Germany 142,

economic collapse 159, 165
educational inequalities 155
financial transfers 161, table 160
integration 262
Social Assistance claimants 151–2
Germany, Federal Republic of (FRG), West Germany 142, 251, 252
  comparison, Britain and Sweden, tables 176, 177
  financial transfers 161, table 160
Gross Domestic Product
  table 1965/85 241
  current expenditure on social protection, table 1980/89 246
  and social expenditure, table 1960/85 243
Gross National Product
  increased share on welfare 27
  proportion of local authority expenditure 1951/75 43
  and public expenditure, table 32
  welfare expenditure as percentage, tables 33, 34
guestworkers (Gastarbeiter) 16, 153–4, 245

health insurance
  private 30, table 31
  tax incentives 63
health services
  expenditure, table 1973/88 56
  Hong Kong 120, 121, 122
  Ireland 215, 220, 226
  and population changes 35
  and quasi-market 63–4
Hong Kong
  community and welfare 130–2
  Community Chest 131–2
  demo-grants 123, 124
  economic success 132–3
  free enterprise economy 107
  politics 107, 126, 133, 134–5
  social disturbances 114, 115–16, 127
  trade union provision for social welfare 114–15
  welfare associations 110–11
  welfare regime 14, 105–40
    delivery 124–32
    lack of coordination 132

linked to economy 117
hospitals
    expansion, Britain 43, 65–6
    Hong Kong 120, 122
housing
    Hong Kong 111–12, 118–9,
    133–4
    Ireland 215, 220
    private 30, table 31
    public expenditure, table
    1973/88 56
    quasi-market 64
    right to buy 63

illegitimacy 44, 190
immigrants
    Algerians to France 16
    and childcare, Sweden 196
    controls 94
    economic migrants 263
    and European Community
    101, 255, 258, 259, 260
    to Hong Kong 135–6
    to Ireland 213
    needed as workers 85, 88
    restriction by Acts 45, 84, 87,
    245
    to Sweden 181, 187–90, 196
    Vietnamese to Hong Kong
    135–6
    and welfare benefits 11, 16–
    17, 84, 86–7, 245
income, household
    comparative figures, tables
    176, 177
    redistribution 177
income support 32, 38, 245, 255
    Britain (Income Support) 27,
    41, 57, 59, 89, 93, 147, 150
    Germany 141, 143, 147, 150,
    152, 153
    safety-net 57, 89, 93
    unemployment 7, 59, 93, 159
    in welfare regime 9, 27–8,
    41, 59, 263
infant mortality 89
inflation 39, 46
    Sweden 184
insurance
    'perverse incentive' 44–5
    privatization 59
insurance, social
    expected in Britain 23, 25–6
    and full employment 3, 23
    German problem 15
International Monetary Fund
(IMF) 46, 249
Ireland, Republic of

economic crisis 212
    welfare regime 14, 15,
    205–37
        crisis 222–5
        modernization 215–16
        post-war transformation
        212–14
Irish Development Authority
(IDA) 213, 216–17
Italy, welfare regime 8, 249

Keynes, John Maynard 1, 2, 21,
23, 241–2, 245, 247
Kilbrandon report 43

labour market see employment
Labour Market Board (AMS),
Sweden 182, 183, 184
laissez-faire see free enterprise
Länder 141, 142, 149, 152, 159
Le Grand, J.54–5, 64–5, 70
lesbians 79, 97, 99
liberal welfare regimes 9, 17,
252
    Hong Kong 105
local government
    cutbacks in services 94
    France 5–6
    Germany 6, 149, 152
    loss of power 69
    and pressure groups 97
    and quasi–market 43
    reform in UK 63–4
    Sweden 180, 186
    employment of women 80
London Living Standards
Survey 91–2
lone-parent families 27, 44, 45,
60–1, 93, 99
    and absent fathers 94
    Germany 150, 156
    and income support 93
    Ireland 221
    Sweden 190, 192, 193–4, 196
    United States 193

Maastricht treaty 72, 224, 230,
231, 256, 261
MacLehose, Sir Murray 117,
118, 134
management, and welfare services 67–8
market economy, and Britain
19, 20, 23, 24
market forces 95
    in education 96
    Hong Kong 110
    and social welfare 62, 110,

252
    Sweden 200
maternity benefits, table 1950/
80 38
maternity leave, Ireland 226,
228
means-tested benefits 9, 26–7,
28, 39, 41, 43, 47, 58
    Germany 142
middle class, and social welfare
55–6
    Britain 144
    Germany 144, 150
    Ireland 208
    Sweden 174, 178
migrants see emigrants; immigrants
minorities, Sweden 187–90
Mishra, Ranesh 3, 5, 16, 70, 72
multi-national corporations
(MNCs) and Ireland 213, 216–
17, 218, 224, 227
Murray, Charles 95
Myrdal, Alva and Gunnar
191–2

National Assistance 26–7, table
38
    reformed 1960s 41
    and women 89
National Health Service
    average costs by age, table
    37
    GP budget-holding 72
    quasi-market 63
    and 'race' 89
    reforms 1974 43
    and women 89
National Health Service and
Community Care Act 1989 63
National Insurance 26
    contributions 34, 148
    history in Britain 144–5
    numbers, table 1950/58 38
    reformed 1960s 41
    see also social insurance
National Insurance Act 1911 84
nationality 81, 84, 100–1
    Ireland 207, 208, 209
    Sweden 187
neo-conservatism 248
neo-corporatism, Ireland 213–
14
new liberalism 28
'new pessimism' 245
new right
    Britain 50–1, 53, 91, 94–5,
    98, 100, 247–8

Germany 147–8
Hong Kong 108

old people
    ageism 82
    care of 99
    comparison FRG, Britain
        and Sweden 179
    Hong Kong 123, 127–9
    increase in numbers 44, 54,
        156, 159
    Sweden 179–80
one-parent families see lone-
parent families
Organisation for Economic
Cooperation and Development
(OECD) 6, 174, 220, 241

Pacific rim countries 106, 108,
109, 122, 128, 247
Papal encyclical 1931 142, 206
parental leave, Sweden 194–5
parental responsibility 94
    Germany 154, 167
patriarchy
    Britain 82
    Chinese families 125
    Ireland 206–7
    Sweden 192, 196–8
pay-related social insurance,
Ireland 218
pensions
    and population changes 35
    private, UK 30, 31, 59–60
    retirement, table 1973/88 61,
        259
    Sweden 179, 180
personal social services
    Germany 157–8
    and local government 43, 45
    public expenditure, table
        1973/88 56
poor
    Germany and UK 150
    undeserving 28, 110, 168
    see also poverty
population
    age structure, Britain 1951–
        2025, 35–7
    Ireland 212, 215
    Sweden 190–1
poverty
    Britain 37, 39
    and European Community
        256
    Hong Kong 122–3
    Sweden 175, 179, table 178
    United States 37

primary care of dependants 45–
6, 66–7, 80; see also carers
private sector 30, 64, table 31
privatization 5, 53
    varieties 62–7
profitability factor 64
Progressive Democratic Party,
Ireland 222, 224
Public Assistance, Hong Kong
123
public expenditure
    funding sources 34
    table 1910/75 32
    welfare expenditure, tables
        1955/76 33, 34
    welfare state 54–5; tables
        1973/88 55, 56
public housing
    Hong Kong 112, 113, 118–19,
        133–4
    Ireland 221
public sector
    debt, table 223
    housing 63
    wages 41, 93
    and women 80, 93
public spending, and Conservatives 51–2
purchaser–provider split 64–5,
72

qualifications, in Germany
154–5
quasi-markets 63–4, 68, 69, 70

'race'
    and benefits 93–4
    and citizenship 28, 77
    and earnings 91, 93, table 92
    and education 96
    and Europe 73, 101
    and feminism 81
    and infant mortality 89
    pathologization of black peo-
        ple 87–8
    and poverty 61
    role in welfare arrangements
        11, 78, 81–2, 245
    Sweden 187–8, 188–90
    unemployed 93
Race Relations Act 1968 87
Reagan, President Ronald, policies under 49, 51, 53
recessions 47, 49, 71
Red Cross, German 157, 158
refugees 17
    to Germany 149
    to Sweden, 181

regulation of services 65, 249
    and European Community
        258–9
religion see church
religious divisions, Northern
Ireland 82
residual welfare regimes
    Hong Kong 105–40
    United States 105
retail price index, and benefit
rates 61
retrenchment in welfare services, table 1970s–80s 248
rights to welfare 27–8

Seebohm report 43
Single European Market 73,
257
Social Assistance (Sozialhilfe),
Germany 141, 148–52, 156–7
    comparison with Britain
        149–50
    compensation principle 152–
        3
    fraud 153
    growing need 149, 150, 151,
        167
    rates set by Association 148
    recipients, table 1970/89 151
    refugees 149
    victims 152–3
    and women 156
Social Assistance (Social
Benefit), Sweden 180–1
Social Chapter/Charter (EC) 72,
101, 253, 254
social corporatism 16, 248
social-democratic model of welfare services 9, 147, 252; see
also Sweden
Social Democratic Party (SAP),
Sweden 173, 174, 175, 179, 191,
192, 197, 199
social divisions, diversity and
interrelations 79–83
social expenditure
    current expenditure on social
        protection, table 1980/89 246
    growth 242, table 1965/85
        241
    Ireland 216–22
    OECD, table 1965/85 241
    proportion of GDP, table
        1960/85 243
Social Fund 59, 94
social insurance
    Britain see National
        Insurance

Germany 141, 143–5
Ireland 215, 218
Sweden, contributions 175
social protection, and GDP compared, table 1980/89 246
social reproduction 80
social security
    expenditure Britain, table
    1973/89 59
    Germany 141, 143–8, 156–7,
    table 1970/89 151
    Hong Kong 122–4
    limited rights for 16- and
    17-year olds 94
    public expenditure, table
    1973/88 56
    review 1985 58
Social Security Acts 59, 61
social services
    Hong Kong, tables 117, 124
    quasi-market 64
social services departments,
local government 43, 45
social welfare
    British colonies 110
    Hong Kong 127–8, 129, 132,
    134–5, 136–7
    Ireland 218, table 1983/90
    217
social workers, and community
care 45
Soviet Union 2, 13
    state planning 20
Special Needs Allowance 123,
124
Special Needs Payments 58–9
squatting, Hong Kong 111–12,
118, 134
state
    Britain 19–20, 22, 25, 49, 50,
    53–6, 59–60
    and family, Britain 44–6
    and family, Hong Kong 127,
    129, 130
    Germany 15
    Hong Kong 107–8, 110–12,
    113, 117, 127–8, 129, 132
    Ireland 206, 207–10, 220,
    221–2
    and quasi-market 64–5
    and social welfare, Hong
    Kong 109
    Sweden 174
    and voluntary agencies,
    Hong Kong 130–1
    and welfare 4–5, 109, 249
    withdrawal, Britain 49, 50,
    53–6, 59–60

State Earnings Related Pensions Scheme (SERPS) 41, 58,
59–60
subsidiarity
    Germany 14–15, 141–2, 154,
    158, 161
    Ireland 206, 215
Supplementary Benefit 27
    alleged effect on family 45
    figures, table 1973/88 61
    numbers, table 1950/80 38
    and women 89
Survivors Speak Out 79, 97
Sweden
    comparison with Britain and
    FRG, tables 176, 177
    and EC 262
    finance of welfare 174, 175,
    tables 176, 177
    political basis of welfare
    state 173–4
    poverty 175, 179, table 178
    social-democratic model 147,
    190
    welfare regime 14, 15, 173–
    203, 252
    women 244
    women at work, table 1966/
    86 146

taxation
    comparison Britain, Sweden
    and FRG, table 176
    Germany 147–8
    Hong Kong 132
    incentives towards private
    health insurance 63
    Ireland 209, 218–19, 224,
    226
    personal, and welfare 27
    policy, British, 1980s 62
    relief, Sweden 177
    source of income 34, 50
    Sweden 174, 175, 177, 193,
    table 176
    thresholds, table 35
    of women in Ireland 226
Thatcher, Margaret 49, 71, 91
    reform of welfare state 2, 50,
    53, 252
trade unions
    Britain 57, 183
    Germany, and social services
    157, 158
    Hong Kong, and social ser-
    vices 114–15
    Ireland 214

legislation against 57
Sweden 173, 179, 182, 183,
184, 186, 196
training
    Germany 154, 159
    Sweden 183
travellers, Ireland, increase 221

underclass 95, 168
    Ireland 221
'undeserving poor' 28, 110, 168
unemployed
    Germany 142–3, 150, 154,
    159, 161, 162, 166, table 162
    Ireland 223, 224, table 1974/
    83 216
    and 'race' 93
    Sweden 181–4
    voluntary 25
    women in Sweden 185
unemployment, rises 46–7, 49,
54–5
Unemployment Benefit 7, 26
    British rates 147, table 1973/
    88 61
    comparison with earnings,
    table 58
    Germany 146–7
    reforms 1980s 57
    Sweden 175, 183
unification of Germany 142, 155
    strains 159–62, 167
    and women 162, 163–6
United States of America
    and Britain 21
    free market policies 49, 51,
    53
    liberal model influence 9, 16
    mixed economy 14
    poverty, battle against 37
    welfare state
    delivery systems 69, 250
    world dominance 2, 13
universalism in welfare services
86, 105
    Sweden 174, 183
user groups 79, 97–8

value-for-money in welfare services 68
voluntary sector 64, 72
    Germany 142, 157
    Hong Kong 110–12, 130–1,
    132
    Ireland 205, 209
    Sweden 183
    see also Catholic Church

wages
  Hong Kong 132–3
  Sweden, table 176
  see also earnings
welfare
  Britain 19, 23–4
  mixed economy likely 4–5,
  19, 23–4
  studies of 77–8
welfare capitalism 12
welfare policies
  Britain, assumptions 20
  disentitlement 5
  historiography 77–8
  welfare rights groups 37, 39
  expenditure increase 39,
  table 40
  and Gross National Product,
  tables 33, 34
  mixed economy 71–2
  modernization 1960s–70s
  41–4
  and public expenditure,
  tables 33, 34
  United States 67–9
  in 1990s 69–74
welfare regime 8–9, 11, 12,
table 14, 17, 19, 20, 21, 46, 73,
74, 106, 108, 139, 147–8, 156,
166, 239–40, 241–2, 252–3, 262,
263
  British
    post-war 20, 23–4, 25, 29
    mixed economy 73, 74
    1980s 69–74
  conservative 8, 14, 141
    German 141–2, 147, 153,
    156, 158, 164, 168

  Irish 205–7, 225, 232–3
  European 257ff
  liberal 9, 17, 252
  residual 74, 106, 118, 145
  restructuring 249–50
  social-democratic 9, 173, 200
welfare state
  attacked, 199, 222
  Britain 53–6, 83–4, 84–90,
  90–101
  data on 6–7, 10
  definition 3–5
  European states 250–3
  European welfare state 14,
  14, 16, 253–61
  Germany 144–5, 166–8
  global context 240–9
  Ireland 214–16, 222
  public expenditure, table
  1973/88 55
  retrenchment in five countries, table 1970s–80s 248
  rolling back 53–6
  Sweden 15, 147, 173–203
welfare system, increase in
demands 39, tables 1950/80 38
women
  and Beveridge Report 21,
  26–7, 77
  British welfare system 24, 78
  as primary carers 46, 65–6,
  80, 158, 228, 242
  family role 44, 66, 79, 83–4,
  242
  and fertility 89–90
  France 244
  Germany 145–6

  and care 143, 156, 157,
  158
  East German inequalities
  156
  and social insurance 145,
  156
  and unification 162, 163–
  6
  health 98
  Hong Kong 125–6, 129
  Ireland 15
    carers 228
    restricted role 205, 210–
    12, 225–32
    working 225–6, 227, 228
  marginalization 10, 79
  motherhood 21, 90
  and poverty 61
  role, British welfare system
  24, 78
  Sweden 15, 184–7, 190–8
    disadvantaged in pensions
    180
    lone mothers' support
    193–4
    paid leave 186
    part-time workers 185
    working 184, 194, 196–7,
    table 185
  and welfare provision 88–9,
  99
  and work 44, 99–100, 126,
  129, 225–6, table 1966/86
  146
  work in social services 88
  see also lone-parent families
work, changes in 98–9
  see also women, and work